T0383005

Advance Praise

Reverse Subsidies in Global Monopsony Capitalism is an important book and one that brings together telling evidence in a compelling way. The authors analyse the injustices in global value chains and, by extension, the global capitalist economy by interrogating the nature of the interactions of the different segments of the chains: from the producers of inputs of the production workers to the suppliers and brand name buyers. They introduce a concept of critical importance to understanding these interactions: the concept of 'reverse subsidies'. Subsidies are widely understood as amounts of funding provided by the state to allow goods and services to be provided or consumed below their cost of production. Reverse subsidies, by contrast, are below-cost provision of goods and services by workers to the profit of suppliers and, more so, brand name companies. This happens because brand name companies download so many costs and risks onto workers—through irregular work orders, low wages or piece rates, delayed payments and rejected goods—that the workers often operate at a loss.

—**Marty Chen**, Lecturer in Public Policy,
Harvard Kennedy School,
Affiliated Professor, Harvard Graduate School of Design, and
Senior Advisor, WIEGO Network

Using reverse subsidies for the basis of analysis is spot on. Continuing to expose the fundamentally unjust economic model that underpins global supply chains is so important and is the pressure that is needed to bring about more effective and sustainable change.

—**Jenny Holdcroft**, former
Policy Director, IndustriAll

An important contribution to the on-going debate organized around the idea of the 'reverse subsidies' extracted from workers and the environment in global value chains.

—**Naila Kabeer**, Professor, London
School of Economics

Reverse Subsidies in Global Monopsony Capitalism is a breakthrough book because it develops the ideas of power, social reproduction, and economic justice—especially related to gender, climate, and caste—through a lens of contemporary global production, organized as it is in complex global value chains, dominated by brand-label firms and subject to deep asymmetries of bargaining power at the level of the firm, the nation, and the household. The focus is on South Asian apparel production, but the implications of the framing and the findings go well beyond this region and this sector to give deep insight into the persistence of underdevelopment in a world economy characterized by rapid capital flow and highly liberalized trade.

—**William Milberg**, Dean and Professor of Economics,
The New School for Social Research, New York

We are happy to note that in this book the authors have integrated homeworkers into the overall analysis of exploitative conditions in global value chains.

—**Reema Nanavaty**,
Executive Director, SEWA

Reverse Subsidies in Global Monopsony Capitalism

This book provides a firm analytical base to discussions about injustice and the unequal distribution of gains from global production in the form of global monopsony capitalism. It utilizes the concept of reverse subsidies as the purchase of gendered labour and environmental services below their costs of production in garment value chains in India and other garment producing countries, such as Bangladesh and Cambodia. Environmental services, such as freshwater for garment manufacture and land for cotton production, are degraded by overuse and untreated waste disposal. The resulting higher profits from the low prices of garments are captured by global brands, using their monopsony position, with few buyers and myriad sellers, in the market. This book links the concept of reverse subsidies with those of injustice, inequality, and sustainability in global production.

Dev Nathan is Visiting Professor at the Institute for Human Development, New Delhi; and Research Director at the GenDev Centre for Research and Innovation, Haryana, India. His research interests range from the nature of global production to development issues of indigenous peoples and gender relations. He co-authored the book *Witch Hunts: Culture, Patriarchy and Structural Transformation* (2020).

Shikha Silliman Bhattacharjee is a lawyer and researcher focused on migration, supply chains, gender, caste, and race in the global economy. She has conducted research and advocacy in collaboration with global institutions like Human Rights Watch, the International Labour Organization, and Global Labor Justice-International Labor Rights Forum.

S. Rahul teaches at the School of Management and Labour Studies of the Tata Institute of Social Sciences, Mumbai. His professional interests are aligned in social analytics and research, especially in the areas of developmental research, labour market, and global value chains.

Purushottam Kumar is a researcher and currently working as a senior programme manager with the Society for Labour and Development (SLD), New Delhi. His research focuses on labour rights in the global value chains of the leather, garment, and seafood processing industries.

Immanuel Dahaghani is a research consultant from Chennai whose work is focused on labour rights and labour welfare in garments, leather, and automobile sectors. He has worked with the Society for Labour and Development (SLD) and the Asia Floor Wage Alliance (AFWA).

Sukhpal Singh is Professor and former Chairperson, Centre for Management in Agriculture, Indian Institute of Management, Ahmedabad. His research interests lie in small producer and worker livelihoods and collectivization of stakeholders in the context of agribusiness value chains and deregulation of agricultural markets in India and the developing world.

Padmini Swaminathan is former Director of the Madras Institute of Development Studies, Chennai, where she also held the post of the Reserve Bank of India Chair in Regional Economics. Her research work covers the areas of industrial organization, labour, occupational health, and skill development.

Development Trajectories in Global Value Chains

A feature of the current phase of globalization is the outsourcing of production tasks and services across borders, and the increasing organization of production and trade through global value chains (GVCs), global commodity chains (GCCs), and global production networks (GPNs). With a large and growing literature on GVCs, GCCs, and GPNs, this series is distinguished by its focus on the implications of these new production systems for economic, social, and regional development.

This series publishes a wide range of theoretical, methodological, and empirical works, both research monographs and edited volumes, dealing with crucial issues of transformation in the global economy. How do GVCs change the ways in which lead and supplier firms shape regional and international economies? How do they affect local and regional development trajectories, and what implications do they have for workers and their communities? How is the organization of value chains changing and how are these emerging forms contested as more traditional structures of North–South trade complemented and transformed by emerging South–South lead firms, investments, and trading links? How does the large-scale entry of women into value-chain production impact on gender relations? What opportunities and limits do GVCs create for economic and social upgrading and innovation? In what ways are GVCs changing the nature of work and the role of labor in the global economy? And how might the increasing focus on logistics management, financialization, or social standards and compliance portend important developments in the structure of regional economies?

This series includes contributions from all disciplines and interdisciplinary fields and approaches related to GVC analysis, including GCCs and GPNs, and is particularly focused on theoretically innovative and informed works that are grounded in the empirics of development related to these approaches. Through their focus on changing organizational forms, governance systems, and production relations, volumes in this series contribute to on-going conversations about theories of development and development policy in the contemporary era of globalization.

Series editors

Stephanie Barrientos is Professor of Global Development at the Global Development Institute, University of Manchester.

Gary Gereffi is Professor of Sociology and Director of the Global Value Chains Center, Duke University.

Dev Nathan is Visiting Professor at the Institute for Human Development, New Delhi, and Research Director at the GenDev Centre for Research and Innovation, India.

John Pickles is Earl N. Phillips Distinguished Professor of International Studies at the University of North Carolina, Chapel Hill.

Titles in the Series

1. Labour in Global Value Chains in Asia
   Edited by *Dev Nathan, Meenu Tewari and Sandip Sarkar*
2. The Sweatshop Regime: Laboring Bodies, Exploitation and Garments Made in India
   Alessandra Mezzadri
3. The Intangible Economy: How Services Shape Global Production and Consumption
   Edited by *Deborah K. Elms, Arian Hassani and Patrick Low*
4. Making Cars in the New India: Industry, Precarity and Informality
   Tom Barnes
5. Development with Global Value Chains: Upgrading and Innovation in Asia
   Edited by *Dev Nathan, Meenu Tewari and Sandip Sarkar*
6. Global Value Chains and Development: Redefining the Contours of 21st Century Capitalism
   Gary Gereffi
7. Capturing the Gains? Gender and Work in Global Value Chains
   Stephanie Barrientos
8. Monopsony Capitalism: Power and Production in the Twilight of the Sweatshop Age
   Ashok Kumar

Reverse Subsidies in Global Monopsony Capitalism

Gender, Labour, and Environmental Injustice in Garment Value Chains

Dev Nathan
Shikha Silliman Bhattacharjee
S. Rahul
Purushottam Kumar
Immanuel Dahaghani
Sukhpal Singh
Padmini Swaminathan

CAMBRIDGE
UNIVERSITY PRESS

University Printing House, Cambridge CB2 8BS, United Kingdom

One Liberty Plaza, 20th Floor, New York, NY 10006, USA

477 Williamstown Road, Port Melbourne, vic 3207, Australia

314 to 321, 3rd Floor, Plot No.3, Splendor Forum, Jasola District Centre, New Delhi 110025, India

103 Penang Road, #05–06/07, Visioncrest Commercial, Singapore 238467

Cambridge University Press is part of the University of Cambridge.

It furthers the University's mission by disseminating knowledge in the pursuit of education, learning and research at the highest international levels of excellence.

www.cambridge.org

Information on this title: www.cambridge.org/9781316512272

First published 2022

Printed in India by Thomson Press India Ltd.

A catalogue record for this publication is available from the British Library

ISBN 978-1-316-51227-2 Hardback

Contents

Figures and Tables

Figures

Tables

Acknowledgements

This book is the product of a Ford Foundation grant to the Society for Labour and Development (SLD) from 2017 to 2019. Our thanks to the Foundation and, in particular, to Srinivasan Iyer who not just supported this work but was also part of discussions as we formulated our analysis over the years. As can often happen with such books, along the way, work done by a number of the authors with various other organizations and in various other capacities also came to be part of this book. Padmini's work as a member of the Madras High Court appointed committee to look into pollution in Tiruppur resulted in Chapter 9. Sukhpal's work with various assessments of Clean Cotton initiatives led to his contribution on cotton production in Chapter 10. Shikha worked with SLD and the Asia Floor Wage Alliance on identifying the spectrum of gender-based violence in garment value chains, which was presented at the time of the International Labour Conference on this topic in 2018. This study is reflected in Chapters 5 and 6. Dev worked with Global Labor Justice in defining issues of labour, gender, and environmental justice and this was the base of Chapter 2. Some of us worked on related research projects on the garments industry with the (International Labour Organization) ILO, where we thank Sher Singh Verick, Sudipta Bhadra, Bharti Birla, and Ayaa Matsura for their support and discussions at various times.

Many of the analyses in this book have been presented in various conferences and meetings. There was a paper on Living Wages at Cardiff University, for discussion at which we thank Jonathan Morris and Jean Jenkins. Chapter 3 was first published in the *Global Labor* Journal, May 2020. Annual Sustainability Conferences of the Center for Responsible Business (CRB) have been the occasion for presenting various parts of the analyses. At various times, some of the authors and SLD have also prepared reports for the Clean Clothes Campaign (CCC). In these and other multi-stakeholder meetings we interacted with persons from all sides of the industry. Our particular thanks to Chandrima Chatterjee of the Apparel Export Promotion Corporation (AEPC), Jalandhar Giri of Shahi Exports, and R. C. Kaser of the Okhla Exporters' Group. Randeeb Sarma is someone we have had discussions with over the years, through his various roles with Gap, Solidaridad, and, now, Marks and Spencer. Raja Shanmugam and other officials and members of the Tiruppur Exporters' Association have been part of our discussions. Rijit Sengupta of CRB too has been part of the journey leading to this book. Renana Jhabvala and other trade union officials from SEWA, AITUC, BMS, and NTUI have at various times also contributed to these discussions and our understanding of issues.

Some of the supplier firm case studies were supported by the Federation of Small and Medium Enterprises (FSME). Lakshmi Menon not just helped us with such firm studies but was an important part of discussions all through the years in which this book was in preparation. Members of the Women in Value Chains have been part of our discussions. In particular, Firoza Mehrotra and Janhavi Dave of HomeNet South Asia, Subhadra Gupta of the Fair Labor Association (FLA), Suhasini Singh of FairWear Foundation, Sabina Dewan of JustJobs Network, Gopinath Parakuni and Rekha Chakravarty of CiviDep, and Rishi Singh, from Bangalore have contributed to our understanding of the garment industry. In the trade unions and related women workers' organizations our major debt is to Amarnath Singh of Garment and Allied Workers' Union (GAWU) and Elizabeth Khumallambam of Nari Shakti Manch, all the participants in the focus group discussions (FGDs) and in the interviews in the National Capital Region (NCR), Tiruppur, and Bangalore. At SLD, Abdul Ahmed and Sonia Wazed provided more than organizational support, along with Meenakshi Kaushik and Jaidev Singh. For a short period of time Anjum Shaheen worked with SLD and prepared some of the field reports. Vijay Baskar, Sandip Sarkar, and Govind Kelkar reviewed some of the chapters. Balwant Mehta provided statistical support and guidance. Somnath Basu, Ashwitha Jaykumar, and Bindita Roy helped with editing. Shikhar Anant Pandey of GenDev Centre for Research and Innovation prepared the GVC flow charts.

At Cambridge University Press (CUP) we have had the support of Qudsiya Ahmed, Anwesha Rana, Anwesha Roy, Aniruddha De, and Purvi Gadia working through the pandemic-induced disruptions. Our thanks to the editors of the CUP Development Trajectories in Global Value Chains series for including this book in the series. Raphie Kaplinsky is the one we have turned to for review and comments over the years. We thank Will Milberg, Marty Chen, Naila Kabeer, Reema Nanavaty, and Jenny Holdcroft for their advance praise in support of this book. We do hope it will contribute to extending the analysis of labour, gender, and environmental justice in global production, and that the concept of reverse subsidies becomes part of the lexicon of global production.

During the years of doing the research and putting together this book there has been an informal core of persons with whom the authors have had frequent conversations. They include Anannya Bhattacharjee, Ashim Roy, Jennifer (JJ) Rosenbaum, Lakshmi Bhatia, Srinivisan Iyer, and Govind Kelkar. They might well be considered co-authors of this book. Though, of course, finally it is the authors who write what they write. Thus, while all these discussions with diverse players have helped formulate our thinking and the analyses in this book, obviously none of the persons mentioned here is responsible for the views and analyses expressed here, which remain the sole responsibility of the authors.

1
Introduction

This is a book about global value chains (GVCs), particularly, but not confined to, those of garments (or apparel). The structure of a value chain is usually taken to be composed of the following coarse-grained tasks: research and development, design, manufacturing, distribution and logistics, sales and marketing, and services. These activities, contributing to the final output and its marketing, are not carried out within the confines of a single firm, or even a multinational corporation (MNC). Rather, they are splintered in GVCs across firms and geographies, held together by an organizational structure, founded on governance relations between the lead firms or brands, including mass retailers and various suppliers.

The two sets of firms, brands and suppliers, are generally located in headquarter economies and supplier economies, respectively, to borrow the terms used by Richard Baldwin (2016). These can also be roughly congruent with the somewhat politically loaded terms, 'Global North' and 'Global South'. It should, however, be understood that all firms within each set of countries need not be only brand or supplier firms. China, in particular, has developed numerous brands or lead firms, such as Huawei, ZTE, Lenovo, Haier, and Alibaba, all with international markets. In garments too, China has the Li Ning brand in sportswear. India, to a much lesser extent, has some brands, such as Tata, Mahindra, Bajaj, and Hero, all in various parts of the automotive sector. On the whole, however, brands are concentrated in the headquarter economies of the Global North, while supplier firms are concentrated in supplier economies of the Global South.

GVCs are not just one other way in which contemporary global capitalism is organized; they can be called the characteristic form of twenty-first-century global capitalism, which is global monopsony capitalism. The World Trade Organization (WTO) and others estimate that as much as 70 per cent of global trade in 2017 was in the form of GVC trade (WTO et al. 2019). The predominance of this GVC form of capitalist organization means that our analysis of injustice in GVCs becomes an analysis of injustice in the global capitalist economy.

The GVC structure starts with knowledge, usually protected under intellectual property rights (IPRs), creating brands with varying degrees of monopoly, or oligopolies, in the product markets (Durand and Milberg 2019; Kaplinsky 2019) in the headquarter economies of lead firms. GVCs have embedded within them a distribution of knowledge among different GVC segments. Knowledge-intensive segments in pre- and post-production tasks are protected under IPRs in lead firms. Production knowledge is distributed among many suppliers in developing economies and is not protected under IPRs. In an unequal world—unequal both in the distribution of knowledge and of incomes and wages—there is the possibility of utilizing these differences to increase the profits of monopolies through the disintegration of production in GVCs.

As a result of IPR-protected product production, if there, for instance, were just five brands of cars, then there would be just five buyers of inputs that make cars; this would give the product monopolies monopsony positions in the input markets. The monopolies on the product market thus simultaneously become monopsonies or oligopsonies in input markets, where a few buyers can bargain with many suppliers to the buyers' advantage. In the resulting distribution of value within the value chain, lead firms or brands earn rents (or super profits), while the suppliers earn just competitive profits. The GVC then becomes a form of global monopsony capitalism.

Before proceeding, a word about terminology. The technical term for a market with few buyers and many suppliers is an 'oligopsony'. A market with few sellers and many buyers is an oligopoly. We substitute the term 'monopoly' for 'oligopoly', understanding that there are really not complete monopolies but firms with varying degrees of monopoly in the product market. Michal Kalecki (1971) uses the term 'degrees of monopoly' in his analysis of the relationship between monopoly profits and workers' wages. In a similar manner, one can also talk of degrees of monopsony, where a few brands as buyers deal with myriad suppliers. Ashok Kumar (2020) uses the term 'monopsony capitalism' as the title of his book on garment GVCs. Dev Nathan (2020) used the term 'global oligopsonies'. We will use the terms 'monopsony' and 'monopoly', understanding them to mean degrees of monopsony and monopoly. The elementary structure of GVCs is then that of brands as monopolies in the product market, and, simultaneously, monopsonies in the input market, dealing with many suppliers, their workers, and a range of environmental services. The

GVC is a form of global monopsony capitalism, bringing together in relations of dominance and value capture brands or lead firms from the Global North with manufacturers or suppliers in the Global South.

Embedding the GVC

The manner in which a GVC is mapped depends on the objective of the analysis. If the objective is to derive business strategies for GVC players, including whether or not to undertake process or product upgrading, then the standard GVC representation given earlier may be sufficient. A more comprehensive analysis even of business strategy, however, may show that the standard GVC representation is insufficient in that the flows are basically unidirectional with outputs of one segment becoming inputs into the next segment and so on. A unidirectional flow does not allow for feedback loops or reflexivity. For instance, results from sales and marketing, such as data from point of sale (POS) mechanisms, are fed back into marketing. Consumers can also feed into design. Von Hippel (2005), for instance, explains that lead consumers play a role in product design, and even in research and development processes.

This type of problem could perhaps be taken care of by introducing feedback loops. This would make the GVC diagram somewhat more complicated and difficult to read. But it would be a necessary introduction to modify the linearity of GVC representation. A more important weakness of the standard GVC representation, however, is that it restricts itself to what may be called the core of the production process, and does not bring into the picture the manner in which this production process relates to what it takes from and gives back to other spheres of the economic system.

For instance, labour power is a commodity input into each and every production segment. This labour power is produced not within the production system itself, but within the household. The key input from the GVC production system into the household is wages. Another input into labour power is from within the production system—the allocation of tasks and accompanying in-house training.

The role of in-house training in carrying out process innovation and bringing about productivity increases within production systems is sometimes considered within GVC analysis, for example, in Brown, Dehejia, and Roberrson (2018) and Nathan and Harsh (2018), or more generally in Ichniowski and Shaw (2003). But the important point that is left out in this analysis of the production of labour power is the role of the household, and of women's unpaid household and care work within it. Theories of social reproduction do, however, deal with the role of the household and women's care work in the reproduction of labour power, for instance, in the collection edited by Tithi Bhattacharya (2017).

The analysis of social reproduction has been joined with GVC analysis by Stephanie Barrientos (2019) in what she calls the Global re-Production Network, or G(r)PN. She argues that 'unpaid labour largely undertaken by women in the home helps cheapen the costs of maintaining and reproducing current and future generations, keeping wages down' (Barrientos 2019: 97). In Chapters 4 to 8, we extend this articulation of social reproduction with core GVC production processes. Here, we consider the relationship between low wages and accelerated work in depleting physical resources and affording insufficient nutritional replacement. This unbalanced equation turns a renewable resource, namely labour power, into one that can be mined or depleted.

Another area where we extend GVC analysis is into considering the production system's relation or interaction with the environment. As Liam Campling and Elizabeth Havice point out, until recently, 'the intersections between firms and the environment were an under-researched dimension of analyses using the GVC framework' (2019: 215). Here too, as with regard to labour power mentioned earlier, the environment links with GVCs as both input and output. For instance, with regard to garment production, as discussed in detail in Chapters 9 and 10, water comes in as an environmental input, while the waste water or effluent is the environmental output. Clean water and the waste cleaning capacity of the river systems are both renewable services. But, like labour power, they too can be overused and depleted.

Apparel and leather product value chains require raw materials produced by farmers and livestock rearers. Here again, there is both an input and an output relationship with their respective production value chains. Raw cotton and animal hides are the outputs of farmers and herders who grow cotton and raise animals. In turn, the price of raw cotton and animal hides is the input of the apparel and leather goods value chains into their livelihoods. Agricultural land is obviously also an input into raw cotton production. With the use and overuse of chemical pesticides, polluted land is another output of raw cotton production. Due to the carcinogenic effects of some of these chemicals, cancer is also an output of the apparel value chain.

A third area of extension of GVC analysis is with regard to interactions of the production system with government tax and revenue agencies. The various tax breaks or outright transfer payments become inputs into production GVCs enabling them to reduce costs. As governments in production countries compete to expand their production base and maintain foreign exchange earnings, lead firms sidestep accountability for contributing to social protection frameworks by locating production in free trade zones and paying wage standards that fall below living wages. These long-standing business practices erode both personal and social safety nets for workers by leaving production-line workers living virtually hand-to-mouth, without supporting personal savings, and transferring the onus of maintaining social and environmental protection to production countries.

Gender, Labour, and the Environment

We extend the analysis of the GVC into two spheres: the household and the environment. The household is a realm with which the GVC has an exchange relationship: the household contributes labour and the GVC contributes wages. Labour in and from the household, however, is gendered, so whether the labour is performed by women or men, is a variable in the analysis. This gendering of labour pertains to not only reproductive work in the household, almost entirely performed by women, but also to labour on garment production lines in the factory, also substantially performed by women. In the factory, there is both a confinement of women to lower sections of the workforce, and specifically gendered forms of harassment and violence that are deployed against women workers (Silliman Bhattacharjee 2020b; AFWA et al. 2018a–c). Women workers are also subject to forms of discrimination that affect them more than men. Gendering of labour also extends to the home as a production site for homeworkers and child labourers. It extends further to the rural households of migrant workers, which provide support as a subsidy that helps keep factory wages down and increase the profits that brands can capture.

Garment factories also have exchange relations with the environment. They extract cheap environmental services, such as fresh water, and return factory-created effluents or sludge into the environment. Resources can be depleted by overuse, beyond the rates of regeneration, as with the extraction of groundwater. But, as the analysis of the Anthropocene has now taught us, humans not only use natural resources but they also co-create the environment. The sludge, piling up in scattered areas around Tiruppur, or the coloured waste water that has turned the River Noyyal in Tiruppur or the Buriganga in Dhaka black, are stark reminders of the co-creation of natural resources by humans. This book takes a step in the direction of bringing this co-creation of resources into the analysis of production. It is a step in going beyond the human–nature binary that is characteristic of economic analysis as a whole.

The extension of GVC analysis into the household and the environment is laid out in Box 1.1, including a schematic representation in Figure 1.1 and accompanying text.

Box 1.1 Garment GVCs—Main Production Segments with Tasks and Inter-relations with Households and the Environment

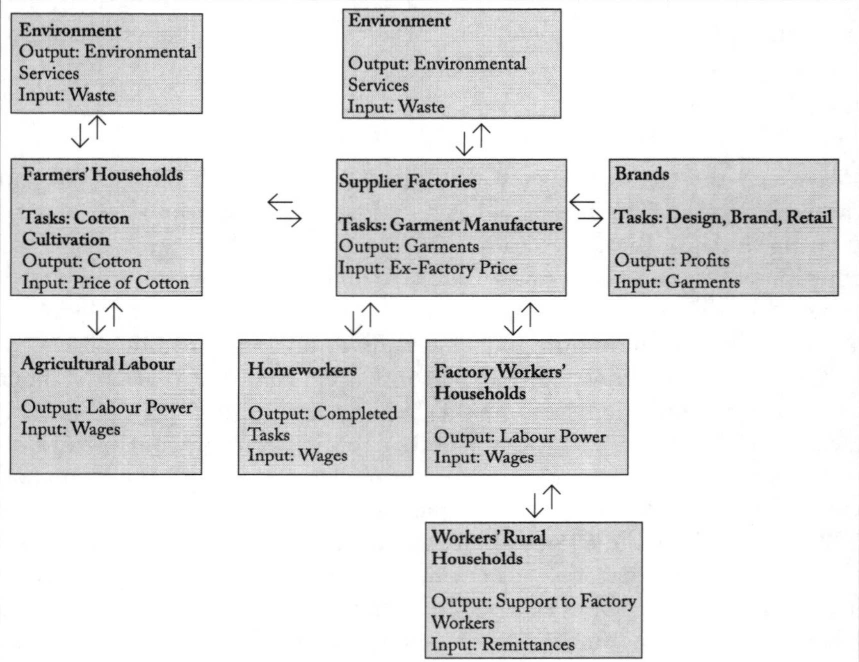

Figure 1.1 Garment GVCs—Main Production Segments with Tasks and Inter-relations with Households and the Environment
Source: Created by the authors.

This is an extended GVC representation. The second horizontal row of boxes represents the core of the GVC with its task segments: cotton cultivation, carried out by farmer households; garment manufacture, carried out in supplier factories; and design, brand, and retail carried out by brands, which are the lead firms. We set aside the transformation of cotton into fabric, which itself comprises a number of segments.

There are horizontal flows of value, in monetary terms, from one segment to the other. Farmer households supply raw cotton, receiving the price of cotton. Supplier factories turn fabric into garments. These garments are supplied on contract to brands, where suppliers receive the contracted ex-factory prices. In the process of exchange between suppliers and brands, we abstract from logistic and insurance costs that result in free on board (FOB) prices. The brands, through monopolized pre-production design and post-production branding and retailing tasks, turn these garments into profits.

The row of boxes below the second horizontal row represent the households and their labour inputs into the cotton cultivation and garment manufacture segments. Farmers receive labour from agricultural labour, which might also include child labour.

The garment factory, in a similar fashion, receives labour inputs from factory workers' households. These include labour inputs from homeworkers, who take up tasks outsourced from factories. Both factory and homeworkers receive wages, either on time-rate (factory workers in general) or piece-rate (homeworkers and factory workers). Factory workers likely maintain connections with the households of their rural origin, in which case they would supply remittances to the rural households and possibly receive some forms of material support.

The row of boxes above the second row represent the environment and the environmental services provided to the two segments of cotton cultivation and garment manufacture. In both cases, there is a supply of environmental services, such as clean water or cultivable land. The environment, in turn, receives untreated or treated wastes from both cultivation and manufacturing segments.

This is a representation of how we have extended GVC analysis in this book, relating both households and the environment into the overall analysis, and not treating them as just separate parts. In the concluding chapter, we will go back to this figure and expand upon the relative magnitudes of the two-way flows between different actors in the garment value chain.

Articulation

How does one connect and understand the relationships between spheres of social reproduction and the environment with the core production system of GVCs? In the examples mentioned earlier, the relations between production and the different socio-economic spheres could be expressed by additions to input–output tables. There could be a row for social reproduction and the manner in which it provides labour power as an input into production and receives wages as an output from production. Similarly, there could also be a row for environmental services that provide water as an input into production and receive waste as an output from production.

Adding rows to the input–output tables, however, is just a representation of what occurs in the interrelations between different spheres. It does not explain why these effects come about; why, for example, wages of women garment workers tend to be well below living wages. Or why environmental services are provided free or well below cost, while environmental wastes are passed on as externalities.

In trying to conceptualize the way in which these inter-actions occur one must note that these are not necessary structures. They can be changed. For instance, wage rates for women garment workers that are well below living wages are not a necessary structural feature of GVC production. Nor can non-valuation of environmental services or wastes be seen as a necessary feature of GVCs. Wages and environmental inputs and consequences are both constitutive of GVCs and present-day capitalism. However, the manner in which these different spheres relate can vary in different geographies and over time. Put another way, the structures of these interrelations are both contingent upon existing conditions and can vary over time.

We bring this contingency and variability into the interrelations between GVCs, gender, and the environment through the concept of articulation. Articulation may be between different modes of production, such as social reproduction and economic production, or between environmental resources and production. Articulation is very different from reflection, where relations in one sphere merely reproduce those in another sphere. Harold Wolpe, who formulated the concept of articulation in the context of the South African homeland economy providing subsidies to wages (and thus profits) in mining, explained it as follows: '... the social formation is not given a necessary structure. It is conceived of as a complex concrete object of investigation which may be structured by a single mode, or by a combination of modes, one of which is dominant' (Wolpe 1980: 34).

The concept of articulation is explained more fully by the cultural theorist Stuart Hall as follows:

> By the term, 'articulation', I mean a connection or link which is not necessarily given in all cases, as a law or fact of life, but which requires particular conditions of existence to appear at all, which has to be positively sustained by specific processes, which is not 'eternal' but has constantly to be renewed, which can under some circumstances, disappear or be overthrown, leading to the old linkages being dissolved and new connections—re-articulations—being forged. It is also important that an articulation between different practices does not mean that they become identical or that one is dissolved into the other. However, once an articulation is made, the two practices can function together as 'distinctions within a unity'. (Hall 1985: 113–114)

The concept of articulation can be used to investigate relations between different socio-economic spheres, such as between social reproduction and core GVC production. It has been used in this manner by Stephanie Barrientos (2019) to analyse the interrelations of gender and GVCs. The concept of articulation can also be used to look into relations between different segments of a GVC. Governance in GVCs, as formulated in Gereffi, Humphrey, and Sturgeon (2005), is also a form of articulation of lead firms with suppliers in GVCs. In the governance analysis itself, different forms of governance are identified, such as captive, modular, and relational.

The importance of articulation as structure is that the structure is not given 'as a law or a fact of life' (Hall 1985: 113). Rather, it is a structure that is brought into being in certain circumstances and can evolve with changes in the relations between different constituent parts of the structure. Choices are made, for instance, by monopsony producers with regard to their relations with suppliers. These relations with suppliers are usually presented as the only possible solutions in market economies. But monopolies in product markets do have a choice about the type of relations they establish with their suppliers (Helper 1991). The articulation of relations of monopoly brands with their suppliers is not something that is fixed and given, but is a matter of strategic choice. The concept of articulation helps emphasize the choice that exists in brand–supplier relations.

What the earlier discussion shows is that articulation is not a substitute for analysis. As Hall mentioned, '[T]here is no reason why anything is or isn't potentially articulable with anything else' (1985: 114). The analysis has to establish what is articulated with what, the power relations within them, the structures that result, and even how the structures do or may change. John Pickles and Adrian Smith (2016) use articulation to explore the ways in which structures of the garment industry changed in some countries of East Europe. Stephanie Barrientos (2019) also uses the concept of articulation in analysing social reproduction in GVCs.

In this book, we will discuss the articulation of core GVC production with social reproduction, the environment, and the government. We will also discuss (Chapter 11) the articulation of different segments, pre- and post-production segments with production segments in GVCs. Understanding power relations in forming and re-forming structures in and around GVCs is essential to our study of articulation across these domains.

We argue that the articulations in contemporary GVCs may be such as to create subsidies in the functioning of GVCs. But these articulations do not give a necessary and unchangeable structure to the interactions of different segments in a GVC. Articulation allows for policy that could change the nature of the interaction. This approach moves away from a deterministic understanding of these relationships that does not allow for choice and, therefore, forecloses policy shifts. Whether in the relation between monopsonist brands and suppliers, or the garment industry and the environment, there are policy choices at firm, industry, and also national and international levels. This approach provides a framework for policy interventions to influence the choices made by firms, brands, or suppliers in GVCs. In the concluding chapter, we discuss how policies do and can influence the choices made by brands and suppliers in GVCs. We take a position that calls for shifting policy to eliminate the unjust subsidies currently rampant in garment and many other GVCs.

One aspect of articulation is the relation where brands dominate suppliers. This monopsony structure enables brands to capture most of the productivity increases by suppliers as argued by Kaplinsky (2005) and shown in Chapter 11 in the context of garment GVCs in India. But here too, one should not presume that there is no choice available to the suppliers, however dominated they may be by the brands. There are constraints but, as Kumar (2020) shows, suppliers still have some policy choices by which they can grow and somewhat improve their bargaining power with brands, even if only in a limited manner.

Reverse Subsidies

Subsidies are usually understood to be the amounts provided by states to enable the consumption of goods or services as a public good, either because of their human rights implications or because of the externalities involved in their consumption. The subsidy allows the goods and services to be provided or consumed below their cost of production. Thus, food may be provided at subsidized prices or even free because of the accepted human right to live. Education and health services may also be provided below the usual cost of production or even free. This could be due to a commitment to enable a minimum or threshold level of human capability development. It could also be due to a realization that there are external benefits in consumption of health and educational services, as a result of which it is desirable to ensure threshold levels of consumption of these services. These are consumption subsidies provided to the public as consumers. There can also be production subsidies provided to the producers to promote the production of socially desirable goods, such as safe drinking water.

Both of these subsidies, whether to consumers or producers, are used to ensure socially desirable goals, such as elementary capabilities for a decent human existence. In addition to these subsidies that are expected to have positive outcomes, there are also what are called perverse subsidies, that is, subsidies that have a perverse or socially undesirable effect. This could be with regard to providing polluting fuels at low prices or other industrial inputs that increase greenhouse emissions. If we accept reducing emissions as our goal, a fossil fuel subsidy goes against this goal and is likely to increase the consumption of fuels that increase emissions. Along with this, the fossil fuel subsidy is likely to impede or retard transition to cleaner fuels.

In this book, we are using a third concept of subsidy: reverse subsidy,[1] defined as one that provides inputs such as labour power or environmental services at prices below their costs of production and, as a result, becomes a subsidy not for the gendered workers or the environment but a subsidy provided by gendered workers, their households, and the environment to the profits of the capital that employs the workers and uses the environmental services.

Such a reverse subsidy could exist in the case of workers, households, and the environment in relation to domestic capital. In this book dealing with GVCs, we demonstrate this notion of a reverse subsidy in the below-cost provision of labour power and environmental services for use in the production segments of GVCs in supplier countries, with the extra profits being transferred to brands through their monopsony positions vis-à-vis manufacturers.

In order for the subsidy to be a reverse subsidy, there are two features that need to exist. The first, of course, is that there must be a below-cost provision of an input in order to qualify it as a subsidy at all. This is argued with regard to labour power in Chapter 4 as the buying of labour power at a price that is lower than the living wage, which is taken as the cost of producing and reproducing labour power. The second feature is that this subsidy must be taken or extracted from the workers and the environment and captured by lead firms or brands that create and govern the garment GVCs. Taking these two features together, the subsidy itself allows for a cheapening of labour and environmental inputs into production. In addition, the GVC as a structure of monopsony capitalism, with degrees of monopsony of different lead firms or brands, allows for the benefits of cheapening production to be captured by the brands, as shown in Chapters 3 and 11.

The low, below-cost wages and the low or non-existent prices of environmental services would constitute a subsidy to suppliers had the suppliers been able to benefit from these low prices and increase their profits. But as seen in detail in Chapter 11, the suppliers, because of the monopsony relation with brands, are not able to secure any more than competitive profits, the minimum required to stay in business. Consequently, the gains from below-cost pricing of labour and environmental services are extracted or captured by the brands. Because of the monopsony structure of the garment GVC, the reverse subsidies also inhibit accumulation in the supplier economies of the Global South and accrue as super-profits in the Global North.

Some better-known reverse subsidies are the tax breaks and other fiscal concessions provided to investors in the export processing zones (EPZs) and other such areas where GVC production is concentrated. Not so well known, or at least not analysed as reverse subsidies, are the purchase of labour power and environmental services below their respective costs of production. The phenomena of poor and exploitative labour conditions and the negative effects of environmental pollution are both well known. That low wages paid to women and other workers in garment value chains reduce production costs and increase profits has been established in the literature (Barrientos 2019). That brands with their monopsony positions in the input markets capture the benefits of reduced costs of production by suppliers has also been noted (Kaplinksy 2005; Nathan 2020).

Where this book makes a departure from these earlier analyses is in identifying the purchase of inputs, particularly labour and environmental services, at prices below their respective costs of production, as a reverse subsidy. Further, the book shows that the monopsony structure of garment GVCs enables brands as lead firms to capture the profits from a cheapening of production, irrespective of where the extraction of the subsidy takes place. In what follows, we may use the term 'subsidy' alone to identify a reverse subsidy. This is just for the ease of exposition. Where necessary, we may make it clear that the reference is to a reverse subsidy or some other subsidy.

Subsidy in GVCs

Is there a subsidy involved in wages below the cost of the reproduction of labour power in GVCs? If one were to adopt a market-based approach to analysing economic phenomena, then an enterprise paying market wages is perfectly normal, playing by the rules of the market game. But as mentioned earlier, such wages result in part of the costs of labour being borne outside the GVC structure. This provisioning of a part of the costs from outside the GVC, not through a market exchange but as unpaid transfer, constitutes a subsidy.

Neither Harold Wolpe (1985) nor Claude Meillasoux (1981) used the term 'subsidy' in their early analyses of the articulation of modes of production. But one can say that a subsidy was implied in their analyses—a non-market transfer of a part of the costs of producing labour power from outside the system of wages. De Janvry was clear that this constituted a subsidy: 'Wages paid can fall below this cost and employers benefit from a *subsidy* that originates in unpaid labour applied to the peasant plot' (1986: 396, emphasis added). Recently, Tamar Wilson also uses the term 'subsidy', giving an explicit definition, 'By subsidy I mean an economic provisioning that comes from outside the dominant capitalist system but becomes integral and necessary to the functioning and expansion of that system' (2012: 204).

In the discussion in India, Jan Breman (2013; 2020) and Ravi Srivastava (2011) point out that circulation, or the movement of workers between the urban and rural economies, is a strategy through which capital raises profits by lowering the wages paid to labour. Capital both takes advantage of and encourages circular migrant labour through low wages that require migrants and their families to draw some part of their subsistence from the rural households of which they are a part. They may not use the term 'subsidy', but what they are analysing is the same process of rural households providing a subsidy to profits by enabling a reduction of wage payments. What Srivastava (2020: 7) refers to as the full cost of subsistence is another term for a living wage.

In this account of circular migration, the subsidy consists in the supply of goods and services from the rural economy of small-holders, agricultural labourers, and providers of household care services. When we are dealing with subsidies to low-wage, low-knowledge working men who leave their families behind, the providers of these subsidies are the left-behind women. In the case of China, where men and women often migrate together, the left-behind producers and caregivers are grandparents who look after children. In one way or the other, it is the rural families of migrant workers who provide the unpaid work and products that help keep factory wages low. The resulting rural women's labour subsidy to manufacturing wages is not specific to garment or other GVCs, but lead and supplier firms in garment GVCs perpetuate this process through seasonal hiring and by keeping wages down.

The subsidy is extracted through the normal functioning of the economic mechanism, including both the market and states. States do set minimum wages, but as seen in Chapter 4, they are nowhere near living wages. Supplier states have generally adopted a policy of keeping wages low, a policy reinforced by competition to secure GVC-based employment. Contracts between buyers and sellers in the garment industry are set at legally required minimum wages. Sometimes, with market scarcity and a firm strategy to retain workers, wages may be just above the legal minimum. As the data we present in this book will show, wages may be a bit higher in large, integrated full-package suppliers by about 10 per cent, but not by much more.

A major constraint on wages in the labour market in developing countries is that there is a large labour reserve in the rural economy. Migrant workers from rural areas are willing to migrate for a wage even below or just at the legal minimum wage since these urban wages are higher than those in the agricultural and other rural sectors. Low, state-set minimum wages, in combination with the market mechanism in a condition of surplus labour, work to ensure that market-based wages are not much more than the legal minimum. It is instructive to note that the two countries with the highest ratios of minimum to living wages are China and Malaysia, both countries that are said to have substantially absorbed their rural labour surpluses in the urban industry.

These low and subsidized wages are the result of the normal functioning of the state-cum-market system in developing economies. Normal market functioning does not eliminate these subsidies. In the market system, labour and environmental subsidies are externalities. We will return to the question of how to internalize these externalities in order to eliminate reverse subsidies from outside the GVC production system in the last chapter.

Intersectionality

In this book, we deal with the manner in which the household and the rural economy, as also the environment, are articulated with supplier factories and global brands. We could also describe our project as an intersectional analysis of class and gender, in the sites of factory, household, rural economy, and the environment, interacting with supplier and brand relations in creating and distributing profits in GVCs. Articulation can be called a specific form of intersectionality, concerned with power and flows in the intersection between the different sections or sites of production and social reproduction.

The more common use of the term 'intersectionality', introduced by Kimberly Crenshaw in 1989, denotes analysis in which multiple collective identities create the reality of oppression or exploitation. This is also the manner in which the term 'intersectional' political economy is used by Nancy Folbre (2020), in which there are multiple axes of system dynamics, including gender, race, ethnicity, caste, and class. We could say that these are multiple forms of oppression that serve to add to the identity of the garment worker. This would be similar to what Jens Lerche and Alpa Shah (2018) call 'conjugated oppression', using a term originating with Philip Bourgois (1988). Conjugated oppression is 'the co-constitution of class-based relations and oppression along the lines of race, ethnicity, gender and, in India, caste and tribe' (Lerche and Shah 2018: 928).

This type of intersectionality, or conjugated oppression, is something that we discuss extensively in the case of gender and class, pointing, for instance, to the earlier expulsion of women than men from factory production (Chapter 5); and analysing gender-based violence and harassment (GBVH) as a gendered form of supervision on the shop floor (Chapter 6). Both early expulsion from factory production and GBVH are linked to concentration of women workers in the most insecure forms of employment—an articulation of workforce composition with gender that has been well documented in Cambodia, Indonesia, Pakistan, and Sri Lanka. Across these Asian countries, women workers also earn between 10 and 25 per cent less than male workers for similar work (AFWA 2021).

The intersection or conjugation of caste with gender and class is also seen in Chapter 6. Data from the Periodic Labour Fource Survey (2017–2018) show that the Dalits (the ex-untouchable castes) and Adivasis (indigenous peoples) both earn median wages that are lower than other social groups. Here, we build upon and contribute to robust lines of research on labour market exclusion in India at the intersection of informal employment status, gender, and social identity for Dalit, Adivasi, and Muslim workers (see, for example, Kompier 2014). There are also ways in which caste discrimination and oppression are carried onto the shop floor, for instance, in the form of caste denigration and caste abuse. Caste-based discrimination is common in Indian garment factories, especially in Tamil Nadu. Dalit workers are concentrated in the most poorly paid and hazardous jobs in the garment industry, with many factories hiring Dalits only for janitorial work in the factory like cleaning toilets and removing cotton waste from the shop floor (AFWA 2021).

In 2021, moreover, the Asia Floor Wage Alliance (AFWA) documented accentuation of systemic discrimination against Dalit garment workers during the COVID-19 lockdown period in India. Dalit garment workers faced the highest fall in wages when compared to every other social category. The wages of garment workers categorized as general category workers fell by 57 per cent and wages for other backward castes dipped by 55 per cent. By contrast, Dalit workers' wages fell by 79 per cent (AFWA 2021).

Heightened exposure to discrimination and violence for women garment production-line workers with intersectional Dalit identities has been well recognized among the global labour, Dalit rights, and gender justice movements—most recently in response to the murder of Jeyasre Kathiravel, an Indian garment worker and Tamil Nadu Textile and Common Labour Union (TTCU) member who was organizing workers to address GBVH in her workplace. After facing months of sexual harassment by her supervisor, Jeyasre was found murdered in January 2021, catalyzing a movement calling for justice for her murder and renewed commitment by lead firms to end GBVH on garment supply chains. We note these forms of intersectionality of class with caste and ethnicity as something that needs to be further analysed with ethnographic detail.

The Inclusion of Injustice in GVC Analysis

GVC analysis has strong normative content. Power and inequality are quite central to the analysis of GVC structures. Social upgrading, meaning an improvement in the condition of workers and small producers in value chains, was a key component of the University of Manchester–DFID Capturing the Gains research project on GVCs. The references are too numerous to be listed here, but in the recent *Handbook of Global Value Chains* (Ponte, Gereffi, and Raj-Reichert 2019), power and inequality in the distribution of returns from GVCs are quite central to many of its chapters. Problems of gender inequality in the treatment of women homeworkers and of extreme forms of exploitation through child labour have also figured in GVC analysis. There is also significant material debunking the weaknesses and even shams of corporate social responsibility (CSR).

The analysis of poor labour conditions in supplier firms in GVCs has worked in conjunction with movements for their improvement. The early United Students Against Sweatshops (USAS) in the USA, the later Clean Clothes Campaign (CCC) and the Clean Shoes movements in Europe have all had links with research into GVCs. Similarly, the Asia Floor Wage Alliance (AFWA) and other workers' movements in countries including Bangladesh, India, Cambodia, and Indonesia have had sustained links with researchers within these countries. This book is the product of one such connection of research with movements to improve working conditions in the garment value chains. Political philosophers such as Iris Young (2004) also linked with these movements for justice, connecting them with a theory of global responsibility. There have been similar links between research on child labour in GVCs and movements to end child labour, whether in programmes of the International Labour Organization (ILO) or, more recently, the Freedom Fund. Exposure of bonded labour and forms of modern slavery, as in the Coltan supply chain from the Congo (Nathan and Sarkar 2010), are part of the staple of GVC analysis. Exposure of environmental harms and double standards have been somewhat less part of the vocabulary of GVC analysis, though that is changing.

At the same time, there is also analysis of the benefits that countries and workers in developing countries have acquired from participation in GVCs. Wages in even the most sweatshop conditions in garment production are higher than the available alternative in labour surplus economies. For millions of women in supplier countries, employment in garment factories has been the route to paid work (Kabeer 2002, 2015). As a GVC worker from a Latin American country told a researcher, 'We have always worked hard. NOW we are paid for it' (Barrientos 2019: xix, emphasis in original). The benefits from participation in GVC employment do not, however, wipe away the fact that this participation may be in highly exploitative forms of precarious employment.

In this book, we are concerned with injustice in what may be called normal forms of employment in garment GVCs. These regularized structures and conditions of employment in garment GVCs are, for the most part, distinct from experiences of 'modern slavery'. The ILO Global Estimates of Modern Slavery focus on two main issues: forced labour and forced marriage. The forced labour estimates included in the Global Estimates of Modern Slavery include forced labour in the private economy that is imposed by private individuals, groups, or companies across sectors; forced sexual exploitation of adults and commercial sexual exploitation of children; and state-imposed forced labour (ILO-WFF 2017: 9). This focus on private actors and violent states echoes the philanthro-capitalist narrative that locates the cause of modern-day slavery in the individual deviant behaviour of 'criminal slaveholders' and recruiters who prey on the 'weakness, gullibility, and deprivation' of the 'enslaved' as a result of the supposed lawlessness in much of the developing world (Bales 1999: xvii, 11, 29).

While modern slavery is a matter of violating these accepted laws and norms, the everyday injustice of reverse subsidies laid out in this book are structurally reproduced by brands and their suppliers that largely follow the rules of the game. The key rules of the game, in this case, are: first, the costing of labour power in production at or around national minimum wages and, second, inadequate or no payment for environmental services carried out in the production countries. Both of these forms of costing do not in fact cover the costs of producing the concerned labour power or environmental services.

Our argument, briefly, is that the extraction of labour and environmental subsidies are forms of injustice that result from following the accepted rules of the GVC game. In order to establish this proposition, we define what constitutes subsidies in the employment of labour and the use of environmental services in GVCs, taking garment GVCs to illustrate the problem. We start with establishing that subsidies are extracted from gendered labour and the environment in garment GVCs. The gendered labour subsidies result in the inability of workers and their families to attain elementary levels of capabilities (Nussbaum 2000; Anand and Sen 2000). Environmental subsidies degrade natural resources with long-term sustainability implications for the planet and people. This is what makes the labour and environment subsidies matters of basic justice. While the subsidies are extracted in different locations, the factory, the household, and the environment, the monopsony relation between brands and suppliers enables the capture of these subsidies by the brands from across these domains.

Here, the experiences of garment workers in Asia during the global COVID-19 pandemic are instructive because they represent a 'systemic edge'—a site of analysis at the margins where techniques of governance are often most visible and most brutal (Sassen 2014: 211). As COVID-19 precipitated seismic shocks to economic security and public health on garment supply chains globally, brands refused to take or share any responsibility for either suppliers or their workers. Instead, some of them even refused to pay suppliers for orders already delivered, a step from which they stepped back only after exposure in the international media threatened them with a loss of reputation (Anner 2020). Refusal to pay for orders already delivered and cancellation of orders for which suppliers had purchased inputs left suppliers without cash. There was a knock-on effect, with suppliers not paying wages to workers. Labour contractors went so far as to switch off their phones in order to avoid workers asking for their dues.

The main point from this account is that the risks of business were basically transferred to suppliers from the Global South and, in turn, to their workers. While the owners of supplier factories would surely have been able to secure their consumption needs from their savings, worker incomes were pushed below the poverty line, with women workers falling even more behind the poverty line than men. In addition, women had to compensate for services formerly purchased from the market that they could no longer afford, such as health services, by increasing unpaid care work. With governments of the supplier countries doing little, again with differences between countries, workers and their families were forced to reduce consumption, deplete savings, increase debt taken on usurious rates of interest, and increase unpaid care work just to stay alive—in order to be able to return to work when the brands from the Global North once again required their labour.

Even with all the excesses of brands (for example, non-payment for orders already delivered), suppliers and their workers have no alternative but to remain available when the orders are revived. That is the reality of global monopsony capitalism, where myriad suppliers and their workers from the South, in a condition of overall labour surplus, face a few brands (including mass retailers) from the Global North. Of course, there are also a few emerging brands, most from China and also a few from India, that are likely to have acted in such a manner. That only shows that one must pay attention to new emerging forces in global monopsony capitalism, but it does not alter the basic picture of the burden of the current global recession in garment production having been pushed onto suppliers and workers from the Global South. The certainty that suppliers and workers in the Global South will be there, even if with somewhat weakened bodies, when the brands require them is what underlies the behaviour of brands in carrying out wage theft in the current recession. This analysis at the systemic edge reveals the subsidies extracted from workers under monopsony capitalism that cut across sectors and geographies.

There is one rule of the game that we do not discuss in this book. This is the unequal remuneration for the same tasks performed in different countries, specifically as between headquarter and supplier economies. This difference, leading to labour arbitrage, is the basis of GVCs. This, in some analysis, is the nature of imperialism in the contemporary world (Smith 2016; Nathan 2018). It was this difference in remuneration to the same factor in different countries that Arghiri Emmanuel called the 'imperialism of trade' (1972). If labour performing the same tasks, say stitching a garment or carrying out the programme of information technology (IT) software, were not differently remunerated across countries, there would be no GVC.

While we do not go into this question of 'equal pay for equal work' across countries, trade unions and other workers' organizations—including in

Bangladesh, Cambodia, China, India, Indonesia, Malaysia, Pakistan, and Sri Lanka—have advanced the concept of an Asia Floor Wage to address labour competition among supplier countries. Foundational to the AFWA, the Asia Floor Wage seeks to halt a race to the bottom in wages and working conditions by allowing the standard of living for workers between countries to be compared regardless of the national currency. The AFWA bases their calculations on the following assumptions: a worker needs to be able to support themselves and two other 'consumption units' (1 consumption unit = 1 adult or 2 children); an adult requires 3,000 calories a day to be able to carry out physical labour; and in Asia, food costs account for half of a worker's monthly expenditure and non-food costs for the other half. The Asia Floor Wage must be earned for a work-week of maximum 48 hours, not including bonuses, allowances, or benefits. The Asia Floor Wage is calculated in PPP$—Purchasing Power Parity $—which is an imaginary currency built on the costs of consumption of goods and services by people. The Asia Floor Wage is revised periodically by conducting fresh food basket surveys, and within intervening years by the use of a formulation based on Consumer Price Indices for each supplier country (Bhattacharjee and Roy 2016).

Responsibility

Are brands *responsible* for labour and environmental conditions along the value chains in which their products are produced? Or, are they merely utilizing existing conditions in the Global South? One way in which brands could be held to be responsible for value chain labour conditions is that since the brands capture the bulk of profits in these value chains—and since these labour and environmental conditions, by keeping labour and environmental costs low, contribute to brand profits—brands are indirectly responsible for the human and environmental costs of these reverse subsidies. But there is another way in which it can be argued that brands do not just utilize existing supply conditions but also *choose* or fashion them in ways that maximize their profits—a process in which they are often aided by authorities in supplier countries. This is a stronger sense in which brands could be held to be directly responsible for conditions in their value chains, right down to the difficult-to-monitor levels of homeworkers and the informal economy.

If brands are to be held accountable for injustice to workers in their value chains, they must be held responsible for the conditions under which workers are employed. As we discuss in more detail in Chapter 2, monopsony brands choose particular strategies in supplier relations. They could have stable relations with fewer suppliers. Such stability would also enable suppliers to carry out technological advances and innovations. On the other hand, monopsonists can also choose a strategy based on myriad suppliers with little commitment on orders. This dominant choice enables short-term maximization of profits, but works against setting up a GVC with more productive suppliers with better gendered labour relations. It is this choice of relations with suppliers that gives brands responsibility for the conditions under which workers are employed in factories and other production sites, such as homes.

Vision

Central to the vision guiding the analysis in this book is that the GVC system should incorporate a base level of well-being for producers, women and men production-line workers and producers of raw cotton, and also for other users or producers of environmental services. We define that base level as being the elementary level of capability development that is considered consistent with human dignity, translated into conditions of decent work. At the environmental level, the notion of full coverage of the costs of environmental services provides a base for the costs of environmental services that should be covered within a GVC.

This approach resonates with Kate Raworth's *Doughnut Economics* (2017), where an acceptable level of human capability development is the basis of a just global production system. We extend this definition of a just global production system to include providing the full costs of environmental services. The under-pricing of labour and environmental services from supplier countries and the capture by brands of the resulting excess profit are part of the 'unsustainable inequalities' that relate to the analysis in Lucas Chancel's book of the same name (2020).

These issues of justice in global production, however, do not deal with the issue of the economic system not exceeding the environmental limits, or the outer ring of Raworth's doughnut, which, again, should not be breached by the GVC production system. Not exceeding environmental limits is a matter of sustainability, which we mention in the book, but do not deal with in depth because that would require a separate book in itself.

Research Methods

The arguments in this book are based on structural analysis of garment value chains and situated analysis of how these global processes impact the daily lives of workers on production lines, with a focus on women workers in precarious employment. This type of argument is well advanced through a mixed methods approach, including macro-level data analysis and survey and ethnographic research.

The scale, relevance, and application of our argument is certainly global and, in many ways, cross-sectoral. Therefore, this book includes examples from production contexts across the globe. However, our understanding of GVCs at the level of how they are experienced by workers is concerned with process—how features of value chain production are operationalized and the impact of these features on workers. Our accounts in these areas are rooted in original empirical research into the experiences of garment workers and supplier firms in garment value chains.

Our analysis of garment GVCs in India includes engagement with more than 350 garment workers in survey or discussion formats; situated in relationship to analysis of unit data from India's Annual Survey of Industries (ASI), Periodic Labour Force Survey (PLFS), and other data from the National Sample Survey Organisation (NSSO). It also includes the findings of interviews with about 60 supplier firms in garment production clusters. Finally, it draws from findings from a 2021 study on wage theft in the garment industry, conducted by AFWA, including surveys of COVID-19 impacts on 2,185 workers across 189 factories located in Bangladesh, Cambodia, India, Indonesia, Pakistan, and Sri Lanka (AFWA 2021).

In addition, this book includes an extended case study of environmental impacts in a particular production area in India. In Chapter 9, where we consider environmental subsidies, we include the experiences of one of our authors as a member of a committee appointed by the High Court of Madras to suggest measures to contain pollution caused to the Noyyal River consequent to the discharge of untreated trade effluents into the river by dyeing and bleaching units in Tiruppur. These components come together to form a deep case study of the Delhi–National Capital Region and Tiruppur garment production clusters, with some fieldwork in Bangalore production hubs.

In our study of living wages and GBVH, we situate our India case study regionally, including original empirical work in Bangladesh, Cambodia, Indonesia, and Sri Lanka. Here, the arguments in this book are grounded in engagement with 883 workers employed in 142 garment supplier factories across Asia.

In studying the experiences of garment workers—a force dominated by young, migrant women—this book engages in network-based rights mobilization as a research practice. This approach seeks to use positions of power in knowledge generation to address extreme imbalances in information and power by strengthening network relations among research participants at all stages of the research process. In short, we anticipate and hope to foster opportunities for this research to strengthen advocacy to advance justice in garment value chains by workers and their allies through the network of trade unions, workers' and women's organizations, and other civil society organizations that made this work possible.

As an approach, network-based rights mobilization also seeks to transform data collection processes into opportunities for two-way participatory learning and engagement. The data collected and presented in this book spans more than five years of collaboration between the authors and labour rights organizations and alliances working at local, national, regional, and global levels of engagement. During this time, our research methods and questions developed alongside discussions aimed at identifying the research required to inform the development and implementation of standards to protect workers' rights. Such an approach joins a line of scholarship committed to 'pragmatic solidarity' (Farmer 2003)—not only perceiving social inequalities but also challenging and transforming inequalities of power (for example, Holmes 2013; Chatterji 2015).

For instance, in the lead up to the 107th Session of the International Labour Conference, a global coalition of trade unions and worker rights organizations released the research discussed in Chapters 5 and 6, detailing patterns of gender-based violence in Walmart, Gap, and H&M Asian garment supply chains. These reports by the AFWA and Global Labor Justice–International Labor Rights Forum (GLJ–ILRF) aimed to make sure that the experiences and recommendations of low-wage women workers—employed in sectors and supply chains that rely on their labour—were lifted up in order to create a strong ILO Convention that will guide employers, multinational enterprises, and governments in working with trade unions to eliminate gender-based violence in garment supply chains and other workplaces. On 21 June 2019, the General Conference of the ILO adopted the ILO Violence and Harassment Convention, 2019 (C190) and Recommendation 206 (R206). ILO C190 and R206 represent a framework for realizing a shared commitment among workers, employers, and states to end workplace violence, including GBVH.

Outline of the Book

Chapter 2 sets out the analysis of labour and environmental injustice issues in GVCs. Starting with the framing of global justice issues, it lays out the minimum gender and labour standards that are generally accepted as basic requirements for gendered labour justice. In terms of labour standards, requirements for basic justice are related to the ILO's Core Labour and Decent Work Standards. Transgression of these standards amounts to gendered labour injustice. We also extend the notion of injustice to the provision of environmental services at prices below their costs of production and the manner in which costs are imposed as externalities on producers or other users of environmental services. Chapter 2 closes by addressing the brand's or lead firm's responsibility for their choice of supplier relations and consequent impacts on gendered labour and the environment.

Chapter 3 is a broader analysis of the brand or buyer–supplier relations in GVCs, and their impacts on labour conditions. It sets out the dual monopoly–monopsony structure of GVCs, created by IPRs-protected product monopolies. The knowledge level in GVC production segments, carried out by suppliers, is related to supplier margins and profits. Where supplier margins are restricted to the normal competitive level, employment conditions tend to be generally poor, with wages around the national minimum and a preponderance of precarious employment. With higher knowledge levels in supplier segments, and particularly where there is some form of reputational capital, there are generally better forms of employment, both in wages and in employment security.

After these initial chapters set out an economic analysis, the context of justice in GVCs, we move to a detailed consideration of gender, labour, and environment issues in garment GVCs. The empirical base for our analysis is mainly from two garment clusters, Tiruppur and the National Capital Region (NCR) in India. We supplement this empirical foundation with empirical material from other garment supplying countries in Asia, including Bangladesh, Cambodia, Indonesia, and Sri Lanka. The three sites in which we consider the extraction of subsidies are the factory, the household, and the environment. The chapters on extraction of subsidies are divided into parts corresponding with these sites—first, the factory, followed by the household, and then the environment.

This next part deals with gendered labour subsidies in the factory base of garment GVCs. Chapter 4 discusses the concept of living wages and its application in Asian supplier economies. Living wages are taken to include a monetization of women's unpaid household and care work. We compare living wages with minimum wages in Bangladesh, Cambodia, China, India, and Sri Lanka. Against this regional backdrop, we provide an empirical examination of wages in the garment clusters in India. The very low level of legal minimum wages forces workers to accept and even seek substantial overtime work.

Chapter 5 deals with the manner in which labour subsidies are extracted from women's bodies through a routine practice of 'overuse and discard'. It shows that most women workers in Asian supplier countries are made to work long hours in conditions that exact a high physical toll and then discarded from factory employment, often by the ridiculously young age of 35, with empirical data from India, Bangladesh, and Cambodia.

Complementing more familiar analysis on GBVH as a form of injustice by itself, Chapter 6 details how GBVH also functions as a form of supervision in garment factories. The chapter begins with a typology of different forms of GBVH in garment production lines. It then discusses the manner in which, under pressure of shortened lead times and uncertain orders, GBVH is used to extract high intensity work, most visible in the frequent phenomenon of fainting by women at work. All of this contributes to the 'overuse and discard' discussed in Chapter 5.

The next part goes beyond the factory to the households of workers. Chapter 7 shows how the rural economy contributes to meeting the costs of production of labour power during periods when workers are laid-off, during illness and in retirement. The rural household plays the key role of providing social security, as was shown when migrant workers returned during the 2020 employment shutdowns due to the impact of the COVID-19 pandemic and its economic consequences on garment supply chains. Chapter 8 deals with the household itself as a production site, for the production of labour power for factory workers; and for the various production tasks carried out by homeworkers, the 'invisible workers' in many value chains, including child labourers.

The next part deals with environmental subsidies in the garment GVC. Chapter 9 deals with the costs of success in the Tiruppur knitwear cluster in India. It shows how the unmitigated discharge of effluents, particularly from dyeing and printing units, blackened the River Noyyal and groundwater in the region. This reduced agricultural productivity in the region and undermined secure drinking water. The chapter points out that when mitigation measures, such as reverse osmosis (RO) treatment units, were taken up, the environmental degradation was considered entirely a local matter. The brands that ultimately captured the value from keeping down the costs of environmental services were not even seen to be part of the problem. There was a cognitive failure in not linking the monopsony brands and their profits with the environmental problems they caused.

Chapter 10 deals with subsidies in cotton production. It explains how United States (US) subsidies for their cotton farmers depress world prices and have serious livelihood consequences, particularly in West African countries. The overuse of water and the degradation of the soil by pesticide and other inorganic chemical residues are thrown into relief by the health consequences of cotton production in the state of Punjab, where the cotton belt is also known as the cancer belt. Cotton production also has extraction of labour subsidies, with high levels of child labour in both BT cotton pollination and the harvesting of raw cotton.

Chapter 11 returns to brand–supplier relations in the garment GVC. Using primary data from interviews with management in supplier factories and secondary official data, it shows that suppliers fall into two groups in their responses to shortened lead times and uncertain orders. One group uses labour-intensive methods such as increasing overtime or increasing the use of precariously employed labour. The other invests in technology and better management practices, including employing workers with employment security and some increased benefits. The investment in technology, management, and labour does not, however, seem to result in an increase in profit rates. This could mean that brands are able to capture the benefits of reduced costs. What the suppliers in the second group do get, however, is an increase in orders and thus turnover. There is also some increased bargaining power among these large suppliers. This was demonstrated during the 2020 recession—brands cancelled payments, even for goods already supplied, but not to large suppliers. Collective action by suppliers in Bangladesh, supported by media exposure fuelled by researchers (Anner 2020), also brought about a partial reversal of brand actions with brands paying for completed products without demanding discounts. The chapter concludes that severe constraints faced by suppliers could, to an extent, be overcome by supplier collective action and also by the forward-looking strategies of suppliers.

Chapter 12 concludes the book with a summary of the main findings followed by a discussion of some ways in which the movement for justice in garment GVCs to eliminate or reduce reverse subsidies could be carried forward. It stresses the importance of collective action by workers, with leadership of women in these actions; collective action by suppliers; ethical consumer and shareholder actions in the headquarter economies of the big brands; and even the coming together of a movement of movements to build a countervailing power to global brands, in other words, to global monopsony capitalism.

Notes

1. An earlier use of the term 'reverse subsidy' is by Tina Rosenberg (2007).

FRAMEWORK

2

Gender, Labour, and Environmental Injustice in Global Value Chains (GVCs)

Introduction

This book deals with injustice in global production. Injustice means the absence of justice. Consequently, what we need to define is what constitutes global justice. The absence of the constituents of justice would then make for injustice. How do we identify the constituents of justice in global production? This book is about economic relations or politico-economic relations between actors and the outcomes they produce for gendered workers and the environment in the context of relations between suppliers and brands in what we have called global monopoly-cum-monopsony capitalism.

We define basic economic justice for gendered workers as the provision of the foundational capabilities for a dignified human life. These foundational capabilities are protected by labour standards, starting with the International Labour Organization's (ILO's) core labour standards and extending to encompass living wages and bodily integrity. The acquisition of an input, whether labour power or environmental services, at prices below their cost of production or reproduction, constitutes a reverse subsidy that is unjust in that it deprives gendered workers of the requirements for a dignified human life and results in the deterioration of the environment. After dealing with economic justice for gendered workers, the chapter sets out the main features of environmental justice, in terms of raw material, manufacturing segments, and post-consumption waste.

In matters of justice, it is also necessary to identify actors responsible for injustice. The chapter then deals with whether we can hold brands or lead firms responsible for labour and environmental subsidies extracted at the level of supplier firms. Since brands or lead firms capture the majority of value added in the value chain, they should also be required to take major responsibility for the labour conditions in which this value is extracted. More importantly, however, brands or lead firms make choices in terms of supplier relations. They could choose to have a small number of suppliers with whom they have stable order relations, or, they could have short-term relations and unstable orders with a large number of suppliers. Their use of monopsony positions to create the latter type of short-term, unstable orders with myriad suppliers is a strategic choice. Since supplier relations are a choice rather than a compulsion, brands are directly responsible for how their terms of engagement with the suppliers impact workers and the environment in their value chains.

Framing Global Justice in GVCs

Global justice problems which are linked to the GVC organization of cross-border operations are problems that affect people who are residents of more than one state. Through colonialism and international trade and investment, the world had become strongly interconnected such that regular and even daily economic matters transcend national boundaries. As Sanjay Subrahmanyam and other historians argue about early modern history (1997), there is and has been an interconnected history connected across nations and regions, predating colonialism.

We can identify some phases in these economic connections. From an irregular trade, there was a movement to a regular trade that separated production from consumption (Baldwin 2016)—the spice trade that brought Europeans to India and other parts of Asia and the slave trade that connected Africa, Europe, and the Americas are quintessential examples of this separation of production from consumption—in the first case that of a commodity, spice, produced in Asia and consumed in Europe, and in the second case, human beings as labour power, born in one place, Africa, and exploited in another place, the Americas. The interconnectedness through trade, which is often initiated or even regularly carried out through force, forms one phase of global economic connections. Another phase of economic interconnection is established with the extraction of revenue from colonies, whether it is gold from South America or taxes in North America and India. This was extended to the investment of capital to earn continued profit, such as the investment of British loan capital in the Indian railway system.

GVCs and the splintering of production have extended this interconnection on a regular, even daily basis, across multiple countries. As we write, the COVID-19 pandemic starkly reveals the interconnectivity of the world created by GVCs. Life-saving drugs and vaccines are mainly created in publicly funded research institutes, or, less frequently, in the research and development (R&D) labs of Big Pharma in the Global North, but are now beginning to be created in India and China, as in the case of the COVID-19 vaccines. They are then produced in bulk with active pharmaceutical ingredients (APIs), mainly produced in China, and then turned into formulations in India. This is a level of interconnectedness that needs to be distinguished from that of simple trade or even investment. The interconnectedness can be characterized as an articulation of production processes across countries. Some might prefer to use the term 'entanglement' to describe this interconnectedness. At this stage, we will not go into which term is more appropriate to characterize the nature of interconnectedness, but we would like to point out that GVCs bring a level of interconnectedness that is structurally deeper than a straightforward exchange of goods—such as cloth for wine, in Ricardo's famous example of commodity trade.

As a result of the changes in international connections, the jurisdictional specificity of rights has also changed. This did not occur just with GVCs, but began even earlier, reaching a new level of global jurisdiction with GVCs. The 1948 Universal Declaration of Human Rights recognizes the moral equivalence of all persons. More specifically, it recognizes the right to 'just and favourable remuneration', which is specified as one allowing for 'an existence worthy of human dignity' (Article 23, Universal Declaration of Human Rights [United Nations 1948]). The Indian Constitution of 1950 also lists a similar right to receive fair remuneration, not as an immediate right, but as a guiding principle of state policy. It states that state policy should secure to all citizens, women and men equally, 'the right to an adequate means of livelihood', and even 'equal pay for equal work for both men and women' (Article 39, Constitution of India).

Who Are the Subjects of Economic Justice?

The fact that some social structural processes have global reach (Young 2004), with GVCs being quintessential examples of structural processes with global reach, extends obligations of justice globally. Nation states are inadequate frames of reference for the analysis of a global phenomenon working across and within borders. There is 'an inherently transnational dimension to the politics of claims-making relating to … women workers in global value chains' (Kabeer 2015: 51). Therefore, the 'who' of the justice problem has to be extended with the 'all-affected principle' (Fraser 2009: 24). In Chapter 3, we lay out who is affected and implicated in the dual monopoly–monopsony structure of GVCs that produce unjust outcomes across borders.

Discussions and the framing of justice are all too often carried out and then implemented by political elites and intellectuals involved in formulating and implementing policy. Such discussions often respond to movements or pressures from below, but the framing of the problem and its judicial solution are typically matters decided from above. We argue that this kind of policymaking needs to be revised in order to democratize the formulation of justice issues, so that the 'who' of justice appear not only as recipients of benefits from policy but also as participants in framing justice issues and deciding on policies. The introduction of workers (as the 'who' of justice) into the process of consultation and decision-making brings a reflexivity into the political process (Fraser 2009: 29). As a consequence, the 'who' are implicated in both the 'what' and the 'how'.

The ILO brings together tripartite constituencies—governments, employers, and workers—of the now 187 member states, to set labour standards, develop policies, and devise programmes promoting decent work for all. As such, social dialogue and meaningful engagement with trade unions and worker organizations is a requirement to uphold international labour standards. Engagement with trade unions and worker organizations is also essential in ensuring that initiatives to advance justice in garment value chains are informed by worker experiences and accountable to workers. Initiatives that do not include a role for trade unions and worker organizations are not sufficient to catalyse the critical transformations required to end unjust subsidies.

What Is Involved in Economic Justice?

Capabilities can be considered at two levels: basic or elementary capabilities and advanced capabilities. The first would include nutrition, education, health, protection of bodily integrity, and freedom of expression (Nussbaum 2004: 13). Over and above these basic or elementary capabilities, there are advanced capabilities, such as those related to higher or tertiary education and a fulfilling career. The boundary between basic and advanced capabilities is flexible and can change over time. For instance, in the aftermath of the COVID-19 pandemic, access to the internet can be seen as a basic capability where it was earlier an advanced capability.

Congruent with this widely accepted notion of basic capabilities, basic injustices can be defined as those that violate requirements for basic human existence, including worker rights (Young 2004). In the labour rights discourse, there is a set of core labour issues, which can be taken as the minimum essential capabilities for workers to secure a modicum of justice. These are set forth as core labour rights, adherence to which is implied in the countries' membership of the ILO. They include freedom of association and effective recognition of the right to collective bargaining; the elimination of forced and compulsory labour; the abolition of child labour; and the elimination of discrimination, including gender discrimination, in respect of employment and occupation. There is no need to ratify these core standards; mere membership of the ILO implies the acceptance of these core values.

In this chapter, we extend this widely accepted definition of basic injustice to include those relations where economic transactions take place below the cost of production. In the case of labour, this would be where wages are below the cost of production of labour power, or below a living wage.[1] Since defining the core labour standards, the ILO has also formulated what is called the decent work framework. This includes fair income, security in the workplace and social protection for families. The inclusion of fair income in decent work goes somewhat beyond what is contained in the core labour standards. Defining what is a fair income is something we will take up in Chapter 4. At this point, it suffices to mention that a living wage is the manner in which we will define the base level of fair income. Economic transactions below the cost of production also include those where environmental costs are not included in formulating the price of a commodity. Degradation of resources, such as water, or provision of environmental services, such as waste sinks, are both examples where environmental costs are not included in the calculation of commodity production prices.

There are issues of economic inequality in the world economy which are also part of the GVC structure. This is the difference in payment in different countries of the world for the same or similar work. For instance, computer programmers or technicians in India earn far less than people doing the same work in the USA. In fact, such differential payment is the basis of GVCs, which capitalize on international differences in payments to people possessing the same capabilities. While this is a question of inequality, we do not include it within the ambit of *basic* economic justice issues since it would not fall under the category of urgent rights or essential capabilities. However, unequal remuneration for similar tasks does need to be noted as part of the problem that needs to be resolved in order to reduce global inequality.

Value Distribution within Value Chains

At the same time, there is also an inequality in the distribution of income among lead and supplier firms in GVCs that needs to be brought into discussions about basic labour justice. This is related to the prices paid to suppliers and the return that GVC suppliers get, which, in turn, is related to the manner in which labour costs are calculated—in particular, the minimum wages at which labour remuneration for low-skilled tasks are calculated. It may be difficult to apply the same yardstick of justice to the differential profit rates of firm owners in different GVC segments. However, the low prices secured by supplier firms (and supplier economies) under GVCs can come into the discussion at least in an instrumental or derivative manner (Beitz 2001: 107), that is, as an inequality that needs to be dealt with in order to ensure basic labour rights, such as living wages for workers in supplier economies. The profits of supplier firms may still remain at around the competitive minimum, but the price level needs to be adjusted for suppliers to be able to bear the higher costs of improved labour standards. Therefore, though supplier prices may not appear as an independent issue in economic justice, they need to be adjusted in order to allow labour costing on the basis of living wages. The question of higher supplier prices will certainly be part of any discussion on the conditions under which living wages can be realized.

In considering questions of economic justice, it is necessary to consider the 'rules of the game' and whether they constitute, in Rawls' phrase, fair terms of cooperation (Rawls 1995). Competition and the search for maximum profits result in the acceptance of market-determined wages and prices paid to suppliers. Market-determined wages, particularly in labour-surplus economies, are well below living wages and market-based valuations of environmental services ignore external costs. These rules are embedded in the economic structures that create GVCs. In order to achieve economic justice, we must then consider ways in which the rules can be modified. This approach to changing the rules of the game will be discussed further in the next section of this chapter.

How to Achieve Economic Justice

The 'how' of justice includes both the organizational structures and processes that can be used and the agents who can be involved in achieving justice. The organizational structure for delivering global justice—economic and otherwise—is very much a work in progress. There is an evolving structure of international governance, but one which is still highly deficient. Since we are concerned with the enhancement of justice, we should look for changes in structures that are feasible while also envisaging more forward-looking structures, even though they may be realized only in the future.

Global justice, involving justice between agents in different countries, would necessarily have to go beyond national boundaries and national organizations. Therefore, it would not be possible without 'constructing or coordinating many other agencies' (O'Neill 2001: 198). The organizational structure would need to be multi-layered, situated at the global, national, and local levels of GVC functioning. In addition, the organizational structure should not be expensive to approach in order to be reachable by local unions and even individual workers. Hence, the processes will need to be developed so that protocols are specified for constructing and coordinating agencies and organizations across borders.

Both lead and supplier firms are involved in GVC employment. In the employment of labour in supplier factories, the supplier firms are direct employers, while brands or lead firms are indirect employers. Extending the manner in which Indian jurisprudence has interpreted direct and indirect employers, the lead firm that directs and controls the GVC can be designated as the principal employer. Consequently, while the responsibility for justice (labour, environmental, and fiscal justice) is shared between direct and indirect employers, it does not imply an equal responsibility. There is a differentiated responsibility, differentiated on the basis of power and the distribution of profits within GVCs. As argued by Young, 'The power to influence the processes that produce unjust outcomes is an important factor distinguishing degrees of responsibility' (2004: 381). The processes here are the business practices of lead firms, such as costing labour below the living wage or of reducing lead times in the service of orders. Therefore, the lead firms that govern and run GVCs and which also monopolize the profits from them should bear the main burden of paying for and implementing measures for workers to secure justice. However, supplier countries and firms also share some of the responsibility in implementing schemes to improve justice in GVCs, at least to the extent of implementing agreed schemes. Thus, there is a shared but unequal responsibility, with the chief responsibility lying with the lead firms of the Global North, who can be designated as the principal employers of labour in supplier firms in the Global South.

The ILO-supported national tripartite structure for bargaining on wages and other working conditions includes only one set of employers, along with representatives of workers and governments. These are the national or direct employers in supplier firms. In GVCs, however, the prices that suppliers get, which determine their capacity to meet wage demands, are contracted with the lead firms. Consequently, both the direct employers (supplier factory) and indirect or principal employers (buyer or brand companies) need to be brought into the bargaining process, changing the tripartite into a quadripartite structure (Nathan 2013).

In the United States (US), at the national level, a quadripartite structure was set up to negotiate on wage and employment issues in the aftermath of the 1911 Triangle Shirtwaist Factory fire in New York (Anner, Bair, and Blaisi 2014). Such a structure, including both brands and suppliers, will have to be recreated, this time at an international level, in order to enable bargaining that results in binding agreements. One may say that a beginning in fashioning such a structure was made in the post-Rana Plaza Accord in Bangladesh, which was a binding agreement that included brands, suppliers, and workers' representatives, with the ILO also playing a role. Before the Accord, employment and working conditions were matters to be agreed upon only between suppliers and workers, with brands not being involved. With the Accord, brands have been brought into negotiations with suppliers and workers' representatives. The Accord builds upon the success of historical trade union initiatives in securing supply chain accountability and also represents new innovations to secure transnational accountability in the context of global garment production networks—by collectivizing global brands and requiring their dedicated investment in factory infrastructure. The Accord has been acclaimed as a 'new model of corporate accountability' in contrast to corporate social responsibility reliance on voluntary standards for brands and retailers (Anner, Bair, and Blasi 2014: 2).

Although the Accord is a step forward in providing a contemporary model of lead firm accountability, the enforceability of this agreement has been limited, due in part to reliance on third parties for enforcement. Accordingly, the organizational accountability structure developed by the Accord should be developed to locate both representation and accountability at the nexus of workers, both through their unions and directly, and the state. An organizational structure that is too expensive for workers to approach (whether through their unions or otherwise) would negate the possibility of justice.

Basic Economic Justice: Gender and Labour

From the earlier discussion, we can formulate certain minimum labour standards required for developing the essential capabilities that are necessary for a dignified human life for the majority women workforce in GVC production segments located in supplier countries in the Global South. A failure to adhere to these labour standards constitutes basic injustice.

In defining these labour standards, we start with the ILO's core labour standards:

- Abolition of all forms of forced labour (including modern slavery, as it is now being termed)
- Abolition of child labour
- Non-discrimination, particularly gender discrimination, in employment
- Freedom of association for all workers

We add to these a living wage as the minimum wage, including in piecework.

Gendered Distribution of Labour

Women's work most often includes significant unpaid care work. Exclusion of women's unpaid work in wage calculations is a matter of injustice. If this supposed non-economic work were equally distributed between women and men, it would not matter as an issue of justice. However, when it is entirely skewed against women, and this skewed distribution of unpaid care work has consequences for women's paid work and bodily health, then it does become a matter of justice. For instance, due to the comparative ability of younger women to physically sustain a combination of paid and unpaid work, along with high production quotas, women workers age out of factory employment at a remarkably young age. In India, employment data show that there are very few women above the age of 35 years and no women above the age of 45 in garment factories. As such, the short employment life of women workers and the consequences for their economic security constitutes a basic injustice.

To the rights that must be afforded to women workers in the interest of justice, we add 'protection of bodily integrity' (Nussbaum 2004: 13), which would involve freedom from sexual and other forms of gender-based violence, both within the workplace and in travel to and from the workplace. The importance of this urgent right has been underlined by the ILO's recent formulation of a comprehensive convention on this issue in 2019 (Convention No. 190).

Finally, we include employment security in our criteria for considering gender justice in GVCs. For women garment workers on production lines, significant employment is through labour brokers, referred to as contractors in Indian law. Labour contractors facilitate consistent access to a flexible low-wage workforce for supplier factories and brands and regular temporary employment stints for workers. They also, however, short circuit access to employment security, benefits, and wage increases that come with permanent positions. The availability of a pool of workers facilitated by contractors, moreover, makes it easier for garment factories to blacklist workers who attempt to unionize. By undermining freedom of association and collective bargaining, contractors contribute to foreclosing opportunities for worker governance on garment supply chains. While employment security and its impact on freedom of association is not a part of the ILO's core labour standards, it is included in the Decent Work agenda, which has been incorporated in the sustainable development goals (SDGs).

The foregoing analysis of basic and gender justice leads us to advance the following minimum labour standards:

1. Abolition of all forms of forced labour, or modern slavery
2. Abolition of child labour
3. Non-discrimination, particularly in terms of gender, in employment
4. Freedom of association for all workers
5. Living wage as the minimum wage, including in piecework
6. Employment security
7. Incorporation of domestic care work in calculations of living wages

8. Protection of bodily integrity or freedom from sexual and other forms of gender-based violence and harassment (GBVH)

In the interest of advancing these labour standards, we direct attention to the need for a just distribution of income along GVCs, particularly the distribution of income between lead and supplier firms which is fundamental to providing living wages to workers. We recognize that there will be financial costs involved in improved labour standards, such as the increased costs of paying an adult rather than a child worker or paying living wages. These higher costs need to be factored into price-fixing in GVC negotiations and the distribution of value along the GVC.

Having set out the manner in which we approach economic justice in a globalized world, we now turn to how outcomes in GVCs appear as matters of injustice.

Subsidies as a Measure of Injustice

Injustice, we argue, is sustained by subsidies involved in the transactions between parties in GVCs—both lead firms and suppliers, typically mapping onto the Global North and Global South, respectively. A subsidy can be defined as the condition where a commodity is purchased below its cost of production. Wages below the living wage and the practice of costing products while ignoring the costs of environmental services and degradation both count as subsidies to the profits of lead firms. *The extent of the subsidies, the extent of below cost extraction from gendered labour and the environment, would then be a measure of the extent of injustice in various transactions.* In this manner, we could say that in India where wages for garment workers are 25 per cent of the cost of labour (living wage), the extent of the labour subsidy extracted is higher than in China where wages are 45 per cent or Malaysia where wages are 54 per cent of the cost of labour. There is yet more of a labour subsidy in Bangladesh, where garment sector wages are not even 20 per cent of the living wage. This difference between the price of a commodity and its cost of production is the measure of unjust subsidies that is utilized in this book.

These wage levels are unjust subsidies, in that they deprive the producers of the labour power (workers) of the resources necessary to cover the cost of production. Of course, not all subsidies are unjust. Typically discussed subsidies promote consumption of public-cum-private goods, such as educational and health services, so that their consumption does not fall below a socially desired minimum. In this book, however, we are mainly concerned with unjust labour and environmental subsidies.

In order to determine whether prices paid by lead firms are sufficiently low to result in extracting subsidies, we would need to have a clear idea of the costs of production, and then see whether a commodity is purchased at a price below that cost of production. In a conventional analysis of GVCs, however, the focus of value accretion is on the production system, including pre- and post-production activities, such as design, branding, and marketing, respectively. However, this boundary setting ignores the fact that materials and energy flow into and out of the production system in a highly complex system of inputs and outputs. Environmental services flow into the production system, while environmental waste flows out. Similarly, wage labour produced by care work in the household flows into the production system from the household, while wages flow out of the production system and into the household. To know whether these flows involve subsidies, it is necessary to have an idea of the costs of production of the various inputs, including labour power and environmental services.

Production Price

GVCs come into existence when there is an international splintering of production due to differences in production costs across different countries, even with these countries utilizing the same technology. The basis of the difference in production costs is that of differences in what Marx (1958) termed the production price, which includes the cost price of the various inputs needed to produce the output, plus a normal or average rate of profit on capital deployed in production.

In the cost price of various inputs, we are particularly interested in two inputs—labour power and environmental services. The cost of production of labour power is the cost of various inputs, such as food, care work, and other household resources, that go into producing labour power, which will be discussed in detail in Chapter 4. This cost of production of labour power would vary from one country to the next on the basis of the economic development of the country. In high-income countries, for instance, the cost of owning and running cars would be included in the costs of production of labour power, but this may not be so in low- or middle-income countries. However, there are still identifiable and calculable costs of production of labour power in each country. These costs include the usually unpaid labour of women in providing various domestic work contributions, such as turning raw food into cooked food.

The cost of production of labour power was related to what Marx (1958) called necessary labour—the labour required to cover the wage cost. Taking the normative position that wages should cover the cost of production of labour power, then necessary labour is that which is performed by the worker to cover this cost. The labour after the wages have been covered becomes surplus labour, which is captured by the employer. When the wage is below the cost of production of labour, one may say that the employer does not return the cost of production of labour and that this is an addition to profit, above the profit that the employer earns from capturing surplus labour.

Marx did not include the costs of environmental services in his formulation of production price, though he did recognize that natural resources were also a source of value. Business costing practices also ignore the costs of environmental services except those which are explicitly priced, such as water or compensation that has to be paid to those who suffer from the external effects of production. Otherwise, environmental services are 'free' gifts to enterprises.

Production prices give us the value of inputs. The production price can then be used as a standard for judging market prices, ascertaining whether they are above or below the cost of production. The market price for labour power is the prevailing wage. If the wage was higher than the cost of production, then the worker would get a premium on the sale of labour power. In the more likely situation of labour surpluses in developing countries, the wage would fall below the cost of production of labour power. In a GVC segment, if the wage was below the cost of production of labour power, that would clearly be a situation where the cost of production was being met somewhere else. For instance, the cost might occur within the household, where the worker might be forced to consume less nutrition than what is required to sustain the body for production, a process we refer to as body mining and discuss in Chapter 5. The wage shortfall may also be made up by resource transfers from the rural household of the worker, discussed in Chapter 7. In both cases, part of the costs of production of labour power is being met outside the GVC system itself.

What we have outlined in this section with regard to labour power may also occur with regard to environmental services. Wherever environmental services are provided for free or below cost, the difference will be provided in some other part of the economy—for instance, the agricultural sector—subject to what are called externalities. These externalities are the unacknowledged costs borne outside the core production system of the GVC. Since they are not compensated by the GVC production system, they can be called subsidies to the GVC.

Subsidies and Rights

How does this subsidy become a matter of rights and justice? The fact that prices are below the cost of production is, at first glance, an economic matter. Such prices and the accompanying negative profits should then drive such enterprises out of business. That is an economic matter, one of economic sustainability.

In a Lockean manner, one may argue that a person, who is the producer of a commodity such as labour power, has some rights over the product, including the right to sell that commodity since she or her household has put their labour to use in creating labour power. However, while such a right may be accepted, is there a concomitant right to sell labour power at a price that secures value equal to its full cost? Such a right cannot be claimed for the usual type of enterprise. As pointed out earlier, it is through fluctuations of prices, which do not cover the cost of production of products made with older, less-productive technologies, that adjustments in the economic structure take place.

The matter is different though where the seller of the commodity is a person whose nutritional status or well-being is entirely dependent on that wage income. This would hold true for both workers and farmers who produce cotton, since in both cases there is a link between the commodity income and the standard of nutrition or well-being. In such a situation, the economic factor is complemented by a human rights factor, the right to live with dignity. Therefore, the economic factor of the sale of a commodity below its cost of production needs to be supplemented by a human rights argument for a standard of well-being in order to develop a rights argument. Accordingly, we propose that the prices of commodities that form the basis of the well-being of the sellers (be they workers or farmers producing cotton) should cover the costs of production or at least equal the production price of that commodity, remembering that the production price includes a normal profit on capital employed.

In the capitalist market, an enterprise that fails to meet its cost of production would soon go out of business. Such an exit or bankruptcy would not constitute a matter of justice in that it cannot be argued that every enterprise has a right to exist in the market. However, if we consider the households that produce labour and raw cotton as enterprises, they consist of labourer and farmer households comprised of human beings. While as sellers of labour power or cotton, they are subject to market forces; there is a strong sense that they should not be subject to the same exigencies of market results as other enterprises. There is a long tradition that argues that labour power, although it is a commodity, cannot be subjected to the vicissitudes of commodity markets. In Chapter 4 (on living wages), we argue that labour should acquire value (wages) at least equal to the cost of production of labour power. We make this argument in the context of workers and the sale of labour power as a commodity on the market. However, it can be extended to farmers as enterprises.

Part of the vision guiding the analysis in this book is that the GVC system should incorporate a base level of well-being for factory workers, producers of raw cotton, and also for other users or producers of environmental services.

We define that base level as being the acceptable level of well-being or capability development that is considered consistent with human dignity.

Environmental Justice

Just as there is a tendency for the production segments of GVCs to be located in developing countries with lower wages, there is a similar tendency for the more polluting segments of GVCs to be located in these countries as well, where the costs of environmental regulation are likely to be lower than in developed or high-income countries. Is such concentration of pollution in developing countries a matter of environmental injustice?

The concept of intergenerational equity put forward by James Tobin in 1974 sparked a discussion on environmental sustainability as justice. Much earlier, Mahatma Gandhi referred to natural resources as something that were lent to us by our children and derived from this the obligation to hand over these resources in at least as good a condition as we had received them. Environmental justice first came up as a political issue during the American Civil Rights movement of the 1980s, when it was pointed out that landfills and other such polluting activities were overwhelmingly located in areas where African-Americans lived. This was due to the political expectation that there would be less of the 'not in my backyard' type of opposition in low-income areas (read: African-American areas) as compared to high-income areas (read: White American areas). Subsequently, environmental justice was defined as a matter of over-concentration of polluting activities in low-income or minority areas. The US Environmental Protection Agency defines environmental justice as the 'fair treatment and meaningful involvement of all people regardless of race, colour, national origin, or income, with respect to the development, implementation and enforcement of environmental laws, regulations and policies' (USEPA 2021). This definition also brings procedural matters, such as the 'meaningful involvement of all people' in developing, implementing, and enforcing laws and policies.

Later, at the international level, the term 'environmental justice' was used by Anil Agarwal and Sunita Narain (1991) to refer to the unequal rights of developing and developed countries in terms of the volume of emissions they were allowed, acknowledging that developing countries had to increase their use of energy and thus incur more potential emissions in order to increase their incomes and carry out development.

The costs of implementing activities, such as setting up and running effluent treatment plants to counter pollution, depend both on the costs of that activity and also on the extent of the enforcement of environmental protection laws and rules. Where enforcement is weak, we get pollution havens where environmental costs are low or even non-existent. The low costs of pollution control are then added to low production costs to increase the attractiveness of low-wage pollution havens as sites for GVC production segments. In the same way that we call for living wages to be part of the prices paid to suppliers, we call for the costs of environmental precautions, clean-ups and services to be calculated as part of the prices paid to suppliers.

Distribution of Value and Emissions

The idea of environmental justice requires the fair treatment of all participants. How does one interpret fairness in terms of GVCs? One way would be to start with the distribution of value within a GVC and require that the attribution of the distribution of, for example, carbon dioxide (CO_2) emissions correspond to the distribution of value within the value chain. The distribution of value within a chain is usually referred to as 'value added'. However, the value that accrues within a segment is related not only to the value of inputs provided along with a 'normal' profit but also to the value captured through the position of actors within the market and in value-chain contractual relations. Value capture represents more correctly than value addition the process of value accretion in different value segments.

A calculation of the shares of Swedish garment brands and suppliers, both direct (garment factories) and indirect (meaning input suppliers), and CO_2 emissions associated with each set of actors is given in the following Table 2.1. The share of value captured by lead firms or brands is clearly well above their share of emissions associated with garment production.

Table 2.1 Swedish Garment Lead Firms and Their Suppliers, Shares of Value (Value Captured) and CO_2 Emissions (%)

	Value Captured	**CO_2 Emissions**
Lead	43	13
Direct Supplier	26	26
Indirect Supplier	31	57

Source: World Bank (2020: 128).
Note: The 'value added' field in the original table has been changed to 'value captured' for the reasons stated earlier.

The activities of lead firms are mainly those of design, branding, and marketing. These are all low-emission activities. However, the production activities of direct and indirect suppliers are emission-intensive. The shifting of such activities to regions with poor environmental regulations is part of the reorganization of production through GVCs. This places a higher burden of environmental costs on suppliers and supplier countries, who should ideally be required to bear a proportionately lower share of the burden. How this sharing of burdens can be made proportionate to the consumption of emission-producing commodities is something that needs to be explored.

What is important is to see a GVC as an integrated whole producing a product, along with environmental waste. The GVC as a whole is responsible for both production and its associated waste. While the responsibility for dealing with waste in production lies with all the firms in the chain, there should be a differentiated responsibility, which could depend on the shares of GVC actors in value captured or on the distribution of the consumption of GVC production in different countries. We will look at the manner in which environmental costs are dealt with in different GVC segments—extractive and manufacturing or production.

Extractive Segments

By April 2015, in the Economic Justice Atlas, there was a list of 1,354 cases of environmental struggles, the majority of which were in the extractive phase of resource use. There have been exposures and campaigns around rare minerals, such as coltan extracted under the supervision of armed gangs with forced labour and child labour in the Republic of Congo (Nathan and Sarkar 2010). Coltan is an essential component of electronic products.

The extractive segments are located at the beginning of the value chains. Production is often carried out in remote areas using non-intensive methods. They are often the supply chain segments with high levels of forced or modern slave labour. There have been attempts to boycott materials extracted through such extreme forms of exploitative labour. The Kimberley process of certifying diamonds by verifying that they are not 'blood diamonds' seems to have been successful. However, the attempts at certification usually place the costs of securing certificates on the producers, as the example of certified wood from Ghana and Indonesia given in the next paragraph shows.

The European Union (EU) has introduced Forest Law Enforcement Governance and Trade (FLEGT) licences for wood. The cost of securing these licences is borne by the wood exporters. The result of this additional cost is that some wood exporters have shifted to less burdensome markets such as those in China or other emerging economies. It has also increased the power of larger suppliers as they rent out licences to small exporters (Acheampong and Maryudi 2020). The main issue of justice is whether the cost of such certification should be borne by the lead firms, who are actually the ones that secure a large portion of the value from the GVCs.

Furthermore, extractive activities, such as mining, often result in the displacement of indigenous people from their traditional livelihoods of small-scale agriculture and gathering of forest products. Procedural justice requires that these indigenous people agree to the use of their lands for mining, while also requiring the creation of new livelihoods for those destroyed. The requirement of consent has now been formalized in the doctrine of Free and Prior Informed Consent (FPIC), which is part of the United Nations General Assembly's Declaration on the Rights of Indigenous Peoples (2010). From the Philippines and India, there are reports of the implementation of this doctrine. In the case of the Niyamgiri Hills of India, the indigenous people rejected the proposal to set up a Korean-owned steel plant in an area that they considered sacred.

Manufacturing Segments

In manufacturing segments, there are two kinds of environmental costs involved: one is the use of resources, such as water and the other is the release of waste into the environment. In the first case, a reduction in the use of the resource, such as water, contributes to a reduction in cost. In such cases, some brands such as Levi's have supported the adoption of technology that reduces water use. Given their position as monopsonist buyers, it is likely that the reduction in costs in manufacturing will be captured by the brands.

The other type of environmental cost is an external one. For instance, the water of the Nooyal River that flows through the Indian knitwear cluster Tiruppur was contaminated by the waste released into the river. The cleaning and setting up of effluent treatment plants was undertaken by the government, with some contributions from the suppliers. However, there was no contribution from the brands (see Chapter 9). Similarly, when the Indian leather cluster near Chennai was cleaned up in order to eliminate the use of chemicals banned by the EU, the brands did not make any contribution to the expenses. However, there was some technological contribution from GIZ, the German technology aid agency (Meenu Tewari, 2020, personal communication).

What we see is that brands have been willing to support a reduction in the use of resources through the transfer of technology, which results in a reduction in costs. Given their monopsony position as powerful buyers, they are likely to secure the benefits of this cost reduction. On the other hand, brands have played no technological or financial role in the environmental clean-ups that are required by the production activities they govern and profit from.

Post-Consumption Waste

GVC analysis usually includes only production activities, pre-production activities such as design, and post-production activities such as branding and marketing. A more complete approach, however, would also include post-consumption or waste management activities. Waste management can be seen as a GVC by itself, involving the transporting of waste, its treatment for the recovery of usable materials, and the use of these materials in subsequent production. For instance, 95 per cent of ship waste, by weight, consists of steel that can be re-smelted and used in construction (Frey 2015), while electronic waste includes plastic, silver, and rare earths, such as coltan, all of which can be reused in production. Economic analysis, however, has usually ended with the purchase of the product for consumption. However, growing consciousness about the need to develop forms of circular economy, where the waste of one cycle becomes the input of the next cycle, has led to the analysis of post-consumption waste value chains, for instance, in Bangladeshi electronic waste (Lepawsky and Billah 2011).

The movement of waste treatment away from high-income countries to pollution havens in low- and middle-income countries (LMICs) is best seen in the case of ship-breaking (Frey 2015). After World War II, ship-breaking was concentrated in the US, United Kingdom (UK), and Japan. Then it shifted to Spain and Turkey in the 1960s, and then to Korea and Taiwan in the 1970s. Since then, the industry has been located mainly in India, Bangladesh, China, and Pakistan. Ninety-five per cent of shipping tonnage is broken up in these countries, with 5 per cent remaining in the UK.

There is minimal regulation of environmental matters in ship-breaking yards in Bangladesh and India. Of course, as the recent World Bank report on GVCs puts it, many LMICs do not implement environment protection regulations in order to not lose their cost advantage in attracting foreign investors (World Bank 2020: 119). In addition, they also fear losing the employment that is made possible, even if it is toxic employment. A day's work in the Indian ship-breaking yard at Alang in Gujarat is said to be equivalent to smoking 10 to 15 packs of cigarettes a day (Frey 2015). Together with the high incidence of physical injury, this surely gives workers in ship-breaking very short working lives. If ship-breaking is an older form of waste recycling, two newer streams have now gained in importance—plastics and electronics.

Whether it is electronics, including mobile phones, or other consumer products, including garments, the monopolist nature of competition promotes quick replacement with minor changes in the sequences of models. This happens in the case of mobile phones and computing devices through the 'need' to keep replacing gadgets, or, in the case of garments and accessories, through the promotion of 'fast fashion'. These practices promote high levels of waste. At present, manufacturers have no responsibility for the 'after-life' of their products. Consumers discard them and they end up in waste recycling centres in developing countries. Dramatizing the social and environmental impacts of garment waste on the communities where they are disposed, the 2020 short film *Textile Mountain* traces the path of unwanted garments from Europe to informal settlements in Kenya, where they clog waterways, creating long-lasting and detrimental health and environmental consequences. Where the cost of recycling or discarding used goods is brought within the ambit of the manufacturers' responsibility, then there is a greater possibility of promoting a circular economy with reduced waste. Japan has begun the process of making manufacturers responsible for dealing with the after-life of their products.

Responsibility

A GVC is a structure and the injustices that result in them are produced by structural processes. These processes are based on connections between different agents in the structure, between lead firms and suppliers, and between suppliers and the workers involved in producing the goods and services. However, different agents in this structure have different measures of power and ability to influence outcomes. This differential power, manifested through monopolistic and competitive markets, respectively, results in different distributions of net income within the value chain. For instance, the business practices of lead firms result in contracts with suppliers based on minimum, rather than living, wages. Here, a connection can be drawn between the lead firms' business practices and the unjust labour outcomes, leading to the conclusion that lead firms can be held responsible for injustice in GVCs.

Of course, the supplier firms which directly employ labour in production are also involved as agents in the structural process of the GVCs. As agents profiting from the structural process of GVCs, even if that profit is minimal, the supplier firms that directly hire labour in production also share some responsibility. However, we should attribute responsibility on the basis of the power that different agents deploy in the process and the profits that they secure from the GVC.

Based on these criteria, the extent of power that competitive supplier firms hold in GVCs is minimal compared to the power of monopsonist lead firms. Furthermore, the distribution of net income from GVC production, which will be discussed in Chapter 3, is also very unequal between lead firms and supplier firms. Thus, although there is a shared responsibility for poor and unjust labour conditions, the responsibility is unequally distributed. The lead firms with their monopoly–monopsony power and high share of net income have both the power and the means with which to undertake measures that can reduce unjust labour and environmental outcomes.

Supplier Relations as a Strategic Choice of Monopsony Brands

A brand, a firm with some monopoly power in the product market, will also have an equivalent monopsony power in the input market. For instance, assuming that all firms in the sector use the same technology, an automobile maker that accounts for 50 per cent of the product market would also account for 50 per cent of the input market. This power gives the monopsonist a choice in what relations to set up with its suppliers. To look at this issue, we utilize Susan Helper's (1991) analysis of suppliers in the automobile industry.

Helper argues that firms with monopoly power in the product market have to choose the type of supplier relations they want to set up. They could set up committed supply relations, involving some long-term commitment to buy from the suppliers. Such long-term relations also foster technical change. Using Hirschman's terms, she characterizes such a supplier relation as one where there is voice and frequent interactions between the buyer and the supplier. In a sense, this is what in the GVC literature is called relational governance, involving much exchange of information between the buyer and the supplier (Gereffi, Humphrey, and Sturgeon 2005). On the other hand, a brand could also set up short-term contracts with suppliers, without any commitment to continue the contract. This is the exit option that would be feasible where there are numerous suppliers, competing with each other to secure orders from the brand. The monopsonist uses this competition among suppliers to secure short-term gains. This would be a captive governance relation, with low barriers to entry.

A brand has an option between these two supply structures: one, where there are many suppliers with short-term contracts, and the other, where there are a few preferred suppliers that have, or can expect, long-term contracts and can even be confident in carrying out technical change. Helper points out that firms with power in their final-product market can use that power to change the structure of their input markets. 'Such firms can act not only to minimize the cost of inputs on a given cost curve, but also to affect the location of the cost curve itself by altering barriers to entry in their supplier industries' (Helper 1991: 789).

Brands in the garment industry do have degrees of power in their final product markets. There is a strategic choice, or choice of business strategies, for them to make in setting their supplier base. As Helper points out,

> There is a conflict between selecting suppliers who offer the best terms at any given point (a strategy that requires a high ability to exit from current relationships) and developing vendors with improved capabilities (a strategy that requires a long-term commitment and the development of mechanisms for technical assistance and other types of administrative coordination). (1991: 823)

Brands choose the strategy of keeping their exit options in order to utilize competition among suppliers. Keeping suppliers in a position to earn just about the minimal profit rate, has, as we will see in Chapter 3, implications for wages and the quality of employment. It is this choice to adopt a strategy of not building commitment to longer-term contracts that constrains improved wage and other employment conditions among suppliers. As we will see in Chapter 11, in the few cases where some longer-term relations have been built, there is some improvement in employment conditions.

It is this choice by brands of the strategy of short-term contracts with myriad suppliers that is the basis for holding brands responsible for labour conditions in their value chains. This strategic choice of brands can itself be traced back to the compulsion of brands to maximize shareholder value, which itself is based on the tyranny of quarterly returns. The compulsion, if any, is not of the market as such but of short-term shareholder returns, compounded by financialization, in the monopsony capitalism that constitutes GVCs.

Conclusion

Basic justice requires that economic transactions of wages and other employment conditions enable workers and their families to acquire the elementary capabilities understood as constituting reasonable human living. Wages below that level would then constitute a subsidy provided by workers to increase profits. Irrespective of where the subsidies are extracted, since the brands capture the excess profit, this becomes a reverse and unjust subsidy to increase brand profits. Similarly, production costs below the level required to cover environmental use and harms at the extraction, production, and waste level also become an unjust subsidy. Since brands or lead firms bear responsibility for their strategic choice of supplier relations, they have a principal responsibility in mitigating gendered labour and environmental conditions in garment GVCs.

GVC operations based on existing market prices result in the extraction of various types of gendered subsidies from both households and the environment. For GVCs to be sustainable, both redistributive and regenerative forms of buyer–supplier relations are needed. Is that possible and, if so, how can that be brought about? Our central argument in this book is that the price of labour power or wages needs to be adjusted to cover the costs of production of labour power, and that prices of environmental services, such as water, should also be adjusted to cover the costs of provision of such environmental services.

Notes

1. It should be noted that a living wage, or even a minimum wage, does not form a part of the ILO core labour standards. Wages are expected to be relative to the level of development. This differentiation in wage levels for the same capabilities in countries with different per capita incomes is what gives rise to the phenomenon of global supply chains. However, there is an ILO Convention (No. 131 of 1970) and national laws in 90 ILO member countries that fix minimum wages. This is a minimum wage which cannot be reduced either by collective agreement or individual contract. Furthermore, the 1919 ILO Constitution called for the 'provision of an adequate living wage' as the basis of social justice. The earlier 1914 Declaration of Philadelphia also referred to 'a minimum living wage' for all employed workers.

3

Knowledge, Global Monopoly–Monopsony Capitalism, and Labour

This chapter explores the relations between the structure of global value chains (GVCs) and labour employment in developing countries where downstream suppliers are largely concentrated. As laid out in the introduction to this book, this starts with knowledge, usually protected under intellectual property rights (IPRs), creating oligopolies or monopolies with degrees of monopoly in the product markets in the headquarter economies of lead firms. In an unequal world—unequal in the distribution of knowledge, incomes, and wages—there is the possibility of utilizing these differences to increase the profits of product monopolies through the disintegration of production in GVCs.

GVCs have embedded within them a distribution of knowledge among different GVC segments: knowledge-intensive segments in pre- and post-production tasks, which are protected under IPRs in lead firms; and production knowledge distributed among many suppliers in developing economies that is not protected under IPRs. The monopolies on the product market then appear as monopsonies in input markets, where a few buyers can bargain with many suppliers to the buyers' advantage. In the resulting distribution of value within the value chain, the lead firms earn rents (or super profits), while the suppliers just earn competitive profits.

Before proceeding, let us revisit our terminology, as clarified in the introduction, once again. The technical term for a market with a few buyers and many suppliers is an oligopsony, while that for a market with a few sellers and many buyers is an oligopoly. Not only is oligopsony a somewhat clumsy word, but it is not very commonly used. The term 'monopsony' can be extended to describe a market where a few players on one side deal with many players on the other side. In this way, there are brands with degrees of monopoly in the product market and also degrees of monopsony in the input market.

The relationship between lead firms and suppliers has been analysed under the rubric of value chain governance (Gereffi, Humphrey, and Sturgeon 2005). The theory of supplier firm governance divides them into three types of governance, in which we emphasize differentiation based on the knowledge level of the tasks performed. Suppliers in captive governance are characterized by the low-knowledge level of tasks performed, as seen in the manufacture of garments or shoes. There is an intermediate level of knowledge in supplier firms in modular governance, as seen in automobile and electronics assemblies. Finally, there is a higher level of knowledge in suppliers in relational governance, as seen in the case of information technology (IT) software services. The knowledge levels required and power of supplier firms have a corresponding effect on the knowledge levels required of the workforce employed in supplier firms and also on whether firms need to retain workers with their embodied knowledge.

Apart from differences in the knowledge levels required in supplier firms, there is a connection between profits and wages. According to Michal Kalecki's theory of distribution (1971), wages are related to profits, which are, in turn, derived from the degrees of firm monopoly: in a GVC, firms with rents will tend to have higher wages than firms with competitive profits. This vertical relation of the inter-firm distribution of profits within a GVC is combined with horizontal relations, such as labour market conditions and gender roles and responsibilities, to result in wages and other employment conditions in supplier firms, such as security of employment. Thus, the knowledge level of tasks carried out by suppliers in GVCs affects the employment of workers in these supplier firms through the knowledge level required of workers, whether suppliers need to retain the embodied knowledge of specific workers, and also the power-based distribution of profits within the GVC.

Keeping in mind the analytical structure just outlined, this chapter puts forward the proposition that the knowledge level of production segments carried out by supplier firms are reflected in working conditions within these firms. Low-knowledge production segments, such as garment and shoe production, would hire mainly labour with low wages and low job security. Medium-knowledge segments, such as automobile or electronics assemblers, would have mainly labour with medium wages and more workers with relatively better job security. High-knowledge segments, such as IT services, would have labour with high wages and higher proportions of employees with job security.

The chapter substantiates this proposition with empirical data on the relations between the knowledge levels of supplier firms and the quality of employment. We do this in terms of two variables: wages and security of employment. Our set of case studies across GVC suppliers, located for the main part in Asian countries, is in line with expectations. Corresponding to the three forms of governance—captive, modular, and relational—are differences in bargaining power between suppliers and buyers. There is little or no power in the case of captive segments; some, but not much, power in modular segments; and substantial power in the case of relational segments.

Our emphasis is on the role of knowledge—whether protected through IPRs and earning rents or commoditized and earning just competitive profits—in determining the nature of employment in GVC manufacturing or production segments. The resulting inter-firm distribution of rents and profits is reflected in wages and employment conditions. There could, however, be variations around this structure. Firm strategies for upgrading could result in higher wages and more secure employment, as firms seek to build firm-level capabilities by retaining skilled labour. Gender relations affect women's employment possibilities as they are constrained by unpaid care work and child-bearing responsibilities. Labour market conditions of surplus labour, as in most supplier economies, would restrict both increases in wages and improvements in employment conditions. These labour market factors in combination with constraints on supplier profits would limit the ability to use workers' associational power to increase wages. It is only in the condition where suppliers themselves have some measure of oligopoly power based on reputational assets (Kaplinsky 2019) or difficult-to-acquire knowledge of specific production niches, such as denim production in the case discussed by Ashok Kumar (2020), that workers could secure some redistribution of higher profits as wages, in the manner of Kalecki's analysis.

The analysis in this chapter does not claim to be a set of hypotheses that have been tested by large-scale, cross-country survey data. Rather, it provides an analytical structure relating knowledge and knowledge-based power on the quality of employment in global production networks (GPNs). This analytical structure can both be tested and refined through cross-country and cross-segment empirical investigations into GPNs.

The Monopoly–Monopsony Relation in GVCs

A GVC has a lead firm, which is usually a brand or a large retailer located in a headquarter economy (Baldwin 2016) or a developed economy in the Global North, and tiers of suppliers in supplier economies of the Global South. There is a division of tasks between these different tiers of firms. For instance, a brand may keep pre-production tasks (such as design and branding) and post-production tasks (such as marketing) to itself, while it outsources basic manufacturing to producers and intermediate input suppliers. There is also a distribution of revenue along the chain, which gives a GVC a structure of inequality, making it dependent upon the market structure within which different GVC units operate and on the relation between firms within a GVC.

However, a somewhat neglected dimension of a GVC is that it also involves a division of knowledge in the performance of tasks along the value chain. The knowledge required for the performance of pre-production (design) and post-production (branding and marketing) tasks is usually retained by the lead firm itself. The carrying out of pre- and post-production tasks becomes the core competence (Prahalad and Hamel 1990) of the lead firm. In their interactions with suppliers, lead firms try to keep suppliers out of the key competencies of design and branding, though often unsuccessfully (Kaplinsky 2019).

The output that lead firms market is protected through IPR regimes, whether of codified knowledge resulting in patents or of tacit knowledge resulting in copyrights and trademarks (Durand and Milberg 2019). In the garment industry and agro-food industries, IPRs are mainly of the tacit variety, embodied in designs and brands, which have also been called reputational assets (Kaplinsky 2019). However, reputational assets do depend on some form of knowledge—for instance, that of design, which is then guarded through a trademark. Patent knowledge is usually codified, but subject to IPR protection. Tacit knowledge can also exist in the production of niche products that may not have patent production. That is the case with the manufacture of denim fabric, which makes it a difficult-to-enter segment, giving the denim producers, who tend to be large, some form of market power.

The consequence of such IPRs is that intellectual monopoly capitalism has become the dominant form of contemporary capitalism (Pagano 2014). There are a few dominating brands or companies in each sector—for example, Apple, Samsung, Huawei, and three other Chinese brands are now present in the smartphone market. This is a form of monopoly created through technical IPRs. There are also monopolies created through brands, that is, reputational assets. For instance, Mars, Mondelez, Nestle, Ferrero, Hershey, and Lindt together account for 60 per cent of the global market for chocolates; Starbucks, Dunkin, and JAB together have 78 per cent of the United States (US) chain-coffee stores (Statista 2019, 2020). However, the monopolies are subject to erosion, as other firms copy or otherwise develop the knowledge required, changing the composition of the monopolies (Kaplinsky 2019).

In the contemporary world, where the knowledge of manufacturing is spread quite widely across the world, we get the second condition for the creation of a GVC. This is the separation of the task of conception from that of execution. The spread of execution or production capabilities means that the separation of conception from execution is not an intra-firm division of labour between management and labour, as discussed by Pagano, but an extension of Adam Smith's intra-firm division of labour to the inter-firm and even inter-country level.

Since the capabilities required for production are quite well distributed around the world, there are many suppliers, in contrast to the monopsony of a few lead firms as buyers. The suppliers usually function in a competitive market, with competition within a country and between countries. The global garment value chain is an iconic example of the GVC relationship, with monopsonistic lead firms on one side and the many garment suppliers on the other. However, as we will see in this chapter, the numbers of suppliers vary with the ease or difficulty of acquiring the knowledge and capabilities required to perform the required tasks in a segment. This is also likely to modify power relations between buyers and suppliers to such an extent that some suppliers may themselves be monopsonistic, and there may be a shift in bargaining power and the distribution of value within the GVC in favour of monopsonistic suppliers. These variations in the balance of power within the value chain will be analysed later.

Thus, GVCs are based on a dual monopoly–monopsony relationship—that of lead firms in both product and input markets. However, the two monopolies are connected. Firms with a monopoly in the product market appear on the global stage as input buyers. The few output sellers or monopolies become the few input buyers or monopsonies. The monopoly on the product side, protected by global IPR regulations through the 1994 WTO Agreement on Trade-Related Aspects of Intellectual Property Rights (TRIPS Agreement), allows these product monopolies to appear as monopsonies on the input side involving the many suppliers. The crucial factor is the monopoly created or supported by IPR protection. Thus, privatized knowledge, whether in the form of the explicit knowledge of patents or the tacit knowledge of copyrights and trademarks, is the critical factor enabling the creation of a GVC, with a separation between conception and execution.

The specific question addressed in this chapter is: What is the impact of this GVC structure on the employment of labour? In this chapter, we deal with this question at two levels. First, we consider differences in the employment of labour at the inter-country level, with a focus on the nature of differences in labour employed in the sites of conception and execution. Second, we examine the employment of labour at the suppliers' end with differences in the intra-firm distribution of labour, based on the nature of tasks in production. We will now deal briefly with the inter-country differences.

The division of knowledge in a GVC also results in knowledge-intensive segments, such as pre- and post-production tasks, requiring more educated and high-skilled labour than production segments. For instance, in 2009, the Information and Communication Technology (ICT) segments in the USA and China show exactly the opposite composition of their respective workforces—the proportion of high-skilled labour was about 45 per cent in

Table 3.1 Distribution of Skilled Labour in the US and China, 2009

		Low-skill	Medium-skill	High-skill
All Industries	USA	10	60	30
	China	65	30	5
ICT	USA	10	45	45
	China	45	45	10
Construction	USA	20	70	10
	China	55	40	5

Source: Approximations from Tables 2.21 and 2.22 in Degain, Wang, and Meng (2017: 58–59).

the US industry, while it was just 10 per cent in China. On the other hand, the proportion of low-skilled labour in the US ICT industry was just 10 per cent, while it was 45 per cent in China (Degain, Meng and Wang 2017: Figures 2.21 and 2.22; see Table 3.1).

In the industry as a whole, too, the proportion of low-skilled labour in 2009 in the US was around 10 per cent, while it was 65 per cent in China (see Table 3.1). The compensation per hour also varied between these skill levels, with US remuneration ranging between three times that of China for low-skill workers and more than four times for high-skill workers in the ICT sector (Degain, Meng, and Wang 2017: Figures 2.21 and 2.22). This is an aspect of global inequality embedded in GVCs into which we do not go any further in this chapter, except to point out that it is related to the double monopoly in product and input markets. This skews the distribution of profits in the value chains and makes the condition for labour performing similar tasks to be very differently remunerated in headquarter and supplier firms.

Knowledge in Production Segments

How do relations between lead and supplier firms, or vertical relations (Neilson and Pritchard 2009) in GVCs, affect employment conditions in supplier firms? Pagano argues that 'the skills of workers are likely to be properly developed only when a secure legal access to property rights on *disembodied* knowledge is available' to the firm where the worker is employed (2014: 1421–1422). While '*embodied knowledge* (i.e. the knowledge that cannot be separated from the worker capabilities) is strictly related to that of *disembodied knowledge*' (Pagano 2014: 1420), these forms of knowledge are differently valued and protected by property rights. This would mean that workers in lead firms, with IPRs, are more likely to have strong employment security, as lead firms attempt to retain the embodied knowledge of workers. On the other hand, in supplier firms that do not have knowledge protection through IPRs, there would not be a similar attempt to retain the relatively lower and easily replaceable embodied knowledge of its workers.

While this distribution holds at a broad level, there are a number of aspects that condition these vertical relations. One is the distribution of value between lead firms and suppliers within the chain. Distribution of value is related to the distribution of market power within GVCs: monopolistic in the case of lead firms, and competitive in the case of suppliers. This results in a distribution of value within the GVC—super profits or rents to the lead firms and only competitive profits to the suppliers (Nathan and Sarkar 2011). Pre- and post-production tasks capture a major share of the value, compared to manufacturing tasks (see the depiction by Stan Shih of the famous GVC smiley curve in Shih 2010).

Other aspects relate to the business practices of lead firms in GVCs and their impacts on employment conditions (wages, security of employment, and so forth) in supplier firms. The ability to carry out tasks, however, is based on possessing the required knowledge and capabilities. Thus, the distribution of tasks can also be termed the distribution of knowledge within a GVC. In Lakhani, Kuruvilla and Avgar (2013), the knowledge in a production segment is characterized by how it is coordinated or governed. The different forms of governance in Gereffi, Humphrey, and Sturgeon (2005) can be used to characterize knowledge in the production segment.

Governance and Distribution of Value within GVCs

How does the distribution of income in a GVC vary with the governance type? In this section, we see that income distribution can be examined in the cases of captive, modular, and relational governance. We do not consider hierarchical governance within a firm since the distribution of revenues within the branches of a firm is a matter of bureaucratic decision-making within the firm, and is often based on tax considerations. Furthermore, we do not take up market linkages separately. Instead, the analysis of captive, modular, and relational governance structures can be extended to the distribution of revenues for similar products in market linkages.

To illustrate the different forms of market linkages, it is important to clarify the difference in forms of market linkages. Let us consider software and other office inputs, such as stationery. The software for operating personal computers and office stationery are both usually bought through market linkages. However, a personal computer's (PC's) operating software, being a knowledge-intensive and complex product with intellectual property protection, has allowed Microsoft to have a great deal of monopolistic authority, which has enabled it to become one of the largest companies in the world. On the other hand, suppliers of stationery and related office inputs sell commodified and undifferentiated products, and therefore do not have much pricing power in the market. Market-linked governance is not a homogenous category in terms of its implications for inequality. Some products may have monopoly power while others may not, with different implications for inequality within the value chain.

Captive Governance

Captive governance is so called because suppliers have little bargaining power. For one, the knowledge required for production is relatively easily acquired. As such, there are many suppliers relative to the number of buyers. This monopsonistic market structure gives the buyers much more power while bargaining with suppliers. It is regularly reported by suppliers in India, Bangladesh, and many other countries in Asia (Cambodia, Indonesia, and so on) that brands are able to squeeze supplier prices by insisting on open costing, where every item of cost is brought into the bargaining structure. They also threaten to take their business to some other country. Suppliers in India point out that they are often told by buyers that suppliers in Bangladesh or Vietnam were offering a particular price, and asked whether they (the Indian suppliers) could match it. The result is that suppliers' margins are at the bottom of the hyper-competitive margin, often resulting in suppliers reducing wage costs by forcing workers to perform low-paid overtime work.

As an example of the low-income share received by suppliers on GVCs, consider the summary calculations for garments from one supplier in India in Table 3.2. These calculations are for garments with embellishments, for which the free on board (FOB) share of the retail price is higher than for basics, such as T-shirts, where the FOB price would be around 10 per cent of the retail price. A calculation for men's polo-necked shirts from Bangladesh in 2006 showed the FOB price as just 10.86 per cent of the US retail price (Miller

Table 3.2 Retail Prices and FOB Shares in 2016 (USD)

	US retail prices	Indian FOB prices	Indian share of retail price (%)
Ladies' top	25	8.50	34.0
Ladies' dress	34	11.00	32.3
Kids' top	20	5.50	27.5
Kids' dress	25	6.50	26.0
Ladies' skirt	34	8.00	23.5

Source: Authors' fieldwork.

2013). The FOB share went up to 25 per cent in the case of five-pocket jeans (Miller 2013). Both material inputs and the complexity of the product affect the suppliers' share of the retail price.

The higher share of retail prices retained by supplier firms may reflect higher costs of distribution or higher profits, or a combination of the two. However, the skewed distribution of income within the value chain undoubtedly results in high profits for global apparel brands. This distribution has become increasingly skewed over time. Liz Clairborne or Phillips-Van Heusen had gross profit margins of around 35 per cent in 1991. Walmart had a gross profit rate of above 20 per cent in the same year. At the upper end, Woolworth had a gross profit rate of above 32 per cent (Applebaum and Gereffi 1994). Accelerating unequal distribution across GVCs, in 2017, Ralph Lauren, Gap, and Levi's had gross profit rates of 57 per cent, 37 per cent, and 52 per cent, respectively (Nathan 2020: 140). These numbers contrast sharply with the 10 per cent or lower profit rates of Indian garment suppliers (Chapter 11).

The results from our study of supplier–buyer relations in the Indian apparel industry are corroborated by a study of Bangladesh (Anner 2019b) reporting that supplier profits declined by 13.3 per cent from 2011 to 2016. In Cambodia, too, trade unions and worker rights organizations report a decline in supplier profits, contributing to rising workers' production targets (CENTRAL, 2020, personal communication). Thus, in captive governance, with the apparel value chain as an example, there is a skewed distribution of income within the value chain, resulting in higher profits for global apparel brands and lower, competitive profits for suppliers.

During the fieldwork undertaken by the authors in 2017 and 2018, apparel manufacturers in and around Delhi pointed out that during the period of the Multi-Fibre Agreement (MFA), when quotas were given to each exporting country, suppliers were able to quote lump-sum prices with margins of around 25 per cent. When the MFA ended, there was intense competition among Asian supplier firms and countries. Margins went down. After the Great Recession of 2008, supplier margins went down even further. With intense competition among firms in different countries, buyers were able to push down prices until margins were less than 10 per cent.

Modular Governance

In modular governance, the knowledge required for production is more complex than in captive governance, but it is codified. As a result, there tend to be fewer suppliers than in captive governance. Nevertheless, the shares of producers are quite low, as seen in one of the major cases of modular production in GVCs—consumer electronics. As such, in modular governance, like captive governance, there tends to be a high level of inequality in income shares, with low margins for contract manufacturers and high margins for leading brands.

A calculation along the iPhone value chain is a well-known example of the low share of the assembler and the high share of Apple in the distribution of income along the value chain. While Apple captured an extraordinary 58.5 per cent of the price of an iPhone, component suppliers received only 14.3 per cent, while the Chinese firm assembling the iPhone secured just 1.8 per cent of the value chain's income (Chan, Pun and Selden 2016).

The distributions of income along the value chain discussed here translated into inequalities in the margins of different actors in these value chains. The operating margins of major electronics-contract manufacturers like Hon Hai (Foxconn), Flex, and Jabil Circuit were as low as 3.53 per cent, 1.84 per cent, and 2.20 per cent, respectively, in 2015 (Raj-Reichert 2018: 25). Gross profit margins were higher—between 6 to 10 per cent. Volumes or total revenues were also high, enabling a reasonably high total profit, but the competitive market in contract manufacturing and the threat of losing market share to low-cost competitors keeps margins low (Raj-Reichert 2018: 37–38). The effect of razor-thin profit margins is that medium-sized firms cannot invest in research and development (R&D) (Ernst 2012). If firms are large in terms of size, then high volumes would enable them to undertake substantial investments in R&D.

At the other end are the gross profit margins of the lead firms or brands. For Apple, the gross profit margin went up from around 20 per cent in 1997 to almost 40 per cent in 2015, while gross profit margins for Dell hovered around 20 per cent in the same period. Notably, HP's profit margin went down from about 28 per cent in 1997 to about 18 per cent in 2015 (Raj-Reichert 2018: 38–39). HP was functioning in an increasingly commoditized low-end PC market, while Apple operated in a high-end, differentiated market, commanding a premium over all other smartphone and PC makers.

Relational Governance

In relational governance, there are close and frequent interactions between the buyer and the producer or supplier. IT services are a good example of the frequent interactions involving design, architecture, programming, testing, and initializing services. Indian IT services have tended to belong to the middle or lower segments in the IT value chain, consisting substantially of programming, testing, checking, and maintenance services. However, even in these services, there is frequent interaction while providing the services and the buyer is dependent on the quality of the services supplied. Within the group of 50 or so Indian IT service providers having the highest quality certification, a few have built a reputation for quality and reliability, which enables them to charge a premium rate for their services. Indian IT majors, such as TCS and Infosys, include a margin of around 25 per cent in the price at which they offer their services. IT firms with lesser reputations such as HCL or Tech Mahindra charge a slightly lower rate (Sachitanand 2018). These high margins show that IT software service suppliers have some market power, which is likely due to their reputational assets and tacit knowledge.

It is interesting to note that supplier pricing systems in apparel (captive governance) and IT services (relational governance) have moved in opposite directions. In the IT industry, Indian suppliers initially set costs on the basis of person per day and equipment costs, with a margin added to this cost. The founder of Infosys, Narayana Murthy, gives a poignant description of how big clients utilized competition among suppliers to push down prices (Murthy 2009). However, as they established their reputation for outsourced services in the world market, the Indian IT service suppliers shifted to quoting lump-sum prices with much higher margins.

Supplier Prices and Wages

The distribution of value within a GVC impacts wages, as predicted by Kalecki's theory of distribution, where wages are based on the degree of monopoly within which a firm operates (1971). Several studies support the Kalecki proposition that workers' wages are positively connected to the rents earned by the firms. Empirical studies in countries such as the US (Mishel 1986: 91), Belgium (Dobbelaere 2005), and India (Pal and Rathore 2014) support Kalecki's assertion that there is a link between high mark-ups and the demand for higher wages by unions.

The connection between a firm's ability to mark up its prices and demands for higher wages is fairly straightforward. Firms that can mark up prices can cover an increase in costs due to higher wages. With their mark-up power, they operate in a cost-plus product market. In such a situation, the workers' demands for higher wages are likely to be conceded. In situations where firms have to regard prices as unchangeable, such as in a competitive market situation, they cannot cover increases in costs through a mark-up. Where industry-level bargaining does not take place, suppliers in a competitive market would resist an increase in wages.

Rather than being just a derivative relation between profits and wages, there can also be a two-way relationship. As argued in the literature (Ichniowski and Shaw 2003), there can be a co-determination of wages and profits. Paying higher wages and generally better conditions of work can improve the firm's performance. In Chapter 11, we discuss just such a relationship in the garment industry. However, there is a caveat. Due to the monopsony situation, the benefits of increased productivity of suppliers were mainly captured by buyers. More productive suppliers' margins were not different from those of other, less productive suppliers; a median rate of profit of 10 per cent for the former as against 9 per cent for the latter. The benefit that the more productive suppliers secured was larger orders and, as a result, faster firm growth. Profits increased but margins did not.

Other vertical relations that affect labour are the manner in which buyers determine labour cost, and the short (and falling) lead times. Given the competition among suppliers, lead firms determine labour cost at the level of prevailing national minimum wages, which are usually far below living wages (Bhattacharjee and Roy 2016). Costing also reflects an assumption that production will include particular working conditions. For instance, supplier costing in garment supply chains in India reflect 10-hour days, including 2 hours of overtime, rather than 8-hour working days. Such projections lend insight into the routine practice by suppliers of paying only normal wages for overtime rather than the double wage rate required under many labour law regimes (Nathan and Kumar 2016).

Accelerated production timelines without adequate lead time drive worker production targets. Production targets are typically set based upon samples made by highly skilled sample tailors. Regular line tailors may not be able to complete daily quotas (Nathan and Kumar 2016). Short lead times and corresponding high quotas lead suppliers to demand high-speed turnover and forced overtime from garment workers (Vaughan-Whitehead and Caro 2017). As we lay out in Chapter 6, attempts by supervisors and line managers to drive worker productivity expose women workers to industrial discipline practices, including verbal and physical abuse.

Horizontal Relations

Supplier firms and their workers are situated not only in vertical GVC relations with lead firms but also exist or are embedded in social and economic relations within their own countries. These include power and market relations between employers, employees, and states in supplier countries. Factors that impact wages and employment conditions in developing countries include both local laws and local labour market conditions.

The state of the labour market is obviously of importance in matters like wage-setting. With developing countries going through the transformation of shifting surplus labour from agriculture into manufacture and services, there is an 'unlimited' supply of workers available at or just above the existing rural wage (Lewis 1954). As long as this surplus labour exists, wages in GVC-related manufacturing would not face the labour market's pressure for an upward revision. With the passing of this transition, as is occurring in China (Fang and Wang 2010), there would, however, be a general upward pressure on wages. At the same time, there might also be specific labour shortages for particular types of workers.

National institutional factors in supplying countries are not the creation of GVC lead firms. Child labour, for instance, existed before the initiation of GVC-based production and continues even in the production of non-tradable goods, such as in roadside eateries or auto repair workshops in India and other countries. Similarly, systems of forced or bonded labour are both older than GVC-related production and also exist independently of GVCs.

While these national conditions may not be created by GVC-led firms, they may contribute to the profit model of brands and lead firms. Allain, Crane, LeBaron and Behbahani (2013) argue that child labour and forced labour have to be understood as part of the business practices or business strategies of lead firms. Notorious examples of conflict-related forced labour include mining diamonds and coltan—a rare metallic ore used in the production of electronics and mined from civil war–torn areas of the Congo (Nathan and Sarkar 2010).

Gender relations and the division of labour within households affects how women interact with the labour market. In the absence of institutionalized childcare, women's responsibility for childcare often leads them to leave the labour force during child-bearing and child-caring years. This causes them to not only lose seniority but may also prevent women from accepting promotions linked to transfers, a feature that has been well reported in the IT industry in India (Kelkar, Shrestha and Veena 2002). In one way or the other, unpaid and unshared care work often leads to women workers being unable to achieve the potential employment quality they are capable of based on their educational and knowledge endowments.

Labour Outcomes in GVCs

How does a GVC's distribution of tasks relate to employment conditions? In answering this question, we consider pre-production (design), production (manufacture), and post-production (branding and marketing) as a coarse-grained division of tasks within a value chain. However, to understand labour outcomes in each of these segments, the level of analysis has to shift from the firm to the worker or employee. In such an analysis, we need to move from the coarse-grained division of labour between GVC segments to the fine-grained division of labour in tasks performed by workers and the capabilities required for their performance.

Knowledge and Employment Quality

Employment has many features, including wages and employment security. In this chapter, we focus on employment security as a measure of job quality.[1] Although this is just one dimension of employment quality, it is a meaningful barometer. Employment security is fundamental to economic security at the individual and household level. Permanent workers also typically have greater access to promotion and seniority-based wage increases—increasing the likelihood that, over time, the workers have access to greater than minimum wages. Finally, household economic security is negatively correlated with child labour, forced labour, and modern slavery since these practices are typically associated with very high levels of economic precarity. As such, using economic security as a benchmark for job quality captures many, although not all, of the labour conditions that, we argue, are fundamental to just labour relationships in the global economy (Chapter 2). After setting out our framework for analysis in this chapter, in subsequent chapters, we extend our analysis of job quality to include the range of rights specified in achieving just labour relations.

The relation put forward in this chapter is not between knowledge as such and employment quality, but between how a firm's knowledge is reflected in bargaining power and employment quality. For complete clarity, the connection we are making is not between how the knowledge that workers possess correlates with their employment quality, though that relationship may also exist. Instead, we are concerned with how the knowledge level of GVC supplier firms in production segments influences bargaining power and profits in the GVCs; and how bargaining power and profits, in turn, inform the quality of employment. In a sense, we apply Kalecki's theory of how degrees of monopoly determine the distribution between profits and wages to GVCs.

The knowledge level of a GVC supplier firm is related to the power that the supplier has in the GVC and in turn the profits that a supplier can earn. Thus, low-knowledge tasks in captive governance carry with them no power in GVC bargaining and therefore correlate with providing only minimal competitive profits. Medium-knowledge tasks in modular governance without many competing suppliers give some power in bargaining and a medium level of profit. High-knowledge segments in relational governance provide some bargaining and price-setting power, thereby leading to higher profits.

In understanding quality of employment (reflected by employment security), and the knowledge base of workers, we distinguish three levels: high, moderate, and low. This gives us nine possible combinations of knowledge and quality of employment (Figure 3.1).

High (3)	High knowledge; low job quality [G]	High knowledge; moderate job quality [H]	**High knowledge; high job quality** **[I]**
Moderate (2)	Moderate knowledge; low job quality [D]	**Moderate knowledge; moderate job quality** **[E]**	Moderate knowledge; high job quality [F]
Low (1)	**Low knowledge; low job quality** **[A]**	Low knowledge; moderate job quality [B]	Low knowledge; high job quality [C]
Knowledge level (K) of tasks/ Job Quality (Q)	**Low (1)**	**Moderate (2)**	**High (3)**

Figure 3.1 Knowledge Levels and Job Quality
Source: Created by the authors.

In our analysis, the segmentation of the labour market by job quality is related to the knowledge level required to perform the tasks assigned to the GVC supplier. The 3x3 matrix in Figure 3.1 is a framework for classifying links between firm knowledge and bargaining power, and firm knowledge and job quality. From this analysis, we can advance a simple theory or hypothesis: the level of job quality is determined by the knowledge level of a task performed in a GVC segment. This hypothesis is consistent with the relationships described in the highlighted cells along the diagonal. GVC suppliers performing low-knowledge tasks are likely to have a low-quality employment structure, medium-knowledge tasks are likely to have a moderate-quality employment structure, high-knowledge or knowledge-intensive tasks are likely to have a high-quality employment structure.

Our use of the term 'employment structure' does not imply that all jobs in a particular GVC supplier would be of the same low, medium, or high quality. Instead, there would be proportionately more jobs of each category in the relevant employment structure. In fact, any GVC supplier would not offer jobs belonging to only one knowledge level and/or quality. In garment production, for instance, there are comparatively low-knowledge level assembly-line tailors and helpers—positions overwhelmingly held by women workers, moderate-knowledge level sample tailors, and high-knowledge level design tailors. This distribution of workers at different knowledge levels can also be represented by the diagonal in Figure 3.1, illustrating the link between knowledge and employment quality within a single firm rather than between GVC supplier firms.

The analytical scheme described here, relating the knowledge level of the GVC segment via bargaining power in GVCs with employment quality, helps in bringing both order and awareness of causative factors into discussions of empirical case studies within this book and beyond. The quality of employment in GVC segments can be categorized as low, medium, or high and compared to the knowledge level of production in that GVC segment. These relationships, however, are not static. Policy and institutional interventions have the capacity to move employment outcomes positively in a rightward or upward direction.

Empirical Case Studies

In this section, we relate the analytical scheme presented earlier to empirical observations through the examination of a number of case studies. These case studies consider employment characteristics across three types of GVC relations: captive and low-knowledge segments, modular and intermediate-knowledge segments, and relational and high-knowledge segments.

The framework set out in the preceding section was inferred from a summary of multi-sector, multi-country case studies, mainly in the collection *Labour in Global Value Chains in Asia* (Nathan, Tewari and Sarkar 2016). The 19 case studies in that book covered garments, agri-food products, tourism, leather products, mobile phones, telecom services, automobiles, call centres, and IT software services. These case studies, and some others from the Capturing the Gains research programme, are summarized below to show the links between knowledge levels of supplier firms and employment conditions.

Low-Knowledge, Poor Employment Quality Segments

GVCs of low-knowledge segments, such as garment and shoe manufacturing, agro-food production, and tourism services, all provide employment with low levels of security and high levels of supply through brokers, along with the hyper-mobility of workers. Wages are low, at or around the national minimum wage.

Work in these low-knowledge segments is often outsourced from supplier factories to both 'shadow factories' and home-based workers, with even worse conditions of employment. There are a high proportion of women in these segments, with women overwhelmingly dominating the homeworker segment. Agricultural production in GVCs, such as cocoa (Barrientos 2014) and fresh vegetables and fruits (Evers, Amoding, and Krishnan 2014), are often carried out on small farms, subsuming within them the labour of women and men as self-employed workers for GVCs.

Moderate-Knowledge, Intermediate Employment Quality Segments

Modular-governance GVCs, such as electronics assembly or automobile manufacture, require knowledge that is of moderate complexity, but highly codifiable. These GVC segments also require workers with a reasonable level of education, instead of the mere work process understanding required in garment manufacture or much of agro-processing. Orders, however, are volatile, particularly in electronics, and this leads to substantial employment of temporary and agency workers (for Thailand, see Holdcroft 2015) and, correspondingly, low employment security in some countries and high levels of overtime in others (for China, see Chan, Pun, and Selden 2016; for Malaysia, see Samel 2012). Supervision is of the Taylorist variety, with the pace of work set by the speed of assembly lines.

Modular governance also encompasses work in back-office services, such as call centres handling customer care that requires a knowledge of English or some other European language. While educational requirements go up in comparison to electronics or automobile assembly, these roles do not have more complex knowledge requirements. In these contexts, new forms of electronic work monitoring, such as measuring the time spent on performing a task, have led to methods of surveillance referred to as digital Taylorist forms of office work (Noronha and D'Cruz 2016). These modular governance GVC segments provide an intermediate quality of employment.

High-Knowledge, High Employment Quality Segments

In relational-governance GVCs, such as in IT software services, the knowledge requirements are more complex, involving some of the design besides the development and maintenance of IT systems. However, even in this, there is a division of labour, with design often undertaken in headquarter economies and system development and maintenance undertaken in developing countries. Indian IT firms, for instance, are concentrated in the middle- to lower-complexity sections; though they are moving into design and full-package supply (Sarkar, Mehta, and Nathan 2013; Ahmed 2018).

In IT software GVC segments, workers are required to have a high level of knowledge and employment is comparatively secure. However, the drive to reduce costs makes employees vulnerable to 'bell curve' methods of dismissal, where a certain percentage of employees who are at the bottom of the curve are dismissed each year. The earnings, however, are consistently higher than for employees of comparable qualifications in other sectors (Sarkar and Mehta 2016). This is possible due to increased margins—from 17 per cent to 25 per cent—in the IT software services industry. In the manner of Kalecki's hypothesis, higher rates of profit in IT services enable and can lead to higher wages.

Interaction with Other Factors

How do additional factors—other than the knowledge level of the task distribution in GVC supplier firms—influence employment quality outcomes? The relationships between firm knowledge types and job quality can be modified by firm strategy, such as building capabilities to move into higher income-earning activities (Nathan, Saripalle and Gurunathan 2016). For such upgrading, a supplier would need to retain more of the knowledge embodied in workers and thus provide more secure employment. When profits remain low and orders are unstable, then the poor quality of jobs in low-knowledge tasks is reinforced. However, the redistribution of rents to supplier factories in a GVC or the stability of orders could together enable higher wages and more secure jobs.

The relation between knowledge levels of supplier firms and employment is also moderated by the contexts within which firms function, such as national labour market regulatory institutions and the state of the labour market. National institutional factors, particularly labour laws, obviously influence the nature of jobs. To take an example from China, the Contract Labour Law (Lan and Pickles 2011) increased employment security for workers in general. China also has a regulation that restricts flexible labour to less than 10 per cent of the total workforce of an enterprise. There may well be breaches of these laws, but their existence changes the context in which employment relations are decided. Similarly, the state of the labour market influences both employment security and wages. At the national level (in developing countries), the overall scarcity of labour can push up wages, as has happened in China. Even local labour scarcity, increased by language ability, can lead employers to offer more secure jobs.

Gendered domestic responsibilities negatively impact women's labour market participation. The need to combine domestic responsibilities, especially childcare, with paid work can force women to choose insecure and low-paid, but flexible work from home rather than more secure and better-paid, but inflexibly scheduled work in factories (Pani and Singh 2012). Across captive, modular, and relational governance, women employed in garment, electronics manufacturing, and IT software service suppliers have been seen to be far less represented in higher levels of the workforce. In the IT sector, this has been related to the inability of women to accept transfer-linked promotions (Kelkar, Shrestha and Veena 2002). Gendered workforce barriers reduce the quality of women workers' jobs below that predicted by their supplier firms' knowledge levels.

Workers' associational power (Silver 2003) can also positively influence labour market outcomes. The extent of this positive influence, however, would be limited by the knowledge level of tasks carried out by supplier firms since the possibility of improvements in labour outcomes, particularly wages, is restricted by the position of the supplier firm within the GVC. Suppliers in the easily acquired knowledge segments of commoditized production would earn competitive profits and this would restrict the wages that could be paid. Only suppliers that establish reputational assets, as is the case with the major Indian IT service suppliers who can set margins of up to 25 per cent; or suppliers that have difficult-to-acquire knowledge of niche production, such as denim production, as mentioned earlier, would be able to go above market wages. Although associational power can influence wages even in these contexts, there is a limit to what can be achieved, a limit set by the generally low, competitive profits earned by supplier firms in GVC segments that perform low-knowledge tasks.

Knowledge and Power

This chapter foregrounds the role of knowledge in both driving the distribution of income within GVCs and in the nature of employment in GVC segments. Knowledge, however, does not on its own or directly produce these effects. Knowledge works through power in the market or bargaining relationships within the GVCs. Knowledge, then, is the base of power in this analysis. However, unless knowledge can be used to affect bargaining relationships, it would not produce results either in changing the distribution of income or in the nature of employment.

The first manifestation of knowledge as the base of power presented in this chapter is in the oligopolistic nature of lead or headquarter firms in GVCs. Oligopoly can also be termed the 'degree of monopoly' to use Kalecki's phrase. Technical knowledge protected through IPRs, and reputational assets protected through brands and trademarks, or through the possession of hard-to-acquire tacit knowledge, all create degrees of monopoly in the product market. These same monopolies reappear as buyers in the supply of inputs, including fully manufactured products. Faced with many suppliers, the monopsonistic buyers are able to confine suppliers to competitive margins.

When suppliers are able to protect the knowledge in their supply of inputs as chokepoint technologies—whether sophisticated components in the automotive industry or platform technologies, such as computer operating systems—bargaining power shifts in favour of such IPR-protected suppliers. Similarly, suppliers of niche inputs with complex and tacit knowledge requirements, as in the case of denim producers, may hold some bargaining power. Finally, suppliers, such as in IT services, who have acquired reputational assets may be able to bargain for increased margins. In each of these cases, however, it is only when knowledge can result in greater bargaining power that it results in higher margins or a higher rate of profit.

The next level of analysis considers the effect of knowledge as power on profit rates, and in turn on employment conditions, including wages. In straightforward Kaleckian terms, the degree of monopoly affects profit rates: profits are higher with a higher degree of monopoly. This improved rate of profit affects the intra-firm bargaining power of workers. Where the supplier firms' margins are higher, in suppliers with some IPR protection, and reputational or niche knowledge assets, then workers can also bargain for higher than market wages. An employee of a large niche denim supplier explained, 'Smaller garment companies I have worked for never had the profits for us to demand higher wages … Even if [a large supplier] lies to us, we can find out the truth easily because it is a big public company' (Kumar 2020: 134).

Conclusion

GVCs are a combination of two kinds of monopolies. The first is a monopoly in the product market, created through some form of IPR protection. The second is monopsony in the input market. This monopsony enables the lead firms in GVCs to capture a substantial portion of the value added in the value chain, including the subsidies from gendered labour and the environment.

The knowledge level of tasks performed in GVC supplier firms impacts the bargaining power of these firms and is therefore substantial in determining the quality of employment in supplier firms in the Global South. A low knowledge requirement of tasks performed by supplier firms gives them little bargaining power and results in low, competitive profits that set limits to the possibility of increasing wages and improving the quality of employment. A medium knowledge requirement gives suppliers some, but not much, bargaining power and an intermediate quality of employment. Generally, it is only in cases where supplier firms have acquired IPR-protected or reputational assets, and consequently increased their bargaining power, reflected in higher profit rates, that employment quality improves along with the increase in profits over competitive rates.

This chapter lays out the relation between supplier firm knowledge, working through power in bargaining, to produce differences in rates of profit.

Firm profit rates, in turn, affect workers' bargaining power within suppliers. The next step in this analysis will be to identify the conditions under which workers' embodied knowledge increases their bargaining power vis-à-vis supplier firms of different types. In subsequent chapters, we consider how firms' capabilities, reflected in rates of profit, interact with worker characteristics, including gender.

Notes

1. This section is developed from Nathan (2016).

FACTORY

4

Living Wages and Labour Subsidies

In this part, we deal with the factory as the site of extraction of subsidies from labour. This extraction is carried out through the payment of wages below a living wage, which is the cost of producing labour power. In this chapter, we outline the concept of living wages and demonstrate their calculation for major supplier countries of Asia, such as India, Bangladesh, Sri Lanka, and China. We then compare the living wages for these countries with national minimum wages, which are often the basis for labour costing in contracts between brands and suppliers. Further, in the case of India, we also look at the actual wages paid, to see the extent of extraction of labour subsidies.

The subsidy from labour is extracted in two ways. First, through the overuse, particularly of women workers' bodies and, second, through support to garment workers by their rural households. The first method of extracting labour subsidies, through the overuse and discard, particularly, of the bodies of women garment workers, is dealt with in Chapters 5 and 6. The second method of extraction is dealt with in Chapter 7, where we discuss the role of the rural connection in sustaining workers during times of need.

This chapter begins with an account of brand–supplier relations in garment GVCs, setting the context for the discussion of workers wages that follows. It then sets out the concept of living wages and the manner of their calculation, including how we can take account of women's unpaid domestic work. We then provide an analysis of wages in two major Indian garment clusters, along with national-level secondary data on wages in the garment sector. Using official survey data on wages and profits, we put forward the proposition that wages in supplier firms are constrained by the low level of profits earned by these firms, and the national minimum wage base of contracts by supplier firms in monopsonistic global value chain (GVC) relationships with lead firms. These firm-level characteristics that lead to low wages are reinforced by worker characteristics, such as gender and low educational levels.

Low wages in the garment industry are usually explained by features of workers in this industry—with low educational levels and a high proportion of women in the workforce. However, when we look at wages and employment conditions of similarly poorly educated workers in other GVC production segments, leather products, automotive components, pharmaceuticals, and IT services, we find that similarly educated workers have very different wage and employment conditions in those sectors.

Taking note of these differences, we argue that the nature of the GVC segment and its profit rate account for these differences, briefly that—in the manner of Kalecki's analysis (1971)—the degree of monopoly in the production segment determines or sets limits to wages in these segments. The higher the degree of monopoly, the more workers of the same educational characteristics or performing the same occupational tasks are paid. Supplier firms that earn higher profit rates can and usually end up paying higher wages to workers at the same skill and education level when compared to firms that earn lower profit rates. This suggests that labour subsidies vary and do not exist at all in some sectors, such as information technology (IT) services, where workers with low educational levels are paid above the living wage.

Garment Manufacturing Segments

Garment manufacture is the quintessential easy-to-enter supplier segment. The products do not have intellectual property rights (IPR) protection and the knowledge required to manufacture garments is quite easily acquired. Garment manufacturing spread around the developing world, supported by the Multi-Fibre Agreement (MFA), which mandated export quotas for each country. After the end of the MFA in 2004 and with the Great Recession in 2009, there was a consolidation of suppliers. With the COVID-19 depression, there is bound to be a further consolidation of garment suppliers. Nevertheless, garment manufacture remains the most widespread among manufacturing GVCs, more widespread than shoe and leather product manufacturing.

The ease of entry due to easily acquired knowledge contributes to the existence of large numbers of suppliers faced with increasingly oligopolistic lead firms, including brands and large retailers. Among garment suppliers, China dominates the scene. However, increasing wages in China, in conjunction with the geo-strategic regionalization of value chains, is leading to some movement out of China into mainly Bangladesh and Vietnam. Chinese manufacturers are countering this by undertaking mechanization and even robotization (such as the use of Sewbots) to reduce manufacturing costs. However, supply chains are stickier than usually imagined. There are costs in reorganizing supply chains, which means that locational shifts are mainly at the margins, where additional supplies are being sought. Some of these locational shifts are being undertaken by Chinese suppliers themselves, by investing in African countries or Cambodia to reduce costs. This mimics the triangular trade that the East Asian suppliers undertook in the 1990s when they fulfilled orders for the United States (US) and the European Union (EU) by sub-contracting to Chinese suppliers. Now, Chinese (and even Indian) suppliers are sub-contracting to countries in Africa.

The monopolistic structure of brands and large retailers is being strengthened by the COVID-19 depression, as it happened during the Great Recession. However, the growing importance of large domestic markets, such as China and India, also means the entry of new brands and large retailers from the Global South. These are not international brands, though a few, such as the Chinese Li Ning, in sportswear are becoming international. Again, in the current COVID-19 depression, export suppliers, such as those in India, are turning to supply the domestic market, so far supplied mainly by numerous tiny and small units in the unorganized sector.

Another trend since the 2008 Great Recession is the change in the business practices of garment lead firms. Fast fashion pushed for a shortening of lead times, giving an advantage to countries with better-organized logistics and trade facilitation. This is an area in which India lost out to competitors, such as Vietnam and Bangladesh, in not being able to attract lead firms looking for alternatives to China. The shortening of lead times has also privileged large units, which can be more agile in switching product lines and delivering on time.

As will be discussed in more detail in Chapter 11, Indian suppliers have responded to these changes in market demand in two ways. One is to invest in improved technology, such as laser cutting, to reduce fabric wastage and thus costs. Such improvements in technology have usually been accompanied by the employment of permanent workers instead of precariously employed contractual workers, as the former tend to be much more stable in factories and develop skills that suppliers wish to retain. The other response has been to increase the extent of overtime to meet shortened lead times. Such firms are losing out on orders as brands shift to more efficient and nimbly organized large firms. In the COVID-19 depression situation, discussions in July and August 2020 with owners and managers in Tiruppur and the Delhi region reveal that large units have full order books, while medium-sized units are working at around 50 per cent capacity. The small units, often unregistered workshops that used to take up the excess orders of medium and large units, are largely without orders. Homeworkers are also languishing without much work.

The garment export industry as part of a GVC was established in the Global South to utilize the difference in wages and environmental costs to manufacture goods more cheaply than in the factories of the Global North. This labour and environmental cost arbitrage, using differences in the prices of the same commodity in different markets, is the base of GVC production. What this means is that the same work of, say, stitching garments, or cut-make-trim, as it is referred to in the industry, is remunerated differently in the Global North and the Global South. Such differential remuneration for tasks performed in different parts of the world has long been an aspect of inequality in the world. One might say that this has been a feature of the world from the time of the Great Divergence from the 1800s, which pushed per capita incomes in the industrialized world well above that in the rest of the world, which was then mostly colonized. The contemporary differential remuneration for the same tasks was analysed by Arghiri Emmanuel as the imperialism of unequal trade (1972). It was seen as the source of imperialist super profits in Smith (2016) and Nathan (2018).

This differential remuneration is not our concern in this book. We are concerned here with the divergence of wages in supplier factories in the Global South from the costs of production of labour power in the same countries of the Global South. For this analysis, we first take up what constitutes a living wage and how to calculate it.

Living Wages

The concept of a living wage has long been recognized in international human rights statements and standards, beginning with the founding of the ILO (1919). In fact, the ILO Constitution recognizes living wages as foundational to global peace and harmony. According to the UN Declaration of Human Rights, 'Everyone who works has the right to just and favourable remuneration ensuring for himself and his family an existence worthy of human dignity' (United Nations 1948) Following numerous struggles to increase wages in the US, the New Deal recognized living wages as a necessary standard and women's unpaid domestic labour (Bhattacharya 2017).

In this book, our assessment of whether there are subsidies in a transaction is based upon the costs of purchasing required inputs. Wages, for instance, are paid in order to purchase labour power. According to Marx, the value of labour power is the value of the means of subsistence necessary for the maintenance of its owner, the worker (Marx 1958). For a worker, this maintenance includes the goods and activities needed daily to create labour power; over time, through sickness and retirement, and to restore labour power on a generational basis (Bhattacharya 2017: 120).

Rather than valuing these goods and activities at the minimum required for human survival, we consider the wages required to enable a decent level of capabilities. As such, living wages should be established relative to the country concerned and adjusted over time. Our approach is consistent with Adam Smith's articulation of the necessary minimum as 'not only the commodities which are indispensably necessary for the support of life, but whatever the customs of the country renders it indecent for creditable people, even of the lowest order, to be without' (Smith 2000: 399–400). This requirement of 'decency' was made more explicit by Marx, who argued that since labour power was a product of history, it depends on 'the conditions with which the class of free workers has been formed' (Marx 1958: 275). Here, Marx emphasizes that Smith's concept of wage decency has historical and moral elements.

The framework we advance defines living wages as those that afford workers with the necessary capabilities to function both at work and in society at large. For instance, in the contemporary world, owning a mobile phone—or even a smartphone to access the internet—may now be considered a necessary element in wages. Perceptions of what may be needed to take part in the life of a community may differ between countries. According to Sen,

> This will impose a strain on the relatively poor person in a rich country even when that person is at a much higher level of income compared with people in less opulent countries. Indeed, the paradoxical phenomenon of hunger in the rich countries—even the United States—has something to do with the competing demands of these expenses. (Sen 2009: 89–90)

Calculating Living Wages Based on Household Expenditure

As set out in the preceding parts, living wages—or the costs of a decent lifestyle for a worker and his or her family—can be calculated by adding up the costs of food, housing, healthcare, educating children, and participating in the social life of the community. The Asia Floor Wage Alliance (AFWA 2017a) and Anker (Anker and Anker 2017) methodologies for calculating living wages include the following components: costs of food for an adequate nutritional intake, clothes, housing, and other expenses; plus a small amount for 'discretionary expenses', meant to cover contingencies.

Both of these methods assume that a worker's household consists of two adults and two children—a norm also accepted in Indian wage calculations based on the recommendations of the 15th Indian Labour Conference. A man is counted as one consumption unit, a woman as 0.8 units, while children are 0.6 units each, totalling three consumption units in a household. While this standard for calculating household size assumes child dependents, dependents may in fact be aged and non-working parents. In garment production countries, which by and large lack robust universal pension systems, parents of garment workers are unlikely to have much (if any) savings. In India, even though there is a system of old-age pensions, the amount is just INR 500.00 per month (or USD 6.60 per month in August 2020). Not only is it common for aged parents to be de facto dependent upon younger earning members of the household but it is also a norm in India.

While similar in approach, there is some distinction in the expenses incurred under these standards. For instance, when applied to the context of Tiruppur, India, the Anker methodology assumes a daily calorie requirement of 2,236 calories per person. By contrast, the AFWA method of calculations, which are meant to apply across Asia, set a calorie requirement of 3,000 calories—consistent with Indonesian government estimates of the number of calories required for employment that requires moderate physical activity. Also, the AFWA method assumes an equal distribution of net income between food and non-food items based on consumer surveys in some developing countries. Thus, the food basket is calculated and then multiplied by two to arrive at the wage requirement for one person. By contrast, Barge et al. (2018), in applying the Anker methodology in Tiruppur in 2018, used actual estimates of non-food expenses, including housing. By this method of calculation, food constituted less than half of the total household expenditure.

Despite these methodological distinctions, the AFWA and Anker household expenditure calculation methodologies reach similar conclusions. For India in 2016, the Anker standard for household consumption is INR 18,830.00 per month. Similarly, for India in 2015, the AFWA standard for household expenditure is INR 18,727.00.

Accounting for Unpaid Domestic Work in Living Wages

Under capitalism, wage and domestic labour have been bifurcated and gendered along patriarchal lines. Over time, some commodity-producing functions, such as raising personal livestock for food, were separated from the daily lives of working-class families. Food and other commodities purchased with wages, however, still had to be prepared for household consumption: food had to be cooked, houses had to be maintained, and children, the sick, and the elderly required care. With the rise of proletarianization, men earned wages while women provided unpaid domestic labour, including care labour. Women's work became invisible, while men were the visible providers.

In line with the invisibility of women's domestic labour, all too often, living wage calculations have failed to account for women's unpaid domestic work. While living wage calculations typically include the cost of food items—

vegetables, grain, fruits, meat, eggs, milk, and so on—they rarely include costs associated with the processes of cleaning, preparing, and cooking required for these foods to be consumed. Similarly, houses and clothes need to be cleaned regularly. The resources required for these tasks are assumed to be available as unpaid work performed (almost by default) by women. The one aspect of domestic work that has, to some extent, entered into living-wage calculations is childcare. While childcare is yet to be included in Indian calculations, it is a feature of living-wage calculations in Europe (Anker 2011).

The number of hours spent on unpaid domestic work is not insignificant. Time-use studies for India show that it comes to almost 6 hours (351.9 minutes) per day for women and less than an hour (51.8 minutes) per day for men (OECD 2018). If we account for this unpaid work, the total working time at the individual and household level increases very substantially. A woman in India working 8 hours in a factory and doing unpaid domestic work is likely to work for more than 14 hours per day. This does not include the time spent travelling to and from work or overtime hours. By contrast, a man in India working 8 hours in a factory would work for about 9 hours per day. Women's unpaid domestic work hours in India are notably higher than in other garment-producing countries. In China, for instance, this total number of unpaid domestic work hours for women is a little less than 4 hours (234.0 minutes). This decrease in unpaid work from the Indian context can be accounted for by both the additional time spent by men, that is, 1.5 hours (91 minutes), and common practices of purchasing various household services, including cooking and care work.

While they reach a similar conclusion on standard household expenditures, the most fundamental difference between the AFWA and Anker methodologies pertains to the number of assumed earners per family. Based on census data and their own local surveys, Anker and Anker (2017) base their wage calculations on having 1.58 full-time workers per family. AFWA, by contrast, argues for living wage standards that allow one worker per family to cover household expenditures. This approach integrates unpaid domestic work, largely performed by women, into living wage formulations by ensuring that living wages are sufficient to cover the labour of one adult family member dedicated to unpaid domestic work (AFWA 2009). This analysis of household domestic labour requirements is supported by Stabile (2008) who points out that if every member of a family must work in order to earn enough to properly sustain a family, then they will be hard-pressed to complete unpaid domestic work requirements.

In households with two working adults, AFWA argues that families require this second income to cover hiring paid care workers and acquiring household services. Not surprisingly, in countries including Thailand and

China, workers' families often buy cooked food instead of cooking food at home. However, this is only possible if wages are high enough for the household to purchase cooked food instead of cooking and also to buy other domestic services. While higher wages can afford women workers the option of substituting commercially produced services for unpaid domestic work, purchasing domestic services reduces, but does not entirely eliminate, domestic work, and particularly care work. As such, feminists have long demanded that we not just recognize domestic work but also redistribute household labour between women and men.

Having seen the ways in which living wages can be calculated, we now turn to a comparison of living wages with wages as they exist. We begin with a discussion of how different supplier countries in Asia, such as Bangladesh, Cambodia, China, India, Malaysia, and Sri Lanka, all fare with regard to comparisons of national minimum wages with living wages. This is followed by a detailed discussion of wages in India, including a comparison across sectors.

Garment Worker Wages

With the preceding framework for understanding living wages as a benchmark, the remainder of this chapter compares living wage calculations with actual wages earned by garment workers in supplier countries. We briefly compare national minimum wages with living wages in Bangladesh, Cambodia, China, India, Malaysia, and Sri Lanka, and then focus on a detailed discussion of wages in the garment sector in India, including a comparison across sectors. Our analysis of wages in India reveals the comparatively higher wages earned by similarly situated workers employed in production segments of leather products, automotive components, pharmaceuticals, and IT services. As such, we argue that GVC segment characteristics, rather than worker characteristics alone, account for low wages in garment factories.

Wages for garment workers in GVC supplier segments tend to be set around the legal national minimum wage. In fact, national minimum wage standards are the basis for calculating labour costs in contracts between lead firms and suppliers in garment and other labour-intensive manufacturing segments, such as shoe manufacturing. In 2013, national minimum wages were 46 per cent of the living wages in China, 26 per cent of living wages in India, 19 per cent of living wages in Sri Lanka and Bangladesh, 25 per cent of living wages in Cambodia, and 54 per cent of living wages in Malaysia (AFWA 2013). In 2020, AFWA living wage calculations for India amounted to INR 26,000 per month while minimum wages (which vary from state to state) are set at about INR 9,000 per month.

Garment Worker Wages in India

Our case study of garment worker wages in the Indian garment industry begins with a macro-level national analysis of wages from the Annual Survey of Industries (ASI) data for the period 2010 to 2015—the last year for which unit data is available. Here, our analysis of ASI data looks at growth trends in the per capita wage of workers in the garment industry in India; and a comparison of per capita wages among workers and non-workers—including supervisory, management, and administration, and other staff who are not directly involved in the production process.

This national-level analysis provides a backdrop to our case study on garment worker wages in Tamil Nadu and the Delhi National Capital Region (NCR). Here, we use ASI data to consider the growth trend of per capita worker wages in the garment industry in Tamil Nadu and Delhi. We supplement this analysis with primary data on garment worker wages in these areas, collected through primary field surveys.

Per-capita monthly wages in the Indian garment industry

Table 4.1 compares per capita monthly wages of workers in the garment industry in India over time, providing insight into actual and real wages in micro, small, and medium enterprises (MSME) and large firms. Here, actual wages refer to the wages paid to the worker and real wages reflect the deflation of these wages in relation to the 2010 Consumer Price Index (CPI).

Table 4.1 Per Capita Monthly Garment Worker Wages (INR)

	Actual Wage[1]		**Real Wage[2]**	
Years	**MSMEs**	**Large Firms**	**MSMEs**	**Large Firms**
2010	4,410	4,350	4,410	4,350
2011	5,201	5,201	4,775	4,775
2012	5,536	5,962	4,654	5,019
2013	6,205	6,692	4,684	5,080
2014	6,874	7,452	4,897	5,293
2015	7,817	8,547	5,262	5,749
Trend Growth Rate	**12%**	**14%**	**3%**	**5%**

Source: Computed from ASI unit records of ASI 2009–10 to 2014–15.

Notes: 1. The actual wage refers to wages paid to the workers in the corresponding year.

2. The real wage refers to the wage deflated by the CPI. The base year for real wage calculation here is 2010.

Actual wages in MSMEs have grown from INR 4,410 to INR 7,817 in contrast to the large firms which reported a wage growth from INR 4,350 to INR 8,547. These figures indicate a significant difference in the per capita wages of workers between MSMEs and large firms. Contextualizing this actual wage growth, however, while the actual wage has grown at a rate of 12 per cent and 14 per cent, respectively, in MSMEs and large firms, real wages have grown only at the rate of 3 per cent and 5 per cent, respectively.

Comparison of Wages in Tamil Nadu and the Delhi Area

Tamil Nadu and the Delhi NCR are two major garment clusters in India. Our case study of these production hubs compares actual wages from ASI unit records with minimum wages protected under India's Minimum Wages Act, 1948, and living wages calculated by the AFWA. We further contextualize this official data with findings from our field research on garment worker wages in these clusters.

Figure 4.1 reports monthly per capita wages of workers in Tamil Nadu and Delhi from 2010 to 2015 for MSMEs and large firms, respectively. Overall, wages in large firms who produce for the export market and occupy a comparatively higher position in the GVCs are higher than wages in MSMEs at any given point of time.

Figure 4.1 also shows that wages in both MSMEs and large firms are higher in Delhi than in Tamil Nadu. This gap between wages in Delhi and Tamil Nadu is even wider in the case of MSMEs when compared to large firms. Notably, wages in large firms in Tamil Nadu progressively declined between 2013 and 2015, while wages in large firms in Delhi increased steadily from 2011 to 2015. The distinction in wage growth patterns in these clusters can be accounted for in relation to the distinct products and processes at play in these areas. The Delhi region produces more value-added products

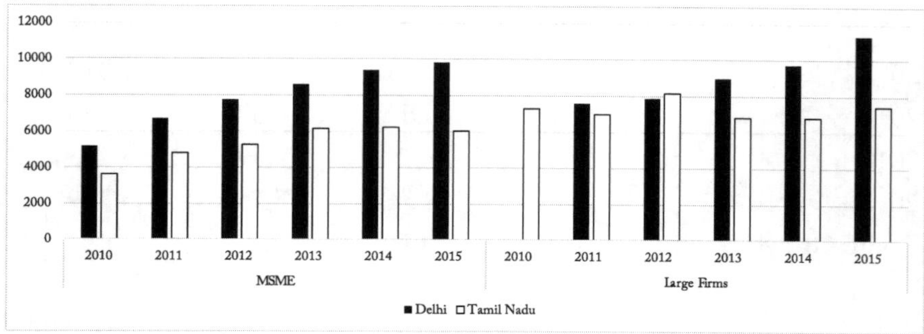

Figure 4.1 Monthly Wages of Garment Industry Workers in Tamil Nadu and Delhi

Source: Computed from unit record of ASI 2009–10 to 2014–15.

with embellishments, while Tamil Nadu clusters focus on fashion basics. As such, the comparative skill level required for embellishment and higher value garments provides greater bargaining power for these firms than for firms producing fashion basics. Large firms producing fashion basics in Tamil Nadu, competing with other global production clusters producing fashion basics in monopsonistic GVC relationships with lead firms, have minimal bargaining power. Their lower power in bargaining is reflected in the lower wages in the cluster where suppliers maintain their profit margin by reducing wages.

Figure 4.2 facilitates the comparative analysis of living wages with statutory minimum wages for garment workers in Tamil Nadu and Delhi. We use the 2015 data, including a living wage calculated for India by the AFWA and official government data on minimum wages. Figure 4.2 also contextualizes these minimum wages as actual wages, reflecting deflation in relationship to the 2010 CPI.

In this figure, we compare living wages with the lowest minimum wage category, since garment workers are most often paid minimum wages or less. In Tamil Nadu, the minimum wage we use is INR 3,796 per month compared to Delhi minimum wages at INR 9,022 per month. This figure, then, can be taken to represent the wage situation of the lowest wage workers: the predominantly female workforce employed as sewing machine operators and helpers on garment production lines. Workers employed in higher-skilled and remunerated positions would earn closer to living wages—but this does not represent the vast majority of the workforce. It is evident from Figure 4.2 that neither the minimum wages nor the actual wages garment workers earn come close to meeting living wages.

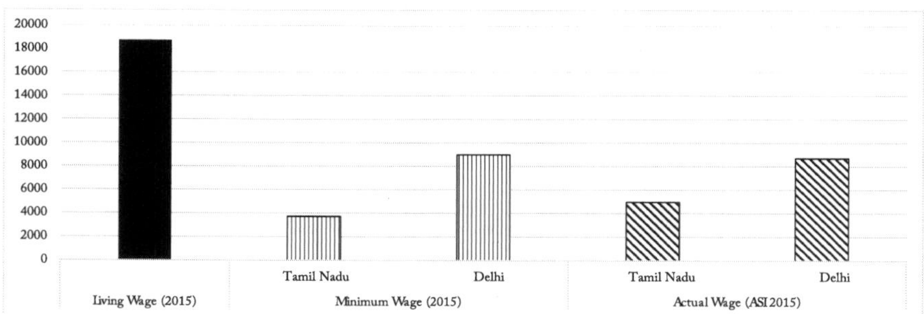

Figure 4.2 Comparison of Living Wages, Minimum Wages, and Actual Wages in Asia

Source: Living wages are referred to from AFWA, minimum wages from the *Report of Working of Minimum Wages*, Government of India, and worker wages computed from the ASI unit records.

Notably, our field research found that, in practice, garment worker wages may not be in line with even the minimum wage standards. In Delhi, we found that per capita wages paid to garment workers are less than the statutory minimum wages. In 2017–2018, the lowest statutory minimum wage level was INR 9,022, and the highest statutory minimum wage level for skilled workers was INR 11,000. Workers, however, reported that their actual wages were only INR 8,736. In Tamil Nadu, by contrast, workers reported being paid actual wages that are slightly higher than the lowest statutory minimum wage. This meant that the extent of wage subsidy was higher than reflected in the minimum wage in the NCR and a bit lower than reflected in the minimum wage in Tiruppur.

Factors Contributing to Low Wages in the Industry

How can we account for the low wages earned by workers on garment production lines? We answer this question by considering two sets of factors: supplier characteristics, including position within the value chain and associated bargaining power, and worker characteristics, including gender, nature of employment, and skill level. As laid out in Figure 4.3, these supplier characteristics interact with worker characteristics to drive down wages. This wage subsidy, however, is not evenly distributed along the value chain segments. Instead, due to the structure of monopsonistic value chains, suppliers retain a minimum profit while buyers earn super profits.

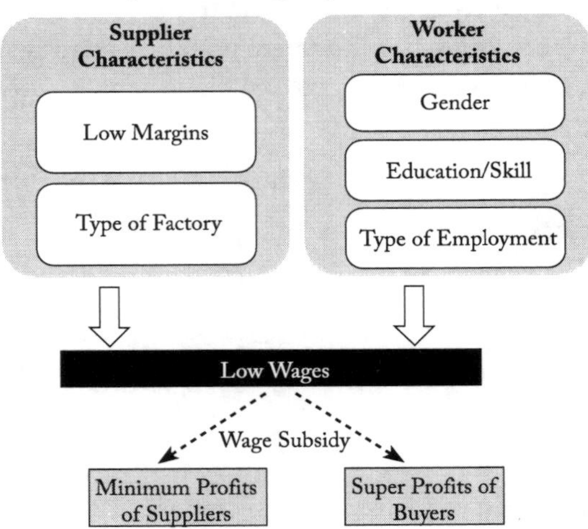

Figure 4.3 Relationship between Supplier and Worker Characteristics in Producing Wage Subsidies
Source: Created by the authors.

In this section, we illustrate these factors and their interrelationship in the Indian garment production segment through an analysis of the margins earned by suppliers in relation to the wages and working conditions in these segments. Situating this analysis in relation to the structure of value chains in India more broadly, we consider the relationship between profit margins and workers' wages in not only garment production segments but also leather, auto-components, pharmaceuticals, and IT segments.

Worker Characteristics and Business Practices in Low Wage Segments

As depicted in Figure 4.3, supplier firm and worker characteristics interact to produce distinct wage outcomes for workers on GVCs. Table 4.2 provides a summary of a comparative wage survey we conducted in Delhi and Tiruppur garment production clusters. Our survey included 80 workers in Tiruppur and 60 workers from the industrial areas in the Delhi NCR. In the sections that follow, we analyse this data in relation to our qualitative findings from the field to distil core drivers of low wages in the garment industry in India. These include gender, type of employment, skill level, industry overtime practices, worker knowledge about wage rights, and role of labour collectives.

Table 4.2 Average Monthly Wages (INR) among Garment Workers in Tiruppur and Delhi, Disaggregated by Gender, Type of Factory, Type of Employment, and Skill Level (2017–2018)

Gender	
Men	9,369
Women	8,967
Type of Factory	
Tier 1	9,817
Tier 2 and Tier 3	8,557
Type of Employment	
Contract Labour/Daily Wages	8,198
Regular Employees	9,965
Skill Level of Workers	
Unskilled	7,559
Semi-skilled	9,370
Skilled	9,392

Source: Primary data, n = 140.

Gender as a Driver for Low Wages

Table 4.2 includes the wage gap between men and women workers who were surveyed. While, on average, male workers earned INR 9,369 per month, women workers earned INR 8,967. Notably, this wage gap of approximately INR 400 per month is significantly less than the wage gaps reported in the 2017–2018 Periodic Labour Force Survey (PLFS) which reported a gender gap in wages of around INR 3,000, with men earning significantly more than women workers in the garment industry.

In Tiruppur, workers explained that differential wages between men and women workers reflect industry hiring practices. In the Tiruppur cluster, our field investigations confirmed that at the time of entering employment, men are typically afforded salaries that are between INR 1,000 and 1,500 greater than the salaries paid to women workers. We also found that firms have a practice of hiring young women workers for a fixed period of time, making an initial payment to their families, and then paying monthly subsistence wages to the worker every month. These and other gendered hiring practices, discussed at greater length in Chapter 6 on 'Gender-Based Violence as Supervision', segment the garment workforce along gender lines, with significant implications for wages and working conditions.

Type of Employment as a Driver for Low Wages

Our discussion of the type of employment as a driver for low wages considers distinctions between workers in regular employment and workers in contractual or daily wage employment—including workers employed seasonally and paid by piece rate. As set out in Table 4.2, while regular employees earn around INR 10,000 per month, contract and daily wage employees are paid INR 8,100 per month. While the literature has recognized the disproportionate benefits that accrue to highly skilled workers when compared with less-skilled workers in GVCs, our analysis suggests that regular workers may also benefit disproportionately when compared to contractual or daily wage workers.

Type of employment often articulates with gender to produce lower wage outcomes for women garment workers. In Sri Lanka, for instance, 17 per cent of women employed in garment factories are employed as manpower or trainee workers, while only 8 per cent of men are employed in this capacity. Manpower workers earn lower wages than regular workers and have limited if any access to social security benefits and employment security. AFWA researchers documented a 10 per cent pay gap between men and women workers in Sri Lanka. In Pakistan, women garment workers are also disproportionately concentrated in casual employment, earning lower wages with less access to benefits than their male counterparts (AFWA 2021).

Purchasing practices by lead firms in GVCs perpetuate such wage inequality within firms (Wang, Thangavelu, and Findlay 2018). Our fieldwork found that factory owners and managers attribute the practice of hiring a large number of contractual workers to unstable orders that ebb and flow by the season. Notably, large units have found solutions to this problem, such as developing production facilities for various markets. But most units close for a few months each year.

Low Skill Level as a Driver for Low Wages

Finally, Table 4.2 lays out the impact of skill level on worker wages. We classify workers into three categories: unskilled, semi-skilled, and skilled workers. We assigned these skill levels based on worker reports which mentioned whether they had participated in any formal skill training programmes, and according to the nature of the work they undertake within the factory. While unskilled workers are paid an average of INR 7,500 per month, semi-skilled and skilled workers are paid around INR 9,300 per month.

Skill level classifications, however, are linked to employment status. Factories that recruit production line tailors on a contractual employment basis routinely classify them as unskilled—and this is particularly the case for women workers. As such, wages are lower than the wages afforded to employees who are considered skilled and are employed on a regular basis. Unskilled women workers earn around INR 1,800 less than their male counterparts, and semi-skilled workers earn around INR 1,600 less than their counterparts. The practise of classifying employees as unskilled is, moreover, strategic, in allowing factories to hire workers with wage thresholds that meet the lowest minimum wage category.

Skilled women workers, by contrast, earned more than skilled men workers in the garment industry. Our investigation of these findings revealed that skilled women workers tend to maintain employment in the same factory for a long period of time and therefore accrue seniority benefits that raise their pay above the pay of their male counterparts.

Overtime Work and Wage Theft as a Driver for Low Wages

Working hours in an industrial unit are one of the most basic defining features of working conditions. Overtime is a common practice in most labour-intensive industries, and the Indian garment industry is no exception. However, it is important to highlight some specific aspects of overtime in the garment industry. First, overtime reported by workers does not refer to overtime beyond the 8-hour workday, and instead refers to work beyond normal factory working hours, which are usually 10 to 12-hour workdays. Second, workers report that overtime payments do not meet legal standards: only 12 per cent of the total workers surveyed received double payment for overtime work and 88 per cent reported that they were paid the same wages for overtime duty. This institutionalized practice of including 2 to 4 hours of overtime within the standard requirement for earning minimum wages, combined with routine and inadequately remunerated overtime, constitutes large-scale wage theft.

Despite overtime being paid below statutory requirements, however, workers reported viewing overtime as a desirable way to earn more wages—in fact, due to the low wages in the industry, for most, it is only with overtime pay that they can sustain their families. Not surprisingly, these institutionalized patterns of unpaid overtime impact workers differently on the basis of gender, skill level, and employment status. Women, for instance, reported working more overtime than their male counterparts.

All regular and contractual workers across skill levels, however, reported working increased overtime hours during peak season. Regular workers earning fixed pay (especially skilled workers) reported being made to work overtime without additional payment during peak season. Low-skilled and contract workers reported being made to work overtime by firms and being paid overtime—however, as previously explained, these overtime payments fall below statutory minimum standards.

During the global COVID-19 pandemic, unprecedented wage theft across the sector precipitated a humanitarian crisis for garment workers across Asia. During the pandemic-induced recession, brands unilaterally engaged in order cancellations, reduced new orders, demanded discounts, deferred payments, refused to pay for goods that were already produced, and demanded shorter lead times. The costs of the unilateral actions taken by brands were then passed on by suppliers to their workers in the form of unprecedented wage theft practices.

In 2021, the AFWA joined with garment workers' unions across six major garment production countries in Asia to study the impact of the COVID-19 pandemic-induced recession, and the actions of global apparel brands, on the lives and livelihoods of garment workers. Through engagement with 2,185 garment workers employed across 189 factories in Sri Lanka, Pakistan, Indonesia, India, Cambodia, and Bangladesh, AFWA documented widespread wage theft practices. For each country, the study documented the percentage loss in workdays, percentage of wage theft, and whether workers were pushed below the international poverty line (Table 4.3).

Table 4.3 Impact of Brand Actions during COVID-19 Pandemic on Poverty Levels, Employment, Wages, and Debt of Workers, 2020

Country	Percentage of workers surveyed who were pushed below the international poverty line (during peak COVID-19 period)	Percentage of loss in work days	Percentage of wage theft	Wage theft estimates per factory surveyed (million USD)	Percentage increase in workers' debt
Sri Lanka	78%	21%	23%	1.38	200%
Pakistan	81%	26%	29%	2.2	196%
Indonesia	78%	20%	21%	0.73	198%
India	93%	26%	23%	1.15	137%
Cambodia	10%	6%	6%	0.7	64%
Bangladesh	96%	23%	27%	N/A	202%

Source: AFWA (2021).

AFWA (2021) also presented a detailed framework for understanding supplier employment practices that resulted in wage theft (Table 4.4). These practices include changing employment status from more to less secure, layoffs and termination, misreporting wages, and targeting particular categories of workers—including pregnant workers, older workers, and union leaders. As a result of these practices, workers experienced a spectrum of wage theft practices, including loss of wages, reduction in wages due to demotion, reduction in employment-related benefits, loss of terminal benefits, unpaid or underpaid overtime, coercive extraction of unpaid labour, and loss of social security. These practices also precipitated an increased wage gap, both along gender lines and between regular, contractual, and casual workers, and on a caste basis in India.

Table 4.4 Cascading Effect of Brand Actions on Suppliers' Employment Practices

Exercise of Managerial Power and Leverage over Workers	Employment Practices	Forms of Wage Theft
1. Malafide Use of Power to Change Employment Status	• Failure to recognize seniority of workers (such as rehiring older workers on fresh contracts or terminating senior workers without following due process) • Replacing more secure employment with more precarious employment (such as rehiring regular workers as contractual or casual workers) • Wrongful designation of permanent workers as short-term contract workers	• Reduction in wages due to demotion • Reduction in employment related benefits due to shift in contract type
2. Arbitrary Practices to Impose Workforce Flexibility	• Layoffs and termination to reduce size of workforce • Coercive intensification of work by smaller workforce • Extension of the work day of smaller workforce	• Loss of terminal wage benefits • Loss of wages • Unpaid or underpaid overtime
3. Use of Deceptive Practices to Evade Liability Under Labour Law	• Manipulation of work-related documentation (such as mis-reporting reduction in wages, number of work days, number of overtime hours) • Termination or wage theft under the guise of disciplinary action (such as in the case of workers for joining protests, taking sick leaves, or being unable to rejoin work on the date set by the employer due to COVID-19 restrictions)	• Loss of wages • Unpaid or underpaid overtime • Loss of terminal benefits

4. Unethical Practices to Leverage Vulnerability in Workforce Demographics	• Replacement or termination of pregnant workers, older workers, union leaders and members, and female workers over male worker • Rehiring male workers over female workers and non-union members over union members • Layoff of female workers over male workers • Layoff of contractual and casual workers over regular workers • Forcing casual or contract workers to work longer hours without payment	• Loss of terminal benefits • Loss of wages • Rising gender pay gap • Rising wage gap between regular, contractual, and casual workers • Coercive extraction of unpaid labour
5. Blatant Leveraging of Weak Labour Rights Enforcement Mechanisms	• Blatant reduction or denial of bonuses, social security, provision of creches, and so on	• Loss of key social security provisions

Lack of Knowledge of Wage Laws by Garment Workers as a Driver of Low Wages

Among the workers we spoke to during our field investigation in Tiruppur, none were aware of the minimum wages. More than 50 per cent of the workers we spoke to in Tiruppur were migrants from north Indian states and, as such, language barriers played an important role in their lack of knowledge about labour standards. In the Delhi NCR cluster, by contrast, migrant workers share a common language with the locals and are therefore far more connected to the society around them.

Despite this communication advantage, very few of the contractual or daily wage workers we spoke to in the Delhi NCR cluster were aware of minimum wage rates. In the Delhi NCR cluster, contractual employees were most often hired by an external contractor. The contractor, in turn, supplied workers to the factories based on demand. These hiring agents facilitate consistent access to a flexible low wage workforce for supplier factories and brands, facilitate regular temporary gigs for workers, but short circuit access to employment benefits and wage increases that come with permanent positions. Workers reported that these hiring agents did not inform workers about minimum wages, overtime benefits, or any other labour rights protections.

Workers who understand that they face wage violations, moreover, rarely have evidence of the payments they receive. Only one-fifth of all of the workers that we surveyed across the two clusters reported that they received payment slips. Very few contractual or daily wage workers received payment slips, and none of the workers from the Tier 2 and Tier 3 firms received payment slips. A lack of awareness about wage protections, along with a lack of transparency in payment practices, combine to further drive down wage standards across the industry.

Weak Labour Collectives

The bargaining power of the workforce is a major factor that influences labour rights and worker welfare. None of the workers interviewed were associated with any trade unions and some of the workers were not even aware of the concept. The only collectives in the clusters were the grievance redressal committees formed by the firms, and the workers had non-union representation in the same.

Most garment factory managers actively try to prevent unionization. They join with labour contractors in taking steps against those who try to unionize. Trade union representatives and union affiliated workers described the negative implications of large subcontractors on freedom of association. The availability of a pool of contract workers makes it easier for garment factories to blacklist workers who attempt to unionize. By undermining freedom of association and collective bargaining, contractors contribute to foreclosing opportunities for worker governance on garment supply chains.

By contrast, research has demonstrated the role of strong labour collectives in raising and securing minimum wages. In Indonesia, for instance, the gender wage gap is higher in the provinces and significantly lower in the older industrial regions where unions are stronger and a long history of labour struggles has achieved significantly higher minimum wages. In the low minimum wage areas of the provinces, women reported earning 25 per cent less than their male counterparts, while in the older industrial regions, the wage gap was minimal (AFWA 2021). These findings suggest that strong trade union activity has the capacity to win and enforce minimum wage standards, levelling the playing field for male and female workers.

Supplier Characteristics in GVCs

In Chapter 3, we put forward the proposition that the bargaining position of firms in GVCs affects wages and working conditions for their employees. We propose that firm bargaining power in GVCs has an impact on wages and working conditions, irrespective of whether the firm utilizes IPR-protected production systems, and across firms with distinct rates of profit. Our proposition is grounded in the Kalecki (1971) thesis that wages in an enterprise would be related to the degree of monopoly of that firm in the product market. The degree of monopoly results in differences in profit rates, which, in turn, affects wages that workers can secure. Broadly, wage rates would increase with enterprise profit rates.

Returning to Figure 4.3, on the relationship between supplier and worker characteristics in producing wage subsidies, this section considers the role of supplier characteristics in setting wages for workers in the garment industry. These supplier characteristics interact with the worker characteristics described in the previous section.

GVC Position of the Factory as a Driver for Low Wages

Tier 1 firms that secure export orders directly pay higher wages (INR 9,800) than the sub-contracted Tier 2 and Tier 3 factories (INR 8,500). Our fieldwork found that Tier 1 factories have proportionately more regular employees in their payrolls than either Tier 2 or Tier 3 factories. Tier 1 factories also have a stable quantity of orders; and stable orders promote regular employment. Due to the instability of orders for the Tier 2 and Tier 3 factories, firms resort to recruiting labour according to their immediate need, and on a piece-rate basis where payments are low. This is consistent with our argument that firms that are higher in the GVC structure have greater bargaining power than those lower down, and that this bargaining power tends to correlate with higher wages and better working conditions.

We re-examine this proposition beyond garment GVCs through an investigation of wages and working conditions in a number of industries—garments, leather shoes, automotive components, pharmaceuticals, and IT services, all of which are well integrated into value chains—mainly global, but also domestic. In looking at these relations, we combine firm data from the ASI (CSO 2015) and labour data from the PLFS (NSSO 2018). The ASI data is used to calculate the margins in these industries, which we have averaged over a six-year period. They are calculated as the total output minus total inputs, divided by total inputs. PLFS data is used for wages and other working conditions, such as social security.

In making such a comparison across different GVC suppliers that cross sectors and employ workers with different education and experience, it is not sufficient to just compare overall worker wages. The educational composition of the workforce in these supplier industries varies from workers in the garment and leather industries who have not completed high school to workers in IT services who are mainly college graduates. Therefore, to effectively demonstrate that differential profit rates do play a role in wages, we first look at the interaction between margins in various industries and their respective wages. After this, we compare wages for the same educational levels in sectors with different profit rates.

In Figure 4.4, which provides a distribution of margins and associated wages, we observe that industries with lower margins are reporting lower wages compared to the others. For instance, garment and leather, which report margins of 6 per cent and 7 per cent, respectively, report wages around INR 7,000 and INR 8,000, while IT services, which reported a margin of 14 per cent, also reported an average monthly wage of INR 25,000. We can see a linear trend with respect to margins and wages from the figure, which is drastically higher in the case of IT.

This figure indicates that the position of the industry (supplier characteristics) in GVCs has a definite impact on the wages of the workers. This may be considered to be preliminary and not at all conclusive, as there are several variables that need to be controlled to conclusively argue that supplier characteristics exert influence over wages. In particular, we need to see these from the comparative frame of the worker's educational characteristics, which will act as controls.

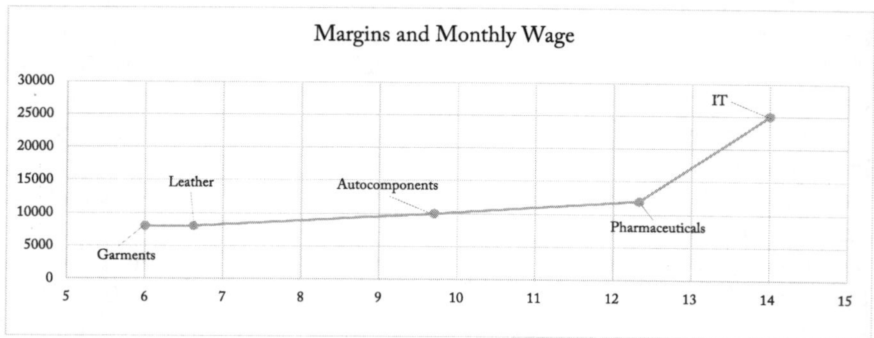

Figure 4.4 Distribution of Margins and Wages

Source: Computed from ASI unit records 2016–17 and PLFS unit records 2017–18.

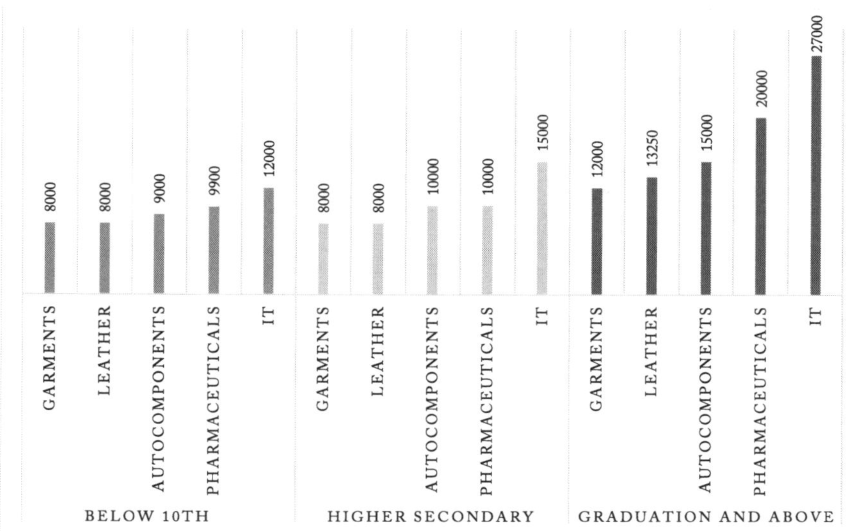

Figure 4.5 Distribution of Monthly Salary across Industries with Respect to Educational Attainment
Source: Computed from PLFS unit records 2017–18.

Figure 4.5 shows a distribution of monthly salary across industries in relation to educational attainment. Overall, we see an increase in wages in relationship to education across all industries. Wages in garment and leather have increased from INR 8,000 to INR 12,000 and INR 13,250, respectively, as worker educational attainment moved from below matriculation (the 10th standard in school) to graduation and above.

However, in testing the validity of our proposition that firm position within a GVC has an impact on worker wages, comparing monthly wages within a particular band of educational attainment is of particular interest. It may be noted that workers from the IT industry earn the highest in any educational category. This is true for a worker with educational attainment below the 10th standard in school, and also for a worker who is a graduate or holds higher degrees.

Taken together, the findings in Figure 4.5 present a picture in which wages are influenced not only by the educational qualifications of the workers but also the nature of the industry—or its location and role in value chains. In short, a worker with any level of education earns more when placed in the IT industry compared to the garment or leather industries. The deciding factor in these outcomes is that the profit margins in the garment and leather

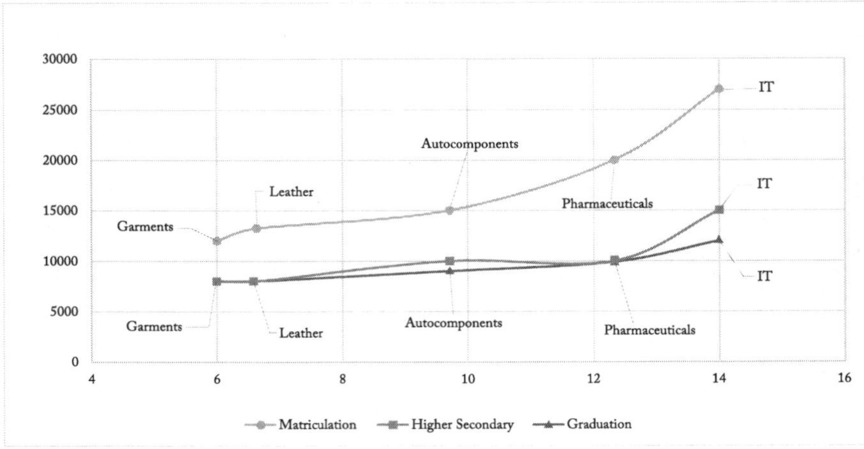

Figure 4.6 Margins and Wages of Workers by Education Level

Source: Computed from ASI Unit Records 2016–17 and PLFS Unit Records 2017–18.

industries are quite low, and in the IT industry is relatively high. This is further reinforced if we compare wages for the same educational levels with firm profit margins.

In Figure 4.6, we are looking at the interaction between margins, wages, and worker education levels. The margins fall in a clear hierarchy—they are the lowest for garments at 6 per cent, and not much higher for leather shoes at 7 per cent; then 10 per cent for auto-components, 12 per cent for pharmaceuticals, and 14 per cent for IT services—which is the highest. In IT services, the large Indian suppliers have considerable market power due to their reputational assets and enjoy a better position in the GVC, which in turn is reflected in their margins.

A worker who has matriculated in the garment or leather industries earns around INR 7,000 to INR 8,000. For the same education level, that earning goes up to INR 10,000 in pharmaceuticals and INR 12,000 in the IT industry. Trends across all educational categories suggest that industry margins have a definite impact on worker wages. Put in another way: wages go up even for workers belonging to the lowest educational category as we move from garment to IT.

In Figure 4.7, we are looking at the interplay between margins, worker education levels, and the percentage of workers who have access to social security benefits. We analyse social security benefits in order to better understand the relationship between working conditions and margins.

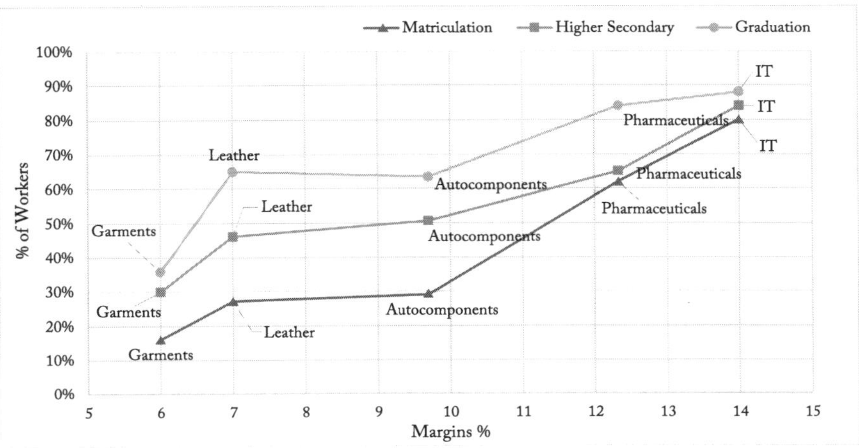

Figure 4.7 Margins, Social Security Benefits, and Education of Workers
Source: Computed from ASI unit records 2016–17 and PLFS unit records 2017–18.

Apart from the auto-components industry, we see a linear increase in the number of workers receiving social security benefits for all educational categories as margins increase. It is particularly evident in the case of workers who have attained matriculation: while hardly 15 per cent of workers in the garment industry have access to social security benefits, 80 per cent of workers in the IT industry have access to social security benefits. This advances our case that working conditions, as represented by access to social security benefits, are influenced by firm margins. In short, the proportions of workers receiving social security benefits (even at the lowest educational level) goes up as firm margins increase: from the lowest level in garment, improving slightly in leather and auto-components, and showing real improvements in pharmaceuticals and IT services. In short, if we control for the individual worker characteristic of education, we observe that the margins a firm earns have a definite effect on the working conditions for employees.

In Figure 4.8, we look at worker gender, wages, and firm margins across the same set of industries. The gender gap in wages is not only one great concern in academic and policy discourse but is also considered to be a dominant driver in wage outcomes. In our analysis, however, the relationship between the workers' gender, wages, and firm margins is quite interesting. Wage disparities are quite similar across manufacturing segments (garments, leather shoes, auto-components, and pharmaceuticals) but virtually disappear in IT services. IT services are the most knowledge intensive of these sectors and gender wage differences seem to disappear, though other forms of gender disparities may well exist.

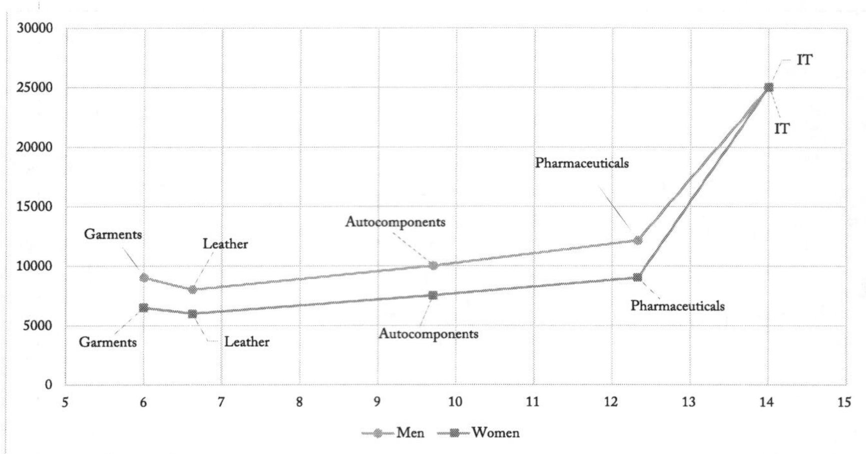

Figure 4.8 Gender, Margins, and Wages
Source: Computed from ASI unit records 2016–17 and PLFS unit records 2017–18.

On the basis of our analysis, we argue that wages and working conditions vary with the margins earned in different GVC supplier enterprises. Kalecki saw this working through the varying strength of trade unions, increasing with profit rates. We demonstrate that wages and employment conditions vary with the position of the suppliers in value chains, in relation to the profits earned by these suppliers. Since this is the case, wage subsidies—that is, wages that are below living wages—are likely to intensify as profit rates earned by the suppliers go down.

Thus, we see that wages depend on both firm characteristics—including distinct bargaining power with lead firms, ranging from no power at all to some, even if limited, bargaining power; and worker characteristics—such as gender, educational level, and skill. In general, firm characteristics or positions in GVCs are a hard constraint on wages. However, this need not be the case. Firm strategies that seek to increase productivity and efficiency through investment in technology and enhancing worker capabilities stand to increase bargaining power. At the same time, these wage increases are likely to be limited and not move wages substantially towards living wages. However, there is a co-determination of employment or working conditions and firm performance, which would modify the strict constraint of existing profit rates on wages. A study by Nathan and Harsh (2018), for instance, provided empirical examples of such firm strategies.

Conclusion

In this chapter, we began by setting out the benchmark of living wages, including goods and services, and domestic services, for a worker and their generational families. We argue that the costs of unpaid domestic services also need to be included in the calculation of living wages. With this framework in mind, our living wage calculation comes to about INR 20,000 per month at 2019 prices (roughly USD 300 per month). Across supplier countries in Asia, actual wages are much less than living wages, ranging from 19 per cent of living wages in Bangladesh to 46 per cent in China and 54 per cent Malaysia, with India at 26 per cent. This difference between actual and living wages then becomes a subsidy—provided by the worker and their household—to brand or lead firm profits in GVCs.

Looking at actual wages in different GVC segments (garments, leather shoes, auto-components, pharmaceuticals, and IT services), we saw that wages of workers of the same educational levels varied across these industries, consistent with firm profit rates. Industries with higher profits had higher wages for the same educational levels. This establishes that firm characteristics or positions in GVCs, summarized by their profit rates, are also determinants of wages and working conditions. In setting wages, these firm-level characteristics interact with worker characteristics—such as gender, education, and skill levels—and industry practices, such as unpaid overtime, to meet fluctuating demand from lead firms. Firm profit rates are a hard constraint on wages, even where trade unions are established. However, firm strategies that seek to increase productivity and efficiency may lead firms to increase wages and working conditions in order to improve firm performance.

Appendix 4A

Table 4A.1 Gender-Wise Monthly Wage (INR) Distribution

Location				**Type of Factory**			
	Men	Women	Total		Men	Women	Total
Tiruppur	8,056	7,531	7,936	Tier 1	10,281	9,682	9,817
Delhi NCR	11,338	9,924	10,772	Tier 2 and Tier 3	8,877	8,090	8,557
Total	9,369	8,967	9,245	Total	9,369	8,967	9,245

Type of Employment				Skill Level of Workers			
	Men	Women	Total		Men	Women	Total
Contract Labour/ Daily Wages	8,481	7,768	8,198	Unskilled	8,419	6,699	7,559
Regular Employees	10,292	9,859	9,965	Semi-Skilled	9,796	8,141	9,370
Total	9,369	8,967	9,245	Skilled	9,261	9,688	9,392
				Total	9,369	8,967	9,245

Source: Primary data.

Notes

1. While our case study refers to the Delhi NCR more broadly, we use Delhi ASI data here because ASI data is not disaggregated for the Delhi NCR. Delhi wages would tend to be higher than for other parts of the NCR.

5

Extractive Labour Subsidies

The Overuse and Discard of Women's Labour in Garment Production

As laid out in Chapter 4, labour-intensive production processes and payments below living wages are structural features of the global garment industry. Chapter 4 laid out a framework for understanding how global value chains (GVCs) drive down wages and structurally reproduce labour subsidies. This chapter, and Chapter 6 that follows, zoom in on the impact of wage subsidies borne by garment production line workers—a predominantly female workforce of internal and international migrants employed at the base of global production networks.

How do women production line workers subsidize the functioning of garment value chains? This chapter presents a two-part framework for understanding the extractive labour subsidies borne by women workers on garment production lines: overwork subsidies and discard subsidies. Each of these labour subsidies is largely experienced by women workers through bodily and embodied processes. Overwork subsidies refer to subsidies extracted from women workers through exploitative labour practices in the garment sector. In order to meet the fast-fashion production targets, garment workers on production lines work extended hours for below living wages.

Overwork subsidies manifest as physical calorie deficits: garment production line workers earn wages that permit them to afford food amounting to fewer calories per day than they expend working on production lines. This calorie deficit is magnified for women who also expend energy on unremunerated care and reproductive work. Prolonged calorie restriction has severe health implications, including reduced fertility and weaker bones. In short, women workers on garment production lines subsidize the global garment industry by absorbing health impacts with long-term consequences. These health impacts are compounded by poor working conditions, including long hours performing repetitive manual tasks under exposure to heat, noise, dust, and chemicals.

Yet another subsidy, which we refer to as a discard subsidy, captures the costs borne by women garment workers when they age out of garment sector employment. Due to industry preference for women below the age of 35, young women workers provide overwork subsidies resulting in long-term health costs until they age out of employment—typically before they become eligible to receive seniority or severance benefits. These outcomes for women workers are not just technical shortcomings in the organization of work but also structural outcomes of global garment production regimes.

This account of how lead firms on garment supply chains exact overwork and discard subsidies from women garment workers is derived from two 2018 studies conducted by Asia Floor Wage Alliance (AFWA), Global Labor Justice–International Labor Rights Forum (GLJ-ILRF), and Society for Labour and Development (SLD), and one conducted by SLD with Clean Clothes Campaign (CCC) in 2018. From January to May 2018, AFWA, GLJ-ILRF, and SLD researchers studied experiences of violence, including extractive labour practices, through engagement with 150 women garment workers in Dhaka, Bangladesh; Phnom Penh, Cambodia; West Java and North Jakarta, Indonesia; Bangalore, Gurgaon, and Tiruppur, India; and in Vavuniya District, Northern Province, Sri Lanka. This sample included workers from 37 different supplier factories (AFWA et al. 2018 a–c). SLD, along with CCC, conducted a study of 37 women workers, of whom 21 were women working in two 'Gold Standard' H&M suppliers (that is, factories certified to be of the highest labour standards) in north and south India (CCC 2018). Finally, this study draws from AFWA 2021 research on wage theft during and in the aftermath of the COVID-19 pandemic, including surveys conducted with 2,185 garment workers employed across 189 factories in Sri Lanka, Pakistan, Indonesia, India, Cambodia, and Bangladesh (AFWA 2021). This primary data is contextualized in relation to the scholarship on gender and the global economy.

Practices of unremunerated, forced overwork with wages linked to impossible targets among low-wage workers—and women garment workers in particular (Custers 1997)—have been well documented through field-level studies for at least two decades. This chapter builds upon and contributes to this line of research by explaining the structural reproduction of these extractive labour practices on garment GVCs that are rooted in fast-fashion brand purchasing practices. We argue that justice in GVCs depends upon remedying extractive labour practices that displace the costs of production onto the bodies of low-wage workers through overwork and discard subsidies with devastating long-term health consequences for women workers. Providing the full costs of labour on garment supply chains is critical to facilitating labour contributions to economic systems of production without exceeding human limits.

Overuse Subsidies

Accelerated Work, Extended Working Hours, and Low Wages

Across Asian garment value chains, women make up the vast majority of garment workers and are concentrated in low-wage production jobs where they are hired on short-term contracts. Within these roles, they are driven to reach unrealistic production targets both by accelerating the pace of work and working for extended hours. These working conditions are endemic to the structure of garment supply chains and intimately linked with, first, the asymmetrical relationships of power between brands and suppliers described in Chapter 4 and, second, brand purchasing practices driven by fast-fashion trends and pressure to reduce costs.

Current brand purchasing practices reflect the rise of fast fashion. Where the norm was four style seasons each year, the Zara brand pioneered monthly styles and even two-week cycles. Today, fast-fashion brands commonly release between eight and ten style seasons each year (Nathan and Kumar 2016), accelerating production cycles and shortening lead time. Short lead times, high quotas, and irregular, repeat orders for high-demand items require supervisors and line managers to demand high-speed turnover, drive worker productivity, and, as laid out in Chapter 4, hold workers overtime (Vaughan-Whitehead and Caro 2017).

In a 2018 study by AFWA, GLJ-ILRF, and SLD, women from Bangladesh, Cambodia, India, Indonesia, and Sri Lanka all reported being forced to work overtime to meet production targets. Women workers in divisions ranging from sewing, trimming excess thread, quality checking, and packaging are assigned production targets. Targets vary by garment type but typically require workers to be accountable for every minute they are at work.

Women in Phnom Penh described group production targets of 380 pieces per hour per line—with 38 workers per line. Notably, while prior to increases in the Cambodian minimum wage there had been up to 50 workers per line, at the time of writing, this number decreased to around 38 in order to maintain stable wage costs. According to a 2018 research by the Cambodian Center for Alliance of Labor and Human Rights (CENTRAL 2018)—including consultations with 41 workers at 10 factories and analysis of payslips from 7 factories—over the years, line-based production targets have increased, while the number of workers per line has gone down. Cambodian garment workers interviewed for this study also reported threats of termination based on a 'three strikes you're out' system for failure to meet production targets or for making minor production mistakes. The increase in production targets also impacts piece-rate workers, many of whom have seen no wage increase and only an increase in their minimum expected workloads (CENTRAL 2018).

In India, Indonesia, and Sri Lanka, women more commonly reported individual production targets. Indian women in Gurugram described typical targets as 30 to 40 pieces per hour. However, during heavy production periods, they may be driven to meet inflated and unreachable targets of up to 100 pieces an hour. At a maximum, women workers in Gurugram reported being able to produce 90 to 95 pieces per hour, 5 to 10 per cent short of the required targets. In Indonesia, women reported being required to produce 90 to 120 pieces every 25 minutes, with timed intervals to determine if targets were met. In Sri Lanka, production targets can escalate to 200 to 250 pieces every 30 minutes for less complicated garments.

Across Asian garment production networks, women reported that workers who fell short of their targets may be prevented from taking lunch breaks, not allowed toilet breaks, or forced to stay overtime. For instance, women workers in Manesar, Haryana, India, reported that overtime hours for most workers amount to a minimum of 3 hours per day and routinely stretched until late at night. To take Sunday off, workers report being made to work as late as 4 am on Sunday to complete their Saturday shift. While Indian legal standards require suppliers to compensate workers for food expenditures during overtime work hours, this supplier factory provides a mere INR 79 (USD 1.22) to workers engaged in overtime late into the night. During high-intensity production cycles, women may work days on end without a break. A woman tailor from a supplier factory in Gurugram described having to work 21 days continuously without a break.

Women reported that they would be allowed toilet breaks only if they were able to keep up with the required work quota. In order to keep up with production quotas, women said that they drank less water so that they would not require any toilet breaks. One can imagine what such practices would to do women workers' kidneys. In Pakistan, women workers described being made to work more than 10 hours a day without a break, locked within the factory gates to make sure they don't leave before the production targets are met.

In Chapter 4, our findings in Tiruppur and Delhi revealed a sustained industry practice of requiring overtime without compensating workers at legal standards. Similarly, workers in Cambodia described forced overtime as a characteristic management practice. All Cambodian workers surveyed reported working in excess of 50 hours a week, with some reporting an average of 60 hours per week. One worker explained:

> We are forced to do overtime when demand is high. If we don't, we are threatened that our contracts will be terminated. If we ask to take leave, we are threatened with termination.

Forced overtime is most common during the garment high season, which overlaps with Cambodia's hottest season. From April to August, workers report being forced to work up to 14 hours a day—as well as on Sundays and national holidays—in the sweltering heat, without an adequate supply of clean drinking water or any breaks.

Workers also reported being required to work when they are ill. A Sri Lankan woman worker, employed in the Vavuniya District, Northern Province, Sri Lanka, described the consequences of resting, even when she is sick:

> Even if we are sick, still we have to finish our work on time. We have a room to rest if we are sick, but if I use that room, I will be blamed by my supervisor for missing the target. Our supervisors don't like us even opening the door of the room. If we get rest there, we won't be able to finish our tasks.

Cambodian women workers described even harsher consequences for resting while ill. A woman worker employed in Phnom Penh, Cambodia, said: 'When workers ask permission for sick leave, the administration officer threatens to force them to submit a letter of resignation instead.'

Calorie Deficit

Women workers produce garments for global fast-fashion retail markets under caloric and nutritional deficits because the food they can afford does not sustain the length and rigour of their workday. In a 2018 focus group discussion with SLD researchers, women working in a supplier factory in Gurugram, Haryana, India, discussed the challenges they faced in purchasing nutritious food:

> We buy low-quality food products and dresses that are cheaper. We usually cook potatoes with flatbread. Milk products, meat, and fish are far from our reach.
>
> We carry some of the food grains from our native place so that we can save money on food. Even basic food items are much more costly over here.

In Tiruppur, India, a woman worker reported that she did not even earn enough to buy food from the canteen at the factory where she worked:

> Our salary is so low that I can't afford the food that is available in the factory canteen. Even that is out of my reach. I carry my own lunch box.

Calorie deficit is exacerbated by the harsh timing penalties for arriving late to garment factories, which drives many women workers to skip meals. A garment worker in Tiruppur, for instance, stated that even if she is a minute late, she loses her wage for an hour. To reach the factory on time, she has to skip breakfast. Such practices of skipping breakfast in order to get to work on time are also reported in Swaminathan and Jeyaranjan (1999).

In a supplier factory in the Vavuniya District, Northern Province, Sri Lanka, women workers reported paying for the food they received at lunchtime but receiving smaller quantities than male workers:

> Our food portions are different according to our gender. At lunch in the company canteen, male co-workers and supervisors receive more food than we do.

Data gathered by tracking monthly food purchases by 95 workers employed in a range of garment factories in Cambodia, compared with recommended amounts and workers' body mass index (BMI), revealed that workers were found to intake an average of 1,598 calories per day, around half the recommended amount for a woman working in an industrial context (McMullen and Majumder 2016).

Introduced by Nathan, Shaheen, and Dehaghan (2018), the term *body mining* refers to the physical toll on women that results from this poor nutritional intake, combined with no weekly rest day, and the physical demands of work. Their study found that among 38 garment workers (21 women and 17 men) in two garment factories in India, 33.3 per cent of women fainted at work and 28.6 per cent received a glucose drip within the previous year. All of the women who reported fainting had worked overtime. These findings were confirmed in a 2018 study by SLD where, among 75 women surveyed, 40 per cent had received a glucose drip in the last year.

Body mining is intimately tied to the oligopolistic nature of GVCs in the garment industry, and the attendant weak bargaining position of suppliers explained in Chapter 4. In order to compete to win production bids from brands and retailers, garment suppliers with low bargaining positions on GVCs project labour costs based upon minimum wages rather than living wages, and 10-hour workdays, including 2 hours of overtime, rather than 8-hour working days. Due to this practice, suppliers routinely pay only normal wages for overtime rather than the double-wage rate required under many labour law regimes.

Calorie deficit is only compounded for women workers who also expend energy on unremunerated care and reproductive work—including for the women in Tiruppur, who reported not being able to afford food in the canteen and therefore had to prepare food to carry to work. This understanding of women's work as including domestic, wage, and non-wage work has been well established for nearly 20 years through analysis of time-use surveys (Hirway 2002), and scholarship on the multidimensional nature of women's work, the multilayered contexts in which their work is situated, and the adverse repercussions of overwork for women's well-being both within the workplace and in their domestic environment (for example, Swaminathan 2004). As we have done in this chapter, analytic frameworks for understanding the effects of excessive labour on well-being incorporate the *length of the working day*, the *incidence of work intensity* (Floro 1995a), and the *time required to recover from fatigue* (Swaminathan et al. 2004).

Notably, in the 2018 study by Nathan, Shaheen, and Dehaghani, where one-third of the women surveyed had fainted at work, and more than one-quarter received a glucose drip within the last year, no man reported fainting. This finding is contextualized by the authors in relation to anaemia among Indian women, a common condition due to the discrimination in access to food and women's heavy burden of unpaid work at home. According to a randomized survey conducted by India's Employees State Insurance Corporation in 2014, 60.6 per cent of garment workers surveyed were anaemic (Ceresna-Chaturvedi 2015).

Extractive labour practices rooted in capitalist relations of production and patriarchal social norms governing women's unpaid household and reproductive work interact and heighten calorie deficit, malnutrition, and attendant health consequences. Padmini Swaminathan (2004) detailed this interaction in her examination of the interaction between women's work at home and garment factories in the Chengalpattu district, near metropolitan Chennai, Tamil Nadu, India. Swaminathan found that almost all women respondents reported that they did not have enough time to complete their household work and eat before leaving for the factory. As a result, the first solid meal taken by these workers was scheduled for around noon but frequently cut short in the drive to complete production targets. These conditions, leading to routine stomach aches and acidity, persist to date.

In the 2018 study by AFWA, GLJ-ILRF, and SLD, women workers—like those in Swaminathan's earlier study—described having their lunch breaks postponed in order to meet production targets. A woman worker from a factory in Gurugram, Harayana, India, explained: 'If the piece is urgent and not complete, our lunch hour is shifted back. The in-charge tells us to finish the urgent pieces and then break for lunch.' Prolonged calorie restriction over time has severe health implications, including reduced fertility and weaker bones.

As a result of falling incomes, layoff, and termination, garment workers experienced high levels of hunger and food insecurity during the COVID-19 pandemic. According to a 2020 survey of 396 workers conducted by the Worker Rights Consortium—including workers from Bangladesh, Cambodia, El Salvador, Ethiopia, Haiti, India, Indonesia, Lesotho, and Myanmar—77 per cent of workers reported that they or a member of their household had gone hungry since the beginning of the pandemic. Twenty per cent reported experiencing hunger on a daily basis, while 34 per cent experienced hunger at least once a week. Eighty-eight per cent of workers reported reduced household food consumption, and 80 per cent of workers with children skipped meals or reduced food intake in order to feed their children (WRC 2020).

Unsafe Working Conditions

The health implications of body mining are compounded by unsafe working conditions, including long hours performing repetitive manual tasks under exposure to heat, noise, dust, and chemicals. Long hours sitting hunched over machines leads to back pain, ulcers, piles, and exacerbate reproductive health issues including irregular periods and excessive bleeding. Women working as checkers report varicose veins as a result of long hours standing and checking garments. Women working for a supplier factory in Gurugram, Haryana, India, described severe pain in their legs.

> Standing for the whole day causes leg pain. My back becomes stiff. My calves and heels start to pain—the pain is continuous.
>
> Sitting at the sewing machine for the whole day, for 12 hours, with only a half-an-hour break leaves my legs swollen. By the evening it is very difficult to walk due to the pain in my legs. I cannot even stand up while working or take a walk to stretch my legs. I just have to sit until I complete my target.

Other routine health consequences for women garment workers include respiratory illnesses, such as tuberculosis, irritation of the upper respiratory tract and bronchi, and silicosis from sandblasting. Prolonged exposure can progress to chronic, obstructive pulmonary disease (Ceresna-Chaturvedi 2015).

Exposure to high temperatures and high levels of chemical substances, exacerbated by poor ventilation systems and inadequate nutrition among workers, make episodes of mass fainting a regular occurrence. In 2017, the Cambodian National Social Security Fund identified 1,603 cases of fainting across 22 factories. Ninety-eight per cent—1,599—of these cases were women.

Cases of fainting include individual workers and multiple workers within a factory fainting at once. On 4 August 2017, Meas Sreyleak, a 25-year-old Cambodian woman, died on her way from the factory to the hospital after she fainted at work and hit her head on the sewing table. Women who worked with Sreyleak reported that she had been feeling unwell on the day that she died. She had a sore throat but was made to work two hours overtime. Her family received USD 1,000 from the factory to help defray funeral expenses. On 6

July 2017, Neom Somol saw a colleague faint in the factory and attempted to help her get to a medical clinic. In the process of doing so, she fainted herself, her head hit a wall, and she died at the factory. At another factory in Phnom Penh, 150 workers fainted over two days (30 and 31 August 2017) due to the combination of high heat and exhaustion.

The extreme health consequences associated with extractive labour practices in garment supplier factories is well known to major garment brands. As early as 2011, Swedish fashion brand H&M responded to 284 Cambodian workers fainting at M&V International Manufacturing in Kompong Chhnang Province—an H&M supplier. More than 100 workers were hospitalized. H&M reported launching an investigation (McPherson 2011). The investigative report commissioned by H&M blamed the fainting on 'mass hysteria' caused by work-related and personal stress (Butler 2012). This explanation capitalizes on gendered tropes that blame women workers for the consequences of extractive labour. Investigation by labour researchers revealed a more robust explanation at the intersection of body mining and unsafe workplaces: malnutrition, prevalent among Cambodian garment workers, makes them more susceptible to exposure to harmful environments (McMullen and Majumder 2016).

Mass cases of fainting among garment workers in Cambodia are the most widely reported to date but such cases are not isolated to Cambodia. On 19 March 2018, 52 workers collapsed from breathing toxic fumes in a garment supplier factory in Ekala, Sri Lanka. That day, the branch union secretary for the factory encouraged workers to leave the workplace due to widespread difficulty in breathing, nausea, stinging eyes, and vomiting. Instead, workers continued to work to meet their production targets. The assistant factory manager attributed the smell to machine maintenance and took no action to address worker complaints. By 10:40 am that day, workers began collapsing and 52 workers were rushed to the hospital.

Unsafe workplace practices that result in physical injury extend beyond the factory. On 10 November 2017, *Campost*, a Khmer language newspaper, reported an accident involving a truck carrying 68 garment workers on their way to work. Five workers were seriously injured. The paper attributed the accident to negligence by the driver, leading the truck to flip over.

Health Impacts for Pregnant Women Workers

For women garment workers, the overlap between years of factory work and reproductive years is common. The health repercussions of extractive labour subsidies in the garment sector are heightened for pregnant women. A 2017 study of the lived experiences of six pregnant workers in Bangladesh—all of whom were migrants—found that pregnant workers reported heightened stress that they will lose their jobs if they cannot meet production quotas due to their pregnancy. As a result, although the women respondents had access to factory-based clinics, they reported that they did not visit the factory doctor for ante-natal check-ups when they first suspected they were pregnant in order to hide their pregnancy from supervisors until their pregnancy became visible. Due to their long working hours, women also reported being unable to seek early ante-natal care at government hospitals. Factory doctors reported that pregnant women may develop hypertensive disorders and diabetes due to working for long hours in one position, compounded by work-related stress (Akhter, Rutherford, and Chu 2017).

The stress associated with employment termination during pregnancy is widespread across Asian fast-fashion supply chains. Women workers from supplier factories in Bangladesh, Cambodia, India, and Indonesia reported either witnessing or experiencing employment termination during pregnancy. In Sri Lanka, by contrast, trade union leaders reported that permanent women workers are able to access maternity leave. However, due to the reliance on workers hired through 'manpower' or temporary agencies, many women are excluded from these benefits. Workers from supplier factories in Gurugram, Haryana, India, reported that women are routinely fired from their jobs during their pregnancy. Permanent workers report being forced to take leaves without pay for the period of their pregnancy. Contract, piece rate, and casual workers reported that although most of the time they are reinstated in their jobs after pregnancy, they receive completely new contracts that cause them to lose seniority.

Since garment factory workers in Cambodia are predominantly women, a lack of access to adequate reproductive and maternal health services is a significant issue. As early as 2012, workers organizations began reporting that pregnant women were regularly threatened with dismissal from garment manufacturing jobs. This led many women to terminate pregnancies in order to keep their jobs. Women also force themselves to work until the very last day before the delivery, putting their own lives at risk. Most women on Fixed Duration Contracts (FDCs) do not get their contracts renewed after they go on maternity leave (CCHR 2014; Nuon 2011).

During the COVID-19 pandemic, pregnant garment workers faced discrimination including verbal abuse, reduced pay, being forced to resign from work, and termination. In some cases, workers in India reported that pregnant women were forced to go on paid leave in the early months of their pregnancy when they wished to use their maternity leave later on. As a result, many women were forced to resign immediately after the birth of their child since they had exhausted their maternity leave and did not have access to affordable childcare options.

In some factories in India, workers also reported situations where all pregnant women were terminated immediately after the COVID-19 lockdown. One factory went so far as to force all women workers to undergo mandatory ultrasound scans, violating their privacy and bodily rights, and used the results to terminate pregnant women workers. Consistent with the wage theft dynamics described in the previous chapter, none of these workers received full severance benefits. In Sri Lanka, pregnant women workers who lost their factory jobs were unable to find alternate work through manpower agencies since these agencies refused to enroll pregnant women. In Pakistan, women reported that companies did not provide financial support for laid off pregnant workers.

Discard Subsidies

Ageing out of Garment Sector Employment

Workers employed on garment production lines, for the most part, age out of employment by the age of 35. For instance, a 2018 study conducted by the International Labour Organization (ILO) project on Improving Working Conditions in the Ready-Made Garment Sector in Bangladesh in collaboration with United Nations (UN) Women Bangladesh found that more than 86 per cent of the 533 garment workers surveyed were under the age of 35 (Table 5.1). The trend of workers leaving factories when they are between 30 and 35 years old has also been documented in Cambodia, India, and China (Mezzadri and Majumder 2018; War on Want 2011, 2012; Pun, Liu, and Lu 2015).

Table 5.1 Age Distribution of Ready-Made Garment Workers in Bangladesh

Indicators	Male	Female	Total
Age distribution (%)			
15–19	11.6	7.7	9.6
20–24	32.5	31.9	32.2
25–29	29.1	31.9	30.6
30–34	12.7	15.1	13.9
35–39	7.5	9.8	8.7
40+	6.7	3.5	5.1
Total	100	100	100
Mean age (years)	26.7	26.6	26.6

Source: Ahmed and Hossain (2018), supported by the ILO project on Improving Working Conditions in the Ready-Made Garment Sector in Bangladesh (Phase II) in collaboration with UN Women.

Table 5.2 Distribution of Factory Workforce by Age Group and Gender in India

Industry	Age Group	Male	Female
Garments	Below 40	89.0%	90.6%
	40–45	3.4%	9.2%
	Above 45	7.6%	0.2%
Leather	Below 40	69.0%	77.4%
	40–45	7.2%	8.5%
	Above 45	23.8%	14.1%

Source: Calculated from the Ministry of Statistics, Government of India, unit data of Periodic Labour Force Surveys, 2018.

The India data in Table 5.2, calculated from the Indian Ministry of Statistics' Periodic Labour Force Surveys, shows a slightly different picture in the Indian context. Only 9.5 per cent of women workers in the factory are over age 40. There are almost no women left in the garment factories over the age of 45. This can be compared with both men in garments and women in leather factories. Men over the age of 40, like women, comprise about 9.5 per cent of the workforce, but unlike women who after age 45 are no longer represented in the workforce, male workers over 45 comprise around 7.6 per cent of the workforce. When compared with the situation in leather, both women and men are worse off in garment factories. In leather factories, women over 45 comprise 8.5 per cent of the workforce, and men over 45 comprise 7.2 per cent of the workforce. Leather products do not have the same treadmill type of work dictated by fast fashion in garments. This could be the reason why both women and men stay on longer in the leather factory workforce.

Since the global garment workforce is overwhelmingly comprised of women, this industry preference for younger workers manifests as a preference for women below the age of 35. Industry preference for younger women has been attributed to the comparative capacity of women under age 35 to sustain the rigour of meeting extremely high production targets, and the willingness and availability of unmarried, young women to submit to compulsory overtime work (Swaminathan 2004).

Forfeiting Seniority Benefits and Severance Pay

Women workers also subsidize garment production at the time they are terminated or 'discarded' by forfeiting legally mandated seniority benefits and severance pay. In this form of wage theft, supplier factories can cut costs by terminating employment for women workers before they are eligible to receive seniority benefits. Reinforcing the concentration of women in subordinate low-wage roles in Bangladesh, India, and Indonesia, the 2018 study of gender-based violence and harassment on garment production lines conducted by AFWA, GLJ-ILRF, and SLD documented heightened levels of abuse against more senior women workers after they become eligible for benefits. A woman worker in Bangladesh explained:

> For the first four years that I worked as a sewing machine operator, I had a reputation for skill and dedication. After my fourth year, when I was eligible for gratuity, the line chief and supervisor increased my production targets, shouted at me, and referred to me in derogatory terms. I reported to human resources, but they did not intervene. Work became so unbearable that I left the factory.

Women workers in Bangladesh reported that targeting women workers who are eligible for seniority benefits is common. Women who resign due to harassment are considered to have resigned voluntarily, relieving the employer from paying legally mandated benefits. Women workers also report leaving the garment sector due to altercations with managers or supervisors, blacklisting in response to union activity, chronic health issues, and family crisis requiring women's labour within the household (Mezzadri and Majumder 2018).

As discussed in Chapter 4, wage theft through failure to pay severance is prevalent and normalized across the garment industry, robbing garment workers—a predominantly female workforce—of hundreds of millions of dollars. The legal obligation for employers to pay severance and redundancy payments is well established in the national laws of not only many garment-producing countries but also worldwide.

National standards, however, are difficult if not impossible to enforce in the context of global supply chains where global brands and suppliers regularly shift supply chain production across borders, depart from garment-producing countries, and thereby sidestep national laws on severance and redundancy. Over the last two decades, cases of brands moving supply chains, the sudden closure of supplier factories, and the failure to pay severance are widespread, and have been challenged and documented by trade unions and allied organizations in Cambodia (HRW 2013), El Salvador (BHRRC 2019), Honduras (Greenhouse 2010), Indonesia (Silverstein 2019), Eastern Europe—including Bulgaria, Georgia, Macedonia, Moldova, and Romania (CCC 2014)—South Africa, Turkey, and the US (Gate 2006).

During the COVID-19 pandemic, workers who were members of trade unions were among the first to lose their jobs. Sothy, a 36-year old garment worker, described being targeted for union activity.

> The COVID-19 crisis was used by my factory to selectively terminate unionized workers like me. Even in the pre-COVID-19 period, women union members like me have been threatened with termination and cuts in social security benefits. The COVID-19 pandemic was used by the supplier to openly attack workers' freedom of association by unfairly dismissing unionized workers.

In addition to these financial subsidies borne by women garment workers at the point in which their employment is terminated, widespread layoffs of senior and unionized women workers may have significant consequences for the workforce at large: an erosion of tacit industrial knowledge within the workforce that stands to increase the vulnerability of young women workers to not only labour exploitation but also—as outlined in Chapter 6—a spectrum of gender-based violence and harassment (Mezzadri and Majumder 2018; Silliman Bhattacharjee 2020a).

Afterlife in the Informal Economy

Although profit margins for suppliers and brands rely on the profits that come from squeezing women workers and their lack of alternative choices, notwithstanding these realities, women's employment changes household budgets which become dependent on this income—especially, but not only, in women-headed households. Families typically rely on the incomes of older women within the family as an established resource stream, while younger women who enter the workforce bring in a new income stream.

In order to maintain these resource streams, those women garment workers who have managed to accumulate savings may pursue work as local micro-entrepreneurs, as documented by Sandya Hewamanne's 2018 study of women workers in Sri Lanka. However, due to consistent payment below living wages, women garment workers routinely leave garment factory employment with debt rather than savings and upward mobility. In India, for instance, in order to compensate for wages in garment factories that fall below living wages, it is common practice for women workers to access their provident fund (PF) contributions, depleting later access to retirement savings (Mezzadri 2016).

Alessandra Mezzadri and Sanjita Majumder's (2018) analysis of the life history of 20 women garment workers over the age of 40 years documents the employment trajectory from garment factories to the informal sector in Bangalore. Among the women interviewed by Mezzadri and Majumder, 17 out of 20 women left the industry with considerable amounts of debt, ranging from INR 50,000 to 500,000. None of the 20 respondents reported leaving with any savings. After leaving Bangalore's garment factories, women workers took up domestic work in private households and offices, home-based garment work, or agricultural work.

Women who lost their jobs in garment factories during the COVID-19 pandemic also reported entering informal sector employment. In Pakistan, when men suffered wage loss of 68 per cent and 56 per cent in April and May 2020, women lost 80 per cent and 90 per cent of their wages during these months. Women workers shared that after losing their jobs during lockdown, they were less likely to be reemployed than men when factories reopened. As a result, most of the women surveyed in Pakistan who were laid off or terminated turned to informal home-based work or domestic work in order to feed their families. In Bangladesh, garment workers found employment in construction work and street hawking.

6

Gender-Based Violence as Supervision

While Chapter 5 explained the structural reproduction of extractive labour subsidies, this chapter directs attention to the day-to-day industrial relations practices that facilitate labour subsidies. How are labour subsidies extracted from women workers? What are the industrial relations practices used to discipline women workers into working beyond their physical capacity in an industry where they have no long-term employment security? Across garment supply chains, labour subsidies are enforced through routine and entrenched practices of gender-based violence and harassment (GBVH) that function as a mode of supervision within hierarchical workplaces, structured along gender lines. This chapter provides a framework for understanding GBVH in the garment industry as not simply a factory-level problem but rather an industry-wide culture of violence sustained at the intersection of gendered ideologies and social relations, and brand purchasing practices driven by fast-fashion trends and pressure to reduce costs.

Women workers on Asian garment production lines face a spectrum of violence (Table 6.1). Sexual harm, stigmatization, and industrial discipline practices perpetrated against women garment workers are at once locally specific and also part of escalating patterns of violence documented across garment supply chains. Women workers may be targets of violence on the basis of their gender, or because they are perceived as less likely or able to resist. Comprising the majority of workers in garment supply chains in Asia and globally, women workers are also disproportionately impacted by forms of workplace violence perpetrated against both women and men (AFWA et al. 2018a–c).

Table 6.1 Spectrum of GBVH in Asian Garment Supply Chains

	Gendered aspects of violence, including: (1) Violence against a woman because she is a woman (2) Violence directed against a woman that affects women disproportionately due to (*a*) high concentration of women workers in risky production departments; and (*b*) gendered barriers to seeking relief
Forms of violence	
(a) Physical and sexual violence and discrimination	• Assault, including pushing to the floor, beating, and kicking—gendered aspects (1) and 2(*b*) • Slapping—gendered aspects 2(*a*) and (*b*) • Pushing—gendered aspects 2(*a*) and (*b*) • Throwing heavy bundles of papers and clothes—gendered aspects 2(*a*) and (*b*) • Sexual harassment—gendered aspect (1) • Sexual advances—gendered aspect (1) • Unwanted physical touch, including inappropriate touching, pulling hair, and bodily contact—gendered aspect (1) • Rape outside the factory at accommodation—gendered aspect (1) • Overwork with low wages, resulting in fainting due to calorie deficit, high heat, and poor air circulation—gendered aspect 2(*a*) • Long hours performing repetitive operator tasks, leading to chronic leg pain, ulcers, and other adverse health consequences—gendered aspect 2(*a*) • Serious injury due to traffic accidents during commutes in large trucks without seatbelts and other safety systems—gendered aspect 2(*a*)
(b) Verbal and mental violence	• General verbal abuse, including bullying and verbal public humiliation—gendered aspect 2(*a*) • Verbal abuse linked to gender and sexuality—gendered aspect (1) • Verbal abuse linked to caste or social group—gendered aspect 2(*a*) and (*b*) • Verbal abuse targeting senior women workers so that they voluntarily resign prior to receiving benefits associated with seniority—gendered aspect 2(*a*)

(c) Coercion, threats, and retaliation	• Threats of retaliation for refusing sexual advances—gendered aspects 1, 2(*a*) and (*b*) • Retaliation for reporting gendered violence and harassment—gendered aspects 1, 2(*a*) and (*b*) • Blacklisting workers who report workplace violence, harassment, and other rights violations—gendered aspect 2(*a*)
(d) Deprivations of liberty	• Forced to work during legally mandated lunch hours—gendered aspect 2(*a*) • Prevented from taking bathroom breaks—gendered aspect 2(*a*) • Forced overtime—gendered aspect 2(*a*) • Prevented from using legally mandated leave entitlements—gendered aspect 2(*a*)

Source: AFWA et al. (2018a–c).

The spectrum of violence described in this chapter is based upon accounts of gender-based violence on garment supply chains from 150 garment workers employed in 37 factories from across Bangladesh, Cambodia, India, Indonesia, and Sri Lanka. These accounts, collected by the Asia Floor Wage Alliance (AFWA) between January and May 2018, include reports of sexual harm and suffering and gendered industrial discipline practices, including physical violence, verbal abuse, and threats of retaliation for resisting abuse. In order to contextualize cases and types of violence reported by women workers, we conducted in-depth factory profiles of 13 garment supplier factories in Bangladesh, Cambodia, and India that aimed at locating patterns of violence in relation to the distribution of workers by gender across departments and roles. The theorization of GBVH as a tacitly approved gendered industrial relations practice and the approach to address GBVH on production lines laid out at the conclusion of this chapter draw from the 2019 strategic framework developed by the AFWA in their *Step-by-Step Approach to Prevent Gender-Based Violence at Production Lines in Garment Supplier Factories in Asia*.

Gendered Segmentation of the Garment Workforce

For more than two decades, scholarship on gender in the global economy has documented how in varied, locally specific ways, international capital relies upon gendered ideologies and social relations to recruit and discipline workers, producing segmented labour forces within and between countries (Mills 2003). Within garment factories, the vast majority of women workers are employed in the production department. They hold subordinate machine operator, checkers, and helper roles, and are overwhelmingly supervised by male line managers. In these hierarchical workplaces, macro-level gendered societal discrimination seeps into garment factories as GBVH. Violence on garment value chains is gendered not only because women workers may be singled out for violence and harassment, but also because women workers comprise the overwhelming majority of workers in production departments—high-pressure work environments that are significant sites of violence within garment factories.

Departments segregated by gender may also be spatially separate, creating multiple working environments within a factory. For instance, within one Indonesian supplier factory, the first floor includes the production department and accessory warehouse, comprised of women workers supervised by both male and female supervisors. While some men work on the first floor, they work in a physically separate warehouse for final products. The second floor houses the cutting unit, staffed by a mix of male and female workers and supervisors. In this arrangement, women production line workers are not only concentrated in subordinate roles but also in segregated spaces.

Women garment workers may be further segregated by demographic categories. For instance, in a garment supplier factory in Gurugram, Haryana, India—part of the garment clusters for which we examined wage data in Chapter 4—women workers described being separated by age during a routine morning practice of labour segmentation:

> As we enter the factory, we are asked to form two separate lines: one of young girls and another of elder women. They keep us segregated. Young girls work on a different floor than the older ladies. So, in the end, we have no idea how they behave with young girls.

Women workers at a supplier factory in the Vavuniya District, Northern Province, Sri Lanka, described being particularly vulnerable to harassment at the beginning and end of the day as they stand in line to clock-in and clock-out using biometric fingerprinting machines.

> Girls are harassed by male workers in the factory. I have seen supervisors and mechanics pull their hair, hit their buttocks, and touch their shoulders. This happens a lot when they wait in line to use the fingerprint machines.

In these varied accounts of entry into the factory, women workers are sorted, segregated, and subjected to routinized sexual harassment at the beginning and end of the day.

This compounded spatial, role, and age segregation prevents elder women from intervening on behalf of younger women who may face violence and harassment. Sri Lankan women workers also identified young, unmarried girls as particularly vulnerable to sexual harassment from both male managers and co-workers.

> Young unmarried girls are targeted for sexual harassment because they are single. Male co-workers and managers ask young women for their phone numbers. They call late at night. Most single women face harassment in the factory.

More senior and widowed women are also targeted. In an industry where women workers age out of employment by the age of 30, women are considered senior at as young as 26 years old. Shahida, a 26-year-old sewing machine operator, described being suddenly targeted by her supervisor when she became eligible for workplace benefits. Shahida recounted:

> I began working at this factory in April 2013. I earned a good reputation as a skilled and dedicated worker. The line chief and supervisor were happy with my work. After completing my fourth year at the factory, they reversed their attitude towards me. They shouted at me and bullied me. They called me names. I reported this to the factory manager, but he responded by raising my production targets. I couldn't manage to work this way. In March 2018, before reaching my fifth year, I quit the job. It was exactly what they wanted. I resigned and they did not pay me the gratuity I had earned because they said I had resigned from the job myself.

A woman in Bangalore recounted being abused both for being a widow and for being a more senior worker:

> My supervisor came to my workspace at 5:30 pm. He told me to get up from the chair and not to come to work from the next day onwards. 'Go and die at home', he shouted. Another staff member joined in and asked, 'Why do you come to work if you are so old?'

Systematic practices of retrenching senior workers leave young women workers without access to their seniority and tacit experience in responding to workplace violence and, therefore, make them more vulnerable to abuse.

GBVH may be further intensified for women from socially marginalized communities. In India, for instance, women garment workers include migrant scheduled caste, scheduled tribe, and Muslim women. Their intersecting status as migrants, women, and members of marginalized communities increases the risk of exploitation and exclusion from decent work and undermines accountability through formal legal channels (Lerche and Shah 2018).

Gendered Industrial Discipline Practices

The daily race to meet production targets, described in the previous chapter, is sustained through gendered industrial discipline associated with *operatory labour practices*. Referring to the role of workers as basic sewing machine operators, operatory labour practices correspond with hierarchical work relationships, sweatshop discipline, and anti-union management practices (Nathan, Saripalle and Gurunathan 2016). Tied to their ability to reach production targets, women workers reported physical and verbal abuse, coercion, threats, and deprivations of liberty. While both women and men reported these forms of workplace violence, discipline is disproportionately directed at women workers due to their concentration in machine operator, checker, and helper roles within production departments.

Women garment workers in Bangladesh, Cambodia, and Indonesia described constant and relentless verbal abuse that continues from the beginning to the end of their shifts. An Indonesian woman described the stress and humiliation associated with yelling and mocking from her supervisor:

> If you miss the target, all the workers in the production room can hear the yelling:
> 'You stupid! Cannot work?'
> 'Watch out, you! I will not extend your contract.'
> 'You don't have to come to work tomorrow if you can't do your job!'
> They also throw materials. They kick our chairs. They don't touch us so they don't leave a mark that could be used as evidence with the police, but it is very stressful.

When factories in Sri Lanka reopened after COVID-19 lockdowns, women workers reported a spike in production targets—and verbal abuse. Prisha, a 33-year-old garment worker, explained:

> When the factory reopened in June, workers with less than six months experience were terminated. Workers with four to five years of experience like me were shifted to new departments and the production targets were almost doubled. Supervisors and managers engaged in constant verbal harassment, calling us 'whores' and 'bitches'. The work environment was terrible and no one could complete these targets. We were all terminated by September.(AFWA 2021)

In addition to verbal abuse, women reported rough treatment from male supervisors. A woman from a supplier factory in Gurugram described being physically pushed to work: 'The supervisor and master push us by our shoulder or shake it abruptly and roughly with their hand ordering us to work.'

Rough treatment may escalate to physical violence, including slapping, pushing, kicking, and throwing heavy bundles of papers and clothes, especially during high-stress production times. Bundles may weigh between two and four kilograms—a projectile that is approximately the weight of a brick, but unlikely to leave visible marks that would allow the victim to seek redress. Workers reported that physical discipline practices spiked after second-tier management came out of meetings with senior management where they faced pressure to drive workers to meet production targets.

Industrial discipline practices may intersect with sexual harassment and threats of violence on the factory floor. A woman worker, employed in a supplier factory in Gurugram, explained: 'It's very common for the in-charge manager to say, "finish the target or I will ..."—using any number of sexual connotations. They do not say this to men.'

Women workers also described being uniquely targeted for rough treatment. In India, a woman described routine incidents of unwanted physical touch:

> The line manager leans on me when he gives instructions, instead of standing straight. I have asked him not to. I said, 'Masterji, if you move back, I can see what you are explaining.' He stayed leaning on me with his elbow touching my breast. I lost my temper and told him: 'Stand properly! Keep your hands away!'

Other women workers also described supervisors touching women workers, with male workers exempt from physical contact.

> The supervisor in charge knocks into us as they pass by. They pretend it is accidental, but it is not an accident if it happens all the time, with most of us women. It if was really an accident, wouldn't it happen to men?

Physical touch may escalate to physical aggression. In Cambodia, where local workers are supervised by Chinese managers, women reported that physical and verbal abuse escalated due to the frustration with communicating across language barriers. A woman recounted:

> Chinese managers pressure the Cambodian team leaders to shout at the workers to make them work faster. We are called stupid and lazy. Sometimes they beat workers.

A Cambodian woman described an incident where a translator slapped a female worker and later claimed he was joking. No action was taken against the perpetrator.

Public corporal discipline terrorizes not only the direct victim but also women around her. Consequently, violence on the production line is both looming and normalized—a constant threat that drives production with fear. Unchecked violence authorizes progressively more extreme forms of physical and verbal abuse.

A woman worker from Bangalore, India, reported being thrown to the floor and beaten for falling short of production targets, including on her breasts:

> On 27 September 2017, at 12:30 pm, my batch supervisor came up behind me as I was working on the sewing machine, yelling, 'You are not meeting your target production.' He pulled me out of the chair and I fell on the floor. He hit me, including on my breasts. He pulled me up and then pushed me to the floor again. He kicked me.

In response, she filed a written complaint with Human Resources. She described the meeting between herself, the supervisor, and the Human Resources personnel:

> They called the supervisor to the office and said, 'Last month you did the same thing to another lady—haven't you learned?' Then they told him to apologize to me. After that, they warned me not to mention this further. The supervisor and I left the meeting. I went back to work.

Although the harassment from her manager did not stop, she continued to work at the factory because she needs the job: 'My husband passed away and I have a physically challenged daughter who cannot work. That is why I suffer to earn my livelihood.'

The GBVH Escalation Ladder

As described in the preceding sections of this chapter, not only do forms of GBVH associated with industrial discipline practices intersect and overlap but they also escalate in intensity over time. This finding is bolstered by a robust literature on workplace bullying—attempts to undermine or control an individual or group within a workplace with repeated behaviours that typically escalate over time (Chappell and Di Martino 2006). Across sectors and geographies, examples of workplace bullying include assigning heavy workloads, refusing applications for leave, allocating menial tasks (Fox and Stallworth 2006), excessive monitoring, unfair and persistent criticism, judging work incorrectly, blocking promotion (Randle, Stevenson, and Grayling 2007), public humiliation, spreading rumours (Keashly 2001; Lutgen-Sandvik 2008; Namie and Namie 2009), rude, foul, and abusive language (Vega and Comer 2005), and explosive outbursts, such as yelling, screaming, and swearing (Lutgen-Sandvik, Namie and Namie 2009). In the literature on workplace bullying, forms of bullying are further characterized by intensity, persistence (frequency, repetition, and duration), and power disparity between targets and perpetrators (Lutgen-Sandvik 2008; Namie and Namie 2009).

A 2010 study of workplace bullying in business process outsourcing in India, including 1,036 respondents located in six cities, found that 44.3 per cent of the sample experienced bullying, with 19.7 per cent reporting moderate and severe levels (D'Cruz and Rayner 2012). The authors note that in keeping with India's hierarchical society, superiors emerged as the predominant source of bullying, displaying task-focused behaviours. Key informant data, gathered through interviews with lawyers, labour commissioners, trade unionists, and labour activists identified a range of factors that inform whether or not targets of workplace bullying pursue interventions from outside the organization. Barriers to seeking external intervention include professional self-identity, career interests, and a dysfunctional judicial system.

The scholarship on workplace bullying notes similar patterns and practices among bullying, sexual harassment, and violence within workplaces—in terms, for instance, of frequency, severity, and impact on well-being (Table 6.2). In fact, sexual harassment in the workplace has been defined as bullying or coercion of a sexual nature, or the unwelcome or inappropriate promise of reward in exchange for sexual favours (Lin, Babbit, and Brown 2014; Paludi and Barickman 1991). Consistent with these definitions of gender-based violence, the AFWA introduced the term 'gendered bullying' as a subset of workplace bullying that encompasses forms of workplace bullying that are directed against a woman because she is a woman and that affect women disproportionately (2019).

Providing a framework for understanding the relationship between the various forms of GBVH in garment production lines, in 2019, the AFWA developed the concept of a GBVH escalation ladder, based upon distinguishing gendered bullying, more aggressive forms of behavioural GBVH, and employment-practice-based GBVH. *Gendered bullying* includes hostile behaviours that are devoid of sexual interest that function to insult and reject women, including the more mild forms of gendered industrial discipline practices. Gendered bullying practices routinely escalate to more aggressive forms of GBVH—or *behavioural GBVH* practices, including physical and sexual violence and verbal abuse. Behavioural GBVH practices, most commonly perpetrated by male workers in hierarchical positions, including supervisors, line managers, and mechanics, can, in turn, escalate into employment-practice-based GBVH that is rooted in control over job placement and security. Employment-practice-based GBVH manifests as retaliation when women workers refuse sexual advances or challenge factory-level practices.

Table 6.2 Shared Features of Workplace Bullying and Gender-Based Violence on Garment Production Lines

	Workplace bullying	Gender-based violence on production lines
Repeated acts	x	x
Perpetrated by one or more individuals	x	x
Extra-contractual	x	x
Rooted in unequal power relations	x	x
Coercive intentions	x	x
Perpetuated by job insecurity and pressure to perform among target groups	x	x
Fear of retaliation for reporting works through implicit or explicit threats	x	x
Creates a hostile working environment	x	x
Adverse impact on organizations (lower morale, lack of trust, reduced productivity, increased turnover)	x	x

Sources: Rayner and Cooper (1997); Quine (1999); Brake (2005); Hodson, Roscigno, and Lopez (2006); McKay and Fratzl (2011); McCormack et al. (2018); AFWA et al. (2018a–c).

The Nexus between Sexual Violence and Employment-Practice-Based GBVH

Patterns of sexual violence and harassment reported by women garment workers reflect power asymmetries between men and women in hierarchical workplaces segmented along gender lines. Women garment workers report GBVH from men in positions of authority within the factory as well as co-workers. While perpetrators traverse hierarchical and non-hierarchical employment relationships with women workers, reports of sexual violence most commonly featured employment relationships where women held subordinate roles in relation to male supervisors, line managers, and mechanics tasked with fixing their machines. In factories where a majority of male supervisors and line managers oversee an overwhelmingly female workforce, male monopoly over authority can contribute to a culture of impunity around sexual and other forms of violence and harassment. Put another way, behavioural GBVH practices are authorized by control over employment by perpetrators of violence and the looming threat of employment-practice-based GBVH.

Women workers employed in a supplier factory in Gurugram described being moved from line to line depending upon the desires of male supervisors. A woman explained:

> If the supervisor likes a girl and has some influence over the floor incharge, then he will arrange to shift that girl under his supervision. If she refuses she will be fired—they will blame *her* for being unable to achieve targets.

In this example, the authority of the male supervisor is set up in advance of perpetrating GBVH, so that any sexual behaviour is advanced from a position of authority. Refusal by a woman worker will likely lead to termination of employment. In Gurugram, supervisors, floor incharge, and line managers within a factory are often relatives. This interconnected web of male supervision further undermines avenues for relief for women who are targets of sexual advances.

Reports of sexual advances by men in positions of authority are not limited to India. Bangladeshi women reported that it is common for supervisors and managers to pursue sexual relationships with women workers by offering benefits including salary increases, promotions, and better positions. Women rejecting these offers face retaliation, including being fired. These practices are widely acknowledged and function as implicit norms. A woman from Tiruppur, India—the other garment cluster where we examined wage data in Chapter 4—explained:

> If a woman worker does not meet the sexual desires of the supervisor, she may get more overtime hours. She may not be allowed to take her break. The supervisor will start to find fault with everything she does. She won't be able to take leave. She can even be fired.

Sri Lankan trade union leaders reported that women employed through 'manpower'—or temporary work agencies—face routine sexual advances from supervisors who make hiring within the factory contingent upon receiving their overtures. Women reported retaliation from supervisors if they resist advances:

> A woman who does not meet the sexual desires of the supervisor may get more overtime hours, be denied legally mandated breaks or leave, or even fired.

Control over working hours by male supervisors provides opportunities for sexual violence and harassment to extend beyond legal working hours and the factory floor. In Tiruppur, women workers reported supervisors abusing control over working hours to make sexual advances after long night shifts. One woman explained:

> It is a trap. If a supervisor is interested in a woman, he can make her work the half-night shift which gets over at midnight. Then, he may offer to drop her home on his bike. She may not have another option to reach home at night. In this situation, it is easy for the supervisor to exploit the woman targeted.

Women workers in this position face a double bind: either submit to sexual advances from supervisors or risk harassment, robbery, or worse during solo late-night commutes.

The link between sexual predation and management-supervision practices was also revealed in a large sample study of factories in Cambodia. Of the 1,588 women workers surveyed, 23 per cent said that supervisors or managers had offered them shopfloor benefits in return for sexual favours or a sexual relationship (Better Work 2019).

Besides managers and supervisors, women are also at risk from mechanics on whom they depend to keep their sewing machines in order. A Sri Lankan woman recounted:

> A machine mechanic asked me to spend the night with him. I refused. When my machine stopped working, I asked him to repair it. He refused. Then he asked me to spend the night with him. He said if I agreed, he would fix my machine.

While women workers are not directly subordinate to machine mechanics, they are functionally subordinate to these male workers because their ability to meet production targets depends upon machine maintenance. A woman employed in a factory in Cakung, North Jakarta, described the unequal relationships of power between women machine operators and the mechanics they rely upon to reach their targets:

> Male mechanics require a 'tribute' payment in order to ensure that they immediately fix your broken sewing machine. If they are late in fixing the machine, I won't make the production target.

A woman working in a supplier factory in the Vavuniya District, North Province, Sri Lanka, described how the dependence on mechanics can expose women workers to sexual harassment:

> When girls scold machine operators for touching them or grabbing them, they take revenge. Sometimes they give them machines that do not function properly. Then, they do not come and repair it for a long time. After that, supervisors scold us for not meeting the target.

Like the escalation in industrial discipline practices described earlier, unchecked sexual harassment can escalate into more severe cases of violence. Among cases of sexual violence, none of the incidents reported by women respondents took place in the physical factory, they all involved coercion from senior management, either tying sexual engagement to employment or threatening to retaliate if cases were reported.

Women employed in factories in rural areas are further exposed to violence based on their physical isolation. On 1 January 2021, Jeyasre Kathiravel, a 21-year-old Dalit woman garment worker and college student, went missing in Kaithian Kottai, Tamil Nadu. On 5 January, her body was found—she had been raped and murdered, her body discarded in a nearby stream. Exemplifying the GBVH escalation ladder, prior to her death, Jeyasre had reported to friends and co-workers that her supervisor—who confessed to her rape and murder in police custody—had been sexually harassing her within the factory for months. Thivya Rakini, the state president of the Tamil Nadu Textile and Common Labour Union (TTCU)—the union representing women at the factory where Jeyasre worked—explained the context in which the violence Jeyasre faced went unaddressed:

> Her family and co-workers have told us that Jeyasre was being harassed at work but nothing was done. Many workers we have spoken to say they are facing the same problems but either don't know how to report grievances against their supervisors or say they are afraid that if they speak out, they will face retaliation. (Quoted in Kelly 2021)

Fear of retaliation for seeking access to justice in cases of sexual violence are far from unfounded. Following Jeyasre's murder, led by officials of the supplier factory, 50 men invaded Jeyasre's family home to coerce her mother into signing documents releasing the company from responsibility in Jeyasre's sexual assault and murder. Facing late-night intimidation in the dark with no electricity, Ms Kathiravel signed the documents under duress. Ms Kathiravel, accompanied at the time by 10 women union leaders, also fainted due to the aggressive action and was rushed to hospital.

Consistent with the wishes of her family, Jeyasre's assault and murder was widely covered in the national and international media due to advocacy by TTCU, AFWA, and GLJ-ILRF. Accordingly, the details of this case are shared in this chapter. However, cases of sexual violence reported by women garment workers during the 2018 AFWA study are not described in detail due to concerns by women workers and trade unions that publicly reporting these cases of sexual violence could elicit stigma and workplace retaliation against the women who shared their experiences.

Cases where women refused sexual advances and faced termination were more openly shared. For instance, in January 2018, Sulatana, a skilled garment worker with 10 years of experience, was hired as a production-line manager by a supplier located in Dhaka, Bangladesh. Her position as a woman production-line manager is highly unusual since the majority of women workers in Bangladesh are employed in subordinate roles as machine operators, helpers, and checkers. In the weeks that followed, the general manager of the factory made frequent advances. Sulatana recounted:

> He flirted with me, he would touch me on the shoulder or touch me on the head. I tried to ignore him. I thought if I showed no interest, he would stop. It didn't work. On 11 April, three days before the Bengali New Year, the general manager called me to his office and asked me to go out with him on the holiday. I gently refused. The next day, the production manager approached me and asked, 'What is wrong with you? Why don't you spend some time with the boss?' I refused again and explained that I was spending the holiday with my five-year-old son.

On 19 April, Sulatana went to the Ashulia police station to file a complaint. The police refused to receive the complaint because Sulatana had no authentic proof. A few days later, on 22 April, the general manager called her to his office and asked her to resign immediately. When Sulatana approached Human Resources, she was informed that the general manager's decision was final. Neither factory Human Resources nor the police provided viable pathways to accountability. At the time of the interview, nearly three weeks later, Sulatana was still searching for a new job.

These findings reinforce conclusions by Drusilla Brown in her 2016 assessment of the International Labour Organization (ILO) Better Work Programme: the most likely perpetrator of sexual harassment is the line supervisor, and the most likely victim is a woman worker (Brown 2016). Articulating the nexus between sexual harassment, violence, and hierarchical employment relationships that facilitate employment-practice-based GBVH, she explains:

> In the workplace, such conduct may also be seen by others as a condition of their employment or as a requirement for promotion.

Stigma, Victim-Blaming, Retaliation, and Impunity for Violence

Significant barriers to ending GBVH on garment production lines, as in other workplace contexts, have been well established. They include cultures of impunity, challenges in reporting, ineffective systems and procedures, and retaliation—including further targeting, loss of employment, social ostracization, and personal and professional reputational harm (UN Women-ILO 2019; Feldblum and Lipnic (EEOC) 2016).

Further undermining accountability, women report reluctance to report sexual harassment, advances, and violence due to social stigma that may manifest as either restriction on their mobility or victim-blaming. A woman worker described the social consequences that prevented her from reporting sexual advances at work and at home:

> I did not report at work because it is the woman who is blamed. No one sees the man as at fault. I thought, if my husband comes to know about this, he will not let me work anymore. So, I decided to resign quietly without telling anyone anything.

In this instance, social stigma, rooted in family and community patriarchal norms, threatened yet another level of consequences for unwanted sexual advances faced at work: barriers to future employment outside the household. The fear of reporting due to stigma and victim-blaming further constrains access to justice in cases of sexual harm.

For those who decide to seek relief through legal channels, social authority wielded by male supervisors and co-workers may be reinforced through gaps in legal protections and gendered policing practices. Notably, women employed in the garment production hub of Phnom Penh, Cambodia, have no avenue for redress under Cambodian Labour Law for sexual harassment from male colleagues since sexual harassment from male colleagues is not included under Article 172 of the Cambodian Labour Law which governs workplace sexual harassment perpetrated by supervisors. The exclusion of sexual harassment from male colleagues under the Labour Law, combined with a restrictive definition of sexual harassment in the Cambodian Criminal Code, strips female workers from protection against sexual harassment perpetrated by male colleagues.

Even where sexual harassment is an actionable offence, women report barriers to accountability, beginning at the police station. When a woman sewing machine operator in Bangladesh reported repeated sexual overtures from her manager to the police, the police refused to file her case. When she returned to work the next day, she was fired from her job. She learned that the police informed the accused manager that she had visited the police station to report sexual harassment.

Women workers from Bangladesh, Cambodia, India, Indonesia, and Sri Lanka, all described fearing retaliation if they complained about any violations of rights at work, including but not limited to GBVH. A woman worker in Gurugram, Haryana, India, explained:

> Whoever speaks against any injustice is fired. Once I, along with others, went to the manager because our wage was not being paid properly. They did not remove us all together, but within ten days, they used some reason or another to remove each and every one of us.

Routine and ongoing threats of employment termination discourage women workers from seeking relief. For instance, a woman in Phnom Penh explained not reporting the Chinese team leader who threw heavy bundles of clothes at her. Fearing retaliation for reporting the violence, she kept quiet.

Barriers to Freedom of Association

Barriers to freedom of association and collective bargaining on garment supply chains further foreclose important pathways for redress by women workers. Put another way, preventing workers from responding collectively to violence furthers cultures of impunity.

Constant threats of termination create a significant barrier to organizing a union. Workers and union organizers in Indonesia explained that high turnover undermines unionization, worker solidarity, and collective action. Within garment production units, very few workers hold continuous employment for more than a year. By hiring workers on short-term contracts, the contractor and the factory can fire workers in retaliation for engaging in union activities.

The structure of work in garment supplier factories further undermines freedom of association. Long working hours deny workers the opportunity to engage with one another. In Manesar, Gurugram, India, workers are prevented from speaking with one another during breaks in the workday. Workers are forbidden to leave factory premises—during their tea and lunch break, they are required to eat at the canteen inside the unit. Prohibitions on leaving the factory for breaks during working hours, combined with extended working hours—at times up to 17 hours a day—functionally eclipses the potential for workers to exercise their fundamental rights to freedom of association and collective bargaining.

Intersectionality: Gender and Caste

While this chapter has focused on the intersection or conjugation of class with gender in the garment workforce, gender is not the only significant collective identity of women (Folbre 2020). Here, we want to draw attention to the intersectional identities of women who are also from marginalized castes or religious communities. In the case of Tiruppur, a large proportion of women workers are from the Dalit (former untouchable) castes, while supervisors are from non-Dalit castes. This leads to particular forms of casteist oppression on the shopfloor.

Factory work does provide an urban anonymity and as Grace Carswell and Geert de Neve have found (2014), Dalit workers prefer factory to village work for just this reason. But caste-based hierarchy remains there, perhaps below the surface, but nevertheless always present. As Carswell and de Neeve point out, some Dalit workers are careful to hide their Dalit identity. When it gets known, those who formerly drank tea with them might stop doing that. Dalit workers are also concentrated in the most poorly paid and hazardous jobs in the garment industry, with many factories hiring them only for janitorial work in the factory like cleaning toilets and removing cotton waste from the shop floor (AFWA 2021).

Dalit women workers have been subject to specific forms of abuse and oppression, different from economic exploitation. When salaries are paid in cash, the money would not be given in their hands, but thrown on the table. If fault is found with work, the Dalit women would be abused in caste terms, saying that you Dalits are no good as workers. Non-Dalit women do not face similar treatment. Dalit women are also thought to be weaker and less socially well connected and, thus, more likely to be subject to sexual harassment.

In 2021, AFWA documented accentuation of systemic discrimination against Dalit garment workers during the COVID-19 lockdown period in India. Dalit garment workers faced the highest fall in wages when compared to every other social category. The wages of garment workers categorized as general category workers fell by 57 per cent and wages for other backward castes dipped by 55 per cent. By contrast, Dalit workers' wages fell by 79 per cent (AFWA 2021).

These are just a few examples of the manner in which caste intersects with gender and class. This is a topic that requires full analysis by itself, with careful ethnographic material.

Transforming Cultures of Violence on Garment Production Lines

GBVH on garment production lines has negative impacts on the physical, reproductive, and mental health of women workers (AFWA et al. 2018a–c; UN-ILO 2019) and also functions to reinforce gendered power dynamics more broadly. The ILO has highlighted GBVH as 'the most prevalent human rights violation that both reflects and reinforces inequalities between women and men' and identified the workplace as a 'relevant context in which this matter can be discussed with a view to prevention' (Cruz and Klinger 2011).

The UN Guiding Principles on Business and Human Rights (UNGPBHR) calls for business enterprises to carry out human rights due diligence to identify, prevent, mitigate, and account for how they address their adverse human rights impacts (Article 17). This responsibility includes internationally recognized human rights, including the right to be free from GBVH which has evolved as a principle of customary international law under the Convention on the Elimination of All Forms of Discrimination Against Women (CEDAW), and has been applied to the world of work under ILO Violence and Harassment Convention, 2019 (No. 190) (C190) and Recommendation 206.

As clearly structured and bounded arenas within the broader context of social discrimination, industrial workplace contexts provide opportunities for intervention with the potential to cause ripple effects that extend far beyond the workplace. It is both important and possible to intervene constructively to solve GBVH at the workplace, at the level of industrial relationships between working people. However, according to the Committee of Experts convened by the ILO in October 2016 in preparation for framing C190 on Violence and Harassment in the World of Work, gender-based violence is a social rather than an individual problem, requiring comprehensive responses that extend beyond specific events, individual perpetrators, and victims or survivors (ILO 2019: No. 35, para. 9).

Ending GBVH in garment supplier factories that manifest at the intersection of patriarchal norms and supply chain employment practices calls for at least three types of interventions: to hold apparel brands and retailers at the top of the supply chain jointly responsible for brand purchasing practices that create known risk factors for violence, to challenge the concentration of women workers in subordinate roles, and to address gendered cultures of impunity for workplace violence.

At the level of brand accountability, gendered industrial discipline practices can be alleviated through enforceable prohibitions against unrealistic production targets that accelerate production speed, extend working hours, and create high-stress work environments. Enforceable commitments to supplying only from factories that pay living wages, respect working hours, and protect workers from environmental and occupational health and safety hazards can address body mining and other physically extractive labour practices. Brand and buyer commitments to sourcing from suppliers that provide employment security, skills training opportunities, and pathways to advancement into line manager and supervisor roles for women can begin to challenge the concentration of women in subordinate roles. Enforceable commitments to take action against workplace retaliation and to uphold fundamental rights to freedom of association and collective bargaining have the potential to make strong inroads into addressing cultures of impunity for workplace violence.

For enforceable brand agreements to intervene in patriarchal subordination and stigma that fuel GBVH in supplier factories, however, they must also take conscious measures to disrupt gendered power relationships in the workplace and beyond. Accordingly, the remainder of this chapter presents a strategy developed by the AFWA to address cultures of violence in garment supply chains. Building upon the 2018 research findings identifying spectrums of violence on garment supply chains that form the core of this chapter, and more than a decade of work to advance the rights of women workers in production lines, in 2019, the AFWA advanced the *Safe Circle Approach* to address GBVH by catalyzing deep engagement in organizational change processes to prevent workplace violence (AFWA 2019). This focus on prevention is better equipped to safeguard the rights of women workers since securing retroactive relief in cases of GBVH is fraught by unequal power relations between women workers and perpetrators of GBVH (UN Women–ILO 2019); and retroactive relief requires women workers to not only bear the harms associated with GBVH but also the harms that attend redressal processes.

The AFWA *Safe Circles Approach* builds from an understanding of the GBVH escalation ladder described in the preceding sections. The escalation ladder—from gendered bullying to more severe forms of behavioural GBVH to employment-practice-based GBVH—not only provides significant insight into processes that catalyze patterns of workplace violence but also provides valuable locational information to inform targeted interventions to eliminate GBVH. Experience among AFWA member unions has shown that the first forms of GBVH on the GBVH escalation ladder that workers confront take place on the production line between supervisors and workers. Accordingly, the AFWA approach to preventing GBVH seeks to address behavioural GBVH in the production line prior to escalation. This requires catalyzing behavioural change among supervisors, line managers, and mechanics.

The *Safe Circle Approach* involves potential 'victims', 'bystanders', and 'perpetrators' in face-to-face, regular, small group engagement processes designed to address behavioural violence in production lines in garment factories. Consistent with United Nations (UN) Women and ILO recommendations (UN Women–ILO 2019), this approach seeks to develop and sustain a positive organizational culture on garment production lines, co-produced by workers and management who seek to advance the shared goal of preventing GBVH.

The AFWA *Safe Circle Approach* is guided by the following core principles:

1. Support proactive engagement in preventing GBVH among front-line (production line) workers who are targets of violence.
2. Empower women workers to have a constructive voice at work.
3. Facilitate ongoing interaction and consensus building among workers and supervisors who work together at the front-lines (production lines). Workers and supervisors should be selected from each production line to ensure that positive outcomes are distributed across production floors.
4. Design and achieve measurable and observable goals and outcomes aimed at addressing GBVH in production lines.
5. Increase communication or behavioural competence among supervisors and others in hierarchical positions of authority. (AFWA 2019)

Within this transformational change framework, GBVH lists created at the production line and factory level provide a measurable index of behaviours to eliminate GBVH and a mechanism of measuring progressive change. Local development of GBVH lists is important to understand and make visible cultural differences that belie GBVH in particular countries and contexts. Although there are commonalities among garment-producing countries in Asia, in this way, the *Safe Circles Approach* accommodates local differences in language, dress code, and behavioural norms.

This approach combines new perspectives in responding to GBVH in garment factories, with a well-established circle approach as implemented through quality circles (QCs) from other industrial contexts. Workplace safety has already been an important and successful focus for QCs (Saheldin and Zain 2007), suggesting that these strategies can be well adapted in addressing workplace safety issues associated with GBVH. Not only are such initiatives required to safeguard women workers but there is also preliminary evidence that initiatives to address workplace violence stand to benefit brands and suppliers by increasing individual efficiency and production quantity among workers, and ultimately firm productivity and revenue (Rourke 2014; Morris and Pillinger 2016; Lin, Babbitt, and Brown 2014; Brown 2016).

HOUSEHOLD

7
Rural Subsidies

Introduction

Wages below living wages are a subsidy to capital, reducing wage costs. Since in such global value chains (GVCs) the surplus profits are captured by the brands, while suppliers basically get competitive profits, it is the brands that benefit from wages below the cost of production of labour power. But what is the form of this subsidy in social reproduction? Who bears the cost of this subsidy in the reproduction of labour power? The subsidy takes two forms—one is by the mining of women workers' bodies and the policy of 'overuse and discard' of, particularly, women workers in garment factories when they age out of employment; and the other is by externalizing part of the cost of reproducing labour power from the factory and displacing it onto the rural economy of the households of migrant workers. The extractive labour subsidy achieved by mining of workers' bodies was dealt with in Chapters 5 and 6. The rural subsidy in the reproduction of labour power is dealt with in this chapter.

There is yet another rural labour subsidy involved, which is in the production of cotton. This is through, first, low prices of cotton, which do not cover its cost of production, because farmer incomes are insufficient to meet the basic justice requirements of supporting elementary capabilities. The second is wage labour, including child labour, in cotton production that again violates basic justice requirements. This chapter begins with the rural connection of garment workers and then goes on to labour subsidies in cotton production.

Before proceeding to look at other forms of labour subsidies, we note an analytical issue in GVC analysis. GVC analysis is embedded (Gereffi 2019) in, meaning connected with, local economic and social processes. However, most GVC analysis tends to remain within the confines of the core factory—interrogating the relation of buyers and suppliers and of workers in supplier firms with their employers. At best, labour market conditions within which GVC labour takes place are included as a subject of analysis. This chapter shows that there is a need to look beyond the GVC itself to understand its functioning and dynamics. Looking at how the rural economy of left-behind households is articulated within the structure of GVC garment manufacturing, producing wages below the living wage, is an example of an analysis that embeds GVCs in the economy as a whole, including migration sending areas even in the case of segments that are located in the urban economy.

In the research project that led to this book, we also began with a look exclusively into labour and other conditions within the garment manufacturing GVC segment, at best, extending this to compare other similar GVCs, such as for shoes and other leather products. This was reflected in the questionnaires we used for surveying wage and working conditions. There were no questions on the rural connections. It was only toward the end of this project that we realized the importance of the rural connection and began to investigate this aspect of GVC relations. This shows up in the fact that data collection on the rural connections of garment workers was mainly through focus group discussions (FGDs) and not through a questionnaire survey, as was used in investigating wages and working conditions in garment manufacturing factories.

We supplement our FGDs with migrant garment workers with data from a 2018 study conducted by Society for Labour and Development (SLD) on access to rights and entitlements for migrant workers in India, including surveys with 981 migrant and non-migrant workers representing a diverse population of internal migrant workers from target source and destination areas, including migrant men and women from Dalit, tribal, Muslim, and other backward classes (OBC) communities. It includes workers included in garment production, other production, domestic, and agricultural work.

The collapse of the garment export industry in India and elsewhere during the 2020 COVID-19 pandemic further underscored the critical role of the village economy as the safety net for migrant workers on garment production lines. We highlight the importance of rural areas in providing safe harbour for migrant workers through data collected by Asia Floor Wage Alliance (AFWA) between 2020 and 2021. Together with 23 partner unions across Asia, the AFWA study surveyed 2,185 garment workers, employed across 189 factories in Sri Lanka, Pakistan, Indonesia, India, Cambodia, and Bangladesh. This regional data complements our more in-depth discussion of the impact of COVID-19 on migrant garment workers in India that is developed from a June 2020 rapid response survey of 100 workers from the National Capital Region (NCR) and Tiruppur. It both extends the timeline of analysis and situates these early findings in India in relationship to the impact on garment workers in production clusters regionally. Besides this survey, field investigators also carried out telephone discussions with workers who had returned to their home villages.

Reproduction of Labour Power as an Employer Strategy

In the migration literature, there is a tendency to look upon the dual or multi-location household as a strategy to spread risks and be more robust and resilient (Dick and Schmidt-Kallert 2011: 28), or even as part of a life period strategy of Chinese migrants: 'An intermediate period in their life between leaving middle school and settling down to marry and have children' (IOM 2008: 176 in Dick and Schmidt-Kallert 2011). Circular migration being a part of livelihood strategies, whether in a specific period of life or an overall household strategy to spread risks, is well accepted as a type of motivation. Households, however, work within existing constraints. In our case, these constraints include low wages below the cost of producing labour power in the garment GVC or other labour-intensive and low-knowledge manufacturing segments. In this low-wage condition, there is no alternative for aspiring proletarians but to become semi-proletarians and adopt a multi-locational household strategy.

More important, however, for our analysis is the way this rural–urban household connection plays out in terms of allowing employers to pay a wage below the cost of the reproduction of labour power, which then becomes a subsidy. Two processes work to create this subsidy: first, the separation of production in the factory system from the reproduction of labour power in the household and, second, the geographical separation of the two processes.

As the social reproduction theory points out, in capitalism there is a separation of the factory-based process of production and the household-based reproduction of labour power. The reproduction of labour power does involve more than the household as some portion of various services, such as education and health, are publicly provided. In supplier economies, such as India, not much of the educational and health services are provided free by the state. For instance, out-of-pocket expenses account for more than 80 per cent of health expenses in India. Consequently, the household share of basic expenses is quite high. Our analysis focuses here on the role of the household in the reproduction of labour power.

In the separation of production from social reproduction, there are two distinct forms of production relations. The first is the production of wage labour in the industrial system. The second is the production of unwaged labour in the household. In a condition where there is a living wage, one may say that household labour is paid for by the factory owner, but paid through the medium of the worker who is the direct employee of the factory. In fact, Henry Ford, one of the industrialists who understood the importance of the living wage for the sustainability of the economic system, including for the macroeconomic factor of providing effective demand, thought that even workers' wives were subject to his surveillance: 'Ford expected men to keep themselves in good moral standing, their children in school and their wives at home' (Bhattacharya 2017: 147). His company inspectors went to check on the proper conduct of household work by wives. Thus, the unwaged labour of the workers' wives was also controlled and subsumed under the wage labour of male factory workers. This is a form of articulation of waged and unwaged labour subsumed under the patriarchal capitalist factory system.

Even where there was no geographical separation between production and social reproduction, in the sense that both were within the same locality, there could have been a disjunction between actual wages and living wages. It was only with the 1930s New Deal that living wages were accepted as a norm in the United States (US). When, however, there was a geographical separation between production and social reproduction, it was much easier to pay wages below the cost of production of wage labour. If wages were enough to cover the immediate cost of reproduction of the worker's own labour power—even if it was not enough to cover the rest of his family, including his wife and children—and with some excess that could be sent back as remittances, then it could be sufficient to attract rural surplus labour to industrial employment.

When there is a separation of the locations of production and social reproduction, there are flows between household members in the two areas. Workers send back remittances, which go toward the reproduction of the household. On the other hand, they also receive food and care when they go back during lay offs, illness, and retirement. In addition, the social reproduction of the worker's household, including children, their education, and the like, are covered, at least partly, out of the income earned at the source location. These are a part of care labour in social reproduction, which have also been called 'social remittances' by Deshingkar and Farrington (2009).

The rural economy that provides for some of the costs of reproduction is a different economic system from urban industrial GVC segments. It is largely an economy of smallholder peasant farming, along with wage labour in small-scale farm and non-farm enterprises. The rural economy may not be subject to the same tensions as the urban economy of GVC clusters, real estate, and so on. Accordingly, winds of international trade buffeting GVC clusters and the more internationally connected urban economy may not equally affect the rural agricultural rural economy and related non-farm enterprises. This rural economy has been used as a safety net to absorb return migrants in many developing countries.

The role of the rural smallholder economy, run mainly by women, as a safety net was prominently visible in the aftermath of the Asian financial crisis of 1997–1998. Men who lost their jobs in urban construction in Thailand and Indonesia went back to their rural households. In the absence of a state-provided safety net, the rural economy provided the safety net (Nathan and Kelkar 1999). During the Great Recession of 2008, when the world demand for diamonds fell, diamond cutters in the Indian state of Gujarat (which cuts more than 90 per cent of the world's diamonds by weight) went back to their rural households. At that time in India, however, there was a rural safety net, the rural employment guarantee scheme, which provided some daily wage labour (Nathan and Kelkar 2012).

This reverse flow in the reproduction of labour power, whether on a regular basis or as a safety net, was analysed in terms of the articulation of rural and urban economies, or non-capitalist and capitalist economies. In the standard analysis (for example, by Arthur Lewis) of economic development, the role of the rural economy was to provide an unlimited supply of labour that could be absorbed in the urban economy. But the articulation analysis shows another essential role of the rural non-capitalist economy: providing a part of the cost of reproduction of labour power.

The international economy articulation, however, does not have to be only through the relations between GVC suppliers and buyers. It can also be, as was pointed out by Michael Burawoy (2010), between Mexican labour working in US agriculture. In this case, a part of the cost of reproduction of labour, even in the limited period for which that labour is employed in US agriculture, is borne by the the source economy.

Rural Connections in Garment Manufacturing in India

In this book, the term subsidy has been defined as the purchase of a commodity below its cost of production, whether the commodity is labour power or environmental services. Identifying a subsidy, however, is just the beginning of the analysis. The important part is then to identify the persons or actors who are providing the subsidy by unpaid or low-paid contribution to a part of the cost and the process through which this happens.

Discussions with groups of workers in Gurugram and Tiruppur reveal that single male migrant workers regularly go back to their villages of origin for about one-fifth to one-fourth of the year. Workers who migrate with their families do not do that, but single male workers do regularly go back. Where couples are together in the factory area, they both work for wages, whether in the better-paid factories or the poorer-paid workshops and in homework. Men who migrate alone may be married but those who are contract workers, and even lower-rung permanent workers, cannot afford to have their families stay with them. A study of a major source area of migrants, Bihar, reveals that the wives and children stay behind: 'Family members rarely join the migrants at the destination' (IHD 2019: 6). This has led to the feminization of agricultural work (IHD 2019). With families left behind, children are taken care of in the rural household economy.

While single migrant workers are largely men, there are also single women migrant workers. This is so in Tiruppur, where there are single women from the states of north-east India, and also from Odisha in eastern India. In a new garment production centre in Ranchi, the capital of the state of Jharkhand which is a major source area of migrant workers in the country, most of the workers are women. They are from neighbouring villages and stay in various types of dormitories. These single women also leave their families, including children, behind in their villages of origin. In this case, the labour of left-behind men supplements factory wages. In Ranchi, the state government provides a subsidy of INR 5,000 (about USD 66) per month per worker employed. The workers, however, continue to be paid at the prevailing minimum wage and do not get any part of the subsidy provided by the state.

Single male migrant workers go to their villages when they are laid off from factory work. This is quite regular in Gurugram, where there is a concentration of cotton fabric garment production, and factories operate with low worker strength for about three months of the year. Even in Tiruppur, workers go back for about two months in a year. The sustenance of workers during the lay off period is then provided within the rural economy. This is corroborated by the IHD study (2019) of migrant workers in Bihar, which confirmed that, for the most part, migrants were back in their rural homes for at least two months in a year.

When garment workers go back to their villages, the stay at home enables them to recuperate their physical strength for the long and strenuous hours demanded in garment factory work. On their return to urban residences, workers usually bring some grain and pulses with them, since the prices of these food supplies in the rural areas are lower than those in the cities. These grains also add to the subsidy that the rural economy provides to GVC wages.

Managers in the garment industry often say that workers go back for festivals and family occasions. They never tell you that lay offs are the reason for workers going back. In FGDs of groups of about 25 workers each, they all pointed out that they almost always go back when they are laid off. Almost none of these workers were landowners and thus had no compulsions to go back for farming operations. For the few small landowners, their wives or other relatives managed farm operations.

The second situation in which workers go back to their villages is when they fall sick with more than just a cold or a cough. For minor ailments, they undertake treatment in their places of work, sometimes through insurance-provided medical care. But since this medical coverage is not very much, they are usually forced to rely on private medical care—particularly in cases of more serious ailments. On top of this, at such times, they would not be able to work and thus would not earn any wages, while having to bear their own food costs. Nor would they have any caregiver with them. Accordingly, in this situation, they usually go back to their villages, where they can be fed and taken care of.

The 2020 COVID-19 pandemic exposed the role of the village economy as the safety net for garment workers when the garment industry collapsed. Investigations by researchers in Gurugram, Bengaluru, and Tiruppur showed that initially there had been a movement of laid-off single male workers who came from nearby villages returning home. Later, as the government arranged transport, many more single contract workers left. Only those workers for whom factory owners had given wages or provided hostel facilities stayed behind in the clusters. In China and Indonesia, there was organized transport of migrant workers to their villages (AFWA 2021). In Bangladesh, too, there was a movement of garment workers, mainly women in this case, who went back to their villages to sit out the period of closure. From being a safety net in annual slowdowns, the role of the villages changed to become a generalized safety net for migrant workers who had no social security system at their places of work. Further, this safety net role must be seen in the context of brands cancelling orders and abandoning suppliers (SLD 2020, for India; Anner 2020, for Bangladesh).

The third situation in which garment workers go back to their villages is when they retire or are removed from factory work. This is usually the case with low-paid contract and casual workers. Only those who earn more, such as permanent workers, may stay on in urban locations after retiring from factory work. While we have seen this in the garment clusters of Tiruppur and Gurugram, the source area study of migrant workers showed that most low-paid migrant workers returned to their villages on retirement, since '[r]emuneration is often below the minimum statutory wage and is inadequate for family migration or long-term settlement' (IHD 2019: 5). In terms of the type of migration, this constitutes what Srivastava terms long-term circular migration (2020).

Studies at both migration destination and origin areas (IHD 2019; SLD 2018, 2020) showed that proof of local residence is virtually impossible to establish in destination areas for migrant workers. In 2018, SLD conducted a study on access to rights and entitlements for migrant workers in India, including surveys with 981 migrant and non-migrant workers from a range of sectors in migration sending areas in Bihar (Katihar and Purnea districts), Jharkhand (Latehar and Palamu districts), and Uttar Pradesh (Kanpur and Kannauj districts); and destination areas in Delhi (South West district, Kapashera) and Gurugram, Haryana (Dundahera, Manesar, Sikanderpur towns). Our research found that due to the inability to secure residence proof in informal settlements in destination areas, only 6 per cent of migrants, compared with 96 per cent of non-migrant workers surveyed in the Delhi NCR held voter identification cards permitting them to vote in the NCR. No migrant workers held ration cards or accessed rations in the NCR, compared to 79 per cent of non-migrants who held ration cards and 57 per cent that reported consistent access to rations in the NCR.

Recently, the Central Government has taken steps to make a ration card valid in any part of the country. But since many migrant workers leave part of their household behind in the villages of origin, this will not solve the problem of being able to access subsidized food grain in both destination and source locations. Our 2018 study of internal migrants found that 51 per cent of migrants in the NCR reported holding ration cards in home states. While some migrants reported maintaining ration cards in home states in order to maintain access to grain subsidies for their families, others reported being afraid to enroll in the NCR based upon concern that they may both lose rations in their home states and fail to successfully enroll in the NCR. In general, migrant workers reported significantly higher rates of access to rations in Bihar (93 per cent), Jharkhand (89 per cent), and Uttar Pradesh (33 per cent). Barriers to accessing residence proof in destination areas also makes it difficult for their children to access the low-cost government schools in the garment clusters.

These issues are not the same as the legal difficulty of urban resettlement in the case of China's *hukou* system (discussed later), but it does compound the impact of low wages to make migrant workers' urban resettlement even more difficult, particularly for low-paid workers, by making it virtually impossible for them to settle in the urban clusters. The difficulty low-wage workers face in making a transition to permanent urban residence has also been well documented in relationship to the return migration of former textile workers from Mumbai to their villages of origin in the coastal belt of Maharashtra (Mhaskar 2019). The retirement costs of low-wage workers are not borne by the industrial clusters. This is true in not only the new ones, such as Tiruppur, but also older ones, such as Mumbai.

Negative health consequences are part of the reverse subsidy extracted from the rural economy of left-behind women. There is some evidence to show that left-behind wives of low-wage workers, such as garment workers, face health deterioration. The study by Lei Lei and Sonalde Desai (2021), using data from the India Human Development Survey (IHDS) of 2004–2005 and 2011–2012, shows a negative health impact due to low remittances along with additional labour responsibilities, as in care of animals and handling bank accounts. At the same time, left-behind wives in nuclear families also reported increased autonomy, as in managing household expenditures, local travel, and so on.

Rural Connections in Other Supplier Countries

This situation is not unique to India. In Wolpe's initial study of the South African mines (1980), it was mainly the African workers' links to the homelands that were identified as the subsidy provided by the economy of rural households. In China, the well-known *hukou* system has been a legal barrier to migrant workers settling down in the urban areas where factories are located. Studies of the dormitory system in China (Ngai 2005) and of migrants in general, showed, as would be expected, that migrants went back to their home towns on retirement from factory work. Since husband and wife often worked as migrants, left-behind children were taken care of by grandparents, who also had the responsibility of cultivating the fields (Schmidt-Kallert and Franke 2010: 272). Only a few of the second-generation migrants earned enough to manage higher urban living costs, including keeping children with them. The phenomenon of children left behind is said to be quite common in Africa (Schmidt-Kallert and Franke 2010: 279). In China, it was estimated that just 19 million children were staying with their migrant worker families, while 58 million were left behind (Chan 2009).

This type of temporary or seasonal migration where most of the family is left behind has been seen in many other developing countries, for example, in Southeast Asia. For Thailand, Pasuk Phongpaichit and Chris Baker pointed out in 2008 that 'over the last generation, the society has relied heavily on the rural economy and community to provide a cushion for the strains to urbanization. The village has provided a refuge in times of crisis, a counterweight to unemployment and a retreat in old age' (277). Of course, they also point out that this has been less and less effective over time. In one of the plethora of webinars held during the current pandemic, they also said that this rural cushion is much less evident now compared to the time of the 2008 Asian financial crisis.

In extant migration literature, the continued urban–rural connection has been analysed in two ways: as circulatory migration (for example, in Breman [2013] and Srivastava [2011] in India) or as multi-locational households (Deshingkar and Farrington [2009]). In Latin America, Alain de Janvry analysed the phenomenon of the 'semi-proletarianized peasants' (1987: 396). Most famously, the role of the rural economy of the 'homelands' for South

African mineworkers was analysed by Harold Wolpe (1980). With regard to Taiwan's early industrialization, Hill Gates (1979) called this rural–industrial connection, the phenomenon of the 'part-time proletariat'. The phenomenon of the rural–urban connection of sections of the industrial proletariat is well known. It is not something that made its appearance only with GVC-based industrialization in India or China. But it is important to go into the meaning of the continuation of this phenomenon in the context of the manufacturing segments of GVCs.

Global Recession and the Rural Safety Net

The role of India's rural economy in providing a safety net in an economic downturn was dramatically seen as TV screens around the world showed scenes of millions of workers, some with families, trying to get back to their rural homes in any way they could. Many walked, others hitched dangerous and expensive rides, as central and state governments in India tried to prevent these workers from going back after they had been abandoned without payment and left to face starvation. While this sordid story of abandonment in recession involved many tens of millions in both the unorganized sector and those precariously employed in the organized sector well beyond the garment GVC, we focus on how this played out in the garment GVC.

The story of the losses suffered by Indian garment exporters due to buyers' cancellation of orders and demands for discounts on goods already supplied before global lockdowns is now well known. For Bangladesh, a study by Mark Anner (2020), supported by the Bangladesh Garment Manufacturers and Exporters Association (BGMEA) and well-publicized in the *New York Times* and other prominent newspapers, exposed the activities of most brands in cancelling orders that were in various stages of manufacture. For India, the Apparel Export Promotion Corporation (AEPC) conducted two surveys of garment exporters, with 105 and 88 exporters, respectively (AEPC 2020). It was reported by 83 per cent of exporters that orders had been wholly or partly cancelled. For orders cancelled, 72 per cent said that their brands had not taken responsibility for materials already purchased. Almost 50 per cent indicated that buyers were asking for discounts on goods already shipped, 72 per cent of exporters said that they had been asked for discounts of more than 20 per cent, with 27 per cent of exporters saying that they were being asked for discounts above 40 per cent.

The AEPC report also pointed out that 88 per cent of exporters said that they were 'challenged' in paying wages to workers. Being challenged can be understood as being a euphemism for not paying wages to workers. The AEPC (2020) had requested the government to provide funds to exporters to pay wages to workers for 'six weeks or until the situation became normal'. On the contrary, exporters did not even get Goods and Services Tax (GST) and other refunds that they were expected to receive from the government.

In order to assess the situation of garment workers, their sufferings, coping mechanisms, and reactions, the SLD carried out a rapid response survey in June 2020, through telephone contact with 100 workers from the NCR and Tiruppur. Besides this survey, field investigators also carried out telephone discussions with workers who had returned to their source villages. Of the 100 workers surveyed, 57 were women and 43 were men. Overall, 54 per cent (54 out of 100) were permanent workers, 44 per cent were contract workers, while 2 women were homeworkers. Most of the workers were inter-state migrants, with 28 workers in Tiruppur being intra-state migrants from other parts of Tamil Nadu. Of the inter-state migrant workers, 69 per cent were from northern India, with 49 per cent from Bihar. In the analysis that follows, we supplement this rapid response investigation of COVID-19 impacts on garment workers in India with findings from AFWA regional research on COVID-19 impacts on garment workers, including a survey of 2,185 garment workers employed aross 189 factories in Sri Lanka, Pakistan, Indonesia, India, Cambodia, and Bangladesh.

The lockdown in India started on 24 March 2020, so workers had completed three weeks of work for the month of March by then. But of the 100 workers, only 19 received any payment. Notably, those who were paid received payment either in the form of encashing earned leave or as advance payment, where the advance payment was given on the condition that it would be deducted from the overtime work that they would do in future. That payment too was quite meagre, ranging from INR 1,800 (USD 24) to about INR 10,969 (USD 146) per worker. Labour contractors, as would be expected, had abandoned the workers and had even switched off their mobile phones. But it needs to be noted that even the majority of permanent workers, whose dues were from the exporting firms, were also not paid.

Eighty-nine per cent of the 433 workers surveyed by AFWA in garment clusters in Gujarat (Ahmedabad), Haryana (Gurugram, Faridabad), Karnataka (Bangalore), and Tamil Nadu (Erode and Tiruppur) also reported employment shocks at some point in 2020, either in the form of lay offs or terminations. These workers reported an overall wage theft of 23 per cent in 2020 and a sharp decline in wages by 73 per cent during the COVID-19 lockdown period. In April and May 2020, two of the most severe months of the lockdown, workers reported covering 81 per cent of household consumption with debt financing. As a result, 93 per cent of the workers surveyed by AFWA in India reported being pushed below the international poverty line of the World Bank in April and May 2020.

When workers are not paid their due salaries and factories close down, one expects the government to step in and provide income support to the laid off workers. While the government eased liquidity for garment suppliers through tax incentives and by facilitating credit flow, there was no concerted intervention by the government to address the crisis of unpaid wages in the industry. The Government of India (GoI) issued an advisory in March 2020 to all employers' associations to not terminate their employees or cut wages during the lockdown, particularly for casual and contractual workers, but it was not enforced. Instead, employers cited weak finances and limited monetary support from the government. They passed these costs on to garment workers, with AFWA (2021) estimates indicating that 79,600 garment workers across 55 factories in India alone were denied 29.67 million USD as wages due to order cancellations, non-payment of existing orders, and other blatant unilateral exercises of power by brands during the pandemic.

The Indian government also steadfastly refused to provide meaningful income support. Some women workers with bank accounts reported receiving just INR 500, about USD 7; others reported receiving a one-time transfer of INR 1,000–2,000 (USD 13–26) which is barely enough to meet consumption needs for a week. Elementary economic theory tells us that when private incomes collapse, the only way to stave off starvation is to provide income support as an entitlement by the government. The government had set up digital payment systems, which are supposed to reach almost all households. This could have been used to make immediate payments to laid off workers and workers in the unorganized sector. Supply chains of food items were working and with income support, workers could have, in some manner, managed their families.

Only 20 of the 100 workers surveyed by SLD said that they got the extra rations (subsidized food grains) from the government. As discussed earlier in this chapter, given that migrant workers usually do not have any proof of local residence, they do not get ration cards for subsidized food grains in destination areas. Some non-governmental organizations (NGOs) and trade unions provided cooked food for workers during the lockdown. As you travelled around urban spaces, you could see depressing lines of women, men, and children literally begging for food. From their clothes, one could make out they were workers, most likely in the unorganized sector. A little less than one-third of garment workers reported getting some cooked food from some NGOs or unions.

The number of meals that workers and their families could eat was depressingly low. Out of the 97 workers who responded to the SLD telephone survey, 6 workers said that they were able to eat just one meal a day, 69 said that they could manage just two meals a day, and 2 workers managed one meal or sometimes two meals a day. This means that as many as 82 per cent of workers could eat just two or fewer meals per day. What has been described here is workers and their families living at semi-starvation levels. They used their savings—money which they had saved from working their bodies to exhaustion. The savings would usually have been remitted to their families in their home villages. But the cruel manner in which the lockdown was carried out forced these workers to use up the savings meant for their rural households.

The brief survey did not ask whether workers had withdrawn money from savings in their provident fund (PF) accounts, but newspaper reports show that 5.2 million, mainly low-wage workers (those earning less than INR 15,000 per month) had withdrawn a total of INR 13,300 crores (roughly USD 2 billion) from their PF savings (*The Hindu* 2020). Workers usually earmark these savings for their children's educational and marriage expenses. The lockdown, with no social security support, forced these workers to jeopardize their children's future to stay alive.

When the lockdown was announced, many intra-state migrants quickly went back to their nearby villages. The inter-state migrants, however, were stuck in the garment clusters; of course, without work and thus with no income. As noted earlier, not even 20 per cent of the workers were paid by the factory owners. Over time, many migrants went back to their home villages. Many hired expensive private transport. Newspaper and TV coverage reported migrant workers paying thousands of rupees to get a place in a cramped truck or even in a cement mixer. Many used the last of their savings or borrowed money to finance their return.

All of the 433 workers surveyed by AFWA in India—with workers having an average of six years of work experience—reported that they did not have enough savings to tide them over even a two-month lay off period. Accordingly, workers reported reducing consumption costs, especially the costs of children's education, incurring debt, and liquidating assets. The average debt for garment workers increased more than two-fold, from 152 USD pre-pandemic to 360 USD by the end of the 2020. Sixty per cent of workers incurred debt to meet food expenses, while 28 per cent took on debt to pay rent (AFWA 2021).

SLD field investigators also spoke by phone to some of the migrant garment workers who had returned to their villages in Bihar and Uttar Pradesh. They described having to borrow money from local moneylenders at interest rates of 20 per cent per month. A study by SEWA Bharat (2020) also showed that women in the unorganized sectors had borrowed money at interest rates ranging from 5 per cent to 18 per cent per month. These are the kind of interest rates one has not seen for decades in India. This is the return of the *sahukar*, the moneylender, with a vengeance. These returned migrant workers feared that they would be unable to repay these loans and end up losing their meagre lands or even their houses. The refusal of the Indian government to accept its moral and economic responsibility for keeping people out of starvation pushed these workers and their families into destitution.

In Tiruppur, it is estimated that by June 2020, some 40 per cent of interstate migrants had gone back. Many of those that remained were kept, rather confined, in company-run dormitories. The exporters feared that if these workers went away, then they may face an acute shortage of labour when work returned to normal. Workers in Tiruppur complained that they had been confined in these dormitories against their will (Gangwar 2000). Most of them were contract workers. Earlier, they were the most disposable of workers; now they were being cajoled and forced to remain. There were protest incidents in Tiruppur. Many workers from the dormitories in the Nethaji Apparel Park (NAP) were arrested in one such incident. There was another protest incident at the Tiruppur railway station.

While in Tiruppur there were incidents of factory owners trying to detain workers in dormitories, in the state of Karnataka, in which the Bengaluru garment cluster is located, the state government opposed the running of trains to take migrant workers home. Garment and other workers were being treated as bonded labourers. This should be contrasted with the quick arrangements made for middle- and upper-class students, very likely from the upper castes too, to return from their educational centres to their home states. Finally, continued adverse publicity on TV forced the central and state governments to relent and allow trains to take migrant workers who wished to return to their villages.

An important point needs to be made about this widespread return migration. It was sparked by the failure of governments to provide income support to workers. The central government, which has the means to provide income support, refused to take this path. Faced with a GVC-based and government-induced starvation, the only way the migrant workers could survive was by trying to get back to their homes in the villages. It was the refusal of the central government to provide a safety net that was responsible for the mass reverse migration, often on foot or in great hardship, for example, a young girl cycling with her injured father riding at the back. Migrant workers were killed in terrible ways, such as while sleeping on railway tracks or even collapsing just when they were near their homes. Reports in newspapers and on TV point to the frequent harassment they faced from the police along the way. Those on trains were often not provided food or even drinking water. Even the Supreme Court of India refused to intervene in the matter. Only in the first week of June 2020 did the Supreme Court finally ask the governments to make arrangements for the return of migrants and not to take any money for their homeward journey.

Will the migrants come back to the garment clusters? Some have said that they will not return but will seek some paid work in their home villages, however little the earnings might be. Many, however, said that there are few opportunities in their home villages, as one would expect, in a labour-surplus economy. But they have been scarred by their experiences under the lockdown with no safety net in place. The risks to migrant workers in the garment clusters have increased. What if there is another lockdown and the brands, suppliers, and governments all abandon them again?

In October 2020, some of the large suppliers reported having received orders that would require them to utilize their full capacity. But many medium-size suppliers were only working at about 50 per cent of capacity. It is likely that there will be some shortage of labour in the garment clusters when business returns to its earlier levels. This could result in wages going up. Will it also increase the ratio of permanent to contract labour? Reports from the different clusters show that mainly permanent workers were being re-employed to take care of the reduced orders. At the same time, there were reports from Gurugram that older women were not being taken back, while young women were being taken back at lower wages.

Further, there will be price pressure on the exporters. To manage the new price range, there is likely to be a need to reduce costs by increasing the level of mechanization and automation, which, together, would increase the demand for more skilled labour. If exporters need to retain skilled labour, then that could lead to an increase in the proportion of permanent workers. The possible increase in the proportion of skilled and permanent workers would be the result of unprecedented *collective bargaining by exodus*.

In comparison to the complete abandonment of garment (and other) workers by the Indian government, in Bangladesh, the government directly paid some wages to garment workers and then charged this as a loan to the factories. Nevertheless, as the lockdown continued, many workers returned to their village homes. This happened in Indonesia too. What this shows is that the rural economy plays an important role as a safety net in supplier economies that have little or no state-provided social security. The role of the rural safety net in the 2020 recession only dramatically illustrated the articulation of the rural economy with garment employment. Precarious employment threatened to lead to starvation and garment workers had to trek back to their rural homes to find some manner of safety net.

What we have seen in the preceding paragraphs is that migrant garment workers' households in the rural economy bear some part of the cost of reproduction of labour power of left-behind household members and of garment workers themselves in lay offs, illness, and on retirement. With supplier economies lacking in social security measures, the rural economy also acts as a safety net in recessions. We now turn to subsidies provided by rural farm households and rural labour, including child labour, in cotton production.

Farmer Subsidies in Cotton Production

Globally, cotton production and trade are highly distorted by policy and more than 20 per cent of the world's cotton producer earnings came from government support to the sector (Gillson 2004). The subsidies to cotton producers that are given mainly in developed countries matter because they restrict the opportunities for the pro-poor growth that the northern governments endorse at global meetings. This is despite the fact that a very small proportion of the developed country population depends on agriculture for livelihoods as against the situation in developing countries where large proportions of the population draw their livelihoods from agriculture. Leveraging of trade opportunities that would be enhanced by dismantling developed world subsidies requires domestic reforms by developing country governments. This is the first necessary condition for better growth prospects for developing countries from a global justice perspective. Most of the farm subsidies end up supporting overproduction and this is then dumped in the world markets at prices that are in no way related to production costs (Watkins and Braun 2003). Many studies during the early 2000s show that cotton subsidy removal can lead to a global cotton price rise ranging from 2 per cent to as much as 70 per cent (Gillson 2004).

In the case of the US, which accounts for 14 per cent of global cotton production (Sharma and Bugaliya 2014) and a 36 per cent share in global cotton export (Nanda 2019), with 86 per cent of its total cotton production exported, the cost of production of cotton was the highest and it was four and a half to six times higher than India's cost of cotton production. During the 15 years from 1995 to 2010, the US gave USD 37 billion to its cotton producers through programmes, such as counter-cyclical payments, decoupled payments, and commodity certificates. Therefore, the comparative advantage of the US in the global cotton market is artificial and sustained because of high levels of domestic support given to farmers and corporations (Sharma and Bugaliya 2014).

In the US, the top 10 per cent of the recipients, numbering 290,000, received 77 per cent of all commodity payments and the top 1 per cent, numbering 29,000, received 26 per cent of all payments; this was USD 1.5 million per recipient during 1995–2011 (Sharma and Bugaliya 2014). In fact, in the US, 60 per cent of farmers get no support and the largest 7 per cent account for 50 per cent of all government payments.

Similarly, the largest 25 per cent of European Union (EU) subsidy recipients secured 60 per cent of all subsidies (Watkins and Braun 2003). The cotton subsidies to Greek and Spanish farmers were one of the highest in the world and they directly competed with developing countries. In fact, 38 per cent of the loss of earnings in west and central Africa was argued to be caused by the EU subsidies (Gillson 2004).

This can also be treated as a case of 'ecologically unequal trade' in cotton as it leads to distorted patterns of production and use of natural resources with implications for human livelihoods (Martinez-Alier et al. 2016). Subsidies to cotton producers in the US and EU have serious implications for African and other developing country cotton producers because the subsidies encourage overproduction and export dumping, which leads to low global cotton prices. In this manner, cotton farmers in the US become first among equals in the harvesting of subsidies.

The scale of these subsidies can be seen in the amount US cotton farmers received in subsidies, which was more than the entire gross domestic product (GDP) of Burkina Faso and three times that of the African budget of the United States Agency for International Development (USAID). The loss to the African farmers due to cotton subsidies to the American farmers was calculated by Oxfam to be USD 301 million per year. This meant Burkina Faso losing 1 per cent of GDP and 10 per cent of its export earnings, Mali losing 1.7 per cent of GDP and 8 per cent of export earnings, and Benin losing 1.2 per cent of GDP and 9 per cent of export earnings. This is a serious livelihood issue for many households in West Africa as cotton is the only cash crop and 10 million people depend on cotton production (Watkins and Braun 2003), while 50 per cent of cotton-producing households' income came from cotton (FAO and ICAC 2015).

In fact, a 17.5 per cent increase in cotton prices between 1993 and 1998 reduced poverty levels in cotton regions of Burkina Faso by 42 to 50 per cent compared with non-cotton-growing areas where poverty increased by 2 per cent over the same period (Makori n.d.). In Pakistan, where cotton is the largest cash crop and accounted for 56.9 per cent of average crop income and 53.3 per cent of the total income of farming households in Sindh, a fall in world cotton prices led to an increase in rural poverty. It was estimated that a 20 per cent increase in cotton prices could reduce cotton farming household poverty by 22 to 25 per cent in cotton-growing areas (Punjab and Sindh) of Pakistan (Orden et al. 2006).

Cotton farmers in African countries are forced to bear the brunt of lower world prices since their governments do not have the fiscal capacity to provide domestic income support. However, governments in China and India have provided income support in the form of minimum support prices (MSP) for cotton, as also for some other agricultural commodities. China keeps its reference price 20 per cent above the international price. In India, there is an annually announced MSP. But procurement at MSP is restricted to only some states of India. In fact, it is estimated that just 25 per cent of cotton is procured at MSP by the para-state Cotton Corporation of India (GoI 2017). The Chinese government not only pays direct subsidies to cotton producers based on the difference between target price for the season and average market price but also provides subsidies for using high-quality seeds and for transporting cotton from producing to ginning areas.

Dumping undermines the economic viability of competing farmers, whether they grow for the domestic market or for export where dumped commodities compete with their production. Dumping is also harmful to the producers being subsidized in the exporting (dumping) countries because they have to sell in the markets that are controlled by a few trading corporations, that is, in the US. Therefore, the prices they get for their crops are generally lower than their average cost of production. Additionally, dumping creates an economic condition that undermines the environmental aspects of production.

So far, we have looked at subsidies extracted from cotton farmers through the maintenance of low international raw cotton prices. Since cotton production leads to a significant reduction in poverty, it is important to bring justice to global cotton prices for the benefit of small and marginal cotton producers in the developing world. Further, since cotton production involves not only farmers but also agricultural labourers—often women, and even substantial numbers of children—the impact of low prices of raw cotton is also pushed on to agricultural labourers. Thus, there are subsidies extracted from both farmers and labourers through the low international prices of raw cotton.

Labour Subsidies in Cotton Production

Raw cotton production is preceded by hybrid cotton seed production under contract farming arrangements in India. The seed companies arrange contracts for seed production with local farmers either directly or through middlemen called 'seed organizers'. These companies or seed organizers supply seeds to the farmers, set the price of the seed before harvest, and supervise the cultivation of the crop. They also advance capital to the farmers, thus linking markets for output and credit (B. P. Singh 2008). The organizers are usually connected with more than one seed company and assigned the task of identifying seed farmers, supplying them with parent seeds, collecting the produce after the harvest, and giving the seeds to the companies after ginning. Many organizers in Gadwal in Telangana were big farmers who worked with 200 to 500 farmers.

They also give loans at a monthly interest rate of 2 per cent to the farmers for investment towards seed cultivation and also for everyday household expenses.

There is another layer of 'sub-organizers' between the farmers and the big seed organizers to facilitate more effective outreach. Over time, many sub-organizers graduate into organizers. These networks of intermediaries constitute an important institution in the cotton-seed industry where they are central players coordinating and managing the seed supply chain on behalf of private companies. The contracts drawn up between the company and the organizers incorporate terms and conditions like the organizers' commission, production targets, and procurement prices to the growing farmers. There were no agreements between the companies and the farmers and no written contracts between the organizers and the farmers (IHD 2020). In turn, farmers engage contractors to employ labour. The labour contractor receives a commission from the farmer for arranging the labourers. In addition, the contractor also deducts 10 to 15 per cent of the wage payment from each labourer as his commission. Substantial wage amounts are withheld until the completion of the agreement period (S. Singh 2017).

Labour contractors are responsible for recruiting workers, who are mostly migrants. Most of the labour contractors were once workers themselves, belonging to the same community as the migrants from among whom they recruit. Before the season starts, seed farmers approach labour contractors, place their demand for labour, and pay some advance money for travel costs and other needs of workers. The per-day wage rates are fixed in advance and the agreement lasts for one crop season. It is the responsibility of the labour contractor to identify the required number of labourers and ensure that they work for the farmer for the entire agreement period. Each contractor mobilizes between 20 and 100 labourers and places them with different farmers. Farmers do not make any individual agreements with the labourers, instead interacting with labour contractors. Payments are made twice or thrice during the agreement period (S. Singh 2017).

In India, cotton is mostly planted and picked by female workers who account for 65 per cent of the workforce—70 per cent in planting and 90 per cent in picking (ITC 2011). Hired workers received only EUR 1.8 per day in India which, at the time, was only 41 per cent of the living wage. There is also the use of child labour even in family farms which accounted for 30 per cent of all working children in cotton in India in 2019 (Ward and Mishra 2019).

Seed farmers depend mostly on hired labour (86.5 per cent), with 82.5 per cent migrant and 35 per cent child workers. It was found that 78 per cent of the workforce on seed farms were girls and 88 per cent of them were aged between 6 and 14, belonging mostly to Scheduled Castes and Tribes. These children lived in labour camps in groups. They had no fixed working hours.

Sixty per cent attended school for a few years and then dropped out to work in the cotton seed fields. These children were paid wages that were at least 30 per cent less than the adult female wage and 55 per cent less than the adult male wage rate (ILO 2016).

More recently, it was found that 2.3 per cent of the children working in cotton farms were as young as 10 years of age and 37 per cent between 11 and 14 years; one-third of them were illiterate and all were from Scheduled Tribe households in Rajasthan (Banday et al. 2018). What distinguishes child labour in cotton seed production from other industries, such as carpet, bangles, diamond polishing, and limestone, is the large numbers involved and the dominance of girls in this sector. It was estimated that there were 450,000 children in cotton seed fields in India, which far exceeded all children put together in the above-mentioned industries. Further, child labour in these industries is mostly composed of boys; while in cotton seed production, they were mainly girls (B. P. Singh 2008).

In cotton seed production in Gujarat, the labourers, mostly migrants from Rajasthan, generally stay on the farm and are paid INR 50 per day (less than USD 1 per day). Since labourers live on the owners' farms, they are at the disposal of the farmers whenever their labour is needed. Labourers generally work for 13 to 14 hours a day with a two-hour break for meals. They begin work around 5 am and end at 6 or 7 pm. A lunch break of one to two hours (only one hour during peak season) is provided between 12 noon to 2 pm (B. P. Singh 2008).

Researchers have documented serious violations of young children's personal and working rights which included physical violence, bullying, and sexual harassment due to their lack of any power to negotiate or lack of any institutions and stakeholder to protect them against a powerful farmer employer other than the labour contractor himself, who sometimes did stand by the child workers. The living conditions of child workers were very poor with shared accommodation that was not gender-segregated and most of them defecated and bathed in the open. The children reported frequent pain in their fingers and long hours of work besides abuse by the farmer employer. Physical abuse including beating children is used to punish them for poor performance, such as not meeting targets or missing cross-pollinating some flowers.

The farmers who advance money to the parents of the children through the labour contractor ('mate') are also known to exploit the girls sexually as reported by mates and NGO personnel; there have even been reports of some girls taking their own lives due to such exploitation. The mates settle such conflicts by not supplying child workers to such farmers in the next season or not returning their advance for the supply of such labour. Whereas some boys are able to cope with such abuse by running away from cotton seed farms or hiding when the abuse is likely to take place, the girls cannot do so as they find it difficult to undertake the journey back home alone (Banday et al. 2018).

Child labour is used in cotton seed production because it is supposedly more efficient due to the flexibility of young bodies as the work requires repeated bending and getting up (Banday et al. 2018; B. P. Singh 2008). The seed companies do not take action against production organizers and farmers even if the use of child labour is found in cotton seed farms as the company needs production from these farmers. In the early 2000s, the government of Gujarat decided to impose a fine of INR 20,000 if the farmer was found using child labour (B. P. Singh 2008).

Farmers are not willing to forego child labour as it is less costly than adult labour, the children follow orders better, and are supposedly more efficient (Banday et al. 2018). The seed companies argue that seed farmers earn relatively better profit margins compared to other farmers and therefore they should be able to employ adult labour at adult wage rates, putting the blame for the incidence of child labour on the seed farmers. Most of these companies claimed to be socially responsible and did not accept that they were in any way responsible for the use of child labour as they did not have direct contracts with farmers, who were organized and managed by seed production organizers who, in turn, had contracts with these companies. Some also deny child labour, saying it is the family members of the small farmers, including children, who worked on these farms, which could not be treated as cases of child labour.

This is, of course, the usual excuse when indirect employment is used as a business strategy. But seed companies did in a manner admit some culpability. Most of the firms acknowledged the problem of child labour in cotton seed production and later wrote in their agreements with organizers and producers that child labour should not be used in cotton seed production. Seed growers argued that since companies did not pay higher prices to take care of additional costs arising out of the use of only adult labour, they could not afford to remove child labour from their farms. This call for higher prices lends insight into the company role in avoiding or perpetuating child labour in cotton seed farms (S. Singh 2017).

The regulatory role of the state is largely absent in the cotton seed industry (IHD 2020) though there are many acts to protect workers' interests in the sector. These include the Minimum Wages Act, 1948; the Bonded Labour System (Abolition) Act, 1976; the Protection of Human Rights Act, 1993; the Equal Remuneration Act, 1976; the Child Labour (Prohibition and Regulation) Act, 1986, amended in 1999; the Inter-State Migrant Workers (Regulation of Employment and Conditions of Service) Act, 1979; and the Unorganised Labour and Agricultural Workers (Welfare) Act, 2006

(B. P. Singh 2008). But these are rarely implemented. The government also has a role to play in implementing this raft of labour law protections.

Conclusion

In this chapter, we have shown that garment workers were paid much less than the living wage, and depended on their connections with the rural economy to make up some of the shortfall in their wages. A part of the cost of the reproduction of wage labour is borne by the rural economy. Often children and other household members are left behind for the rural household economy, with a large extent of feminization to take care of both the young and the aged. Workers themselves return to their rural homes during lay offs and illness. The precariously employed long-term circular migrants also return to their rural homes after retiring from garment factory work. This is so not only where there are legal restrictions, as in China, on these migrants settling down in urban areas but also without such legal restrictions, such as in India, where the sheer economics of wages well below the living wage prevents such permanent relocation.

We have also seen that the rural economy serves as a safety net during economic downturns, as has been seen during the Asian financial crisis of 1998 in Southeast Asia, in India during the Great Recession of 2008, and also the 2020 COVID-19 depression. Abandoned by brands, suppliers, and governments, precariously employed garment workers, in particular, were forced to return to their rural homes.

Subsidies are also extracted from rural farm and labour households producing cotton. The low international prices of raw cotton are a means through which subsidy is extracted from cotton farmers in developing countries, more so in West and Central Africa. This is an unjust subsidy in that it increases poverty among cotton farmers and is a constraint on their achievement of elementary capabilities for reasonable human existence. This low price of raw cotton, like a low price for labour power and the use of child labour, keeps down the prices of cotton that goes into garment manufacture. Finally, this extracted value is captured by the brands through the monopsonistic market structure in the manufacture of cotton garments.

8

The Household as a Production Site

Homeworkers and Child Labour

So far, we have dealt with the household as a site for the reproduction of labour power. However, the household is also a site for production to perform tasks outsourced from the factories. There are two types of home-based workers. First, those who buy inputs, perform some value-adding tasks, and sell the output. These are called either own-account workers or self-employed workers. Street vendors and hawkers are of this type who operate on their own account. The second type of home-based worker constitutes those who perform tasks specified by an employer. Women in Informal Employment, Globalizing and Organizing (WIEGO), the international network of women in the unorganized sector, refers to this type of home-based workers as homeworkers, and this terminology will be followed here.

The ILO Convention 177 on Home Work defines home work as

> work carried out by a person, to be referred as a homeworker, (1) in his or her home or in other premises of his or her choice, *other than the workplace of the employer*; (2) for remuneration; (3) which results in a product or service as specified by the employer, irrespective of who provides the equipment, material or other inputs used unless this person has the degree of economic independence necessary to be considered an independent worker under national laws, regulations or court decisions. (ILO 2000, emphasis added)

Since we are considering sites of production, it is important to note that to qualify as homework, work must be carried out on a site 'other than the workplace' and carried out 'as specified by the employer'. Since homework is carried out as specified by the employer, it qualifies as part of the global value chain (GVC), where work contracted to the manufacturer of garments is outsourced to a homeworker. The relation between the manufacturer, the exporter, and the homeworker is not of the market type where the homeworker sells goods or services to the manufacturer. Rather, the manufacturer contracts for the performance of tasks, usually embroidery or finishing an almost-finished garment.

These subcontracted homeworkers occupy an intermediate space between independent own-account workers and factory workers (Raveendran, Sudarshan, and Vanek 2013). They differ from own-account workers in that they are not sellers of their output. The finished pieces of work are returned to the factory, via the contractor, and the homeworkers are paid for the tasks performed. On the other hand, unlike factory workers, homeworkers can choose and be flexible about their own work timings, so long as the work is completed in the stipulated time. They are also flexible in that, unlike factory workers, they can utilize other members of the household, usually children but also spouses and others, in completing their work. The other household members, including children who might participate in homework, would then fall under the category of contributing or unpaid household labour.

Homeworkers are the most precariously employed in garment value chains. Under Indian law, with indirectly employed contract labour, the subcontracting factory is considered the principal employer, with responsibility for ensuring the payment of minimum wages and social security payments, such as Employees' Provident Fund (EPF). This, however, does not apply to work that is subcontracted outside the factory. Homeworkers are not covered as contract labour under laws protecting contract workers. There is a clear need to amend the relevant labour law in India to include homeworkers within the ambit of the responsibility functions of the principal employer.

Incidence of Homework

A 2019 survey of 340 garment factories in Delhi and Bengaluru found that 58 per cent of these factories outsourced to homeworkers (Anner 2019a). The phenomenon of subcontracted homework is quite widespread, though not ubiquitous. The incidence of homework in garment value chains in India has fallen over time for reasons that will be discussed later.

Data from India's Periodic Labour Force Survey (NSSO 2018) can be used to look at the incidence and some features of home-based work. Only subcontracted workers who work from their own dwelling are taken as homeworkers in the garment value chains. At this level, we cannot distinguish between those who work for GVCs and those who work for domestic value chains. But that is usually the case with such national-level labour force survey data.

What the PLFS 2018 (NSSO 2018) survey does show is that 32 per cent of subcontracted homeworkers are women and as many as 68 per cent are men.

Among those who were helpers in household enterprises, it was the other way around, with as many as 63 per cent women and 37 per cent men. Even among homeworkers, there is a gender disparity with more women being helpers—who would not get separate remuneration—than men.

The main category in the place of work is 'other than factory', which includes not only their own dwelling, but also 'structure attached to dwelling', 'open area adjunct to dwelling', and 'detached structure near dwelling'. While 69 per cent of women homeworkers worked in their own dwelling, it was lower at 43 per cent for men homeworkers. More men, as homeworkers, are able to detach themselves from domestic work and have a sense of non-domestic labour and a distinct workplace. Women, however, combine domestic work with income-earning work, reflecting the multitasking that women are forced to juggle. It can be expected that working for just short periods of time, interspersed with domestic care activities, would have an effect on women's productivity in the subcontracted tasks. At the very least, there would be the time lost in frequently stopping and restarting work. For more complex work, such as embroidery or applique work, it can be expected that the productivity loss would be higher than in relatively simple tasks, such as tidying garments by cutting threads or inserting the tie into tracksuit pants (Table 8.1).

What are the specific advantages that homeworkers bring to the organization of value chains? They are all related to a reduction in costs, but there are a number of dimensions to such cost reduction. For one, they are hidden workers and are not counted when considering regulations regarding factory workers. There is no minimum wage set for homework, and homeworkers do not qualify for social security benefits, such as provident fund contributions or medical insurance.

At one level, it has been stated that 'homeworkers are particularly difficult to locate and monitor and thus they pose a challenge for companies who are trying to ensure sustainable social practices throughout their supply chain' (Freeman 2003: 107). They are not, however, difficult to locate if the

Table 8.1 Gender Distribution by Place of Work of Homeworkers

Place of Work	Men	Women	Total
Own dwelling	43%	69%	56%
Structure attached to dwelling	46%	28%	36%
Open area adjunct to dwelling	2%	1%	1%
Detached structure near dwelling	11%	4%	7%
Total	100%	100%	100%

Source: Calculated from unit data, NSSO (2018).

trouble is taken to find them. The factory managers and their contractors and subcontractors, who take the pieces to be worked on and bring them back, can locate the homeworkers. They can locate each one of them since if they could not do that, they would lose some of the pieces given for finishing.

In fact, it is not that homeworkers are difficult to locate, it is that it is easy to hide them from so-called auditors or government inspectors. As a factory manager in Pakistan admitted to a researcher, since government inspectors cannot inspect private homes, it is cheaper to simply outsource work to home-based workers (Zhou 2017 in von Broembsen, Harvey, and Chen 2019: 5). Even in the case of violations of whatever regulations do exist concerning the home as a workplace, it is easy to hide them from inspectors.

Besides the ease of hiding them, there are several specific cost advantages of using homeworkers. For one, minimum wage regulations do not apply. As we will see later, the earnings of homeworkers are far below even the minimum wage. In addition, some production costs are transferred to the homeworkers. Rent of the worksite is not included in the costs nor is the electricity utilized. Homeworkers are forced to purchase their own production equipment, such as scissors, needles, and even sewing machines. In setting piece rates, the time required to set up a piece for production, for example, putting a piece of fabric into a frame for hand embroidery, is not taken into account. HomeNet South Asia (HNSA) calculates that these non-wage costs passed on to homeworkers amount to 25 per cent of the piece rate (HNSA 2020). To calculate the effective per-hour earnings of homeworkers, it is therefore necessary to make this adjustment to piece rates.

The poverty condition of homeworkers is evidenced by the low wages at which they work. A study of homeworkers in the garment industry found that most of them were Dalits or Muslims. The incidence of poverty among these marginalized social groups is higher than among other social groups, forcing workers from these social groups to accept very precarious work with lower wages.

Their poverty-related weakness is compounded by their isolation and lack of information. Often the homeworkers do not know the brand or even the factory for which they are working. Even if they did know the names of the factories or brands, their isolation as individual homeworkers has traditionally made it difficult to organize them into collectives and informal sector unions. After the pioneering of India's Self Employed Women's Association (SEWA) in organizing women homeworkers and other unorganized sector workers, the community-based unions of homeworkers have spread around the world and now have a prominent global voice in WIEGO. But despite the abundance of evidence on the importance of homeworkers in GVCs, homeworkers have not been included in most analyses of GVCs, where the concentration has been on the factory as the core of production work. The neglect of homeworkers is a result of the methodological blinders which do not embed the factory and production as a whole within the household economy, whether as the provider of labour power or the site of performance of specific tasks in production. Homeworkers are truly invisible workers not only in the value chain but often in much of the analysis of value chains.

Both information and social isolation have been reduced by the organization of homeworkers. Nevertheless, there are major problems regarding the under-pricing of the labour inputs of homeworkers. Their market weakness makes it difficult to secure higher prices. A study in Pakistan pointed out that when women tried to ask for a higher piece rate, they faced retaliation with the threat of losing what work they had. Homeworkers in Tiruppur in India are reported to have been scared to be interviewed by researchers (Sinha and Mehrotra 2016).

Wage Subsidy

Garment factory workers get paid at around the national minimum wage. Homeworkers, however, do not get even that. Both labour force data (NSSO 2018) and our primary data show homeworkers earning much less than the minimum wage. In Table 8.2, a comparison is made between homeworkers and factory workers.

Table 8.2 shows a substantial difference between the earnings of men and women in homework and factory work. The difference in wages between factory and home work is much greater in the case of women than men—women homeworkers earn just 23 per cent of women factory workers' average wage, while men homeworkers earn 71.5 per cent of men factory workers' average wage. It is likely that men are able to put in more hours at economic work than women, who have to combine economic work with domestic work. It is also likely that there is a difference in the supposed skill levels of women and men, with women performing unskilled and semi-skilled tasks, while

Table 8.2 Gender and Monthly Earnings (INR) of Factory Workers and Homeworkers

Gender	Home-Based Workers	Factory Workers
Men	6,800	9,500
Women	1,500	6,500
Total	3,500	8,000

Source: NSSO (2018).
Notes: N = 456 (home-based workers); N = 712 (factory workers).

men perform skilled tasks. Women homeworkers are disadvantaged not only vis-à-vis women factory workers but also vis-à-vis men homeworkers.

The data in Table 8.2 reflects total monthly earnings, but there could well be differences in the hours worked. Thus, a proper comparison will require a calculation of the earnings per hour. In particular, we are interested in how much of the minimum wage can be covered in a regular eight-hour working day.

For data on hours worked (Table 8.3), we shift from large-scale sample study to primary data collected by the Society for Labour and Development (SLD) in a survey of homeworkers carried out in the garment cluster of Gurugram in the Delhi National Capital Region (NCR). The homeworkers surveyed were women who work on subcontracts from factories, performing specific tasks such as cutting threads and other tasks in tidying up garments.

On average, a homeworker gets around 13 days of work per month and works for around 4 hours in a day. Average monthly earnings from home-based work for a worker in the NCR was around INR 1,268 and per day earnings is around INR 110, with a worker earning around INR 32 per hour. In an 8-hour day, that would amount to a gross income of INR 256 per day. Reducing it by 20 per cent to take account of the expenses incurred by the homeworker would give a daily net income of INR 200, which is around two-thirds of the daily minimum wage of INR 318 even for unskilled work in garment factories in the state of Haryana. Or, to put it another way, women homeworkers would have to work around 12 hours per day in order to earn the minimum wage.

In the SLD survey, the number of days of work women homeworkers got was just 13 per month and 4 hours per day. This provides INR 1,258 per month. The national PLFS for 2017–2018 reported that women homeworkers earned INR 1,500 per month, which was not even one-fourth of the monthly earning of INR 6,500 per month for women employed in garment factories.

Table 8.3 Aspects of Home-Based Work, 2017

Aspects of Home-Based Work	Averages in Gurugram (Haryana)
Worker Age	32 years
No. of days in a month	13 days per month
No. of hours in a day	4 hours per day
Earnings	INR 1,268
Earnings per day	INR 110
Earnings per hour	INR 32

Source: SLD primary data. N = 31 (Delhi NCR).

Another survey of 1,452 homeworkers conducted by the Blum Center for Developing Economies at the University of California, Berkeley (Kara 2019), calculated that women in home work in India earn a daily income of USD 1.12, which is about INR 100, half the net income of INR 200 calculated by the SLD survey.

All the data mentioned earlier point to the fact that women homeworkers in garment value chains are the most deprived, and a per worker wage subsidy is extracted from them that is one-third more than that extracted from women garment factory workers. This data underscores that women homeworkers in garment value chains are the most deprived of decent wages, with a per worker wage subsidy extracted at a rate one-third higher than from women garment factory workers.

There is some data available on the per-hour earnings of women homeworkers from Pakisan, which is quite similar. For Pakistan, a study of 406 homeworkers and their assistants (quite likely children) found that working for 12.4 hours a day, 6 days a week, provided a monthly income of PKR 4,342 (USD 41.42) per month, which was less than one-third of the minimum wage of PKR 14,000 per month (Broembsen, Harvey, and Chen 2019).

Maria Mies studied women lace makers from the village of Narsapur, India, producing for the global market and covered this issue of the earnings of women homeworkers being less than the cost of production of labour power (1982). Mies used the Marxist concept of necessary labour, which corresponds to what we call the cost of production of labour power:

> The lace makers are not only exploited in the same sense as other workers are exploited, i.e. by not being paid for their surplus labour, they are in fact *overexploited*, as with all their work they are not even able to earn enough to pay for their day-to-day maintenance for reproduction. (Mies 1982: 150)

She raises the question: How do they survive if they do not cover the cost of necessary labour? The answer lies in the fact that the bulk of household income comes from agriculture, pointing to what we discuss in this book as the rural subsidy to global production.

Precarity of Homework

Contract labour or workers indirectly employed through labour contractors are indeed precariously employed. But while they do not have any factory-specific identity cards, many would have records of provident fund (PF) payments. In contrast, homeworkers have no official records to prove their existence in the workforce. Their contracts with the intermediaries who provide them work are always verbal. In any case, the factories from which the subcontracting is done do not enter into the picture.

Some aspects of the precarity of homeworker earnings are brought out in the previously mentioned study by Siddharth Kara (2019): about a quarter of homeworkers could be penalized if work was not completed on time and none had any type of contract for the work performed. Put another way, homeworkers have little flexibility on the timeline for completing contract work, but no corresponding employment security. Even in normal, or pre-COVID-19 times, orders given to homeworkers were flexible, depending on seasonal and other fluctuations. Homeworkers, like factory workers, absorbed the fluctuations in orders. But in the COVID-19 lockdown, homeworkers were just abandoned by all, from the brands to the suppliers, contractors, and even the governments.

A COVID-19 lockdown report from WIEGO was aptly titled, 'The World's Most Vulnerable Garment Workers Aren't in Factories' (Broembsen 2020). As with factory-based contract workers, homeworkers in Tiruppur found that the contractors who provided them with work disappeared when the lockdown started at the end of March 2020. As in the case of factory-based precariously employed workers, the homeworkers also found that the contractors had switched off their mobile phones. Of course, they did not make payments to the homeworkers, even for work already delivered back to them. The cascading effect of brand non-payment thus trickled down to the homeworkers. Like contract workers in factories, they too were completely abandoned, with rents and other expenses to bear.

The Household and Child Labour

The household is a site for the reproduction of labour power, as dealt with in Chapter 4, and also the site for production by homeworkers, as we saw in the first part of this chapter. It is also a site for the employment of child labour, though not the only site for child labour.

In the garment value chains, there has been a history of the use of child labour in the factory. This, however, has been substantially reduced after various exposés of child labour being used in the production process of garments or, quite often, handmade carpets. Factories producing for export, whether of garments, leather products, carpets, or handicrafts, usually carry a sign prohibiting the entry of anyone below the age of 18 years. As an owner explained, they prohibit children not only in employment but even from visiting the factory as, for instance, in bringing lunch for their parents working in the factories. There is a fear that there might be an audit at any time, and if children are seen on the premises, it might be reported as evidence of child labour. Nevertheless, there have been factories that have continued to bring in child labour, as shown by the rescue of such children from a Jaipur factory in 2018 (personal communication by the late Varsha Joshi, who led the Child Helpline in Jaipur).

The most usual response to the exposure child labour in garment value chains has been to shift the location of child labour from the factory to the household or to workshops in rural areas where they could escape the regulatory gaze. This has been well documented in the case of both garments (Bhaskaran et al. 2010) and carpets (Venkateswarlu, n.d.). As mentioned earlier, it is difficult to monitor whether children are working or not in the household.

Indian law is somewhat permissive in this matter—it allows children under 14 to work with their parents even on household economic enterprises and adolescents (children between the age of 14 and 18) to work in 'non-hazardous' occupations. Combined with low adult earnings, the result has been a persistence of child labour in home-based work. HNSA points out, 'A decade ago, child labour was rampant in home-based work' (HNSA 2020: 81). However, Kara's study of women and girls in India's home-based garment sector showed that 17 per cent of homeworkers had children working with them (2019). This is much below what HNSA called a rampant prevalence of child labour among homeworkers.

Types of Child Labour

There are two types of child labour. One is children who work as employees. The other is children who work with their parents or family. Of course, nowadays since children working as employees is illegal, children who are in fact employees are identified as family members. When talking to these children both at their workplace and after they have been rescued, it becomes clear that these children are in fact employees who are being passed off as family members (Nathan and Joshi 2018).

These children are often recruited in deceptive ways. Their parents may be promised that they will be sent to school and only work after school. The parents may be given some advance and told that the children will be paid on a regular basis; in practice, the only thing the children are given is some food to keep them working. Often, the children are not allowed any contact with their families; though with mobile phones quite widespread, there may be some, though infrequent, contact. With the advance that has been given to their parents, the children are restrained from leaving their employment. Of course, being in a distant land with no social networks, it would be difficult for the children to even consider leaving their employer. Given that children as wage employees are (*a*) bonded, (*b*) unable to leave the employer, (*c*) paid little more than some food, (*d*) often unable to communicate with their families, and (*e*) they and their families are subject to deception in methods of recruitment, they can be categorized as being in a form of slavery. Since this slavery is for a limited period of time and not lifelong, it can be called modern slavery (Bales 1999).

Child labour as contributing to family labour is very different from child labour as a wage employee. The features of modern slavery mentioned in the previous paragraph are not present in contexts where children work with their parents or family. Both forms of child labour, however, are examples of what is called 'adverse incorporation', that is, the inclusion of children within value chains in a way that is detrimental to their well-being, both present and future (Phillips et al. 2014). This leads us to the question of why this adverse incorporation takes place.

If we assume that parents do not wish ill for their children, then what leads parents, who are the decision-makers in cases of child labour, to decide on a path that is deleterious for their children? In the analysis put forward by Kaushik Basu, the reason is clearly low adult wages (Basu and Hoang Van 1998). When adult wages are low, the very existence of the household is threatened. This leads parents to make their children work as child labourers, whether as wage employees or contributing to family labour. This existential threat to the household also works in a gendered manner. When both parents are forced to work to earn an income, adolescent girls are kept out of school in order to look after younger siblings.

The link between higher adult wages and the reduction of child labour has been seen with the increase of adult employment through the rural employment guarantee scheme, the Mahatma Gandhi National Rural Employment Guarantee Act (MGNREGA). When adult earnings went up with the employment guarantee, there was an observed withdrawal of children from wage labour (Mahendra Dev 2011). Ending child labour on garment GVCs requires stable living wages that lift workers and their families out of poverty and debt.

Reduction in Homework and Child Labour

In garment GVCs, considerable attention has been paid to the issue of employing child labour. The initial campaigns of United Students Against Sweatshops (USAS) in the United States (US) were against the use of child labour by brands in their value chains. In India, there was a considerable uproar when garments with the GAP label were found to be worked on by child labourers.

In the aftermath of this, there have been moves to reduce child labour by reducing homeworking itself. Much of this focused on mechanizing handworked materials, for instance, through the use of multi-head machines to carry out embroidery. Where the work required was somewhat complex, the work was often brought within the factory premises (Nathan and Juneja 2018).

Following the GAP exposure, an attempt was made to reorganize homeworking by providing work in monitored community centres (Tewari 2016). This is similar to the shift in the workplace from the home to community centres in football-stitching in Pakistan (Lund-Thomsen et al. 2012), but the Mewat experiment, which also involved community centres, was not continued. Brands preferred to push for a shift to factory-based work or to shift to distant locations, such as Bareilly in the state of Uttar Pradesh. Shifting to remote locations, with a lower presence of administration, can be cheaper than an investment in mechanization.

These measures, undertaken to protect the brands' reputational assets, have resulted in a reduction in the incidence of homework and, simultaneously, child labour in garment value chains across India. It is not that homework has been eliminated, but it has been reduced. Those who have been researching garment value chains, trade unions, as well as worker activists, all report that one does not see the kind of homeworking that used to be so ubiquitous a decade or so ago. What homework remains has become somewhat hidden, giving rise to the phenomenon of hidden homeworkers.

Conclusion

This chapter dealt with the household as a production site in garment GVCs. It includes homeworkers, a hidden workforce with a substantial proportion of women. Their piece-rate earnings are well below even minimum wages. This non-payment of a part of the cost of production of labour power is a constant feature of homeworkers in garment value chains. The low earnings of homeworkers have also been accompanied by a high incidence of child labour. Together, homeworkers and child labour extend the production system of garment value chains to the household, showing that it is necessary to count the household as a production site to understand wage subsidies in garment value chains.

ENVIRONMENT

9

Tiruppur

The Environmental Costs of Success

Introduction

In this chapter, we look at the utilization of environmental products and services, or ecosystem services, and the manner in which their costs are met within or externalized from the core garment global value chain (GVC) production system, resulting in subsidies. These ecosystem services include provisioning services, such as raw materials and water, besides other materials used in production, such as fuel, biogenic materials, plant protection, and medicinal materials. The garment GVC also uses regulating services, such as waste decomposition and air and water purification. These provisioning and regulating services are used both in garment production and in the production of raw cotton.

Ecosystem services are either secured through market-based exchanges or extracted by non-market appropriation. Market exchanges include the acquisition of fresh water through payment to local municipalities. This may be underpriced, in the sense that it does not cover the replacement cost of the fresh water. It may also be secured free, as in the extraction of groundwater by raw cotton cultivators. The result of such underpriced or non-priced appropriation is the overuse and depletion of a renewable, but exhaustible, resource.

The cost of ecosystem services also includes the use of water (in the form of a reservoir formed by a dam in the case of garment manufacture in Tiruppur) and land resources (in the case of raw cotton cultivation) for the dumping of waste generated in the production process. Garment factories, particularly through their dyeing and printing segments, produce sludge as waste while raw cotton agriculture produces degraded land with inorganic fertilizer and pesticide residues.

Environmental Subsidies

The manner in which ecosystem service subsidies are created may be partly through the market mechanism and partly through non-market mechanisms. Even in market mechanisms, there may be subsidies through underpricing. Non-market mechanisms of appropriation, as in the case of groundwater for the cultivation of cotton, are a clear case of subsidy. How do we decide that there is underpricing and thus a subsidy? Take the case of water for garment factories. We have to use some system of valuing ecosystem services from renewable natural assets. Non-renewable assets would pose a different problem and we do not go into that. There exist a number of systems for valuing ecosystem services, the most prominent of which are that of contingent valuation and of replacement cost.

Contingent valuation is based on the 'willingness to pay' and generally involves the use of user surveys. Such willingness to pay has also been used to assess whether consumers would pay a premium and, if so, how much of a premium, for ethically produced garments. Such contingent valuations have been made compulsory in the United States (US) after the Exxon Valdez oil spill in Alaska in 1989 (Buccholz and Rubbelke 2019). Contingent valuation does not include the cost of providing the ecosystem service. There are also objections to using the subjective willingness-to-pay system.

Another system is that of replacement cost, which would be the cost of replacing or producing the ecosystem service. It could also be the cost of restoring ecological functions. This is more appropriate as it gives a cost calculation, which can then be used to estimate the extent of the subsidy involved in the appropriation of the ecosystem service, whether of a market or non-market type. For instance, there is the reverse osmosis (RO) process of cleaning used water. The cost of such RO-cleaned water can be taken as the replacement cost of producing fresh water for garment factories. In fact, if such a price were adopted for fresh water, there would be an incentive for suppliers, as a group, to install RO cleaning equipment, since there would be economies of scale operating here. A similar method could be adopted in pricing clean soil. What would it cost to produce clean soil after it has been used for cotton cultivation? These are what may be called the full costs of providing clean water and clean soil. If they were integrated into garment GVCs, the prices of garments would reflect these costs. Their non-inclusion in prices becomes a subsidy to garment production where, as we know, the rents go to the brands or buyers.

Capitalist Globalization: Consequences for the Environment

In an earlier paper (Swaminathan 2014), we had located the adverse environmental fallout of the production process in Tiruppur within the framework of the 'treadmill of production' model developed by Schnaiberg (and as explicated in Gould, Pellow, and Schnaiberg 2003). The salient points of the model may be summarized thus: As a social scientist with a technical or scientific background, Schnaiberg tried to understand why US environmental conditions had declined so precipitously since World War II. No matter where he turned or what he read, the dominant narrative always seemed to start with the changes in economic production as the major determinant of the trajectory of ecosystem impacts. From Schnaiberg's perspective, it was production changes that caused environmental disruption.

Going further, the Schnaiberg production model emphasizes that the question of how much we are consuming (that is, growth), is rarely challenged, with the only change being in what we are consuming. Since most policymakers are generally aided by economists schooled into protecting consumerist approaches in the name of safeguarding consumer sovereignty, policies generally focus on expanding consumption and choices. This, apart from being an easy path to take, more often than not absolves both the industry and the state of responsibility for the host of problems that result from such indiscriminate expansion. Thus, production remains largely undisturbed through

- failing to challenge the fundamental structure of the industry in question and
- often blaming poor populations for not engaging in 'enlightened', 'responsible', and 'conscious' consumer practices (Gould, Pellow, and Schnaiberg 2003: 9–12).

More pertinent to the argument of this chapter is the observation by Schnaiberg (noted in Gould, Pellow, and Schnaiberg 2003) that the transnationalization of the economy, which we take to mean integration into GVCs, makes it necessary to include distributional politics in the pursuit of environmental objectives. Inequality, including unequal power relations in GVCs, provides the basis for environmental injustices and anti-ecological survival strategies, forcing producers onto the treadmill of ever-greater effort in the face of ever-diminishing social returns. As we hope to demonstrate through our case study, the manner in which production in the knitwear cluster of Tiruppur is currently organized to cater to the export market has left the Indian government with no manoeuvring capacity either to withdraw from the global market (and risk loss of earnings as well as employment) or to enforce a pattern of production compatible with sustainable environmental standards.

Schnaiberg's 'treadmill of production' has generated considerable discussion; of immense significance to our discussion is the phenomenon that Dean Curran (2017) calls the 'treadmill of consumption'. According to Curran, in contemporary capitalist economies, the 'treadmill of consumption' or what he has also theorized as the 'political economy of *positional* consumption' 'locks individuals into increasing their income and consumption levels merely to maintain their existing levels of social practices and the well-being generated from them' (2017: 28). Curran discusses three types of positional consumption, each of which is aimed at demonstrating how the increased incomes and wealth of some translate into patterns of consumption that others strive to attain in their struggle to effectively participate in social life. This struggle is further intensified by corporate strategies of planned obsolescence, which 'involves the strategy of increasing turnover and profits for corporations through reducing the duration of usability of existing products through a variety of different tactics, including continual cycles of changes in new products that diminish the functionality of previously adequate products and ceasing to support earlier versions of products' (Curran 2017: 39).

In their discussion of the 'global environmental injustice of fast fashion', Rachel Bick, Erika Halsey, and Christine C. Ekenga

> posit that negative externalities at each step of the fast fashion supply chain have created a global environmental justice dilemma. While fast fashion offers consumers an opportunity to buy more clothes for less, those who work in or live near textile manufacturing facilities bear a disproportionate burden of environmental health hazards. Furthermore, increased consumption patterns have also created millions of tons of textile waste in landfills and unregulated settings.... Extending the environmental justice framework to encompass the disproportionate impact experienced by those who produce and dispose of our clothing is essential to understanding the magnitude of global injustice perpetuated through the consumption of cheap clothing. In the context of Sustainable Development Goal (SDG) 12 which calls for sustainable consumption and production as part of national and sectoral plans, sustainable business practices, consumer behavior, and *the reduction and elimination of fast fashion should all be a target of global environmental justice advocates*. (2018: 2, emphasis added)

Several other scholars (for example, Sklair and Miller 2010) approach the theme of the internationalization of production from a different, but equally important, angle. They differentiate between generic globalization and capitalist globalization. The former, according to them, has emancipatory potential (such as in the case of the electronic and communication revolution); in the case of the latter, however, the emancipatory potential of generic globalization is transformed into opportunities for private profit. In discussing the manner in which transnational corporations attempt to appear socially responsible through their commitment to globally approved standards of production as well as through the institution of corporate social responsibility (CSR) programmes, Sklair and Miller point out how these standards are selective in nature and 'bulldozed through in countries that are part of global production chains' (2010: 473). Critiquing the actual practice of CSR as opposed to its received conceptual understanding, Sklair and Miller ask whether CSR under capitalist globalization is 'a sign of a more humane capitalism or a desperate attempt to resolve the contradictions of capitalist globalization?' (2010: 473). Even more trenchant is the following observation that succinctly sums up how the operation of CSR programmes have produced a twisted understanding of the meaning of sustainability to serve the purpose of capitalist globalization:

> … the concept of sustainable development in use here is one which is focused on the development of 'economic growth' and not on sustainability of economic activity. The concept of sustainable development has been captured by the corporations by changing its meaning from the sustainability of the planet to the sustainability of economic growth. The combination of the discourse of sustainable development with that of national and international competitiveness provides a powerful weapon for transnational business. (Sklair and Miller 2010: 490)

Tewari and Pillai (2005) discuss what they call a 'success story', involving the Indian leather industry, which has had to comply with stringent environmental requirements, namely the use of banned chemicals. Their key finding is that while compliance to environmental standards did add to firm costs, it did not adversely impact competitiveness. Their analysis describes in detail the crucial role played by the Indian state, particularly the Ministry of Commerce, to safeguard Indian export earnings. However, it is clear from the analysis that while Germany, the principal importer of Indian leather products, helped push the industry towards compliance both technically and financially, this compliance did not translate into higher prices for the products of the industry. Further, the intervention was undertaken to eliminate the use of banned substances in order to protect German consumers—the objective was not to eliminate or reduce other negative environmental effects around the producing units in India. The intervention by the Indian state notwithstanding, the environmental costs continue to be borne solely by India and the Indian people.

De Neve's (2009) study of the Tiruppur garment cluster demonstrates concretely how the logic of CSR, as practised by Western buyers, has reorganized production so that 'cheap' but quality garments are made possible by subcontracting the phenomenon of non-compliance of standards itself to producers down the line who the Western buyers do not transact with directly. There is a transferring of costs down the line. The result of such unethical behaviour on the part of the Western buyers and consumers is that larger exporters, in their anxiety to demonstrate that their production processes comply with buyer-driven norms, evade compliance by 'devolving' responsibility onto subcontractors by making the latter sign a form. As de Neve points out:

> The crucial point about this form is that it devolves responsibility—and hence risk—for compliance down to the subcontractor. By signing the form and stating that they comply with the codes or standards, it becomes the subcontractors' own responsibility to ensure compliance. In case a subcontractor is inspected by a buyer representative or a social auditor and a violation of regulations is found, it is the subcontractor who will be held responsible and not the exporter, as the latter will be able to refer to the signed form as proof that he was dealing with a compliant subcontractor. (2009: 70)

Thus, apart from reproducing inequalities at the global and local level in the name of compliance with codes and standards, 'the politics of compliance contributes to the consolidation of the power of standard-setting actors by facilitating the devolution of risk, uncertainty and responsibility to the weaker "partners" in the chain' (de Neve 2009: 71).

Scholars have also explored how buyers from the Global North can be made accountable in their home countries for the violations of their subsidiaries and subcontractors located in the countries they source their products from. For instance, Flynn and O'Brien have elaborately discussed the options that could be fruitfully deployed to bring to book some of these transnational corporations despite the fact that these larger-than-state establishments will attempt to not only sabotage every such move but also 'structure their transactions and affairs in such a manner so as to avoid a jurisdiction altogether, with a concomitant effect of lessening investment and commercial activity in that jurisdiction and consequent economic repercussions that flow from that loss of economic activity' (2010: 193).

In the light of this discussion, what this chapter attempts is to discuss how the silencing of the 'costs' of production, particularly environmental, produces a scenario wherein emerging economies end up subsidizing importers and importing nations while also benefitting the consumers located in importing countries, at the cost of workers and the environment in the manufacturing countries. The particular manner in which such production for the global market is organized and the specific way in which international retailing operates ensures that often the buying countries and consumers, who otherwise cry hoarse about the need to be ethical, somehow absolve themselves of any responsibility for the damage that their demand for quality but cheap products causes to the environment and/or health of workers in the producing countries. The governments in producer countries, vying not only to maintain but also expand the production base in their countries so as to maintain the flow of much needed foreign exchange earnings, most often take the easy way out by capitulating to the demands of the producers through lax or almost nil implementation of existing labour and environmental laws.

The rest of the chapter is organized as follows: using the export-oriented cotton knitwear cluster of Tiruppur in south India as an example, we demonstrate how the industry has had to consistently reinvent itself to cater to the ever-changing demands of the global market just to stay afloat. The heavy toll in terms of damage to the river and groundwater that this production has caused, with severe consequences for the livelihoods of those dependent on agriculture and cattle rearing in that area, is the special focus of our discussion. We also discuss the attempts made by governments at different levels—local, regional, and national—to address the environmental issues. At the national level, the issue has always been and still continues to be informed by the perspective that the problem is a local one. We dwell at length on the role of one of our authors as a member of a committee appointed by the High Court of Madras to suggest measures to contain the pollution of the Noyyal River by the discharge of untreated trade effluents by dyeing and bleaching (D&B) units.

Thereafter, we reflect on the specific concerns that our case study has thrown up. While buyers may raise concerns about inadequate attention to labour and environmental standards and even point fingers at the producers, in particular, and the authorities, in general, about agreed norms being violated, our reflection demonstrates how, on the ground, the problem was largely seen as one that was produced locally and which therefore needed to be resolved locally. In other words, members of the committee became a party to the complicity that almost totally absolved buyers from being made partly, if not equally, responsible for falling labour and environmental standards in response to progressive reductions in lead production time and in refusing to demand that environmental costs be factored into the pricing of the products.

Tiruppur: From an Industrial District in the Making to an Environmental Disaster

In a joint paper published in 1994 and another one in 1999, we (Swaminathan and Jeyaranjan) attempted to problematize the varied experience and phases of Tiruppur's transition from an obscure hamlet into India's premier cotton-knitting manufacturing centre. We attributed Tiruppur's phenomenal growth to the dense and complex network linking together its (then) '2500 knitting and manufacturing units, 600 processing units, 300 printing units and 100 embroidery units' (Swaminathan and Jeyaranjan 1994: 1) into an industrial district. Though developed conceptually in the context of more developed countries to capture the characteristics and functioning of particular areas, we found then that the principles of organization that characterize the industrial district model could very usefully be applied in the context of Tiruppur. Tiruppur started catering to the export market from 1980 onwards, and that was also when the industry began to grow.

The spatial and sectorally specialized clustering of firms in Tiruppur allowed the firms to enjoy economies of scale at the level of one or a few machines not just whole factories. Production efficiency was achieved by rapid responses to market needs based on a flexible organizational structure and substantial subcontracting to other small firms to allow the specialization and maximum use of the existing plant and equipment. These strategies increased rather than decreased inter-firm dependency.

While the papers mentioned earlier concentrated mainly on capturing the dynamics of production organization within Tiruppur, and on how Tiruppur was not merely a cluster of firms but 'an Industrial District in the making' (Swaminathan and Jeyaranjan 1994: 13), there was then no engagement whatsoever with the environmental issues that had begun to surface as a consequence of the indiscriminate emphasis on increasing output and foreign exchange earnings through exports. Between 2005 and 2012, as a member of the committee appointed by the Madras High Court to examine and suggest measures to resolve the pollution of the Noyyal River (flowing through Tiruppur) that had occurred due to the indiscriminate discharge—predominantly by the D&B units of Tiruppur—of pollutants into the river, one of the authors had the occasion to study (for more details, see Swaminathan 2014) first-hand the nature of the environmental issues that became increasingly visible. A brief discussion of the nature of the problem is in order and will cover the following:

- the nature of the damage that the growing industry has caused to the Noyyal River flowing through the town,
- the consequences of river water pollution for agriculture and the livelihoods of farmers in the area,
- a discussion of the steps taken to address pollution as a consequence of the intervention by the judiciary in the matter.

Genesis of State Intervention through the Judiciary

What drove the High Court of Madras to constitute an expert committee to address the pollution problem afflicting the Noyyal River in Tamil Nadu? It would be pertinent to refer readers to a succinct account of the trajectory that forced the High Court of Madras towards such a step, namely a High Court Order dated 22 December 2006 wherein the Chief Justice Mr A. P. Shah and Justice Mr K Chandru referred, among other things, to the genesis of the problem, the several attempts made by aggrieved parties to get the state of Tamil Nadu to find a resolution to the problem including through legal measures, and the failure of the state to enforce its own pollution laws and/or court orders—all of which led to the court having to step in again to direct the state to implement its orders.

Beginning in the 1980s and more rapidly during the 1990s, the Noyyal basin area witnessed rapid but haphazard industrialization, particularly in the emergence of knitwear garment manufacturing in and around Tiruppur. The expansion of the hosiery industry led to the concomitant growth of D&B units to serve the industry. The unabated, heavy, and constant discharge of untreated, raw trade effluents into the Noyyal River and the gradual accumulation of pollutants in the Orathapalayam Dam (a dam built to store the Noyyal River water for irrigation) adversely affected not only agricultural operations but also severely contaminated the groundwater and impaired the health of the cattle that drank the polluted river water. This dam, which was completed in 1992, was able to service the agricultural sector through irrigation for an extremely short period of time, that is, only through the years 1992–1993 to 1995–1996.

Struggles by Farmers' Associations: Entry of Courts

Aggrieved by the total failure of the state of Tamil Nadu, represented by the Pollution Control Board (PCB) to check pollution, farmers' associations began approaching the courts to direct the PCB to take action against the polluting D&B units. In response to a writ petition that was filed by an association in 1996, an interim order was passed on 6 March 1997, by which the court ordered the PCB, among other things, to close 114 units and to ensure that these units did not operate until they had installed devices to prevent pollution and obtained the consent of the PCB. The order also required that Common Effluent Treatment Plants (CETPs) should be constructed before 10 June 1997. The affected parties filed a Joint Memo on 11 February 1998 containing an agreement arrived at among the parties which specifically provided in Clause 5 that

> the bleaching and dyeing units agreed to contribute such amount as may be decided by the court as and when this Court decides the liability of all the polluting units in the upstream of Bhavani river, for the purpose of undoing the damage caused by pollution and especially with regard to the cleaning up of Orathapalayam dam.[1]

After recording the agreement as per the Joint Memo, the court passed final orders on 26 February 1998, stating that '... The PCB will be at liberty to open the units covered by the memo for three months.... If they fail to obtain consent within three months, the PCB is directed to implement the Pollution Control and Environmental Laws forthwith. No further extension will be granted in any eventuality'.[2]

Despite the final order passed on the Joint Memo filed by the parties, no steps were taken to implement the order and no efforts were made to get the units to install the necessary equipment and machinery to clean the polluted river water stored in the Orathapalayam Dam. Nor did the association of the D&B units (to whom the PCB had issued a letter dated 14 August 2003 estimating that cleaning up the Orathapalayam Dam would run up costs to the tune of INR 12.50 crores) comply with the PCB's letter of 14 August 2003. The farmers' associations approached the high court again in 2003 seeking the enforcement of the Joint Memo dated 11 February 1998. By the order dated 5 May 2005, the court appointed an expert committee which was directed

> to go into all the terms of reference … and then make an interim report by giving the ways and means to clean the stored water and release the treated water in the river, and for removing the sludge that has formed in the dam area, without delay, and also to suggest an immediate action plan for remediation of the Noyyal river and for preventing the discharge of polluted trade effluents into the Noyyal river.[3]

Illustrative List of Some Crucial, as Yet Unresolved Tasks

The scale and magnitude of the fallout of the pollution caused to the Noyyal River can be gauged to some extent from the following tasks that were entrusted to the committee appointed by the high court for its immediate action.

Sludge Disposal

In the course of its attempts to address the various Terms of Reference (TOR) suggested to it by the court, the committee had to decide on how it would, in particular, contend with TOR (iii) that required the committee to 'suggest ways and means for de-silting or removing the sludge that has formed in the dam area'.[4] The Public Works Department (PWD) informed the committee that the quantity deposited in the dam assessed by the Hydrology Wing of the PWD using the sounding method was of the order of 770,000 cubic metres. This quantity included both the silt brought by the runoff from the catchment areas of the Noyyal River and the solid waste and sediments carried through by the effluents from industrial units. It was realized that it would be very difficult to segregate the individual quantity of silt and solid waste as they would be deposited at random one over the other (and hence mixed) over the water-spread area of 425 hectares since the date of commissioning of the dam in 1992. The committee zeroed in on two options:

- to empty the reservoir, wait for some time for the bed to get dry, and then remove the silt using machinery or
- retain the water in the reservoir itself but remove the silt by using floating dredgers.

What finally clinched the decision in favour of depleting the polluted water in the dam were pleas from farmers and their associations, who wanted the dam emptied of polluted water at the earliest because of its adverse impact on groundwater. The stored water (that was not allowed to flow because of an earlier stay obtained by the farmers) was increasingly seeping into the ground and affecting the groundwater. The committee also realized that the longer the water was stored, the further and more pervasive would be the damage to the groundwater given the topography of the area; the river course is incised and the bottom is a rocky bed. In such conditions, flowing water drains quickly without seeping into the ground while stagnant water finds entry into the ground through the sides and affects the groundwater. This was observed in the tests undertaken during a field inspection by the committee. Also, the livelihoods of farmers dependent on wells for irrigation had been ruined because of groundwater pollution and compounded further by the scarcity of drinking water for people as well as livestock. In September 2005, the dam was rid of its polluted water in phases after the necessary precautions were put in place all along the course of the flow of the water into the Cauvery River. Thereafter, a baby channel was excavated in the dam along the old river course to lead both runoff water and effluent water to the river sluice. From 2005 to date, the river sluice has been kept open since permanent remedial measures have not yet been put in place to deal with the effluent discharge. A few farmers put up a plea that the dam needed to be decommissioned; that the river sluice gates needed to be kept open all the time to allow the water to flow down as though no dam is in existence. This arose from the fact that, as expressed by the farmers, 'a dam constructed for helping agriculture, had become a storage pond for polluters'.[5] Right from its 1st interim report submitted to the court on 20 May 2005, the committee had expressed its concern regarding the huge quantum and continued dumping of solid waste into the river by industrial units. Despite repeated assurances and the fact that the PCB considered the sludge and solid waste to be 'hazardous', the PCB had not and still has not been able to find a place to deposit the removed sludge and solid waste generated by the industrial units. Thus, the inability of the authorities to address the problem of unscientific solid waste disposal by industry in Tirupur adds to the problem of the pollution of the Noyyal River.

The storing of solid waste by the units on their premises and the dumping of waste in the river system itself continues unabated. The packaging in which the materials are stored has been observed to wilt in harsh weather conditions, rendering the storage mechanism ineffective. This solid waste is a potential environmental hazard and finds its way into the river whenever there is heavy rainfall. The executive engineer of the Environment Cell Division has already carried out studies and suggested making solid cement blocks using this solid waste. But further studies on the toxicity of the waste and its consequent effect on human contact have not yet been carried out.

The poor treatment of waste thus had five interconnected effects: (*a*) the river water itself was polluted, (*b*) the groundwater was contaminated, (c) the drinking water became scarce, (*d*) the dam built for irrigation turned into a storage lake for waste, destroying its irrigation function, and (*e*) the sludge from the water treatment was stored around the cluster.

Installation of Measuring Devices

The committee was also constrained to note that there were no measuring devices installed at the outlets to measure the quantity of effluents flowing into the river. In a sense, therefore, the PCB, the one arm of the government in charge of safeguarding the environment of the state, had no clue whatsoever as to what and how much treated or untreated material was being discharged into the river.

During its field visit in January 2007, the committee observed that the baby channel was running full and that some water was also flowing into the river. The committee directed the executive engineer to install a flow-measuring device at the check dam diverting water to the baby channel to measure the quantity flowing into the river. The committee wanted the flow in the baby channel to be measured at the fifth notch nearer to the dam; in this connection, it directed the executive engineer to purchase forthwith a total dissolved solids (TDS) measuring meter and to record the discharge and TDS four times daily including at night.[6]

On 8 April 2007, the committee inspected the dam and observed that the water-spread area was almost dry. The flow in the river had been diverted completely through the baby channel. The discharge at the time of inspection was 46 cusecs.[7]

Mandating Zero Liquid Discharge by Industrial Units

Among the TORs given to the committee, TOR (vi) specifically wanted the committee to suggest ways and means for preventing the discharge of polluted trade effluents either directly or indirectly into the Noyyal River by the cluster of industrial units in and around Tiruppur.

Based on wide-ranging discussions with personnel from the industry, government, farmers, and others affected by the pollution, the committee urged that the following measures be considered for implementation immediately:

- zero liquid discharge (ZLD) into the river by the polluting units,
- industrial units to commence installation of treatment plants towards zero discharge levels on a war footing,
- the Pollution Control Board and other concerned government departments to play a proactive facilitator role to implement zero discharge by industrial units and to encourage completion of the CETP,
- industrial units be directed to produce concrete evidence of having commenced installation of facilities for zero discharge within a period of three months,
- an independent monitoring unit appointed by the court be asked to review and report on the progress made by the industrial units and other bodies once in three months to the court and, based on the progress, advise stakeholders accordingly.

Subsequent reports filed before the high court documented the processes adopted, the progress achieved, as well as the setbacks encountered by the committee in operationalizing the mandate of getting D&B units to achieve ZLD, which the committee had recommended in its very first report and had been accepted by the court through its orders, most comprehensively stated in the high court's order dated 22 December 2006. The different reports of the committee, each of which was the product of a field visit undertaken by all or several members of the committee, highlighted several issues that provided insights into why the process of achieving ZLD has eluded the industry thus far.

The 19th Interim Report submitted by the committee to the high court after its visit to the Noyyal basin site from 1 to 3 October 2011 provides the committee's review of the situation on the ground consequent to the submission of 18 Interim Reports to the court between 2005 and 2011, each of which not only contained details of the committee's field visits but also sought specific directions from the court for the problems identified by the committee as contributing to the pollution of the Noyyal River.

This review report submitted to the High Court of Madras highlighted the continuing damage being caused to the river mainly because of procrastination on the part of the state (both at the state government level and the central government level), in operationalizing its own rules and regulations concerning pollution norms, compounded with an inability to act even when directed by the high court. It underscored the express need for an institutional architecture that would not only bring together various stakeholders, including the relevant departments and wings of the state, to address the various components constituting the problem of pollution but more importantly, it stressed the imperative need to invest the institution with the necessary authority structure to continuously monitor and take action as and when required. This was in line with an important 2004 ruling of the apex court of the country (reasserted in 2009) in *M. C. Mehta v. Union of India*, AIR 2004 SC 4016, in which it was asserted that the protection of the environment would take precedence over economic interest. The relevant section of the ruling is quoted below:

> Development and the protection of the environment are not enemies. If without degrading the environment or minimising adverse effects thereupon by applying stringent safeguards, it is possible to carry on development activity applying the principles of sustainable development, in that eventuality the development has to go on because one cannot lose sight of the need for development of industries, irrigation resources and power projects etc, including the need to improve employment opportunities and the generation of revenue. A balance has to be struck.... If an activity is allowed to go ahead, there may be irreparable damage to the environment and if it is stopped, there may be irreparable damage to economic interest. Precautionary principle requires anticipatory action to be taken to prevent harm. The harm can be prevented even on a reasonable suspicion. It is not always necessary that there should be direct evidence of harm to environment".... The appellate authority has, in fact, considered all these aspects threadbare and held that, if the PCB insists for zero discharge system, it has power to do so and in such circumstances, it is not for this Court to interfere since pollution free India is the present Constitutional goal, as it deals with the right to life of its citizens.[8]

It is clear from this ruling that the entire judicial discourse on this matter as well as the high court–appointed committee's deliberations regarded the issue as one to be resolved locally with support from the state. The TOR for the committee's functioning did not include, and neither did the committee deem it essential, to seek state support to negotiate with buyers for higher prices for the products to compensate for the cost involved in containing pollution, which could have gone some way towards instituting mechanisms aimed at meeting environmental standards.

The Perspectives of Major Stakeholders

Farmers, and their associations, because of whose struggle the issue of pollution of the Noyyal River reached the courts, continue to maintain that the state has let them down by not monitoring the knitwear industry. To reproduce a couple of observations of farmers in their own words:

> As [the industries] earn foreign exchange the stakes are high and the industrialists tend to ignore norms; they also do not operate the treatment plants at night. Who is to monitor this? Do not give water from the New Tiruppur Scheme if [the industries] do not adopt reverse osmosis (RO) process and attain zero discharge. The TNPCB [Tamil Nadu Pollution Control Board] has failed in its duty of preventing setting up of new industries within 5 km from the river. (Remarks made by the president of a farmers' association to the expert committee at a stakeholders' meeting)

> When the dam was built in 1992, it was hoped that it would irrigate and provide water to the surrounding areas. However, because of pollution, 20,500 acres of land have degraded and people of almost twenty villages are affected. Availability of drinking water is a major problem in all these villages; people are forced to fetch water from far off villages. The people are aware that polluted water flowing in the river may not affect the groundwater due to incision and the rocky bed, but stagnant water in the dam has adversely affected groundwater and the wells. When earlier, the farms yielded paddy, sugarcane, banana and turmeric, there is very little cultivation activity now. The question that keeps recurring is: when new technologies and equipments have been introduced by the dyeing industries, why don't these industries introduce new and cleaner production processes? (remarks made by the president of a farmers' association)

The farmers used the adage: 'buying a picture by selling one's eyes' to describe the operation of the industrial units in Tiruppur. According to them, long-staple cotton from Egypt is sent to Tiruppur for D&B so as to protect the Nile River from pollution. European countries have all the technical know-how but do not undertake dyeing and processing in their own lands and rather get it done from developing countries so that their countries do not have to deal with the pollution that such processes cause. According to many farmers, the treatment of effluents was past being remedied and the only solution would be to close the dyeing units and stop exporting garments.

Members of several other farmers' associations repeatedly elaborated on the nature of the adverse impact on agriculture, livestock, and labourers because of groundwater pollution in the vicinity of the dam. According to them, coconut trees had withered, a phenomenon observed by the expert committee as well; further, they reasoned that while drinking water for humans could be procured from elsewhere, cattle tend to drink the polluted water, which, according to the farmers, has resulted in infertility and reduced fertility among them. The specific kinds of health problems identified among humans included hair loss, cancer, and joint pains. Another visible indicator of the growing health problems because of water and environmental pollution, according to the farmers, was the phenomenal increase in the number of doctors, clinics, and speciality hospitals in the district.

The Government of India's Loss of Ecology Authority (LEA) estimated the cost of pollution damage to agriculture to be a little over INR 248 million in the year 2004. Environmental economist L. Venkatachalam (2015) found this estimate to be low, just one-fifth of the damage using the replacement cost method. The replacement cost method included compensation to affected farmers, the cost of cleaning up the river, and restoring the ecology of the river system. This, however, was a very limited estimate of the damage caused by pollution due to the Tiruppur garment industry: 'Due to lack of available data, estimating the total economic damage caused to all the sectors—households, animal husbandry, industry, tourism and biodiversity—could not be carried out' (Venkatachalam 2015: 168).

An important department of the state government directly mandated to deal with issues of the environment in general and pollution, in particular, is the TNPCB. It is significant that, very early on, the committee realized that the TNPCB was part of the problem, given its inability even to answer the basic question of what role it had played in addressing the problem of the D&B units polluting the river, how it perceived the problem, and what information, if any, it had with it regarding the industry, the level of pollution, and the environment in general. Most farmers were critical of the TNPCB and asserted that the continuing issue is not for want of powers of the TNPCB but because of the inability of the latter to function in an effective manner.

Industry representatives were keen on making the committee recognize the importance of D&B to the hosiery industry, the importance of Tiruppur in the global export garment market, and the need for the government to step in so that competition from countries, such as China, can be confronted. They admitted that pollution is a problem; in fact, the president of the Dyers' Association of Tiruppur made a plea for a government subsidy of 50 per cent (25 per cent each from the provincial and central governments) towards installing effluent treatment plants to achieve zero discharge norms. A former member of the legislative assembly (MLA) and also a representative of the Centre of Indian Trade Unions (CITU) deposing before the committee stated that the livelihoods of almost 6 lakh workers were directly dependent on the textile industries of Tiruppur while another 1.5 lakh people depended on it indirectly. Hence, according to him, the government should build the treatment plants and recover the cost from the industry.

Environmental Action as Maintaining Legitimacy

In 2014 (Swaminathan 2014: 236), we interpreted the constitution of the TNPCB, and its mandate to 'regulate' the environment through a 'command

and control' policy (that involves setting air and water quality standards, emission and discharge limits, and so forth) as an acknowledgement that an 'environment' problem exists, that the present system is not sustainable and that change is needed. Nevertheless, through the exercise of being a member of the expert committee, it is apparent that the rhetoric has not yet translated into action that is commensurate with the nature and scale of the problem. We concurred with Handmer and Dovers who pointed out that '[m]any responses to environmental change, and much else besides, are shaped by what is perceived to be politically and economically palatable in the near term rather than by the nature and scale of the threat itself' (1996: 501). In fact, 'from the perspective of global survival, the thrust of these changes—as distinct from the rhetoric—may be further entrenching unsustainable practice. Yet the minor adjustments and policy statements may give the appearance that the problem is being addressed properly' (1996: 504).

At another level, we also noted (Swaminathan 2014: 237) that the state's actions in constituting an expert committee and authorizing the latter to seek redressal of the problem directly from the court, could be explained by what Davidson and Frickel describe as 'efforts of state actors to maintain legitimacy among a given set of civil society actors' (2004: 487). However, and as our description of the committee's work has revealed, the preoccupation by nation-states to respond only to concerns of legitimacy has resulted in a situation where

> nation-state environmental activity will continue to be characterized by incremental, incoherent, and at times directly conflicting political actions that are more often designed to appease political interest groups rather than address environmental degradation and have the potential to become dominated by corporate interests based on this group's ability to co-opt environmental discourse to its own advantage. (Davidson and Frickel 2004: 487)

A similar view is echoed by Eric Bonds in his discussion of 'environmental reviews' undertaken by states ostensibly to 'bring about a more harmonious relationship with nature through better environmental and social accounting' (Bonds 2007: 159). While Bonds accepts that

> the very logic of such reviews biases them from the start in favour of economic interests because they overemphasize the economic benefits of development, underestimate environment costs, and do not consider the distribution of costs and benefits—or how the wealth produced by a venture may be enjoyed by one group of people while the pollution is borne by another. (2007: 159)

He also firmly believes that 'citizens can exercise power over owners and managers of capital in environmental reviews, for instance by producing a crisis of legitimacy or by waging a war of atrophy' (2007: 172).

The agitation by the farmers indeed created a crisis of legitimacy for the provincial government of Tamil Nadu, forcing it to 'act', which it did by setting up an expert committee. In hindsight, we realize that the committee's work can be characterized as environment management, which sought to find a harmony between economic and environmental interests even while furthering private corporate interests (for more details on what constitutes environment management and its implications, see Levy 1997). The committee worked towards mitigating adverse environmental effects of growth without questioning the goal of increased production and consumption. The set of measures put in place by the committee were aimed largely to deflect attention away from demands for more radical changes that would seriously challenge capitalism's hegemony. In this sense, what the committee's work ensured was political rather than environmental sustainability.

Going back to the different ways in which buyers and consumers (located predominantly in the Global North) have eschewed any responsibility for why environmental standards are what they are in producer countries, even while demanding adherence to ethical standards of production, we admit that our entire effort as a committee, to contain the pollution problem caused by the expanding garment cluster in Tiruppur, at no point addressed the buyers in particular as a constituency mainly or even at all responsible for the environmental damage by their acts of omission and commission. While attempts were made (howsoever inadequate) to estimate the different kinds of local losses, the remedial suggestions of the committee neither mentioned the need to negotiate higher value realization from global brands to reflect on the cost of pollution nor did it include ways and means by which the Indian state could have been compelled to highlight, at various international fora, the link between Tiruppur-like situations and unsustainable consumption patterns emanating largely from the Global North, resulting in unsustainable and environmentally damaging patterns of GVC production in supplier countries located largely in the South.

Box 9.1, based on a study in 2019 of the water-stressed Noyyal–Bhavani basin, gives an idea of the key challenges that continue to plague the region while also emphasizing the fact that those who are part of the chain but far removed from it, up to the end-user, remain insulated from the adverse impact that the manufacture of garments continues to have on the lives, livelihood, and the environment of the region.

Box 9.1 Key Issues Related to Water Quality in the Noyyal–Bhavani River Basin

The problem of water pollution in the Noyyal–Bhavani basin is complex and multidimensional. Four key issues related to water quality management emerged as important from key informant interviews.

Incomplete Monitoring of Zero Liquid Discharge

One of the biggest successes from the law suits in the Noyyal sub-basin was the implementation of ZLD. Unfortunately, in the absence of long-term water quality data, we were unable to conclusively assess if ZLD has made a difference. From key informant interviews, it appears that larger units have been able to invest in improved technologies and comply. But anecdotal evidence points to continuing illegal night-time discharges of effluents into sewers by smaller units. Furthermore, many units have simply relocated to outside the basin, sometimes just to neighbouring districts.

Illegal Discharges to Groundwater

One concern that emerged from interviews and field observations was that textile units might have begun injecting effluents into groundwater. The elevated EC levels in groundwater in the Tiruppur district, corroborate this. However, in the absence of systematic plume mapping, it is virtually impossible to understand the extent of such violations.

Inadequate Planning or Enforcement of Textile Sludge Disposal

The implementation of ZLD technology in the textile wet-processing units is anecdotally reported to result in reuse of treated wastewater up to 85–90 per cent with freshwater only required as make-up water. The ZLD process also generates textile sludge that is hazardous in nature and requires safe handling and management. Initially, the textile sludge was required to be stored at the textile units. Later, the dry sludge was permitted to be sent for use as fuel in the cement industry.... It is reported that earlier textile sludge was also being disposed on land ...

Costs of Upgradation

The upgradation of effluent treatment technology including ZLD and associated processes involves large capital investments. As the textile D&B facilities in the Noyyal–Bhavani basin are small-scale units, they lack the ability to invest in expensive treatment processes. Further, given the competitive nature of the global textile market, they are under constant pressure to reduce their costs of production. Further, based on the estimation of the LOEA, the compensation to be paid to downstream pollution-affected farmers was collected by the textile units.

In this context, CETPs were setup with financial support from the Tamil Nadu state government for collective treatment and management of effluents from the small textile wet-processing units. At present, there are 18 textile CETPs in the basin.

However, the twin pressures of adhering to adequate effluent treatment as well as competing in the global textile market is borne entirely by the small and medium textile wet-processing units in the basin. The textile supply chain up to the end consumer is largely insulated from the externalities involved in the manufacture of textiles on the environment, health and livelihoods of people residing in the river basin.

Source: ATREE (2019: 41–42).

Notes

1. High Court of Madras, Final Orders on Writ petition No. 1649 of 1996, passed on 26 February 1998, Chennai, p. 3.
2. High Court of Madras, Final Orders on Writ petition No. 1649 of 1996, passed on 26 February 1998, Chennai, p. 3.
3. High Court of Madras, 'The Interim Report of the Expert Committee Constituted by the Honourable High Court of Madras to Go Into the Questions Formulated in Matters relating to Pollution Problems in Noyyal River', Chennai, 2003, p. 3.
4. High Court of Madras, 'The Interim Report of the Expert Committee Constituted by the Honourable High Court of Madras to Go Into the Questions Formulated in Matters relating to Pollution Problems in Noyyal River', Chennai, 2003, p. 9.
5. High Court of Madras, '3rd Interim Report of the Expert Committee Appointed by Madras Court to Address Pollution in the Noyyal River', Chennai, August 2005, p. 7
6. High Court of Madras, '12th Interim Report of the Expert Committee constituted to address pollution in the Noyyal River', Chennai, January 2007.
7. High Court of Madras, '13th Interim Report of the Expert Committee constituted to address pollution in the Noyyal River', Chennai, April 2007.
8. Supreme Court of India, M C Mehta v. Union of India, AIR 2004 SC 4016, point No. 48, pp. 44–45, Delhi, available at www.ielrc.org/content/e0409.pdf, accessed 4 October 2021.

10
Externalized Costs of Cotton Production

The upstream of agribusiness, which involves how raw materials are procured or where production takes place, is becoming increasingly important due to issues of social and environmental justice, as against downstream agribusiness, which relates to the purchase, use, and consumption of products as part of the product value chain (Schrempf-Stirling, Palazzo and Phillips 2013). It is not just market failures that lead to externalities—which can, therefore, be attended to with market-based systems—but it is also the 'cost shifting' that acts as an externality on those who are either smaller players in the chain or non-participants (Martinez-Alier et al. 2016: 732). Further, agribusiness companies working with primary producers (farmers) are driven solely by the profit motive at most times and tend to ignore the social dimensions of their operations (S. Singh 2016). Examples of such behaviour include abandoning an area if it is found to be unprofitable to continue; excluding small and marginal growers from their operations; and following the practice of 'agribusiness normalization', in which lower prices are offered to producers over time or prices are not raised adequately to cut down costs of procurement (Glover and Kustrer 1990: 63).

Most environmental regulations do not help in enhancing revenue; they typically increase cost and reduce the capacity of businesses to generate cash flow (Boehlje, Akridge and Downey 1995). Engaging in social responsibility is considered the key challenge for global sourcing companies and their suppliers in the developing world though it is more challenging to meet regulations. Even more problematic is the belief that if suppliers from a developing country comply with codes of conduct (CoC), it will improve the workers' conditions and reduce environmental pollution; that is not necessarily the case as the objective conditions prevailing locally are different, for example, overtime and child labour, which are difficult to deal with. More importantly, believing that exclusion of non-complying suppliers is an effective way of securing compliance with codes or standards and, in turn, of improving the conditions of producers or workers and the environment is misplaced as such actions only harm by downgrading such producers or workers (Lund-Thomsen 2008).

Achieving environmental sustainability or upgrading, along with economic and social sustainability, is a part of the 'triple bottom line' or three Ps (profits, people, and planet) of corporate entities (Sindhi and Kumar 2012; Campling and Havice 2019). Corporate entities attempt self-regulation on environmental and social issues due to market-based rationale and incentives, such as risk management, pressure from investors and/or consumers and activists, pressure to retain and attract employees (Graham and Woods 2006), and to create and retain competitive advantage (Campling and Havice 2019). But, this happens only when markets have extensive information about corporate activities, which is often not the case. This creates a scope for governmental intervention in order to make self-regulation effective by placing mandatory provisions (Graham and Woods 2006). Also, implementing proactive environmental strategies can be profitable, and sustainable ways to deal with the natural environment (Aragon-Correa and Rubio-Lopez 2007) and environmental management improves market-related and image-related drivers of economic performance if integrated with other managerial functions (Wagner 2007).

Globally, there are many multi-stakeholder initiatives (MSIs) dealing with sustainability issues in agriculture, such as Better Cotton (BCI), Better Sugarcane, fair trade, Organic Production and Trade, Common Code for the Coffee Community (4C), Rainforest Alliance, Social Accountability International (SAI 8000), and the Ethical Trading Initiative (ETI, UK), which aim at building and mainstreaming sustainability models beyond corporate social responsibility (CSR) (S. Singh 2016). Tackling sustainability issues is more like a strategic CSR which proactively seeks to incorporate larger, chain-wide concerns into a business strategy to address them and create a shared value (Ross, Pandey, and Ross 2015; S. Singh 2016).

At another level, when global trade is neither free nor fair, it becomes important to examine the implications of such trade in terms of social and environmental justice. For example, subsidies for cotton farmers in the United States (US) makes cotton producers and exporters produce and export cotton from the US at prices that do not reflect the realistic cost of production and, therefore, depress global market prices; this, in turn, means that cotton producers from developing countries are not able to compete with their counterparts in the US. The beneficiaries of such subsidies are not necessarily the US cotton farmers but the local cotton and readymade garment brands. They get access to subsidized raw material but do not always pass on the low-cost raw cotton benefit to the value chain partners and consumers. Besides this, domestic production subsidies also depress cotton prices because these do not reflect the real cost of production of raw cotton. It is in this context that the issue of production subsidies in cotton needs to be examined from a social justice perspective as it is public resources that are deployed to support such subsidies. Further, there are subsidies offered on various farm inputs, which have implications for natural resources and their use, including depletion. For instance, free electric power supply to cotton farmers in India for accessing groundwater leads to the depletion of that resource. This cost then does not become a part of the calculation of the Minimum Support Price (MSP) for cotton. Similarly, subsidies on other farm inputs, such as fertilizers and pesticides, also lead to excessive use of such inputs, leading to social and environmental subsidies and externalities, such as poor health and well-being, and, therefore, make a supply chain socially and environmentally unfair. Even MSP protection provided to farmers in India may be seen as a subsidy as it sustains cotton production at a price not supported by the open market, thus leading to overproduction (which would not happen if market prices were to prevail).

This chapter re-examines the raw cotton production sector from a justice perspective, incorporating various dimensions of injustice ranging from state subsidies in competing countries, such as the US, and within India, to the lack of regulatory and social protection measures that make cotton production and its harvesting a loss-making proposition for farmers and farm workers.

This chapter focuses on two aspects of cotton production, various policies around it, such as fiscal subsidies, and the environmental damage caused due to raw cotton production as a part of the environmental justice domain. The second section briefly profiles and examines the context of cotton production in India. The third section looks at the environmental externalities in the growing of cotton and the burden they create on farmers and workers. It takes stock of the magnitude and nature of environmental subsidies and externalities in cotton as a crop and a commodity in India's overall as well as farm economy. It also assesses the sustainability aspects of the cotton regime for the local resource base. Finally, the fourth section examines the state of social and environmental justice in terms of economic and social upgrading due to newly emerging sustainability standard-based initiatives, such as organic cotton, fair trade cotton, and BCI operational in India for many years, in terms of how and whether they help cotton production conditions at the local level for reducing social and environmental injustice.

Indian Cotton in Global Context

Cotton is an important high-value commercial crop across the world though the price of raw cotton forms only 10 per cent of the final retail value of a garment. Moreover, cotton's share in world textile fibre use fell from 70 per cent in the 1950s to less than 40 per cent by the middle of the 2000s (Nelson and Smith 2011).

Globally, 100 countries grow cotton, and it accounts for the largest area (33 million hectares in 2010) under a single crop—2.5 per cent of the world's total arable land (Fayet and Vermeulen 2014). Furthermore, 150 countries trade in it, making cotton the world's most widely traded commodity; one-third of the cotton produced crosses national boundaries and gets consumed in a country other than its producer (S. Singh 2017). India and the US account for 50 per cent of cotton exports globally (FAO and ICAC 2015). China is not only the largest producer but also the largest user (40 per cent of global use) and the largest importer of cotton globally (WWF and Yes Bank 2012). Of the 500 companies involved in cotton trading, the 13 largest companies handle about 25 per cent of the total cotton produced globally. However, cotton is also one of the most toxic crops to cultivate as it consumes 20–25 per cent of global insecticides, 9–10 per cent of global pesticides, and 8 per cent of fertilizers, with just 2.5 per cent area under it (S. Singh 2017); it is also one of the thirstiest commodities along with rice, sugarcane, and wheat (Sneyd 2014). The geography of cotton production has also changed over time, with its area declining in the US and Brazil and going up in Australia, China, and South Asia, with China and India accounting for more than 50 per cent of global cotton production, where 100 million families are engaged in it directly and another 150 million indirectly (FAO and ICAC 2015).

Cotton is a politically sensitive commodity in most of the countries where it is grown because of the roles of the state and trade regulations, and significance for local livelihoods of small producers given the high cotton production subsidies in the US, China, Greece, and Spain, with 10 of the 11 largest producers providing subsidies to cotton cultivators (Nelson and Smith 2011). But 60 per cent of global cotton is still produced by 40 million small farmers (FTF 2012). The developing world accounts for 75 per cent of the global cotton production (S. Singh 2017).

India was the world's largest producer and the second-largest consumer as well as exporter of cotton after China in 2015 (S. Singh 2017); it accounts for 30 per cent of the total global area under cotton, with two-thirds of it under rainfed conditions, whereas globally, only 27 per cent cotton acreage is rainfed. The area under cotton in India was almost double of that in China and 2.5 times that of the US, but yields were only 50 per cent of that in the US and 40 per cent of that in China, thus producing only one-fifth of global output (NCPCR 2011). In India, raw cotton accounted for 11 per cent of India's agricultural exports and 1 per cent of its imports in 2011. There is no doubt that the cost of production per hectare in India varies from region to region and also between rainfed and irrigated areas. The harvesting cost was more similar across regions, especially in central and south India, although in the north, it was 78 per cent higher in irrigated condition than under similar condition in south India. Further, whereas in the north zone, 100 per cent of cotton production is under irrigated conditions, the other two zones have a substantial area under rainfed conditions (WWF and Yes Bank 2012).

Environmental Costs of Cotton Cultivation

Major environmental impacts of cotton cultivation include high water use and consequent groundwater depletion, human toxicity and health effects, environmental toxicity, global warming, eutrophication of surface water, acidification, erosion, land degradation, reduced biodiversity (natural habitats and flora and fauna), soil and water salinization, and high energy use (FAO and ICAC 2015; Kooistra and Termorshuizen 2006). From a management perspective, the major aspects of the environment include pest and pesticides management, water management, soil management, biodiversity and land use management, and climate change management (FAO and ICAC 2015). Major contributors to global warming in cotton production were fertilizers, other field emissions, and irrigation, in that order (FAO and ICAC 2015). It was estimated that pesticides unintentionally killed 67 million birds each year (Kooistra and Termorshuizen 2006). Even in the US, where cotton production occupied 49 per cent of surveyed farms and 10 per cent of the US's total cotton area in 2015, nitrogen use efficiency was as low as 10 per cent, and potash and phosphate use efficiency varied between 12–53 per cent and 19–45 per cent, respectively, across regions (Daystar et al. 2017).

A major worry that continues to plague cotton production from the resource use and sustainability perspective is the massive use of water, which ranges from 7,000 to 29,000 litres of water per kilogram of cotton lint (S. Singh 2019). For every cotton T-shirt produced, 2,700 litres of water is used in the supply chain (Ward and Mishra 2019). When global and Indian numbers are compared, water use in cotton production in India is 8,663 litres per kilogram of seed cotton and 20,127 litres for 1 kilogram of lint cotton against the global average of 3,544 and 8,506 per kilogram of seed and lint cotton, respectively. In India, cotton accounts for 6 per cent of the irrigation water used in agriculture (Ward and Mishra 2019). Along with water usage, low input use efficiency, especially for nutrients (only at 30–40 per cent), remains a major challenge.

Cotton production affects sustainable water use in three ways: water depletion, soil salinization, and water pollution. This is a result of the area under cotton being mostly (85 to 95 per cent) irrigated using the flood or the furrow irrigation methods (FAO and ICAC 2015). The water footprint (WF) of cotton was 42 per cent blue (groundwater), 39 per cent green (rainwater), and 19 per cent grey (polluted water); of the last, 95 per cent was located outside Japan, 50 per cent of it was in the US, and in Europe, 84 per cent was external with major impacts in India, China, Pakistan, and Uzbekistan. Sixty per cent of Clemens and August's (C&A) blue (surface and ground) WF and 18 per cent of grey (freshwater pollution) WF was in India as it procured 42 per cent of its cotton from India (S. Singh 2019).

So far as the environmental impact of cotton production in India is concerned, it required pesticide consumption of 2.7 kilogram per hectare, which is much higher than the national average of 0.8 kilogram per hectare for other crops (WWF and Yes Bank 2012). Further, only 0.1 per cent of the pesticides used reached the target pests, with the rest going into the soil, water, and air, besides causing harm to friendly pests and biodiversity (Ward and Mishra 2019). It was not only the quantity of pesticides used but also the type of pesticides used and their handling, in terms of the pesticide-use behaviour of farmers, which impacted the environment. The effects include the contamination of water sources, long-term persistence in soils affecting other rotational crops, poisoning of fish, wildlife, and livestock, reducing pollinating insects, and air pollution (FAO and ICAC 2015). Cotton is recommended to be sprayed with pesticides seven times, but farmers in Punjab sprayed cotton 30 times (Kumar and Kumar 2016). Pesticides residues have even been found in blood samples of Indian cotton workers (WWF and Yes Bank 2012). In Brazil, rainwater was found to contain 19 different pesticides, of which 12 were used in cotton production. Cotton cultivation also was responsible for the emission of 220 million tonnes of carbon dioxide annually. Incidentally, the WF of organic cotton is only 10 per cent of that of conventional cotton.[1]

With 2.5 per cent of the global area being under cotton, it used 25 per cent of insecticides and 10 per cent of pesticides and 11 per cent of all chemical insecti-pesticides (COAPCL 2012) (an acre of non-organic cotton can consume up to 6 litres of pesticides and 500 kilograms of chemical fertilizers). In India, cotton has 5 per cent area under it, but 54 per cent of pesticide use is in cotton. Pesticides accounted for 11 per cent of the cost of cultivation in 2012–2013 and were next only to seed costs (20 per cent) and human labour costs (15 per cent); these costs did not differ much across farm size categories though small farmers had the highest proportion of pesticide costs in total (12.3 per cent), especially when cotton was cultivated as a monocrop and the grower was a land-owning tenant, not an owner or landless tenant (Ranganathan, Gaurav, and Halder 2018). Pesticides used in cotton accounted for 27 per cent of the total cost of production followed by labour (25 per cent) in Punjab (Gill, Singh, and Brar 2010).

The 'true price' of conventional seed cotton in India was EUR 4.2 per kilogram, of which the farm gate price was only EUR 0.55 and the true price came to be six times higher than that. The environmental cost accounted for 75 per cent of the external cost of cultivation, and the remaining was social cost. The major material costs in the process of cotton cultivation in terms of externalities were water use (35 per cent), water pollution (17 per cent), and income (12 per cent). However, the external cost of certified sustainable cotton cultivation was 30 per cent lower than that of conventional cotton. Of this change, 70 per cent happened due to higher yields in certified farms, 20 per cent due to better environmental condition, especially lower use of various chemical and other inputs, such as water, and 10 per cent came from better social conditions. Even though certified farms used less water for irrigation, water still accounted for 23 per cent of total external costs. However, certified farms were more profitable than conventional farms. The external costs in raw cotton in India were lower than those in cocoa in Ivory Coast but much higher than coffee in Vietnam and tea in Kenya at the farm level (Grosscurt, Ruiz, and Fobelets 2016).

That there are other externalities of cotton production that come into effect with the use of chemical inputs is also evident in the case of Punjab, where the use of chemical pesticides on cotton has led to many human health problems, such as cancer and asthma. The workers applying these chemical pesticides on cotton crop and women cotton pickers suffer from such health hazards. In fact, the cotton belt is now more commonly known as the cancer belt of Punjab due to the increasing number of cancer patients in this region in recent years. Cotton farmers were using chemical pesticide containers for household purposes, and none of the farmers or workers spraying pesticides used any protective equipment. Of the respondents (Kaur 2019), 69 per cent reported skin problems due to pesticides use. It is important to note that the cotton belt occupies 15 per cent of Punjab's land area, but it uses 75 per cent of the total pesticides used in the state. Some villages in the Bathinda district were declared cancer-ridden, and the female reproductive system cancers were more common in some parts of the district. Pesticides were also the common cause of pancreatic cancer, prostate cancer, breast cancer, and brain tumours. There were also reports of infertile married couples in many villages and cases of delayed maturity among boys and girls in the region. In fact, various banned pesticides, such as Monocrotophos and Endosulphan, were still being used in the region on cotton and other crops (Kaur 2019). There are 'cancer villages' in China too, which were an externality of heavy metal pollution caused by the industries in local areas (Martinez-Alier et al. 2016).

In India, 65 pesticides have been approved for use in cotton, of which 18 are linked to cancers in humans as per the World Health Organization (WHO), the International Agency for Research on Cancer (IARC), and the US Environmental Protection Agency (EPA); at least seven of these pesticides belong to WHO class 1A and 1B category of extremely or highly hazardous pesticides. India still permits the use of Monocrotophos despite the Food and Agriculture Organization (FAO) advising many developing countries to phase out this pesticide (PAN 2017). In the cotton belt of Punjab, the correlation between cotton crop and cancer mortality was 0.34, and the cancer mortality risk was higher among females than that among males. The mortality rate became higher with higher exposure to cotton as against paddy (B. P. Singh 2008). There were 108 cancer patients per 100,000 of the population in Punjab compared to the national average of 80; of the total cancer deaths in Punjab in 2013, 46 per cent were in this region (Kumar and Kumar 2016; Kaur 2019). There is also a daily train popularly known as the 'cancer express' that carries cancer patients and their attendants from Bathinda to a charitable cancer treatment centre in Bikaner in neighbouring Rajasthan.

In Gujarat and Rajasthan, where cotton seed production takes place, young boys and girls working to ensure cross-pollination of flowers suffer from exposure to pesticides and later experience stunted growth and development of their bodies; there are also deaths that have resulted in some cases, but these are not made public and hushed up by making payments to the families of such children by the farmers (Banday et al. 2018).

Local Resource Sustainability under Cotton Production

Agriculture is the largest user of fresh water (69 per cent) globally, and cotton is one of the main thirsty crops after paddy and wheat. Most irrigation systems in cotton rely on traditional flood irrigation but the efficiency of such irrigation is only 40 per cent. Water-saving technologies, such as micro irrigation, cover only 0.7 per cent of the cropped area globally (Schwank, North, and Battig 2001), which translates to only 9 per cent of cultivated area in India (Palanisami et al. 2011).

Many cotton-growing areas in India, such as north Gujarat or southern Punjab, suffer from excessive groundwater withdrawal. In Mehsana of Gujarat, for raw cotton as well as cotton seed production, there were thriving and exploitative water markets in operation for decades due to the high cost of groundwater access through deep tube wells—which were under the control of larger landholders. This led to not only groundwater exploitation but also inequity in access to groundwater; and those with poor resources did not have access to tube wells, being forced to buy water from tube-well owners. The landholdings of well owners were double in one village and almost eight times that of the non-owners in another village. In one village, 51 per cent of the farmers did not have wells, and in another, 31 per cent did not have wells;

wells were mostly owned by small, medium, and large farmers in one village, and mostly by medium and large farmers in the other village (Dubhash 2000). However, in Punjab—where there was a large dependence on groundwater and resultant problem of waterlogging and soil salinity in the cotton belt—some experts recommended the expansion of the area under cotton as the crop consumed less water as compared with paddy and wheat; the experts also argued for produce-specific incentives for cotton growers as a water management strategy (Kulkarni and Shah 2013).

In cotton, the indirect water-saving practices in organic farming systems include crop rotation and the reduction in the use of chemical inputs, resulting in the protection of soil structure and keeping plants healthier. Organic practices save 15 to 25 per cent of water compared to conventional cotton production practices; but many times, saving water is not the focus of sustainability projects as either water is available for free or is highly subsidized (Schwank, North, and Battig 2001) as in Punjab, where there has been a free supply of electric power since 1997 to all farmers for pumping out groundwater for irrigation and the state has 1.4 million tube wells (G. Singh 2020).

Social and Environmental Upgrading in New Global Sustainability Initiatives in India

Standards are important to economic, social, and environmental sustainability in the cotton-producing sector where sustainability is routinely sacrificed, not only in the conventional sector, but also within some of the sustainability projects. Standards, however, vary significantly. For example, whereas fair trade standards have 97 indicators of sustainability, organic standards have only 41, and BCI has only 43 indicators (FAO and ICAC 2015). For example, certified cotton lowers external costs by one-third when compared to conventional cotton, but this resulted mainly from higher yields of certified farms, and better environmental and social conditions, in that order. This led to certified farms being 52 per cent more profitable than conventional farms due to a lower use of water and chemical inputs. Certified farms also had better wages and working conditions although underpayment and under-earning was the largest social cost in cotton in India since hired workers earned only 41 per cent of the living wage (Grosscurt, Ruiz, and Fobelets 2016).

Of the total cotton produced globally in 2004, 80 per cent was under conventional farm management, 20 per cent under Integrated Pest Management (IPM), and 0.04 per cent under organic practices (Kooistra and Termorshuizen 2006). By 2015, sustainable cotton production accounted for 12 per cent of the global supply. This percentage has more than doubled in the last three years though only about one-fifth of it is bought as sustainable cotton while the rest is treated as conventional cotton (Truscott et al. 2016; PAN, Solidaridad, and WWF 2017), despite the fact that all sustainability standards rely on market uptake to meet their objectives at the farmer level. All 60 sustainable cotton textile labels and standards in 2015 accounted for just 3.4 per cent of global cotton production, of which only half was sold as standards-compliant (FTF 2015).

Only 3.3 per cent of the cotton produced in India complied with voluntary sustainability standards in 2012, which mainly included Better Cotton and organic, and it was close to global compliance levels (3.4 per cent) (Grosscurt, Ruiz and Fobelets 2016). In 2014–2015, India was the largest producer of organic cotton and was the second-largest producer of Better Cotton in 2015–2016 after Brazil (PAN, Solidaridad, and WWF 2017). Organic cotton uses 91 per cent less water and 62 per cent less energy than that used in conventional cotton production (Ward and Mishra 2019). Most of these sustainability initiatives in cotton are supported by global readymade garment and textile players as a part of their business model individually (for example, IKEA) or as part of a consortium of brands (for example, BCI) or as CSR initiatives (for example, the C&A Foundation). Some of these initiatives also get support from bilateral development and aid agencies, such as the Dutch IDH.

Both organic cotton and Better Cotton have become brands that provide a premium of between 20 and 40 per cent over conventional cotton price (Kaplinsky and Morriss 2019). This kind of producer benefit is quite different from non-brand linked environmental improvements, such as cleaning up and restoring the River Noyyal in Tiruppur. This leads to an important conclusion about brand involvement in environmental improvements: brands invest their own money where they can expect to secure higher margins due to reputational qualities. In the case of leather products using banned azo chemicals in Tamil Nadu, the brands did not invest their own money, but their governments utilized taxpayer money, as in the case of the role of the German state technical agency GIZ, for supporting the threshold environmental requirement. When we look at other countries, the major instance where brands invested their own money in building safety improvements even when they did not get any reputational premiums was the Accord on Fire and Building Safety in Bangladesh. That may well have been due to moral pressure in the wake of the Rana Plaza tragedy in Dhaka that cost the lives of thousands of garment workers due to the collapse of a multi-storeyed factory building.

Organic Cotton Standards in India

Organic cotton accounted for one-third of the cotton use of the top 10 users of cotton in 2015 (Truscott et al. 2016). Globally, 25 companies/retailers consumed three-fourths of organic cotton (*DtE* 2013). Further, most of the fair trade certified farmers were also organic (73 per cent in 2015) (Truscott et al. 2016). In 2014, 77 per cent of farmers reported at least one other certification in addition to fair trade, and 52 per cent reported organic, which was the largest single additional certification (FTI 2016).

In 2014–2015, India's share in global organic cotton was 66.9 per cent, followed by China and Turkey (Truscott et al. 2016), when globally, in 2015, only 1 per cent of the cultivated cotton area was under organic cotton (Ward and Mishra 2019). Put another way, India's certified organic cotton area was more than half of the global organic area in 2014–2015. The major states in organic cotton in terms of area are Madhya Pradesh, Orissa, and Maharashtra (Truscott et al. 2016), and in terms of production, they are Maharashtra, Gujarat, Rajasthan, Madhya Pradesh, Orissa, and Andhra Pradesh (*DtE* 2013).

In the Indian organic cotton sector, which is once again seeing a revival in demand and production, major issues at the farmer level include the availability of non-genetically modified seeds, adequacy and efficacy of an internal control system (ICS) and its cost, and *Bacillus thuringiensis* (Bt) or genetically modified organism (GMO) contamination. In 2010, almost one-third of cotton bought by large global retailers tested positive for genetic modification (*DtE* 2013).

Most organic production organizers, especially private players, use the contract farming system to organize production at the grower end. But the contracts are highly biased in favour of the contracting agencies, protect company interest at the cost of the farmer, do not cover farmer's production risks, for example, crop failure, retain the right of the company to change price, and, generally, offer prices that are based on the open market prices for conventional produce (S. Singh 2009). This means that even a significant premium over market price may not help a farmer if open market prices go down significantly, which is not uncommon in India. The market-price-based price is offered to avoid grower defaults as they can otherwise sell the produce in the open market because of the availability of the alternative market as a result of product symmetry. Thus, the issue of what is fair price for the primary grower in an organic produce chain remains, as there is little transparency in pricing and costing of operations when private players are the organizers of contract farming projects (IFAD 2005). There is also the exclusion of small producers due to high certification costs, smaller volumes, tighter control by chain drivers, and the absence of local markets (S. Singh 2009).

In Orissa, where organic cotton certification started in 2006 and farmers put 46 per cent of their average farm of 2 hectares under cotton, farmers realized higher profits due to soil improvement, no chemical input use and, therefore, lower input costs, and higher area under cotton. Also, a part of the cotton produce (45 per cent) was sold at a 5 per cent premium over the conventional cotton price. However, at the same time, the workload increased for women as most bio-inputs were prepared at home. In fact, most environmental and gender issues in cotton production remain unchanged and challenging (Altenbuchner, Vogel, and Larcher 2017).

In Madhya Pradesh, where organic as well as Better Cotton were being grown in addition to conventional cotton, organic farmers were found to be socioeconomically better off than conventional farmers; yet 35 per cent of the exclusively organic-cotton-growing farmers still self-reported the continued use of chemical fertilizers and 33 per cent reported the use of chemical pesticides. Interestingly, all cotton farmers, including exclusive organic, non-exclusive organic, as well as conventional cotton farmers, on average made a loss in cotton production. This loss ranged from INR 39,824 in the case of exclusive organic cotton farmers to INR 28,482 in the case of non-exclusive cotton farmers, including the opportunity cost of family labour. Profits were realized by 45 per cent of the exclusive organic cotton farmers and 38 per cent of the non-exclusive organic cotton farmers. There were also reports of children below 14 years working in the case of 22 per cent of organic and 31 per cent of conventional cotton farms. The per acre losses were INR 39,823 and INR 32,695 in the case of exclusive organic and conventional cotton farmers, respectively. Similarly, in the case of non-exclusive organic cotton farmers, the per acre loss was INR 28,481. If family labour was excluded, then these losses came down to INR 27,875 in case of exclusive organic, INR 11,840 in case of non-exclusive, and INR 18,007 in case of conventional farmers. The income from organic cotton farming was one-third of the income from all farming activities—notably, the percentage of cotton farming income was higher in the case of conventional cotton farming (38 per cent). However, the overall income from farming was lower in the case of conventional cotton farming households and other household income was much higher when compared to organic cotton farm households (de Hoop et al. 2018).

For workers, organic standards do not have much to offer as they are more about production processes than surplus distribution. The labour issues in organic cotton, whether gender or child labour or wages and compensation, remain as in conventional cotton production as they are not part of the organic standards unlike fair trade. Surprisingly, the International Labour Organization (ILO) report on child labour in cotton does not even mention organic cotton standards and the prevalence of the issue of child labour under these standards (ILO 2016).

Fair Trade Standards in Cotton in India

Fair trade was launched in cotton in 2005 globally, but 60 per cent of fair trade cotton was used for clothing, and fair trade remained only 10 per cent of organic trade. In fact, globally, cotton is one of the three small volume products in fair trade along with rice and sports balls, though, within the Asia Pacific region, it is one of the three main products along with rice and coffee (FTI 2017a). Globally, only seven countries produce fair trade cotton involving 55,000 growers, and the markets are primarily in the United Kingdom (UK) and Europe. Further, cotton farmers accounted for only 3 per cent of all fair trade farmers and workers in 2014 (FTI 2016). Major challenges in cotton for fair trade that remain are competition from synthetic fibres, subsidies to cotton producers in the West, prevalence of child and forced labour, price volatility, poor resource base of farmers, excessive use of chemicals and water, climate change, and geneticall modified (GM) cotton (FTF 2015).

In the Asia Pacific region, 69 per cent of fair trade premiums in 2016–2017 were received by three countries: India, Fiji, and Indonesia (FTI 2016). India's share in fair trade premiums in the Asia Pacific region was 27 per cent as the country had the largest number of fair trade organizations (80), accounting for 40 per cent of those in the region (FTI 2016). India had the fifth-largest number of fair trade farmers, and it was the fourth largest in terms of the number of fair trade farmers and workers in 2014, even though it had the largest in number of fair trade certified plantations in the world. Also, cotton had one of the lowest percentages of women farmers (15 per cent) across fair trade crops (FTI 2016). In 2018, India had 25,000 fair trade certified farmers (Ward and Mishra 2019).

In India, mostly, farmers do not have their own organizations but are under contract production arrangements wherein an intermediary, such as an exporter or processor known as a promoting body, helps farmers in forming a functional organization (FTI 2016). Fair trade, which was launched in India in 2014, faces the following problems: child labour in picking, women labour and their work conditions, and the gender gap in wages. It is also more challenging to implement minimum and equal wage in India because the women may lose work or may face higher exploitation due to the broader social dynamics. In fact, there has been not much difference in the way fair trade and conventional cotton value chains have been run as the same stakeholders continue to make decisions based on similar factors.

The producers are also generally unaware of fair trade standards, principles, processes, and markets, and the improvement in labour conditions and women worker status remains unaffected by and large due to the larger social and cultural environment in which fair trade is embedded. Awareness among producers about child labour only has increased. Fair trade does not differentiate between types of farmers in India, which is reducing the impact it could have had on the poorest of the poor cotton farmers. Further, the producer organizations remain weak and dependent on promoting bodies—non-government organizations (NGOs) or private agencies (Nelson and Smith 2011).

Though there are standards of fair trade for raw cotton, what makes it unfair is the absence of graded prices and the use of lower prices for the last picking. In India, the direct impact on farmer income has been low as market prices were found to be higher than fair trade minimum prices. Further, the very small scale of fair trade operations in cotton has meant that there is no impact on the sector nationally or even provincially (FTF 2012). But, fair trade has complemented the organic trade sector in cotton to some extent though there are only a few players.

Better Cotton Standards in India

The mission of the BCI is to reduce the most significant environmental and social impacts and improve livelihoods of cotton farming communities to make cotton better for producers, the environment, and the future of the sector. The drivers of BCI—Marks & Spencer, IKEA, and others, including some global supermarkets—have committed to move even up to 100 per cent of their cotton use to Better Cotton. Globally, Better Cotton was grown in 22 countries, accounting for 12 per cent of global cotton production in 2015–2016 (Ward and Mishra 2019) and including 1.6 million participating farmers in 2014 (ILO 2016). Fair trade is also, however, seen as a hybrid business model with an alternative market structure that makes use of the same market, creating injustice for the producers in the first place (Delgado and Cruz 2013).

The BCI had its origins in the Better Management Practices (BMP) in cotton attempted by IKEA in partnership with the World Wide Fund (WWF) (Joshi Rai 2011). It is a global multi-stakeholder initiative and focuses on farm-level sustainability—economic, environmental, and social—with six principles as minimum requirements regardless of the geographical location of producers (Sneyd 2014). Since 2010, the BCI has picked up pace in the Indian cotton sector, with major global players adopting the BCI standards.

India has one of the largest numbers of Better Cotton farmers; it also has the second-largest percentage of licensed farmers in total (92 per cent) and the highest number of projects in Better Cotton (18) globally—with these projects accounting for 5.5 per cent of India's cotton area (Ward and Mishra 2019). But India also has almost the highest cost per tonne of licenced Better Cotton and the least uptake of produced Better Cotton among all the producing countries. Although India received the lion's share (more than half) of Better Cotton Fast Track Project (BGFTP) investments in 2013, followed by Pakistan, its contribution to Better Cotton production was only one-fifth of the total and lower than that of Pakistan (Dhingra 2014).

The BCI does not guarantee any major price and income benefits, unlike other sustainability standards. It puts the entire onus of sustainability on the primary producers without commensurate benefits and without questioning the global cotton trade system (Sneyd 2014). In India, the Better Cotton prices were generally around MSP though the BCI does not promise any minimum prices or premiums to Better Cotton farmers. Further, the BCI standards do not include cotton seed production in their ambit; this leaves a large part of the value chain out, which is known for many labour rights violations. In terms of market compatibility and institutional compatibility, the BCI scores better than other sustainability initiatives, such as organic or fair trade or even Rainforest Alliance, as it does not really demand any compliance from partners (Bitzer 2012). The BCI claims that 53 per cent of its farmers were aware of child labour issues in an advanced manner, and another 34 per cent had a basic awareness of the issue (Ward and Mishra 2019).

In the case of Better Cotton in Madhya Pradesh, both exclusive and non-exclusive BCI cotton farmers experienced losses in their cotton production, ranging from INR 24,103 to INR 32,087. Only 51 per cent of the exclusive BCI cotton farmers and 45 per cent of the non-exclusive BCI cotton farmers made minimal profit from cotton production. Of the organic farmers, 40 per cent were exclusive and 60 per cent non-exclusive. The child labour worked out to be 1.14 days in the case of the BCI, which was lower than that in conventional cotton farming (1.79 days) (de Hoop et al. 2018).

The decent work aspect of the BCI in India mainly concerned the status of women, child labour, wages and incomes, health and safety, and forced or bonded labour. There was gendering of tasks (occupational segregation), wage discrimination, women's reproductive health risks associated with pesticide exposure, use of child labour, exposure of children to hazardous working conditions, low wages (even lower than the legal minimum), and prevalence of forced and bonded labour. Many of the issues did not appear in the BCI system as the initiative relied on self-assessment to ensure compliance and producers did not report these issues for fear of being excluded from the programme; however, the BCI took some steps towards addressing these issues through an assurance programme and by conducting an external assessment of BCI itself and also implementing partners through independent verifiers. The global compliance on decent work was reported to be 42 per cent in 2010, which jumped to 74 per cent in 2012 (Usher, Newitt and Merouchi 2013).

Further undermining labour standards, hired labour and wage issues are not addressed in the smallholder category when assessing decent work conditions. Most of the time, the focus of interventions is on child labour and health and safety, which has led to higher awareness of these issues while other issues, such as non-discrimination and gender equality, forced or bonded labour, migrant workers, and freedom of association, receive much less attention. In fact, very few implementing partners target workers as beneficiaries and there is very little evidence of any kind of gender focus or forced or bonded labour focus in implementing partner approaches to decent work. Therefore, there is a need to refine the BCI production principle on decent work (Usher, Newitt and Merouchi 2013).

The BCI projects in India claim that there is 27 per cent lower water use and 29 per cent less fertilizer use and 15 per cent less pesticide use compared to conventional cotton cultivation in the same area (*Economic Times* 2020). By contrast, Primark's sustainable cotton programme in India managed to reduce water use only by 4 per cent (Nanda 2019).

Whereas organic standards focus more on environmental and resource sustainability, it is only fair trade that directly targets social aspects, such as producer incomes and livelihoods. Better Cotton standards aim to improve the quality of fibre and reduce the cost of production. Despite these differences, the overlap between organic and fair trade cotton globally was as high as 73 per cent, meaning the vast majority of farmers who held certifications were both organic and fair trade certified (Ward and Mishra 2019). Also, the BCI is the only cotton-specific standard that is also technology-neutral, allowing the use of GM seeds (Fayet and Vermeulen 2014). Therefore, some standards are easier to implement and scale up than others because if incomes and livelihoods are not the focus, it is much easier to achieve results and scale up the coverage. Also, some standards are more stringent than others, for example, organic and fair trade do not permit the use of GM seeds whereas Better Cotton does, which helped it to scale up in India as farmers were already practising GM cotton production and did not need to change their seed or growing practices, but instead needed to manage the existing practice better, requiring little effort (S. Singh 2019).

Conclusion: Bringing Environmental Justice to Cotton Production

Sustainable chain management is primarily 'the success of working together' or what may be called 'partnership for sustainability'. Sustainable chain management assumes that the chain partners no longer feel responsible for just their own part of the chain but for the whole chain. Usually, the involvement of a broader category of stakeholders—government bodies, NGOs, consumers, and research institutes—is required. The instruments of sustainable chain management include codes of conduct, certification schemes, and sustainability reports on the social and ecological aspects of doing business. Sustainable chain management must not disrupt the culture and lifestyle of local people but should emphasize the importance of creating shared ownership. An effective combination of the local and the global is required.

So far as contracting agencies are concerned, they can bring about better environmental compliance by adopting a procedural justice perspective instead of higher levels of monitoring that may be counterproductive and damage buyer–supplier relationships by generating conflict between buyers and suppliers. Procedural justice includes using unbiased, transparent, and correctable criteria and procedures for making and executing decisions that can improve levels of trust and commitment between the buyer and the supplier. The basic principles include consistency in applying criteria, suppressing bias, using accurate information, affording opportunity for correcting errors, providing adequate representation in the decision-making process, and ensuring ethical treatment (Boyed et al. 2007).

The analysis of cotton subsidies implies externalities of cotton production as it would not be produced in places where it is currently being produced if the global trade in cotton was fair. Therefore, there is scope for the role of various stakeholders in intervening at the World Trade Organisation (WTO) level to ensure that the trade and subsidy agreements are more fairly designed to reduce, if not eliminate, the economic and social injustices created by such trade rules and WTO policies. It is already known from the experience of the last 25 years of the WTO's functioning that the trade is neither free nor fair.

The role of cotton in poverty reduction—though limited as only 50 per cent income comes from this crop, especially in Africa—depends on dealing with issues of fair prices, value chain benefit-sharing mechanisms, and public support services for farmers and marketing systems (FAO and ICAC 2015). One such measure at the farmer level could be crop insurance, which has not worked in the developing world, including India, so far. In fact, India has made crop insurance voluntary now, whereas earlier, it was tied to crop loans from institutional sources.

There is a need to address ecological concerns within contract farming programmes and policies. This can be done through land use planning based on soil depth, soil quality, land slope, and suitable water availability. It is also important to understand previous land use and make it mandatory to follow crop rotation, if necessary (S. Singh 2016).

Environment-friendly processes and products can be used in cotton to lower the externalities of its production as is evident from a study of tomato harvesting in Africa, where tomato farmers used recycled post-harvest equipment, used water, and powered operations sparingly and more of human labour; besides, they used homemade sand filters for water purification, green leaves for refrigeration, and recycled paint buckets for solar ovens (Hilmi 2016).

From a company's perspective, bringing in an NGO is, at the very least, highly recommended. Strong local NGOs in developing countries can play the role of a 'watchdog', providing incentives for and influencing the process of sustainable economic development. They can also play a role in mediating between local knowledge and (traditional) norms and values, on the one hand, and global markets and multinationals, on the other. Furthermore, local NGOs in developing countries are often trusted locally. The experiences of fair trade show that it does not really matter where value is added as long as small-scale producers also benefit from the process. This implies building in guarantees to ensure that the interests of small-scale producers are represented elsewhere in the chain. This can, for example, be expressed by eliminating middlemen, by agreeing on long-term fixed prices to give producers certainty, and by providing agricultural cooperatives access to and/or a financial interest in the (retail) companies at the other end of the chain (S. Singh 2016).

One major insight which emerges from the analysis of various sustainability standards is that some standards are easier to scale up as they demand much less from farmers in terms of disrupting their routine practices. However, they may not significantly impact the social sustainability part of the objective as they are focused not so much on producer or worker livelihoods as on mainstreaming the standards for a larger effect on markets (S. Singh 2019).

For standards to make a difference, the institutional variety in terms of representing different stakeholder interests is crucial. For example, if there is no voice of the most marginalized, such as the farm workers, and they have no agency in terms of participation or no association to create some associational power, then objectives such as decent work or fair work conditions cannot be expected to be met because many times the dominant stakeholders would like to extract all benefits from a sustainability initiative.

Further, social standard compliance is more difficult to achieve than other standards, such as environmental, as it involves working with different communities who do not share the same perspective on the issue and involve cultural, class, and caste questions—for example, on decent working conditions in Better Cotton or fair trade premium payment to workers or gender parity in wages—as many of these issues are locally embedded socially and culturally. However, there is a need to bring in worker interest and labour issues as many sustainability initiatives in Indian agriculture get jammed at the level of small farmer concerns, losing sight of the real workers on farms. Even within commercial networks, worker training and capacity building need to be strengthened.

Finally, for any sustainability initiative to scale up and sustain, the creation and expansion of markets are a must. If the differently produced crop or product does not find a market, the producers would be discouraged from continuing with it. This is a problem all three standards, that is, organic cotton, fair trade cotton, and Better Cotton, face that needs to be attended to proactively with equal focus on markets, including emerging domestic markets, rather than production alone.

Notes

1. See https://www.theworldcounts.com/challenges/consumption/clothing/cotton-farming-water-consumption, accessed on 4 December 2020.

11
Value Capture in Global Monopsony Capitalism

In Chapters 4 to 10, we saw how value is extracted through the purchase of inputs, gendered labour power, and environmental services at prices below their respective costs of production. Such acquisitions of inputs below their costs of production were identified as subsidies. These subsidies are extracted in different nodes or locations: the garment manufacturing factory, the household, including the rural household, and the enviroment. In the framework chapters, we have argued that these subsidies, though extracted at different nodes of the global value chain (GVC), end up with, or are captured by, the brands that govern or are lead firms in these value chains. This argument is similar, but not equal, to the Marxist distinction between the location of value production and realization, where there is a distinction in the firm and country location of value production and value realization (D. Harvey 2017).

In this chapter, we discuss the manner in which monopsony functions to bring about value capture by brands. The analysis in this chapter is built on the primary material gathered from discussions with over 100 suppliers from different research projects during the five-year period of 2016 to 2020. One round of investigations was with about 60 garment suppliers across the Delhi National Capital Region (NCR), Jaipur, Surat, Bangalore, and Tiruppur as part of the International Labour Organisation Apparel Export Promotion Corporation (ILO-AEPC), a quasi-government body study of management practices in Indian garment suppliers (Nathan and Harsh 2018). The management weaknesses reported in this study led to the ILO-AEPC Handbook of Good International Practices in the Garment Industry. This report also formed the basis of a paper (Nathan and Harsh 2018) on process upgrading in the garment industry.

During 2017–2019, the Society for Labour and Development (SLD) carried out a questionnaire-based survey of 45 garment firms in Delhi NCR,

Bangalore, and Tiruppur. The data from this survey was filled out with inputs from senior officials of the firms. Besides these project-based surveys,the researchers have also interacted with various suppliers and brand representatives in many multi-stakeholder initiatives. These interactions date back to our participation in the Capturing the Gains (CtG) research programme between 2011 and 2016.

Information gathered from these discussions do not fit into survey-type results. But they are important in forming impressions of how buyer–supplier bargaining functions. Even from the questionnaire survey, one should not take the numbers to be exact since they are not based on balance-sheet calculations. What is important are the trends they represent, such as a reduction in lead times or a fall in margins.

Information was also gathered from conversations that were not specifically geared to discussing conditions in the firm or industry. For instance, a conversation during a social interaction with a supplier showed that they had a high margin, above 20 per cent, in the manufacture of high-end shirts that retailed for around USD 150. They were clearly preferred suppliers with a long-standing relationship with the retailer. All of these bits of information and even impressions are important in forming a picture of brand–supplier relations.

Analysis and insights from these discussions are triangulated with national survey data on garment producers from the Indian Annual Survey of Industries (ASI). The process, however, is not just one of triangulation; it is also a matter of bringing in insights from these discussions to understand the survey data.

A word about ASI data on firms in garment manufacturing. It includes not just exporters or suppliers to international brands but also includes firms manufacturing for the domestic market in domestic value chains. Much of the manufacturing for the domestic market is carried out in workshops in the unorganized sector, and this data does not find its way into the ASI surveys. Since the ASI surveys corporate firms, some of the large units that produce for both domestic and global markets may be included in the ASI. For instance, Arvind is the largest denim manufacturer in the world, supplying to both international and domestic markets. Goculdas, Aditya Birla, and Raymond all supply to both markets, both with their own brands and as suppliers to brands. Within these units, even if there are separate lines for international and domestic production—since the designs and specifications are different—there are no differences in the equipment used or employment conditions. As we were told, and what seems plausible, one cannot really run a factory with differences in employment conditions between production lines. Overall, we can be confident that the ASI data does not misrepresent the situation of Indian suppliers of global brands.

The rest of the chapter is organized as follows. First, we delineate the business processes that lead to value capture. Second, there is a discussion of the manner in which cost reduction is carried out by suppliers through capability development, of firms, managers, and workers, while the benefit of this cost reduction is captured by brands through their monopsony positions. Third, a section analyses the ASI data on gross vale added (GVA) and capability upgrading. Lastly, this is followed by the concluding section.

The Process of Value Capture

How are the benefits from cost reduction distributed within global garment value chains? The Ricardian theory of rent would predict that if market-driven supply required keeping high-cost producers in the value chain, then the required higher prices would give low-cost producers a surplus profit or rent. In the 1950s, this analysis was modified by Prebisch and Singer (Toye 2003). They pointed out that international markets for primary goods were dominated by oligopolies from the industrial or developed economies, while primary producers were competitors on the supply side. This oligopsony structure of the market for primary goods enabled the oligopolies from the developed countries to push down prices to the new costs of production, and thus the bulk, if not all, of the profits from reduced costs of production were captured by the trading oligopolies of developed countries.

Prebisch and Singer (Toye 2003) argued that the benefits of what is now called process upgrading that reduces costs of production would be captured by the oligopolistic buyers of the primary goods. From this followed the development policy dictum that developing countries should find ways of growth in the manufacturing sector where such oligopolistic value capturing structures were supposed to not exist. Presumably, the manufacturers would sell to final consumers and not to oligopsony buyers. But what if manufacturers in the developing world sell not to final consumers but to corporate buyers who are the lead firms in a GVC structure? Kaplinsky (2005) pointed out that the structures of intra-GVC trade would enable lead firms to capture the benefits of cost reduction by suppliers. The structure of intra-GVC trade is that of monopsony, with few buyers and many suppliers. Where, in addition, the knowledge levels of the GVC manufacturing segments led by the suppliers is low, with relatively easy to acquire capabilities, the profit accumulation is mainly at the buyers' end.

There, however, is an important distinction between the arguments of Prebischand Singer and the case of GVC production. In the former, the process through which the outcome comes about is that of market-based transactions. The GVC case is one of bargaining between brands and suppliers. It is necessary to look into the bargaining process that results in the outcomes we observe, that is, of suppliers getting just the minimal profit with their product prices reflecting the low input costs due to subsidies extracted from the location of different segments of the value chain, that is, the factory,the household of the worker, and the environment.

The results of the bargaining between brands and suppliers must fall within limits that were well expressed by Adam Smith almost 250 years ago. He pointed out that the monopoly price is the highest that can be got, while the competitive price is the lowest that can allow the sellers to continue in their business (Smith 1776/2000). In the bargaining process between the few brands and the very many suppliers, we would expect the price to settle at that which the 'sellers can commonly afford to take, and at the same time continue in business'; of course, that price which the sellers can afford to take is reduced by the subsidies extracted from gendered labour, farm and factory workers' households, and the environment.

The basic process of value capture is quite simple. Labour costing is done on the basis of minimum wages. Minimum wages in India differ by state, but the corresponding minimum wage is the basis for labour costing. Other inputs, such as cotton fabric, or environmental services, such as water, are priced as on the market or supplied in the usual manner in which water is priced, or rather not priced. These systems of labour and environmental pricing mean that the low prices of these inputs reflect these subsidies in the prices of the manufactured garment.

The reflection of subsidies in output prices occurs through the monopsony relation of brands with suppliers. The brands are few in number, and they deal with many actual or potential suppliers. There is competition not only among suppliers in, say, India but also with suppliers in competing supplier countries, such as Bangladesh or Vietnam. Brands are very blunt in bringing such actual or potential competitors into the bargaining process with the suppliers, often saying that we can get this for 5 cents less per piece, can you match that? Having invested capital in factories to manufacture garments, the suppliers must stay in the business of manufacturing garments and have to accept the lowest price at which they can continue in business. Having looked at the basic structure of bargaining in the garment GVC, we look at this process in more detail.

Suppliers reported, as would be expected, that brands and buyers often have a fair idea of cost break-ups. Standard allowable minutes (SAMs) are fixed by the second for every task in stitching a garment. With the open costing system, suppliers are expected to reveal their cost for each input and process item. Brands decide a target price, which does not leave much room for suppliers to increase their margins in any way. The invasive manner in which brands get cost information from suppliers was picturesquely described by one supplier as the brands trying to get into one's bedroom! The requirement to supply detailed cost information leaves little room to bargain on costs. Margins too are fixed between 7 to 10 per cent, inversely related to the size of the order and the extent of complex embroidery required.

The open costing requirement only works for suppliers and not for brands. As pointed out in Chapter 3, among the information technology (IT) software service suppliers, the largest Indian firms with strong reputational assets fix their margins at close to 25 per cent and do not accept contracts with lower margins. However, with high levels of competition and easy to acquire capabilities, garment suppliers are forced to accept margins up to 10 per cent.

Brands are not beyond sharp practices that border on deceit. For example, one supplier said that a brand mentioned a large volume order and asked for a quotation. The supplier, thinking that they could manage with a lower margin on the large order, quoted accordingly. But when the time came to place the order, the brand reduced the order to just about one-tenth of the originally discussed quantity.

Within the broad contours of the buyer and supplier interactions described earlier, there are some variations. Negotiation practices shared by the buyers can be classified into three categories: quotation or tenders followed by negotiation by the brands or buyers, quotation followed by target price, and target price set by the buyers and brands. Supplier firms fell into two broad types. One is of those that followed a capability development strategy based on technological advancement, improvement in management processes, and enhancement of skill, including multi-skilling, of workers. The other type is of those that followed an extensive strategy of increasing the number of precariously employed workers and increasing overtime. As will be seen in the following sections, these two types of firms, named in brief as ones following capability development and labour-intensive strategies, also tended to interact with brands in different ways.

Quotations Followed by Negotiations

This is a practice in which a quotation is asked for from suppliers for specific articles according to the buyer's requirements, followed by a negotiation with selected suppliers. As shown in Table 11.7 later in the chapter, not a single firm adopting a labour-intensive strategy reported this practice and, thus, they have no scope for negotiation,whereas 46 per cent of firms adopting capability development strategies reported this practice, showing that there is some level of negotiation with them. One plausible explanation for this could be the price offered by technologically sound firms that labour-intensive firms cannot match. The labour-intensive firms are mostly left to accept orders that have some target prices or orders that are given a target price after taking quotations from the suppliers.

Quotation on Target Price

Suppliers are supposed to give quotations for specific products with a target price that is slightly flexible. The target price here is fixed by the buyer, and the suppliers have minimal power. The data from the SLD study shows that 74 per cent of firms adopting labour-intensive strategies get orders on the basis of this practice. The problem with this practice is that it brings in competition among suppliers, resulting in a target price allowing the least margin possible. In such discussions, buyers also bring in supposed competitive offers from Bangladesh or Vietnam. Many suppliers reported that even when there is no margin at all,they sometimes have to accept orders just to stay in business.

Target Price

This is the most retrograde buyer–supplier interaction seen in the industry, where the supplier has to produce on a fixed target price. There is absolutely no negotiation process involved in this mode, and suppliers are relegated to a position of mere choosers. According to the suppliers, this practice is mostly followed by buyers or brands that have their own designs and samples and want a simple cut-make-trim (CMT) operation.

Global Buyers Capture Value in Garment GVCs

In this chapter, the core thematic area under discussion from the field survey is the extreme imbalance in the monopsony relationship between buyers and suppliers in the garment GVCs and the corresponding impact upon the economic condition of small and medium enterprises (SMEs). In the SLD primary study, 15 SME units each from three clusters, in the Delhi NCR, Bangalore, and Tiruppur, were covered, amounting to a total of 45 garment supplier firms. The SLD study investigated changes in the business practices of buyers and changes in supplier production systems, either as a response to changes in the brands' demands or to the suppliers' own strategies. It also looked into aspects of the labour situation within the production units and their employment standards.

The three clusters, Delhi NCR, Bangalore, and Tiruppur, produce a different mix of products. Tiruppur is the knitwear capital, largely producing what are called basics, such as T-shirts, with an average ex-factory price of USD 4. Bangalore produces a higher range with an average price of USD 10. The Delhi NCR, on the other hand, produces in the higher range with

Table 11.1 Trend in Ex-Factory Price and Margins across Garment Clusters

	Ex-Factory Price (USD)		**Margins (Per Cent)**	
Location of the Cluster	2011–2012	2017–2018	2011–2012	2017–2018
Delhi NCR	13	17	19	15
Bangalore	8	10	19	13
Tiruppur	4	4	20	12
Total	9	10	19	13

Source: Own fieldwork.

an average price of USD 17. The margin is also the highest for Delhi NCR at 15 per cent as against 12 and 13 per cent for Bangalore and Tiruppur, respectively. There is a reduction in margins in all three clusters, but it is the most in Tiruppur, where it went down from 20 per cent to 12 per cent (Table 11.1). Knitwear is a highly competitive supply product, with competition from Bangladesh, Cambodia, Vietnam, and other countries.

Delhi NCR produces more garments with embroidery and embellishment. These are more niche products in which the cluster has an old specialization. This specialization reaches homeworkers in hand embroidery centres, such as Bareilly, in north India. Embroidery is also more labour-intensive than knitwear, which is largely mechanized.

Shrinking Lead Time and Margins

Over the last decade, there has been a reduction in lead times—from 84 days in 2012 to 63 days in 2018, a reduction of about 25 per cent. This is, of course, the result of the growth of 'fast fashion' pioneered by the Spanish brand Zara, but then copied by most other garment brands. From four sets of designs in a year based on the seasons, garments moved to 12 or even more design sets in a year. Point-of-sale systems transmit real-time information from the retail floor. This is used for replenishing orders that have to be supplied very quickly. Combined with the practice of keeping inventories low, if not eliminating them altogether, fast fashion has led to a substantial fall in lead times. As seen in Table 11.2, the fall in lead times took place in all three clusters.

Strategies Adopted by Suppliers

The advent of fast fashion and global competition has forced suppliers to adopt various strategies to remain competitive and reduce lead times to retain their markets. Based on the management practices (strategy) adopted by the

Table 11.2 Trend in Lead Time across Different Garment Clusters

	Lead Time (Days)	
Location of the Cluster	2011–2012	2017–2018
Delhi NCR	75	59
Bangalore	89	64
Tiruppur	89	66
Total	84	63

Source: Own fieldwork.

firms, they can be classified into two types: those with a strategy of capability or knowledge development and those with a strategy of the intensification of labour. Firm-level capability development has three aspects to it—the adoption of new technology, improvements in management practices, and capability building of the workforce. The labour intensification strategy, on the other hand, consists of increasing the use of precariously employed contract labour and the increase of overtime.

In discussions with owners and managers, we found that their strategic choices were based on a need to remain competitive in the market in terms of price rather than an attempt to move into different product segments. To remain competitive, suppliers carried out both process and functional innovations. Taking on more functions, such as the sourcing of fabric and trimming, and providing full-package supply rather than just CMT manufacture was common. Most suppliers had moved in the direction of functional upgrading in the decade of the 2000s, particularly after the 2008 recession, when there was price pressure from the brands. The trends observed in the last decade (the 2010s), and captured in our firm surveys between 2016 and 2019, were more related to the shrinking of lead times with 'fast fashion'.

Capability development was the strategy measure adopted by suppliers who sought to identify the factors that limited their efficiency and productivity and then to work upon them with improved management practices, involving better knowledge of the internal production routines and requirements to reduce internal delays. The following were some of the factors that suppliers identified: time taken in receiving the raw material, low efficiency of (inadequately trained) workers with low rates of retention, inadequate use or use of old technology, lack of proper stock management, and too many varietiesof garments with very few similar processes of manufacturing.

Reductions in cost are not only brought about by changes in technology, such as those involved in substituting multi-head machines for hand embroidery. Much of it is due to improvements in firm-level management processes that result in better internal supply chains. For instance, one of us has seen a factory so poorly organized that a room full of tailors were sitting idle at their sewing machines, waiting for cut pieces to be brought to them. Poorly organized stock rooms led not just to time wasted in searching for needed inputs but also in the purchase of materials that had already been purchased. Improvements in the management of internal supply chains often result from utilizing business process software. Overall, growth-minded suppliers have been seen to utilize superior management processes when compared to suppliers who were not so concerned with growth (Nathan and Harsh 2018).

Capability development also extended to workers. Attrition rates of workers in excess of 10 per cent per month are common in all these clusters. Firms that went with capability development took measures such as increasing the efficiency of the workers by training and multi-skilling them. This gave an incentive to these firms to retain these workers by giving them a permanent status. These firms also upgraded their machinery, streamlined the product range, and took orders for similar products, keeping required fabric in stock. They adopted more computerized operation systems utilizing enterprise planning software, even if not fully, to rationalize internal supply chains and reduce inventory costs. Firms adopting capability development strategies tried to minimize the insecurity of orders by becoming preferred suppliers and supplying a higher share of their production to long-term buyers.

While many firms opted for a capability building strategy, combining technological upgrading with improved management practices and more skilled workers, others opted for labour-intensive strategies, such as simply increasing the labour force, increasing overtime, and subcontracting to unregistered workshops.

Table 11.3 distinguishes between the type of firms we surveyed based on the management practices adopted in responding to reduced lead time in order to maintain competitiveness. It was reported that 58 per cent of the firms adopt capability building activities, such as technological upgrading or skilling of workers. Traditional labour intensive practices were followed by 42 per cent of firms to respond to reduced lead times.

Table 11.3 Distribution of Firms Based on Main Strategy to Meet Falling Lead Times

	Per Cent of Firms
Capability building	58
Labour intensive	42

Source: Own fieldwork.

Table 11.4 Strategy Adopted and Number of Workers

	Number of Workers (Per Cent)	
	Less than 200	**Greater than 200**
Capability building	44	56
Labour-intensive strategies	100	0

Source: Own fieldwork.

Table 11.4 shows that all firms of relatively small size—which is represented by the category of less than 200 employees—resorted to labour-intensive strategies. Of the firms with a workforce of more than 200 employees, 56 per cent report adoption of technological and/or knowledge-driven strategies.

It is quite evident that larger firms are moving into skilling of the labour force and technological upgrading. On the other hand, smaller units resort to labour-driven strategies of an increase in overtime, increase in labour force, and subcontracting. Skilling and technological upgradation both involve capital expenditure, and smaller players are not in a financial position to adopt the same in the wake of falling margins, or to face the risk that always exists in any investment in capability development. Uncertain orders magnify the risks involved in investment in technological upgrading. This is indicative of the direction in which the industry is heading with respect to the fate of smaller players, who report an adoption of labour intensification to remain competitive with falling lead times and this,in turn, leads to a further deterioration in labour standards of the industry. This becomes an important signpost for the agenda to be taken up for strengthening the industry where technological and skilling support has to be provided for the smaller players in the industry, which is a responsibility of not only the state machinery but also the buyers/brands, which have an important role to play. Larger buyers and brands need to play their part in providing security in orders rather than leaving it to be a season-to-season matter.

Table 11.5 Strategy Adopted and Share of Contract Workers

	Share of Contract Labour (Per Cent)	
	Less than 50 per cent	**Greater than 50 per cent**
Technological or knowledge-driven strategies	89	11
Labour-intensive strategies	52	48

Source: Own fieldwork.

Table 11.5 compares the quality of labour practices with respect to the workforce and the strategies adopted in firms to counter the reduction in lead times. Of the firms adopting capability development strategies, 89 per cent hired less than 50 per cent of the workforce as contract labour. While nearly half of the labour-intensive factories reported more than 50 per cent of contract labour in the total workforce, close to 90 per cent of the capability driven firms has more regular workers. The result is significant from the workers' point of view in that the technological capability-driven strategies require a regular and stable workforce. Operating technologically advanced machinery requires a corresponding development of workers' capabilities. The investment by suppliers in upgrading worker capabilities will only pay off if they are able to retain the workers. This would require the workers to be in the permanent cadre rather than working as contract labour, which is prone to very high attrition rates.

The important question is: What was the outcome of adopting the capability development strategy? Did capability development, with its investment in equipment and skilling, lead to higher rates of return than the labour-intensification strategy? In the SLD survey, firms reported on the changes in their margins in the six-year period from 2011–2012 to 2017–2018.

Table 11.6 shows that while margins were slightly higher for technology or knowledge-intensive suppliers in 2011–2012, by 2017–2018, there was no difference in the margins for the two types of suppliers. The margins of both were 13 per cent in 2017–2018. This shows in a very stark manner that cost reduction brought about by upgrading is essentially captured by the buyers in the GVCs. This leaves the technologically upgraded firms with the same margin as the risk-averse firms with labour-intensive strategies. However, there was some benefit for the capability development firms in that they did get some scope for bargaining with brands and, importantly, larger and more stable orders.

Table 11.6 Distribution of Margins and Lead Times by the Strategy Adopted

	Lead Time (Days)		**Margins (Per Cent)**	
	2011–2012	**2017–2018**	**2011–2012**	**2017–2018**
Technological or knowledge-driven strategies	90	60	20	13
Labour-intensive strategies	70	60	18	13

Source: Own fieldwork.

Table 11.7 Strategy Adopted and Buyer–Supplier Interaction on Prices

	Quotation and Negotiation (Per Cent)	Quotation and Target Price (Per Cent)	Target Price (Per Cent)
Technological or knowledge-driven strategies	46	27	27
Labour-intensive strategies	0	74	26

Source: Own Fieldwork

Table 11.7 shows how the strategy adopted by firms influence interaction with buyers in the bargaining process. Of the firms that adopt capability-driven strategies, 46 per cent reported having some negotiating space with the buyers, which, on the other hand, is completely absent for firms adopting labour-intensive strategies. The quality of negotiation and its influence on prices are still questionable, but it gives the firms a space to discuss the prices and the specification of products. But though limited, having some space for discussion is a positive factor in a limited redoing in brand–supplier relations, a redoing that is too limited to be called a restructuring of bargaining relations.

The data in Tables 11.4, 11.5, and 11.6 shows that suppliers adopting technological- and knowledge-driven strategies are comparatively larger in size both in terms of labour force and production capacity. Firm owners observed that due to the upgrading which they have undertaken, they are able to handle bigger volumes and hence are able to maintain a targeted level of profit, if not a rate of profit. This technological upgrading by the suppliers does not necessarily result in a decrease in value capture by the brands. But it is the increase in the scale of production that keeps the large firms going, despite the advantages of technological upgrading being captured by the brands or the buyers.

Table 11.8 brings in a comparative analysis between the strategies adopted by firms and the increase in the quality of the product, and the increase in the sales price. It is interesting to note that the majority of the firms, irrespective of the strategy adopted, observed that there was an increase in product quality.

Table 11.8 Strategy Adopted and Increase in Product Quality and Sales Price

	Increase in Product Quality (Per Cent)	Increase in Sales Price (Per Cent)
Capability development strategies	89	58
Labour-intensive strategies	95	95

Source: Own fieldwork.

With respect to prices, 95 per cent of firms that adopted a labour-intensive strategy reported an increase in prices. On the other hand, only 58 per cent of firms who resorted to capability-driven strategies reported an increase in sales price. This suggests that firms that adopt technological- and knowledge-driven strategies are not benefitting enough on monetary terms, while the increase in price for the labour-driven firms is mainly due to the nature of products they are engaged in producing—fashion apparel, with more hand embroidery. Large firms seem to concentrate on order size. But there are many small firms, especially in Tiruppur, that produce low-value basics using labour-intensive strategies.

Technological Upgrading and Margins in Garment Manufacture: A Macro Picture

In order to further explore and triangulate the results from the field that adoption of capability development strategies in the Indian garment industry does not fetch much gain for firms, we analysed ASI unit records. Our field-level data and observations revealed that business has been growing in terms of volume but not in terms of returns. In simple terms, the profits and total value addition are increasing, but the margins and worker productivity are not. Here, we analyse ASI micro-data for the garment industry in India from the period 2010 to 2015.

The garment firms we analysed are classified into SMEs and large firms based on the SME classification criteria.[1] We use classification based on investment in plant and machinery to reflect the technological adoption in the industry. Along with investment in plant and machinery, we analyse the value of computer and allied software and per worker value of both to indicate the technological upgrading in the industry. Further, we analyse the trend in productivity by exploring aspects of GVA, profits, margins, and worker productivity (GVA per worker). Finally, we use relational analysis of the aspects indicating technological upgrading in the industry and aspects of productivity to establish the case of value capture in the GVCs.

Table 11.9 reports the trend of various industry aspects that indicate the technological upgrading in the industry. We explore the value of the plant and the machinery, the value of computer and allied software, and per worker value of both these aspects to indicate technological upgrading in the garment industry.

Value of Plant and Machinery

The value of the plant and the machinery per worker is higher in large units than in SMEs. While SMEs show an increase in the value of plant and

Table 11.9 Trend in Investment (in Million INR) in Computer and Allied Software

	2010	**2011**	**2012**	**2013**	**2014**	**2015**	**Trend Growth Rate**
Value of Plant and Machinery (in Million INR)							
SME	3.8	3.8	3.3	4.1	4.3	3.9	2%
Large Firms	143.4	139.3	116.7	111.8	114.8	111.2	-5%
Value of Computer and Allied Software(in 100,000 INR)							
SME	0.86	0.87	0.82	1.20	1.27	1.07	8%
Large Firms	22.97	23.65	18.35	19.58	18.49	16.45	-6%
Per-Worker Value of Computer and Allied Software							
SME	908	868	928	959	1,010	933	2%
Large Firms	2,437	2,067	1,663	1,698	1,355	1,519	-10%
Per-Worker Value of Plant and Machinery							
SME	35,377	38,522	36,241	37,880	38,691	37,960	1%
Large Firms	122,018	139,750	126,761	135,597	116,811	115,748	-2%

Source: Computed from the unit records of the ASI.

machinery, the large firms show a decline during the period. Further clarifying the argument, the trend growth rate of the value of the investment in plant and machinery in large firms during the period 2010–2015 is -5 per cent while that of SMEs is 2 per cent. This clearly shows that there is a declining trend of upgrading in large firms in the garment industry. A possible explanation for the same is the depreciation of the already existing plant and machinery assets. With regard to technological aspects, if the value of depreciation is higher than the value of the investment in a year, it is quite indicative of the lack of technological upgrading in the industry.

Value of Computer and Allied Software

Investment in computer and allied software is specifically indicative of investment resulting in process upgrading in the industry. The value of software per worker in large units is about 50 per cent higher than in SMEs. This confirms the point made earlier that cost reductions in large supplier units are largely the effect of process improvements, resulting in the better organization of work.

As with the investment in plant and equipment, the value of computer and allied software is declining in large firms while SMEs report a growth. SMEs reported a growth of 8 per cent over the period 2010–2015 in the value of computer and allied software, but large firms reported a negative growth of -6 per cent. This further indicates the lack of incentives in upgrading, which forms a key argument posed in this chapter.

With regard to per worker value of computer and allied software and value of plant and machinery, in actual value, large firms report higher value than SMEs. However, the trend shows that the SMEs are reporting an increase while large firms are reporting a decline.

The findings in Table 11.9 are of significance to the core argument made in this chapter. On the one hand, large firms are definitely more technologically advanced than SMEs, but, on the other hand, these large firms are moving away from technological upgrading, which is evident from the decline reported in all aspects indicating technological upgrading. As mentioned earlier, depreciation accounts for the decline, which means that the value of depreciation in large firms is higher than the investment in each year.

Table 11.10 Trend in Aspects of Productivity in the Garment Industry

	2010	2011	2012	2013	2014	2015
			GVA (in Million INR)			
SME	18	21	23	28	31	35
Large Firms	169	219	277	281	330	295
			GVA per Worker (in 100,000 INR)			
SME	1.64	1.95	2.09	2.09	2.49	2.76
Large Firms	1.41	1.95	2.28	2.52	2.79	2.83
			Profits (in Million INR)			
SME	2	1	1	2	3	1
Large Firms	34	22	25	26	46	27
			Margins (Per Cent)			
SME	8	7	8	7	7	7
Large Firms	7	8	10	9	9	9

Source: Computed from the unit records of the ASI.

Table 11.10 looks at trends in different aspects of productivity. GVA and GVA per worker relate to the aspects of productivity from a production point of view. Profits and margins report the productivity aspects from a returns point of view. The rationale of the comparison between SMEs and large firms is that the classification is indicative of the focus on technology and upgrading in the industry.

While GVA and profits are both significantly higher for the large firms, there is no significant difference in GVA per worker and also in the margins between SMEs and large firms. This very well validates the observation from the field that the technological upgrading in the industry has helped firms to increase the volume of production, leading to greater value addition and profits. However, it has neither really translated into higher worker productivity nor higher margins. The GVA per worker is INR 283,000 in large firms and INR 276,000 in SMEs. Margins are 9 per cent in large firms and 7 per cent in SMEs.

The case of technologically upgraded firms here, which are large firms, is of specific interest. While these firms have invested significantly more in technological upgrading and earn a higher gross profit, they have margins similar to the SMEs, which are technologically not on par with the large firms. If we look further into the relationship between productivity and technological upgrading in the garment industry, Table 11.11 shows the bivariate correlation of the aspects under study. Profit and GVA of both large firms and SMEs are positively influenced by the investment in plant and machinery and the value of computers and allied software. However, the other two aspects of margins and GVA per worker show no significant relationship with the value of plant and machinery and the value of computer and allied software. The most significant result here is that margins show no significant relationship with any aspect of technological upgrading, whether in equipment or IT services.

It is important to note that the worker productivity measured in terms of GVA per worker shows no significant relation with respect to either gross investment in plant and machinery and computer and allied software or per capita investment in the same. This was descriptively presented earlier, where we have seen that there is no significant difference in GVA per worker in the large and small firms while there is a large difference in the gross values. It also may be noted that the gross GVA of both SMEs and large firms are positively correlated to per worker investments too. This indicates that the investments are actually increasing the volume of business but not its efficiency.

Is it likely that despite higher per worker investment in equipment and IT software in large firms compared to SMEs, there is no difference in the GVA per worker between large firms and SMEs. Discussions with firms show that investment is carried out in more up-to-date sewing machines

Table 11.11 Relation between Capital Investment, Productivity Measures, and Size of Firms

	Profit	Margins	GVA	GVA/Worker
		SME		
Investment inplant and machinery	.079**	N.S.	.272**	N.S.
Value of computers and allied software	.181**	N.S.	.398**	N.S.
Per worker value of plant and machinery	N.S.	N.S.	.153**	N.S.
Per worker value of computers and allied software	N.S.	N.S.	.055*	N.S.**
		Large Firms		
Value of plant and machinery	.281**	N.S.	.651**	N.S.
Value of computers and allied software	.185**	N.S.	.454**	N.S.
Per worker value of plant and machinery	N.S.	N.S.	.118*	N.S.
Per worker value of computers and allied software	N.S.	N.S.	.044**	N.S.

Source: Computed from the unit records of the ASI.
Notes: * significant at .05; ** significant at .01; N.S. not significant relation.

and ancillary equipment, such as multi-head embroidery machines and other such equipment in non-sewing tasks. All of these increase productivity per worker. Improvements in business processes, such as more efficient stock management and multi-skilling of workers, are also reported to increase productivity (Nathan and Juneja 2018). So, how is it possible that there is no difference in the GVA per worker between large firms and SMEs? It should be remembered that the GVA figures are based on ex-factory prices. Brands are well aware of investments and improvements being undertaken by their suppliers. They can well utilize individual bargaining to secure reductions in prices, citing competitive offers from other suppliers, including those from Bangladesh or Vietnam. The carrot they hold out is that of higher and more stable orders.

Who is really benefitting from the increase in productivity from technological upgrading by the suppliers? It can only be the buyers: the monopsonistic brands that are able to reduce ex-factory prices in order to capture the reduction of costs due to productivity increases.Suppliers have revealed, in anonymous discussions, that they are not compensated for increases in prices of inputs, having to make up by increasing production efficiency. On the other hand, when the devaluation of the Indian rupee would increase the INR equivalent of USD prices, buyers insist on dollar price reductions. Either way, brands are able to take the benefit of price and productivity changes. Larger suppliers seek to compensate for price reductions by becoming preferred suppliers with higher volumes.

Our major observations from the ASI data on garment manufacturers are as follows:

1. Large firms in the garment sectors have a significantly higher investment in technological upgrading compared to SMEs.
2. Large firms in the garment sector have significantly higher profits and GVA compared to SMEs.
3. With regard to margins and worker productivity, however, there is no significant difference between SMEs and large firms. While there clearly would be an increase in physical productivity in large firms, the benefits of this increase in productivity are captured by the brands. Because of this capture by the brands of the benefits of higher physical productivity in large suppliers, we get the quite astonishing result that there is hardly any difference in the GVA per worker between large and SME suppliers.
4. Hence, the technological upgrading in the large firms has only helped them to make their business bigger in terms of volumes.
5. The technological upgrading in large firms does not translate into higher margins.

Comparison with Suppliers in Other GVCs

Innovations or technological upgrading that cannot be protected by intellectual property rights (IPRs) and are easy to copy are features of supplier segments. On the other hand, design and marketing are either protected by IPRs or difficult-to-enter segments. Kaplinsky, Morris, and Readmond (2002) showed that investment in the use of computerised numerical control (CNC) machinery in the South African furniture industry did not provide higher profit rates for manufacturers. The international buyers who concentrated on design and marketing were able to capture the benefits of manufacturers reducing production costs, leading even to immiserizing growth, that is, growth with lower net incomes per unit of production.

A quick comparison of the GVA per worker in the manufacture of leather shoes and the auto-component sector shows that, in the former, there is a 20 per cent difference between large firms and SMEs, while in the latter, that is, the auto-component sector, there is a much bigger difference of around 80 per cent in the GVA per worker between large firms and SMEs. It should be remembered that the auto-components segment includes a number of firms that have IPR protection for their components, such as braking systems or spark plugs. Garment suppliers seem to be quite unique in terms of investment in equipment and computerization not showing up as significant differences in the GVA per worker between large units and SMEs.

Since large suppliers have a higher volume of profits, due to their larger turnover, they do have some scope to provide higher wages. And we have seen that wages and security of employment and other side benefits that are provided are higher in large units (Nathan, Saripalle, and Gurunathan 2016). But the inability to secure a higher profit margin with better employment conditions means that these units can increase wages without reducing profit margins, only if the wage increases are compensated by higher productivity.

Conclusion

This chapter furthered our argument that brands in monopsonistic garment GVCs appropriate or capture the productivity increase and also the subsidies in all the nodes in the value chains—the factory, the household, and the environment. These subsidies result in lowered prices of labour power and environmental inputs, but they do not result in higher margins for the suppliers. Rather, since they contribute to keeping ex-factory prices low, they end up increasing brand profits. It is the capture by brands of the benefits of these subsidies that turns them into reverse subsidies, in the sense that the subsidies are extracted from workers, their households, and the environment, and go to enhance the profits of the brands. In the process, suppliers are left with just about the competitive profit, the minimum necessary to continue in business.

It was observed from both the field-level data and unit records of the ASI that the technological- and knowledge-driven changes adopted by the suppliers have only enabled them in being competitive in the market with respect to pricing. Hence, the margins earned have not really increased with the technological- and knowledge-driven changes in the industry. The study shows that capability development strategies, which consist of technological- and knowledge-driven changes, have helped the suppliers to stay competitive at pricing and securing larger and stable orders. It has not translated into higher margins for the suppliers. Benefits to the workforce in larger firms have been limited to those that relate to increasing the efficiency of production.

Now, regarding value capture in the GVC in garments, it is quite clear that the profit accumulation happens at the higher- or brand-end of the GVCs. The supplier firms, featuring low skill level, minimal knowledge transfer from the buyers, and led by a power asymmetry tending towards the buyers, are held in captive governance ties and thereby belong to a lower bargaining in the GVC. As a result of this lower position, the profitability and productivity of the firms remain low, regardless of the changes initiated. Hence, in a GVC structure of captive governance, the fruits of the technological advancement, which is higher volumes, benefit the brands or buyer firms by keeping ex-factory prices really low. In sum, the governance ties in GVCs and the nature of upgrading in the industry contribute towards the low profitability and productivity of the garment suppliers.

There are two factors that are said to reduce power asymmetry in bargaining. One is the increased competence of the suppliers (Sturgeon and Linden 2007). The other is large size, as described in Kumar (2020). The SLD study looked at the effects of improved competence or enhanced firm-level capabilities through investments in technology and improved managerial and labour processes. The benefits of the increased productivity, however, did not accrue to the suppliers: their margins did not increase. What they did achieve was firm growth through larger and more stable orders. In terms of bargaining with brands, the firms that enhanced capabilities did have some leeway in bargaining. But it did not change the crucial result of margins.

These findings strengthen the point made in Chapter 3 that knowledge and capability enhancement do not translate into greater bargaining power in GVCs unless that knowledge and capability can be turned into some form of IPR, either in the form of legal protection or of hard-to-acquire, often tacit, knowledge. Size by itself could make a small difference, seen, for instance, in that a large Indian supplier, Shahi Garments, did not suffer the same brand demands for discounts during the 2020 recession. Size, through collective action, also enabled Bangladesh garment manufacturers to secure a rollback of brand demand for discounts. We should not negate the importance of these gains, but they cannot be termed as a change in the balance of power within the garment GVCs. A change in the balance of power within a GVC is measured through a change in the relative profit rates earned in the different segments.

The size factor could be looked at by comparing large and SME suppliers. Here too, there was no impact of size on firm performance in terms of the GVA per worker; the GVA per worker was about the same for large and SME units. The large unit discussed by Ashok Kumar (2020) is Arvind Textiles, the largest denim producer in the world. Here, it is the dominating position of this supplier in a speciality fabric market that gives it a better bargaining position vis-à-vis the brands. It is this monopoly position as a supplier of a key input that gives it some bargaining power. A degree of monopoly position is developed from the difficult-to-acquire knowledge of denim production. It is likely, therefore, that there is some increase in margins that can be secured by such a monopoly position in the supply of a key input.

The monopsony structure of the garment GVC enables the brands to capture the value that is produced in different segments and also extracted from input suppliers, such as the worker, her household, both urban and rural, and the environment. This capture of subsidies through low input prices is what turns these subsides into reverse subsidies. Of course, if these subsidies had ended up contributing to higher profits for the suppliers, they would still have been reverse subsidies, but they could have contributed to accumulation of profits by the suppliers. Since they end up adding to brand profits, one could say that they are double-reverse subsidies, reverse in being from gendered workers and the environment and also in being transferred from supplier economies in the Global South to headquarter economies in the Global North.

Notes

1. The classification criteria refers to the one based on 'investment in plant and machinery' and not on the latest update where industries are classified in terms of investment and annual turnover.

12
Conclusion

In Chapter 1, a subsidy was defined as the purchase of a product, such as labour power, or an environmental service, such as water, below their cost of production. The cost of production of a commodity is the sum of the various inputs that go into its making, plus a normal profit for capital. This is Marx's prices of production or also a neo-Keynesian definition of cost. The difference between the cost of production and the price of the product, however, does not just disappear from the value chain. The cost is incurred somewhere, either in the household where labour is reproduced or within the environment. If this incurred cost is not compensated, it appears as a subsidy extracted from the household or environment.

The extraction of the subsidy takes place in multiple locations: the factory and other sites of production, such as worker and farmer households, and also the environment. Thus, it may seem that the subsidy is being provided to or benefiting the producer, which is the factory owner in the value chain. However, monopsony relations in the value chain result in the capture of that subsidy by the brands, who are able to keep supplier prices down to incurred monetary costs. Thus, there is a distinction between the site of subsidy extraction, which is the supplier factory, and the site of its capture, which occurs through the monopsony relation between brands and suppliers. This is important in the analysis of global value chains (GVCs), such as that of garments, where the monopsony structure of the input market enables the capture of subsidy by the brands even when the extraction of that subsidy takes place under the management of the supplier or local authorities in supplier countries.

Consequently, since the subsidy (in terms of lower prices of inputs) translates into lower ex-factory prices of garments, the subsidies are reverse subsidies to brands—from gendered labour, farmer households, and the environment. These are reverse subsidies in two senses. The first is that they are extracted from the weakest and worst-off in the value chain. The second is that they do not accrue to supplier firms; rather, through the monopsony structure, they are transferred to the brands. Not only do they constitute extreme forms of exploitation of gendered labour, farm households, and the environment in supplier countries but they are also a drain from the supplier economies of the Global South to those of the headquarter economies of the Global North.

The purchase of labour power and environmental services below their cost of production provides a simple and economic definition of the term 'subsidy'. However, when does this subsidy become an unjust subsidy?

Not all subsidies are unjust. Many economies provide subsidies to increase consumption of certain goods, such as food, health services, or education, which are provided below their cost of production. We are not characterizing such subsidies as unjust. Instead, they are just subsidies in that they allow all persons to achieve elementary capabilities with regard to nutrition, health, and education.

The reverse relationship exists between the payment of labour power below its cost of production and the attainment of elementary capabilities. Such wages below the cost of production do not allow the attainment of these elementary capabilities and thus violates the requirements for basic human existence—a condition that Iris Marion Young (2004: 385) identified as a basic injustice.

Therefore, an unjust subsidy is one that violates the basis for human existence by preventing the attainment of socially accepted elementary capabilities in nutrition, health, education, and related areas of well-being for a worker and her family. These unmet costs of the production of labour power are extracted from the worker herself, who has a cruelly short working life in the garment factories, usually forced to leave the factory by the age of 35 (or at best 45). The unmet costs are also borne by the homeworker, who works at much less than even the minimum wage, and even child labour, whose present and future are both blighted. The unmet costs are also extracted from the rural household of the worker, which sustains the worker during lay offs, illness, and retirement. The rural household also meets part of the cost, minus the remittances, of maintaining the workers' left-behind families.

Similarly, we can extend the notion of unjust subsidy to environmental services, where they are paid for at a rate below the cost of provision of these services as a result of which the unmet costs are extracted from other users of these environmental services or by a deterioration of the service. Services such as clean water are not maintainable at their socially required level due to the high level of subsidized extraction in the garment GVC. To sum up, we are arguing that subsidies are unjust when they do not enable the attainment of elementary human capabilities.

Besides gendered labour and environmental subsidies, there are other subsidies, particularly fiscal subsidies, provided to production in GVCs—

for instance, export processing zones (EPZs) with their tax holidays and restrictions of labour rights. These and other subsidies provided by the governments of supplier countries are quite well known and are not discussed here as unjust subsidies.

Paying labour wages that do not cover the cost of production of labour power then constitutes an unjust subsidy; unjust in the manner that the costs not being remunerated fails to enable the worker and her household to attain elementary capabilities. In a similar manner, acquiring environmental services at prices that do not cover their costs of production and cleaning lead to the depletion and degradation of the resource.

In a market-fundamentalist or neoliberal approach, the way enterprises work or should work in the market involves trading commodities at the prices at which they are available on the market, along with no interference in the market-based price-setting mechanism. At an analytical level, this market-fundamentalist approach reifies the market and places the interests of capital (global monopsony capital in this case) above all else. In Polanyi's characterization, this is the dominance of the market over society, which we amend to read: the dominance of monopoly–monopsony capital over the global economy and society (Polanyi 1944/2001).

The garment GVC is based on a double monopoly. In the first place, with branding, design, and various forms of protection of intellectual property rights (IPRs), the brands have a certain degree of monopoly in the product market. The monopoly sellers on the product market then appear as monopsony buyers on the input market. Utilizing global differences in the prices of labour power and environmental services, the brands organize production through GVCs. With the monopoly–monopsony structure of garment GVCs, which are really two sides of a coin, the brands are able to reduce costs and increase profits.

In a market-economy system, the assertion that prices should cover the costs of production is a principle that no one can reasonably reject, to use Scanlon's formulation (Scanlon 1998). Even in neoclassical economic analysis, equilibrium prices would have to be such that they cover the costs of production along with a normal profit. When market prices are below the costs of production, it is supposed to generate market exits that would reduce supply and push up prices until they cover the costs of production. This is the neoclassical equilibrium position, where none of the actors in the market has a reason to change their actions.

However, the market for labour power is not something from which workers can exit, particularly in labour-surplus economies—such as those in the Global South. Thus, the equilibrating mechanism does not work to reduce the supply of labour to the level of demand. This leads to employment at wages below the cost of production of labour power and also to unemployment.

The absence of meaningful social security in these supplier economies also compounds the compulsion of the workers to seek employment at almost any wage. As Polanyi argued, this shows that labour is a fictitious commodity, as also is nature. The questions of meeting the normal costs of production do not enter into these market valuations.

In order to develop a critique of this line of economistic thinking, we had to go beyond the core production system of the garment GVC, the factory, to look at its intersection with the worker's household and with the environment to see how labour power is procured from the household, and environmental services from the environment. Only by looking at the manner in which the GVC is embedded in the household and the environment is it possible to reveal how gendered labour and environmental subsidies are extracted.

In what follows, we summarize the manner in which these subsidies are extracted from the household and the environment and captured by the brands in garment GVCs. The analysis in this book, though specific to garment GVCs with much of its empirical base in India (supplemented by data from other garment suppliers across Asia), would also apply to any GVC based on a monopsony structure—what Ashok Kumar (2020) labels 'monopsony capitalism' and we call global monopoly-cum-monopsony capitalism.

Labour Subsidies in Manufacture

While with the gendered production cost of labour power is a living wage, which includes the monetization of domestic care work, wages in the garment GVC are generally around the national minimum wage. This national minimum wage varies from 19 per cent of the living wage in Bangladesh and Sri Lanka, 26 per cent in India, and 46 per cent in China. This means that the wage subsidy as a percentage of the living wage captured from labour varies from 81 per cent in Bangladesh and Sri Lanka, 74 per cent in India, and 54 per cent in China (AFWA 2013).

There can be wage subsidies that can be borne by the state. For instance, in the state of Jharkhand, India, the provincial government pays a subsidy of INR 5,000 per month to each worker employed in garment factories. This wage subsidy was initiated in order to attract Indian suppliers to set up factories in Jharkhand. However, this is an exceptional case of a wage subsidy provided by the state. Furthermore, since the wages the workers get is the minimum wage, the difference from the living wage is still borne by the workers and their rural households.

For the rest, the cost of this wage subsidy is borne by labour in a number of gendered ways. First is the mining of the workers' bodies, largely of women workers but, to some extent, of men too. This overuse-and-discard policy is reflected in the early expulsion of women from garment factories, with very few remaining past the age of 35, whether in Bangladesh, India, or Cambodia.

Women's unpaid care work, which forms a part of the cost of reproduction of labour power, is another part of the subsidy captured from women. In addition, women as homeworkers are paid around 50 per cent of the minimum wage. Along with this, the extreme exploitation of child labour—whether in carrying out work outsourced from exporting factories or on farms producing cotton—is yet another wage subsidy to reduce costs in garment GVCs.

A final form of the labour subsidy is that which is provided by the rural economy of left-behind households of single migrants. These mostly male—and single—migrants (but also an increasing number of single female migrants) are provided consumption support by their rural households when they are periodically laid off, healthcare support when they are ill and unable to work, and consumption during retirement. As dramatically illustrated during the COVID-19 lockdowns, the rural household serves as a safety net when employment in the garment industry collapses.

In all of these ways, wage subsidies provided by labour do not enter into cost calculations in deciding ex-factory or free on board (FOB) prices of garments. Thus, they provide a subsidy that increases the profits of brands. As stated by Stephanie Barrientos, 'The feminization of work in the commercial work of production of consumer and household goods helps keep down the labour cost and final price of those goods' (2019: 97). The final price in the sense of the ex-factory or FOB price is kept down, but that does not necessarily apply to the retail price, given the degrees of monopoly that brands have in the garments' markets.

Some of the labour cost subsidies may be passed on to consumers as consumer surplus. Keeping the prices of basic goods (such as garments) low is part of the current low wage social contract, for instance, in the United States (US) (Freedman and Lind 2013). Cheap garments based on reverse subsidies extracted from labour and the environment in the Global South participate in keeping wages in the Global North low. In one way or the other, the labour subsidy is transferred to the Global North.

Extracting labour subsidies in the factory is made possible by a combination of labour force and industrial-relations factors. The surplus-labour condition in India and other developing countries of the Global South means that workers will accept employment at wages that are just slightly above the rural alternative. This army of surplus labour is a necessary condition for workers to accept employment at wages well below the living wage.

At the factory level, repressive industrial-relations practices, adopted by factory management supported by their respective national governments, are also part of the extraction process. Gender-based violence and oppression on the shop floor is the manner of supervision through which extra work is forced on women workers. In addition, freedom of association is denied to workers, with great costs borne by those who try to form unions. Normal procedures of collective bargaining are closed off, giving rise to what Hobsbawm (1968) called 'collective bargaining by riot', most visible in Bangladesh.

More recently, the mass reverse migration of garment workers from the garment clusters in India was termed a 'collective bargaining by mass exodus' (SLD 2020). The pandemic situation also saw the emergence of collective bargaining by garment manufacturers in Bangladesh, who used their collective power to threaten a boycott of brands that did not meet their pre-pandemic contractual obligations to pay for garments already delivered (Kumar 2020).

Labour Subsidies in Cotton Production

Labour subsidies are prevalent not only in the manufacture of garments but also in the production of cotton. These are of two types. One is subsidies by cotton farmers. This is due to the low international price of raw cotton. The price is kept low by the vast income support provided to cotton farmers in the US, which enables them to sell cotton at international prices well below the costs of production even on US farms. This low international price affects the income of millions of farmers. This is the case particularly in some African countries, where the governments do not have the fiscal capacity to provide income support for cotton farmers. It is less so in India, where the government provides a form of minimum price support to cotton farmers, though just about 25 per cent of cotton is purchased at the minimum support price. Even then, it means that less fiscal space is available for other social security measures.

In cotton production, subsidies are also borne by agricultural labourers who work at rates below minimum wages. There is also substantial child labour involved in cotton cultivation, particularly in harvesting. Child labour, again, is of two types: those working with their families (mainly in cotton harvesting or older girls caring for younger siblings while both parents are at work), and children working as wage labourers who are paid a pittance, whether for pollination of *Bacillus thuringiensis* (Bt) cotton or other processes. These underage employees are often trafficked.

Environmental Subsidies

We now turn to environmental subsidies in both the manufacture of garments and the production of cotton. In socially embedding value chains, it is necessary to look at environmental services and resources that go into making a garment. In Chapter 9, we looked at the destruction of the River Nooyal, brought about by the garment industry in Tiruppur. In Bangladesh, the Buriganga has been similarly destroyed by the discharge of untreated effluents. These are usually treated as 'externalities'. They are external to the garment factory system but not to the people who use these rivers and related water resources.

The first environmental subsidy is in the cheap provision of fresh water for use in garment manufacture. Taking the cost of cleaning water with the reverse osmosis (RO) system as the benchmark price of water, fresh water is provided to factories and related dyeing and printing units at prices far below this cost. There is no charge for the extraction of groundwater, and any water from municipal sources is priced at a fraction of the cost of production of clean water, which can be approximated by the cost of recycling water, within the factory system, through the establishment of the RO or similar water-cleaning processes. The subsidy involved in the underpricing of fresh water is borne by those who are deprived of water by the falling groundwater level in the region.

An associated subsidy is in the overutilization and destruction of the water-cleaning properties of natural resources or the sink capacity of the environment. This is created through the discharge of untreated effluents into rivers and other water sources. These costs are borne by those farmers who live in the garment cluster areas and whose agricultural productivity has been reduced by the pollution of the waterways.

Yet another environmental subsidy is with respect to the accumulation of inorganic residues, resulting in the degradation and eventual destruction of the soil. We should also keep in mind that the Bt cotton cultivation region is labelled the cancer belt of Punjab. These are all subsidies borne by the cotton farmers themselves.

To summarize, subsidies are extracted from labouring households in garment manufacture, from farm households in cotton production, and from all those who suffer from the underpriced water supplied to factories and the pollution of the water from effluent discharges. All these subsidies can be termed unjust and reverse subsidies in garment GVCs.

Who Benefits, or Value Capture

Are these labour and environmental subsidies—whether in garment manufacture or raw cotton production—subsidies to global brands and, thus, reverse subsidies from gendered labour, farmers, and the environment in the Global South to the Global North? Yes, because by reducing the price of inputs, they allow for higher profits. The varying degrees of monopoly positions of brands in product markets translate into degrees of monopsony in the input markets, which are encompassed in the market for manufactured garments. As seen in Chapter 11, supplier profit rates remain fairly fixed, even when suppliers undertake cost-reducing investments. This monopsony relation results in the capture of the gains from productivity increases, mainly by the brands, with suppliers only getting the benefit of higher turnover. Margins do not increase for suppliers unless they also establish monopoly positions in their own technical areas. This occurs only with special areas such as denim production, where a degree of monopoly in supply seems to lead to an increase in margins. Firm size alone without the possession of knowledge that is privatized does provide some improvement in bargaining but does not seem to result in an increase in margins.

Given that brands are the chief beneficiaries of the subsidies extracted from gendered labour and the environment, these are reasons enough to argue that brands have the primary responsibility for rectifying the situation. In a sense, the Bangladesh Accord, under which brands committed to providing funds for improving building safety standards in Bangladeshi garment factories, is an acknowledgement of brand responsibility, due to their having profited from the lower costs associated with unsafe buildings.

The analysis of reverse subsidies in garment GVCs is summarized in Box 12.1.

Box 12.1 Reverse Subsidies in Garment GVCs

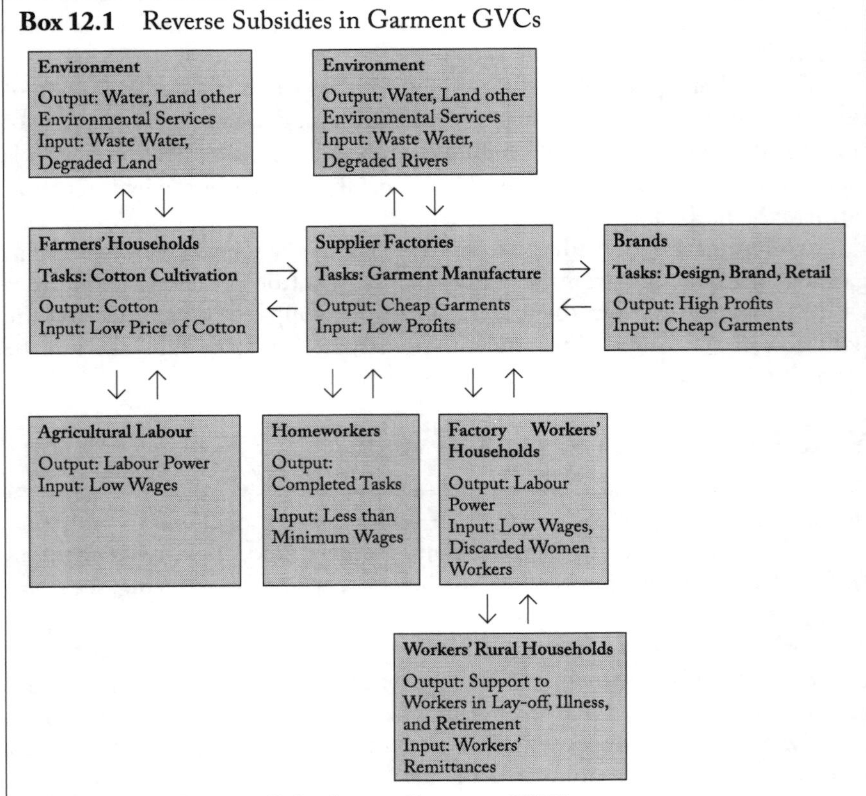

Figure 12.1 Reverse Subsidies in Garment GVCs
Source: Created by the authors.

We now return to the GVC representation in Figure 12.1 to fill out the interrelations between actors. A thin arrow represents a lower value than a thick arrow. This would mean that more is taken out as an output from an actor than is given back and would represent a reverse subsidy.

Starting with the cotton-cultivation segment, farmer households provide their labour (and material inputs) to cotton cultivation. The farmers, in turn, receive labour inputs from agricultural workers, including child labour. Labour from farmers' households and those of agricultural workers are remunerated with low prices of cotton and low wages for labour power.

Environmental services into cotton production include the supply of agricultural land and water, taken to represent all environmental services. These inputs are either unpriced or paid for at prices below the replacement cost of these services. They constitute a reverse subsidy from the environment to cotton cultivation. Cotton farmers provide cotton at prices kept globally low by highly subsidized production of cotton in the US and the European Union (EU). This is the basis of the subsidy provided by cotton farmers, along with agricultural workers and the environment, through cheap cotton into the cotton garments' GVC.

In the supplier factories' segment, this cheap cotton (as fabric, setting aside the processes in the transformation of raw cotton into fabric) is turned into garments. This key process involves subsidies from both gendered worker households and the environment.

The supply of labour power at a wage below a living wage, which is its cost of production, constitutes a gendered labour subsidy. One form of this subsidy is the overuse and early discard of women factory workers. Another form is the extraction of women's unpaid domestic work or care work for the reproduction of labour power. Yet another form of this subsidy is the reliance of low-paid factory workers on support from their rural households, especially in times of lay off, sickness, pandemic-induced lockdown, and retirement.

Homeworkers also provide a subsidy to factory production. They earn only about one-half to two-thirds of the minimum wage. This subsidy is extracted not only through low piece rates but also through homeworkers' provision of their own unpriced inputs into carrying out outsourced tasks.

Factory production also receives a subsidy from the environment. Clean water, often unpriced or certainly priced below its replacement cost, is a key environmental service. The factories, in turn, return untreated or partially treated waste, producing a degraded environment.

These are all subsidies from producer (worker and farmer) households and the environment into the production of garments. The last step of this process is where global monopsony comes into play. In the exchange between suppliers and brands, the low price of garments, due to the subsidies in their production, are transferred to the brands. The suppliers get competitive profits, allowing them to continue in business, while the brands secure the excess profits due to the low prices of the garments. Some of the low prices of the garments may also be transferred to consumers in the brands' headquarter economies in the Global North.

However, are brands *responsible* for labour and environmental conditions along the value chains in which their products are produced, or are they merely utilizing existing conditions in the Global South? Earlier, in Chapter 11 and in the preceding paragraphs in this Conclusion, we have discussed one way in which brands are responsible for value chain labour conditions—brands capture the bulk of profits in these value chains, and low labour and environmental costs contribute to brand profits. There is also another way in which it can be argued that brands do not just utilize existing supply conditions but also choose or fashion them in ways that maximize their profits. This is a stronger sense in which brands could be held responsible for conditions in their value chains. We take up this argument below in our discussion of supplier relations as a strategic choice of monopsony brands.

Supplier Relations: Strategic Choice of Monopsony Brands

Brands do have a strategic choice about the supplier relations they set up. They can choose between a strategy based on a long-term commitment to a supplier and another based on very short-term contracts with suppliers. They choose the strategy of keeping their exit options open in order to utilize the competition among suppliers. Keeping suppliers in a position to earn just about the minimal profit rate has (as we saw in Chapter 11) implications for wages and the quality of employment. It is this choice of adopting a strategy of not building a commitment to longer-term contracts that is a constraint for improving wages and other employment conditions among suppliers. As we saw in Chapter 11, in the few cases where some longer-term order relations have been built, there is some improvement in employment conditions.

It is this choice of short-term contracts with myriad suppliers that is the basis for holding brands responsible for labour conditions in their value chains. This strategic choice made by brands can be traced back to the compulsion of brands to maximize shareholder value, which itself is based on the tyranny of quarterly returns. The compulsion, if any, is not of the market as such but of short-term shareholder returns, compounded by financialization, in the monopoly–monopsony capitalism that constitutes GVCs.

In addition, there are two specific strategies adopted by brands in garment GVCs. The first is eliminating or reducing inventories to a bare minimum. The second strategy is fast fashion, with styles changing not just with seasons but virtually every two weeks. The reduction in lead times, as seen in Chapter 6, has led to enormous pressure on shop-floor routines and also the use of short-term, precarious employment to meet quick changes in orders.

Yet another business strategy of garment brands is to set labour costs in supplier factories on the basis of the prevailing national minimum wages. Existing The main point of our analysis in this book is to show that the price of labour power or wages needs to be adjusted to cover the costs of the production of labour power, and that the prices of environmental services, such as water, should also be adjusted to cover the costs of providing such environmental services. National minimum wages do not necessarily reflect the costs of production. For GVCs to be sustainable, both redistributive and regenerative forms of buyer–supplier relations are needed. Is that possible and, if so, how can that be brought about?

Pricing of Environmental Services

The pricing of environmental services is a major topic by itself. An objective of this book was to show that underpricing or free provision of environmental services is a subsidy that reduces the cost of manufacturing garments—a cost reduction that is captured by brands.

A major input in garment production, including the cultivation of cotton, is water. In cotton cultivation, this water is extracted from groundwater, and the only cost is pumping out and distributing the water. In Tiruppur, much of the water used in the factories and related units carrying out dyeing is acquired from the groundwater for just the cost of extraction. In Tiruppur, there is the additional problem that effluent from the garment units is not treated and directly discharged into the river, streams, and even into the groundwater. Treating and cleaning the water is a cost that should be added to supplier prices, which, of course, is not done.

Pricing water on the basis of the cost of treatment and cleaning through the RO process is said to allow the recycling of 95 per cent of the water (based on a discussion with staff at Arvind Mills, a manufacturer of denim, which is a very water-intensive product). Including the cost of this recycled water, using effluent treatment processes, would create a reasonably proper pricing of the key environmental input of water.

There are scale issues in effluent treatment plants. A large supplier such as Arvind Mills, the world's largest producer of denim, can utilize a cost-efficient water treatment plant for its own production. However, for small and medium garment manufacturers (and dyeing units), there would need to be common area plants.

So far, the costs of these treatment plants are borne locally at the site of production. In cases of large suppliers, they themselves undertake this investment. In the case of area units, it is the government that provides the funding, in some cases with partial contributions from producers. Our point is that the costs of cleaning up environmental negatives and providing environmental inputs need to be integrated into the ex-factory pricing of garments and that brands need to be brought into negotiations on the provision of these services. However, as pointed out in the case of trying to clean up the Tiruppur River, brands are not even considered to be involved in creating these negative externalities.

Way Forward

A higher wage—a living wage that covers the costs of reproducing labour power on both a daily and a generational basis, including the now unpaid labour of domestic care work—would not end labour arbitrage but moderate it. For instance, with wages in the US being around 30 times higher than what they are in India, a doubling of the wage in India and other similar supplier countries would only reduce the benefit that brands secure from labour arbitrage from 30 to 28—a small difference in rents for brands in the headquarter economies of the Global North, but a transition to a decent life for workers in supplier countries. A hypothetical calculation by Miller and Williams (2009) shows that a wage increase of 50 per cent to 100 per cent in Bangladesh would lead to a net retail price increase of 6.8 per cent. This is not a trivial increase, but it is well within the 15 to 25 per cent extra that US consumers are reported to be willing to pay in order to ensure that products are not made under sweatshop conditions (Pollin, Burns and Heintz 2004).

This would involve a redistribution of value along the chain, from brand rents to supplier workers' wages. How can this redistribution be brought about such that brands pay prices that would allow workers in supplier firms to earn a living wage? How we can move forward to establish a market economy system in which prices would cover the costs of production of labour power and environmental services is a question of political economy, a matter of analysing how the required coalitions of forces to bring about such a change can be established.

We have put forward an analysis of the injustices involved in subsidies extracted from gendered labour and the environment. This leads us to some points for transformation, but not a full analysis of the political economy of this transformation. It might even be impossible to put forward such a full analysis of the necessary transformation—almost until it has been carried out. Remember Hegel's quip that the owl of Minerva only takes flight at the break of dawn, implying that wisdom only comes when the phenomenon being studied has almost run its course. Analysis, however, is not for itself but to provide some guidance to policy and action. The point, then, is not to abandon analysis until a process has run its course but to continue to produce analysis that is 'less false' (Harding 2013) than something that preceded it.

The first point that emerges from our analysis is that the nation-state is no longer an adequate site of analysis for the phenomena of unjust subsidies fostered by monopsony capitalism. With GVCs, the inadequacy of the nation-state as the site of analysis is almost a truism. Looking at unjust subsidies where they occur, whether in the rivers that used to run through Tiruppur or Dhaka, will not enable us to take the steps needed to deal with this problem. The process creating the problem has to be framed as not just being local but having global connections. The Rana Plaza tragedy occurred in Dhaka, but it was co-created by the global forces of brands in conjunction with suppliers and lax government regulation. Consequently, the global framing of the problem as occurring through a GVC structure is critical to analysis and related policy.

The second point is that one needs to move beyond uni-dimensional movements to a multidimensional one. The factory, the site of the workers' resistance, is necessarily linked to the household and the environment. From this intersectionality of the factory with the household and the environment follows the necessity of linking labour movements with those of gender and environmental justice. Movements for social security to end the use of the rural safety net are also part of the intersectionality of factory labour with the household.

What this means is that it is necessary to move from single and separate movements to a 'movement of movements' to employ a phrase used by Tom Mertes (2003). Such multidimensional movements against monopoly–monopsony capitalism should also include those in the Global North, such as the moral consumer or moral shareholder and global labour justice movements, which have already played a role in effective campaigns and brand boycotts based on issues of labour, gender, and environmental justice linked to the activities of monopsony capital in the Global South.

As a result of these two factors—global connections and multidimensionality—the countervailing power to monopoly–monopsony capital will not be just that of labour alone but an alliance of women as workers and as caregivers in the household, other workers, farmers, and providers of environmental services, who are forced to provide subsidies to the profits of monopsony capital. The global countervailing power that Ulrich Beck (1992) saw as a necessary counterweight to secure the reformation of the global system will not be that of labour alone but of labour allied with gender and environmental justice movements. The alliance could extend beyond these to include other social movements too. In India, most of the lowest-paid factory workers are not only women; they are also Dalits—groups formerly considered untouchable castes. Consequently, movements for social justice could also be allied to those of workers, women, environmentalists, Dalits, and the rural poor.

Working on Both Sides of the Brand–Supplier Interaction

A change in the wage-environmental price base of garment GVCs can be the result of social forces acting on either side of the monopsony relationship or even on both sides simultaneously. It is necessary to consider the likely factors and forces that could bring about a shift of the supply curve towards higher wages and environmental costs. We will first consider initiatives that could change brands' decisions on supplier relations, even in the absence of changes on the supply side.

'Doing the Right Thing': Individual Brand Initiatives

Many brands have made statements committing themselves to eventually paying living wages to workers in supplier factories. However, not much has been done by major brands. M&S carried out an initiative that involved process improvements to reduce manufacturing costs for their suppliers so that the cost reductions could be passed on to workers as higher wages. It reported an increase in efficiency and even in wages through some form of enhanced production bonus. The important thing about this and similar scaling-up initiatives is that they did not involve the brand paying more. Increases in wages 'were achieved largely as a result of improvement in cut to ship ratio … and productivity—thus enabling buyers to avoid paying more' (Miller and Hohenegger 2018: 15).

On the other hand, some relatively small brands have instituted living-wage considerations. The Alta Gracias factory in the Dominican Republic, initially owned by the brand Knights Apparel, started paying a living wage to its workers (Adler-Milstein and Kline 2017). Being a small brand without price-making power (such as Nike), Knights Apparel had to stay competitive through process improvements to increase productivity. Two other small

European brands, Continental and Nudie Jeans, which have some price-making power (as they serve niche markets), have also introduced living-wage calculations into their supplier costs. Since they only utilize a portion of the production capacity of the two factories they collaborate with in India, they make proportional payments that are distributed among all the workers in the two factories. The extra costs are covered in two ways. Continental, the United Kingdom (UK) brand, added a premium to products made with living wages, explaining the mark-up in the label. Nudie Jeans, a Swedish brand, took a cut from its profits to pay for the higher wages (FairWear Foundation 2016).

This increase in minimum wages was not due to market compulsions. In fact, market compulsions would have worked in the opposite direction to pay only the market wages. They were carried out because '… it is the right thing to do' (Egels-Zander 2015: 121). Egels-Zander also thinks that 'by challenging the status quo and evoking resistance, SMEs can potentially trigger changes in GPN governance' (2015: 121).

The limitation of such individual firm interventions is that there is no guarantee that they will continue. A change in management may result in a different business strategy. There is neither any legal compulsion nor a market requirement to continue a living wage pilot. While such initiatives are useful as pilot schemes in setting examples and showing that they can work, scaling them up to the industry level requires something that affects all brands and buyers across the industry.

Before going on to discuss possible industry-level action, we will discuss three other ways in which firms can be nudged to 'do the right thing'. These are (*a*) the possible role of public procurement, (*b*) the actions of ethical consumers and shareholders, and (*c*) the role of multi-stakeholder initiatives.

Public Procurement

Public procurement does not have to follow the market logic of minimizing costs. It can be carried out with a view to achieve an ethical commitment to living wages while keeping production efficient. Thus, there is scope to extend pressure for the ethical sourcing of publicly procured garments. Public procurement is large and annually amounts to about EUR 1 trillion or an average of 12 per cent of the gross domestic product (GDP) across Organisation for Economic Co-operation and Development (OECD) countries (OECD 2017, quoted in Martin-Ortega and O'Brien 2017: 69). This is a large amount of procurement, so moving it to being carried out on a living-wage basis could have a big impact and set a standard in the global market. However, public procurement has been conducted with the primary objective of the achievement of 'value for money', which contradicts the secondary objective of promoting social and environmental goals (Martin-Ortega and O'Brien 2017: 70).

The International Labour Organization (ILO) Labour Clauses (Public Contracts) Convention, 1949 (No. 94), and Recommendation, 1949 (No. 84), require public buyers to observe socially acceptable labour standards. These, however, apply only to the national sphere. New initiatives, such as the European Fair Trade Association and Swedwatch, have sought to extend this respect for labour standards to the international level (Martin-Ortega and O'Brien 2017).

Some US cities have made extension of living-wage standards to international suppliers mandatory. San Francisco's Sweatfree Contracting Ordinance requires contractors and subcontractors to ensure a living wage adjusted to the country's level of economic development and Purchasing Power Parity Index (PPPI) (personal communication with Nicole Vander Meulen of the International Corporate Accountability Roundtable, ICAR). The cities of Madison (Wisconsin), Los Angeles (California), and Milwaukee (Wisconsin) also have living wage requirements in international production. However, it is not clear whether and how this has been implemented. At this point, what is important to note is the intent behind policies and ordinances.

Ethical Consumers and Pressure on Big Brands

One of the first pushbacks against the power of brands in GVCs was due to ethical consumer movements, chiefly those of student consumers on college campuses in the US. Rejecting the argument of brands that they had no responsibility for labour conditions in outsourced, contracted production, they forced the consideration of labour standards into the supply of college-branded apparel. Campaigns and media exposure of sweatshop working conditions threatened non-complying brands with reputational risk. These campaigns had some substantial effects, such as on the non-employment of child labour in factories and general payment of minimum wages. Current campaigning is trying to extend the pressure to advance living-wage standards.

Paying a living wage would not make much of a difference to the profits of these corporations and their owners. The founder of Zara is now one of the 10 richest persons (who are of course all men) in the world. So, why do they not 'do the right thing'? In the current era of financialization, publicly traded companies are faced with the market constraint of sustaining their share values on the basis of very short-term quarterly results. However, private companies do not face the same constraints and can be more subject to pressure from ethical consumer movements to provide for living wages. Additionally, companies with degrees of monopoly (and thus some price-making power) that can cover increases in costs through cost-plus pricing can also be subject to the pressures of moral consumer movements.

There are three kinds of pressures to which brands can be subjected: one is that of the moral consumer, the second that of moral shareholder movements in the headquarter economies, and the third is that of trade unions and women's movements—local, regional, and global—in the supplier economies. We have already referred to the positive roles played by moral consumer movements and the likely damage caused by the exposure of sweatshop conditions to reputation-conscious brands. Not only do these exposures need to bring out the human rights' violations in sweatshop conditions but they also have to highlight the implications of low wages on workers' health and well-being. As pointed out earlier, for women, low wages with high levels of overtime and poor working conditions, along with the burden of unpaid domestic work, lead to a mining of women workers' bodies. The exposure of this systematic production practice of mining women workers' bodies raises the ethical issue of the manner in which women workers are treated in apparel GVCs. Rousing the moral conscience of society in the brands' headquarter economies is important to bring pressure 'to do the right thing'.

Starting with the Biggest

Some garment brands have greater monopsony strength than others. The Spanish brand Zara, the Swedish H&M, and the Japanese Uniqlo are the three biggest garment retailers in the world. They have a greater degree of monopoly power than other large brands. Whether it is a matter of adjusting their own margins or increasing prices, they can easily take such steps without any threat of collapse. Once these large brands undertake these measures, their wage and environmental payments could become benchmarks for the market. They would have the same benchmarking effects as a shift in OECD member government procurements towards living-wage and environmental-service payment standards.

Multi-Stakeholder Initiatives

There have been a number of what are called multi-stakeholder initiatives (MSIs), usually arising from parties external to the value chains. There is the Ethical Trade Initiative (ETI), the ILO's Better Work Programme, ACT (or Action, Collaboration, and Transformation), the German-Dutch Sustainable Textiles Cooperation Agreement, and the IndustriAll Global Framework Agreements (GFA). They all include some kind of statement about the brands' intentions to implement living wages. However, as pointed out in a study of 13 brands by Remi Edwards, Tom Hunt, and Genevieve LeBaron

(2019), there is little evidence that these MSIs are increasing the payment of living wages. The MSIs do not include any legally enforceable commitment to living wages. 'All this suggests that some companies are seeking to outsource their living wage commitments to external institutions, rather than modifying their core purchasing practices' (Edwards, Hunt and LeBaron 2019: 16).

Legal Regulation in Brands' Home Countries

Industry-level actions would generally require some form of regulation by the concerned governments. 'Doing the right thing' can be made a requirement by legislation in the home countries of brands. There are now various due diligence requirements with regard to forced labour or modern slavery. Due diligence is required all along the value chain. However, there are no mandatory requirements on compliance with labour or environmental standards in supply chain operations. A major weakness of due diligence is that it does not involve trade unions and workers' representatives. Due diligence should have a tripartite structure, with representatives of brands and suppliers, along with government and workers' representatives. In the manner in which due diligence is now carried out, it amounts to nothing more than a statement by the brands that all labour and human rights issues have been dealt with.

Since the brands (and also the consumers) of these headquarter countries benefit from GVCs, which are key parts of their own economies, it is only reasonable to expect that just standards meeting production costs in terms of labour and environmental services should be respected around the world. Many countries have legislation that makes their firms accountable for corruption carried out in their operations anywhere in the world. As Genevieve LeBaron (2020) asks, should brands also not be made legally liable for labour and, we would add, environmental standards around the world? But countries of the Global North seem reluctant to have similar measures with regard to respecting just labour and environmental standards. As we complete drafting this book, in November 2020, a majority of Swiss cantons rejected a plan to hold corporations liable for such violations abroad (Illien 2020). Of course, legal liability needs to be calibrated according to the seriousness of the violation of justice. Child or bonded labour and sexual and gender-based violence in supply chain establishments would count as more serious violations than, say, failure to pay overtime. But there is strong resistance to requiring global corporations to pay attention to matters of justice in overall labour and environmental standards outside their headquarter economies.

The cheapening of basic consumer goods, such as garments and footwear, is a part of the current social contract in the US and, one might add, many European countries, other than in Scandinavia. As argued in Freedman and

Lind (2013), the US has moved away from the post-Second World War social contract, which was formulated in the Roosevelt period, of full employment and living wages, to one of low wages, made up, in part, by cheap consumer goods. GVCs, with unjust gender, labour, and environmental pricing, make cheap goods available in the high-income countries of the world. As pointed out earlier in this chapter, consumer surveys have shown a willingness to pay from 10 to 15 per cent more for goods known to have been produced with ethical standards. The obstacle to a realization of such changes in pricing is clearly the short-term profit maximization of the monopoly-cum-monopsony brands and a social contract based on cheap labour.

The next set of initiatives laid out in this chapter could be taken up on the suppliers' side. These include actions by suppliers themselves, as well as trade unions and civil society organisations (CSOs). There is also some discussion about the role of governments in supplier countries and global instruments, such as binding agreements (and even a tax), to cover the unjust subsidies in GVCs.

Changing Supplier Bargaining Power

The characterization of prices of labour and environmental services below their costs of production as unjust subsidies leads to a call for the prices of these commodities to be changed to reflect these full costs. Is that possible in a market-based economy? Henry Ford was one of the first to actually institute a living wage for workers. He realized that the mass production of cars required workers who could buy those cars. This was the birth of the working middle-class.

The difference between GVC monopsony capital and the Ford model is that, unlike the latter, the former does not depend on workers employed in garment supplier factories for their market. Jeans and other garments produced by low-paid workers in India and Bangladesh are sold mainly in the Global North. A small but increasing part of this production goes to upper- and middle-class markets in the Global South. Overall, however, there is a geographical distance between production and consumption within GVCs.

There is a pressing need for a strategy to realize a minimum living wage that can be derived from the Ford example and Helper's (1991) analysis of the three-firm monopoly in the US auto industry. Monopsony firms have a choice between supplier strategies: either a short-term strategy utilizing competition among suppliers or a longer-term commitment with fewer suppliers. The former choice would dampen innovative cost reductions by suppliers. The latter choice would promote innovation for cost reduction, following increases in wages.

This argument has a resonance with Ashok Kumar's analysis (2020). He argues that the growth of large-scale suppliers with a degree of power in bargaining relations with brands can bring about a redistribution of revenue within the garment value chain. To this, we would add the caveat that this would work where the supplier has some form of scarce knowledge, even if it is not protected by IPRs. The world's largest denim supplier, Arvind Mills in Bengaluru, which is one of Kumar's examples, has built a difficult-to-replicate knowledge of denim production. This gives it a certain strength while bargaining with buyers.

The growth of such large-scale producers could allow higher profits for the suppliers. In turn, this could lead to higher wages and better working conditions, such as a greater proportion of permanent workers. This would reduce what we have identified as the unjust subsidy of low wages, even if the wage has not reached the living-wage level. This analysis has to be tempered, however, because our research found that in India, large garment suppliers did not benefit from higher profit rates, but only through larger volumes. Therefore, one can put forward the proposition that it is not size by itself but the possession of specific capabilities that are not easily acquired that enables suppliers to improve their bargaining position.

Can such a change in bargaining positions be brought about by suppliers combining together in relationship to brands? There was a recent instance of such a combination by suppliers in Bangladesh, organized into the Bangladesh Garment Manufacturers' Association (BGMEA). During the 2020 COVID-19 pandemic lockdowns, the BGMEA threatened a boycott of a brand that did not pay for goods already delivered. The brand was forced to relent and make the payments (Kumar 2020) in order to continue manufacturing garments in Bangladesh.

Such collective action has not been forthcoming from Indian suppliers. When a German brand forced a discount on Indian suppliers, one of them got in touch with us to tell us the story. In Bangladesh, the brand repaid the forced discounts, but not in India. However, the supplier was unable to get other Indian suppliers to jointly take up the matter with that brand. This illustrates the weakness of Indian medium-sized suppliers and their inability to overcome this weakness through collective action, which is one way in which suppliers can improve their bargaining position with monopsony brands. In another instance, in 2018, the Tiruppur Exporters' Association (TEA) asked members not to accept brand demands to reduce US dollar supplier prices because of the devaluation of the Indian rupee. However, this was not followed by members who succumbed to brand pressures to give up the benefits of rupee devaluation.

There are two factors that appear to be at play in the failure of Indian suppliers, which are largely small and medium enterprises SMEs, to overcome collective action problems. India's traditional low-trust social relations, where trust extends only to family limits, has its effect on economic organization. As Bloom et al. (2013) pointed out in a study of the textile mills of Mumbai, owners do not increase the number of units they own beyond a number that family members, as managers and accountants, can control. We would add that they do not allow size-wise growth of units beyond what they can control with male family management, though one can notice some changes, with some families accepting women from their own families in managerial positions. In discussions with small and medium units, we have noted a reluctance to give up management control to a professional structure, which a large unit would require. Such lack of trust is also an obstacle in developing collective action since each one suspects the other of being willing to compromise with the buyers. Of course, this is exacerbated by the competition among suppliers for orders. However, the same brands operate across countries, so it would be useful to study why collective action has been easier among suppliers in Bangladesh compared to India.

Another factor in the failure to develop collective action by Indian suppliers could be the absence of local government or other administrative departments in these conversations. In Bangladesh and China, relevant government departments, including local government administrations, have played roles in bringing suppliers together and supporting them in bargaining with brands and other lead firms (see Fuquan et al. 2016, for tourism in Yunnan). This has not happened in India. Even during the COVID-19 pandemic, the Government of India confined itself to appealing to brands to stand by their commitments; but there was not even a suggestion of action against brands for the failure to honour their contractual commitments.

Trade Unions and Other CSOs

Obviously, trade unions are also important actors in creating pressure to establish and implement living wage standards. The global garment industry has created major pockets of worker concentration in supplier countries—for example, the East Coast of China, Phnom Penh in Cambodia, Hanoi in Vietnam, Dhaka and Chittagong in Bangladesh, Tiruppur and the Gurugram-Faridabad-Noida region in India, and so on. Such concentrations of supplier factories have the possibility of strengthening the associational power of workers through unions. In addition to traditional unions, there are also associations of women workers organized by feminist groups of various persuasions. When they are combined in regional associations—such as Asia

Floor Wage Alliance (AFWA) or in global unions as part of IndustriAll—the workers' associational power is further strengthened. However, in a situation of a labour-surplus economy, or one with a permanent reserve army of labour, one cannot count on union pressure to raise wages. Setting up living wages as a normative standard provides an important counterpart to the fight for living wages by trade unions and workers' organisations.

As mentioned earlier, it is necessary to supplement workers' movements with those for gender and environmental justice and also with global labour justice movements in the brands' headquarter economies. It is also necessary that women secure leadership positions in trade unions and workers' councils. For instance, in June 2018, AFWA and Global Labor Justice–International Labour Rights Forum (GLJ-ILRF) called upon Gap, H&M, and Walmart to address gender-based violence documented in their supply chains by proactively working with the AFWA Women's Leadership Committee (WLC) to pilot enforceable brand agreements in supplier factories with trade unions aimed at eliminating gender-based violence and discrimination, and expanding broader indications of women's collective empowerment. Such initiatives, led by women garment workers' collectives, have the potential not only to identify context-specific risk factors for violence but also to address gendered imbalances of power within supplier factories (Silliman Bhattacharjee 2020b).

In order for trade unions to have a role in labour disputes and in addressing working conditions, however, workers must have the right to form trade unions. Many EPZs do not allow workers to form trade unions. As significantly, many suppliers (usually with support from their governments) take action against the formation of trade unions. Workers who take the initiative in forming unions are routinely dismissed from employment. Brands are well aware of these actions but do nothing about them.

Binding Agreements

A major problem in achieving living-wage standards is that brands are not subject to legally binding agreements to set prices that would enable living-wage payments by suppliers. The 'jobbers' agreement' in New York a hundred years ago was just that—a legally binding agreement on supplier prices and workers' wages between brands, suppliers, and workers (Anner, Bair, and Blaisi 2014).

Most agreements on labour standards, including the GFAs, have been indicative rather than binding. Following the Rana Plaza tragedy, a breakthrough was achieved in establishing the legally binding and enforceable Accord on Fire and Building Safety in Bangladesh. This agreement, mainly signed by European brands, instituted legally binding commitments to provide money for upgrading factory building infrastructure in Bangladesh. This could be a precedent for moving on to legally binding agreements about wages and other labour conditions. A number of brands have come together with IndustriAll, committing themselves to business practices enabling living wages. Such agreements should be legally enforceable under national laws (IndustriAll 2017).

Such agreements would also require a redressal mechanism. In the words of the UN Guiding Principles on Human Rights and Business, there needs to be a mechanism to 'remedy' violations of agreements on human rights—in this case, living wages. This would bring a fourth party to the process. This can only be the ILO; an ILO, however, with stronger powers to remedy violations (Nathan 2013). If the world can have an International Criminal Court, why can there not be an International Labour Court? There would be opposition from brands and other buyers, as was evident when they opposed the ILO adopting any regulation on global supply chains at the 2016 International Labour Conference. With the globalization of production through GVCs, the national framework has become woefully inadequate to deal with transnational violations of workers' human rights. The globalization of economic processes has proceeded far in advance of any regulatory or governance mechanism of GVC economic affairs (Gereffi and Mayer 2006).

Supplier Governments

Governments in supplier countries try to keep wages low and attack trade union rights, supposedly in order to create more employment in labour-intensive manufacturing. However, as labour surpluses decrease and there are wage increases, local governments in China have worked with suppliers to improve bargaining strength and combine more stable orders with better employment conditions and technological investments to increase worker productivity. In Sri Lanka, the government worked with suppliers in the Good Garments campaign (Goger 2016). However, in general, governments such as those in India, Bangladesh, or Cambodia have not supported attempts to increase wages and have supported anti-union actions instead. Even official minimum wages are not strictly enforced; on the contrary, inspection and regulation have been relaxed. Again, in the quest for manufacturing employment, they have not taken action against or tried to mitigate the harmful environmental effects of garment production. Instead, as in the Tiruppur case, they have taken such action only when it has become a political issue with potentially destabilizing electoral effects.

Can governments of supplier countries combine to increase wages in garment export industries? Such a coalition is unlikely, given not just the competition between these countries but also the widely held notion that cheap labour is what is needed to attract garment export orders. However, where there are strong supplier organizations (as was seen in the case of Bangladesh), governments could work with them to secure better supplier conditions, including stability of orders.

A GVC Tax for Redistribution

We have seen that some redistribution of income within a value chain is needed in order to advance from costing based on minimum or market-based wages to costing based on living wages. While moral consumer movements in headquarter economies and trade unions in supplier economies are applying pressure for such an advance, the market-based mechanism of short-term valuation and the monopsony power of brands together obstruct such a move. In the long term, the economic development of supplier economies is likely to push up wages, but should we wait for such a long-term development?

Given the monopsony power of brands and the failure of global governance to address its consequences, one can propose a GVC tax for redistribution, as suggested by Srinivasan Iyer (personal communication, October 2017). This would be a tax paid by brands that do not include a living wage in the prices paid to supplier firms to the extent of the difference between existing and living wages. As mentioned earlier in this section, a tax equivalent to the doubling of wages in supplier firms in India would reduce the advantage from labour arbitrage from the notional USD 29 to USD 28. This is not of such a magnitude that it would end the GVC-based growth of employment in supplier countries. That, of course, is not our objective. If redistributed to workers in supplier firms, the tax would be sufficient to advance to living-wage employment conditions. It is also likely that such a tax would increase product prices and reduce consumer surplus in the headquarter economies.

Living wages in, say, China or Turkey would be much higher than in India or Bangladesh, given the difference in the levels of development between these two sets of countries. Thus, a GVC-tax based movement to nationally determined living wages would not eliminate competitive differences between supplier countries at different levels of development. While redistributing a small portion of the value currently captured by brands, it would be a major move towards eliminating unjust labour subsidies in garment GVCs.

It is clear that establishing and administering such a tax would require the a global governance system that is not in place today. However, conversations about such a GVC or extreme labour arbitrage tax could still take place, just as there is a discussion of a Tobin tax on international financial flows despite no such mechanism existing for its implementation. Without thinking of or imagining such a redistribution process, one cannot work towards bringing it about.

GVCs and the Reduction of Subsidies

The fact that garment GVCs exploit both workers and the environment has been seen in the chapters of this book. The question we face is: Is that the only way in which GVCs can function? With regard to labour and wages, there are historical examples, as in New York garment manufacturing. Even before the spread of GVCs, there was a value chain separation between the brands or retailers and manufacturers in New York. The tripartite agreement between brand or retailers, manufacturers, and workers through their unions showed that workers could be paid a living wage within the value chain system. In the context of GVCs, this has not yet occurred, but this does not mean that it cannot happen. In fact, if one assumed that this could never happen, then there would be no scope or meaning for a trade union or related activities that seek to strengthen and utilize workers' associational power.

The same position is valid with regard to environmental subsidies. Just because capitalism has historically relied on 'cheap nature' as a law of value (Moore 2015: 14) does not mean that it is the only way in which global capitalism in the form of GVCs can exist. Through the Organization of the Petroleum Exporting Countries (OPEC), the oligopolistic strength of crude oil owners changed the earlier regime of cheaply priced oil. In the case of garments, the producing countries are too many, but such developments cannot be ruled out. Some increases in wages have been secured, particularly in countries such as China and Malaysia, where labour shortages have emerged.

The unethical practices followed in GVCs can be reduced and even eliminated over time. Will that mean the end of GVCs or even of capitalism as such? Costanza et al. (1997) point out,

> If ecosystem services were actually paid for, in terms of their value contribution to the global economy, the global price system would be very different from what it is today. The prices of commodities using ecosystem services directly or indirectly would be much greater. The structure of factor payments, including wages, interest rates and profits would change dramatically. (1997: 259)

An Indian proposal to pay farmers for non-commoditized ecosystem services (that is, other than food and recreation, which are provisioning and cultural services that could be marketed) would bring a substantial redistribution of the GDP towards farmers (see the proposal in Devi et al. 2017). However, this would be a welcome redistribution within capitalism, to which industrial capital would have to respond, possibly with more efficient use of employed workers and machinery.

Fresh water is a critical natural input that is often taken free from nature. In the use of groundwater, only the costs of extraction are taken into account, often leading to its depletion as a renewable resource. Would pricing fresh water lead to a crisis that would end capitalism? In the generation of hydel power in Switzerland, the upstream cantons were paid for the water they supplied to urban electricity generation. This provided for a redistribution of national income with a share for rural cantons from the generation of electricity. Many hydel schemes in Nepal, China, and the Philippines pay upland communities for the supply of unpolluted and clean (non-sandy) water (for an early review of such schemes, see Nathan and Jodha 2004). A similar move, for instance, would be for Nepal to charge India for the water it supplies through the Himalayan system, which would enable Nepal to secure a higher share of India's income from the use of Himalayan water from Nepal. Neither did the payment to the Swiss rural cantons end Swiss capitalism nor would payment to Nepal for Himalayan water end Indian capitalism.

As pointed out earlier, the rise of OPEC from the mid-1970s not only raised the price of oil but it also redistributed income shares within oil with a rise in the share of oil-owning countries. In addition, the period from the end of the Second World War until the mid-1970s, which is referred to as the Golden Age of Capitalism, saw a rise in the share of wages in the GDP of high-income countries.

Neither of these substantial changes in factor shares and reductions in the environmental or labour subsidies led to the demise of capitalism. Instead, it triggered adaptation, namely the search for cheaper ways of producing, in fact, promoting the rise of globally splintered production to take advantage of low wages in what were then low-income countries in Asia and Latin America. Changes in both labour incomes and payments for environmental services would similarly trigger moves toward reorganization and innovation in order to reduce production costs and quite likely accelerate the adoption of automation, but that would end neither capitalism nor GVCs. Instead, they would be reorganized on a more just and sustainable basis.

Transformative Change for Social and Environmental Sustainability

The changes in labour conditions in garment value chains through various multi-stakeholder initiatives, whether through the GFAs or through the ILO's Better Work Programme or in larger supply factories, have been what can be called incremental changes, that is, they have yielded some benefits without, however, changing the basic underlying labour practices of wages far below living wages, extensive overtime, supervision-related gender-based violence, the early expulsion of women workers from factory work, often high levels of informalization in factory employment, and continuing precarious homework paid even less than national minimum wages.

What is needed is to fashion a path moving from soft to hard regulation in the movement from incremental to transformative change, building on the gains of the former. Transformative change is defined as that which is (*a*) progressive, in a normative sense of social justice; (*b*) systemic, addressing various factors simultaneously and in an interrelated way; and (*c*) long term, cannot be easily reversed in the short term (UNRISD 2016: 32). In the case of labour standards in garment value chains, transformative change can be defined as that which brings about decent work conditions. This would be a radical change enabling workers to achieve the basic capabilities for human existence. This would reduce or even eliminate the current system of reverse subsidies.

While one can define the achievement of decent work conditions as constituting transformative change, the important, and difficult, task is to outline a pathway to achieving such transformational change. Below we outline such a possible path.

Existing compliance codes, including those of the Global Framework Agreements, are based on ILO standards. It is not that the standards are basically weak. Where there are weak standards, it is usually due to national labour laws. For instance, Indian law allows for precarious employment in the form of contract labour or endless fixed-term contracts, without a path to permanency—as there is in China, for instance.

What is needed it to consolidate all the codes on the basis of ILO Conventions, with a clear statement about living wages as the wage standard and the elimination of precarity. Such a consolidation into one ILO convention would be like the Maritime Labour Convention (MLC) adopted by the ILO in 2006, which regulates labour and environmental standards in the shipping industry and now covers more than 90 per cent of all shipping (Ryder 2020). Such a convention, as is the case with the MLC, should have a tiered-wage system, based on different living wage bases for low income countries (LICs), lower-middle income countries (LMICs), upper middle income countries (UMICs), and high income countries (HICs).

What about an implementation mechanism—one that moves from soft regulation to hard regulation? The MLC has a national implementation mechanism as ports of call are authorized to inspect, and, if necessary, detain, ships for labour and environmental standards. Special units of export customs' authorities could play such a role in export garments. They could be authorized and trained to inspect and, if necessary, detain garment shipments found to be in violation of both labour and environmental standards.

Having formulated a global garment convention based on relevant ILO conventions, it is necessary to build a political coalition that could bring it about. The major brands, such as Inditex, Uniqlo, H&M, M&S, Gap, and so on, already have commitments to paying living wages and minimizing precarious employment. They, along with mass retailers Tesco, Carrefour, and Walmart, are critical to initiating a convention-framing process. While governments in general have committed to decent employment standards as part of SDGs, one could begin with governments from the Global North, such as the Scandinavian governments, the EU, and others that have formulated global due diligence requirements.

The difficult part would be to get governments and suppliers from the Global South to accept the standards. But the tiered-structure of wages could work to convince them that they can still compete on wage standards, though there are developing country status limits to wage competition. In accommodating living wage and other labour and environmental standards, there would obviously have to be an increase in ex-factory and FBO prices. This might help convince suppliers that they could join in such efforts. For instance, some large Indian suppliers, such as Arvind, the largest producer of denim in the world, and the Aditya Birla Group, have both joined the International Apparel Coalition, which has a stated commitment to living wages and workers' associational rights.

Obviously, international trade unions and alliances, such as the International Trade Union Confederation (ITUC), IndustriAll, Asia Floor Wage Alliance (AFWA), major unions and associations of informal workers, such as SEWA and WIEGO, would play a key role in even initiating a process of discussion of a global garment convention. However, as we have pointed our earlier, it is necessary to build a 'movement of movements', bringing together workers' organizations with moral consumer and trade movements, women's movements, and environmental movements.

All of the above would be an ambitious agenda but not something that is beyond imagination. As the world emerges from the most severe economic crisis since the 1930s Great Depression, it is necessary to imagine a new global social contract that can end reverse subsidies and promote both social and environmental sustainability.

Bibliography

Acheampong, Emmanuel, and Ahmed Maryudi. 2020. 'Avoiding Legality: Timber Producers' Strategies and Motivations under FLEGT in Ghana and Indonesia'. *Forest Policy Governance* 111 (February). DOI: https://doi.org/10.1016/j.forpol.2019.102047.

Adler-Milstein, Sarah, and John Kline. 2018. *Sewing Hope: How One Factory Challenges the Apparel Industry's Sweatshops*. Berkeley: University of California Press.

AEPC. 2020. *AEPC Study: Impact of COVID on Indian Apparel Exports.*Apparel Export Promotion Corporation. https://aepcindia.com/system/files/AEPC%20Covid%20Study%208%20May%202020.pdf, accessed 27 October 2021.

AFWA. 2009. 'Perspective: Asia Floor Wage and Gender'. Asia Floor Wage Alliance. https://protect-eu.mimecast.com/s/Ok6ECzKPPtKLY8qI4W0Bk?domain=archive.cleanclothes.org, accessed 9 October 2021.

———. 2013. 'Living Wage versus Minimum Wage'. Asia Floor Wage Alliance. https://cleanclothes.org/livingwage-old/living-wage-versus-minimum-wage, accessed 9 October 2021.

———. 2017a. 'Asia Floor Wage: What Is It and Why Do We Need One?' Asia Floor Wage Alliance. https://archive.cleanclothes.org/livingwage/afw/what, accessed 9 October 2021.

———. 2017b. 'Asia Floor Wage in Local Currency (2017) Asia Floor Wage Alliance. https://archive.cleanclothes.org/livingwage/afw/asia-floor-wage-in-local-currency, accessed 9 October 2021.

———. 2019. *Asia Floor Wage Alliance's Step-by-Step Approach to Prevent Gender Based Violence at Production Lines in Garment Supplier Factories in Asia.* https://asia.floorwage.org/wp-content/uploads/2019/10/AFWA-Step-by-Step-approach-to-Prevent-GBV-May-2019.pdf, accessed 9 October 2021.

———. 2021. *Money Heist: Covid-19 Wage Theft in Global Garment Supply Chains*. Asia Floor Wage Alliance. https://protect-eu.mimecast.com/s/yhmdCKZXXuLJy8WTnw45d?domain=asia.floorwage.org, accessed 9 October 2021,

AFWA et al. 2018a. *Gender Based Violence in the GAP Garment Supply Chain*. Asia Floor Wage Alliance (AFWA), The Center for Alliance of Labor & Human Rights (CENTRAL), Global Labor Justice (GLJ), Sedane Labour Resource Centre/Lembaga Informasi Perburuhan Sedane (LIPS), and SLD. https://www.globallaborjustice.org/wp-content/uploads/2018/06/GBV-Gap-May-2018.pdf, accessed 9 October 2021.

———. 2018b. *Gender Based Violence in the H&M Garment Supply Chain*. Asia Floor Wage Alliance (AFWA), The Center for Alliance of Labor & Human Rights (CENTRAL), Global Labor Justice (GLJ), Sedane Labour Resource Centre/Lembaga Informasi Perburuhan Sedane (LIPS), and SLD. https://globallaborjustice.org/wp-content/uploads/2018/05/GBV-HM-May-2018.pdf, accessed 9 October 2021.

———. 2018c. *Gender Based Violence in the Walmart Garment Supply Chain*. Asia Floor Wage Alliance (AFWA), The Center for Alliance of Labor & Human Rights (CENTRAL), Global Labor Justice (GLJ), Sedane Labour Resource Centre/Lembaga Informasi Perburuhan Sedane (LIPS), and SLD. https://asia.floorwage.org/wp-content/uploads/2019/10/GBV-walmart.pdf, accessed 9 October 2021.

Agarwal, Anil, and Sunita Narain. 1991. *Global Warming in an Unequal World*. New Delhi: Centre for Science and Environment.

Ahmed, Nazneen, and Md Iqbal Hossain. 2018. 'Study on Garment Workers in Bangladesh'. Improving Working Conditions in the Ready-Made Garment Sector in Bangladesh, ILO. Mimeo.

Ahmed, Neetu. 2018. 'Strategic Change in Indian IT Majors: A Challenge'. In *Development with Global Value Chains: Upgrading and Innovation in Asia*, edited by Dev Nathan, Meenu Tewari and Sandip Sarkar, 229–246. Cambridge: Cambridge University Press.

Akhter, S., C. Rutherford, and C. Chu. 2017. 'What Makes Pregnant Workers Sick: Why, When, Where and How? An Exploratory Study in the Ready-made Garment Industry in Bangladesh'. *Reprod Health* 14 (1): 142–151.

Allain, J., A. Crane, G. LeBaron and L. Behbahani. 2013. 'Forced Labour's Business Models and Supply Chains'. https://www.jrf.org.uk/report/forced-labour%E2%80%99s-business-models-and-supply-chains, accessed September 2018.

Altenbuchner C., S. Vogel, and M. Larcher. 2017. 'Social, Economic and Environmental Impacts of Organic Cotton Production on the Livelihood of Smallholder Farmers in Odisha, India'. *Renewable Agriculture and Food Systems*, 373–385. DOI:10.1017/S174217051700014X.

Anand, Sudhir, and Amartya Sen. 2000. 'Human Development and Economic Subtainability'. *World Development* 28 (12): 2029–2049.

Anker, Richard. 2011. *Estimating a Living Wage: A Methodological Review*. Geneva: ILO. https://www.ilo.org/wcmsp5/groups/public/---ed_protect/---protrav/---travail/documents/publication/wcms_162117.pdf, accessed 20 September 2018.

Anker, Richard, and Martha Anker. 2017. *Living Wages around the World*. Cheltenham: Edward Elgar Publishing.

Anner, Mark. 2019a. 'Predatory Purchasing Practices in Global Apparel Supply Chains and the Employment Relations Squeeze in the Indian Garment Export Industry'. *International Labour Review* 158 (4): 705–727.

———. 2019b. 'Squeezing Workers' Rights in Global Supply Chains: Purchasing Practices in the Bangladesh Garment Export Sector in Comparative Perspective'. *Review of International Political Economy* 27 (2): 320–347.

———. 2020. *Abandoned? The Impact of Covid-19 on Workers and Businesses at the Bottom of Global Garment Supply Chains*. State College: Penn State Center for Global Workers' Rights (CGWR).

Anner, Mark, Jennifer Bair and Jeremy Blaisi. 2014. 'Towards Joint Liability in Global Value Chains: Addressing the Root Causes of Labor Violations in Global Production'. *Comparative Labor Law Policy* 35 (1): 1–43.

AP and WRC. 2017. 'WRC Factory Investigation: Rio Garment'. Worker Rights Consortium. https://www.workersrights.org/factory-investigation/rio-garment/, accessed 17 December 2020.

Applebaum, Richard P. 2004. 'Fighting Sweatshops: Problems in Enforcing Global Labour Standards'. In *Critical Globalization Studies*, edited by Richard P. Applebaum and W. I. Robinson, 369–378. New York: Routledge.

Applebaum, Richard P., and Gary Gereffi. 1994. 'Power and Profits in the Apparel Value Chain'. In *Global Production: The Apparel Industry in the Pacific Rim*, edited by Edna Bonacich, Lucie Cheng, Norma Chinchilla, Norma Hamilton, and Paul Ong, 42–62. Philadelphia: Temple University Press.

Aragon-Correa, J. A,. and E. A. Rubio-Lopez. 2007. 'Proactive Corporate Environmental Strategies—Myths and Misunderstandings'. *Long Range Planning* 40: 357–381.

Arnold, Caroline E. 2010. 'Where the Low Road and the High Road Meet. Flexible Employment in Global Value Chains'. *Journal of Contemporary Asia* 40 (4): 612–637.

ATREE. 2019. *Contextual Water Targets Pilot Study: Noyyal-Bhavani River Basin, India, May*. Bangalore: Ashoka Trust for Research in Ecology and the Environment.

Auvray, Tristan, and Joel Rabinovich. 2017. 'The Financialization–Offshoring Nexus and the Capital Accumulation of US Nonfinancial Firms'. https://hal.archives-ouvertes.fr/hal-01492373/document, accessed 22 December 2019.

Bair, Jennifer, and Marion Werner. 2013. 'The Place of Disarticulations: Global Commodity Production in La Laguna, Mexico'. *Environment and Planning, A* 43: 998–1015.

Baldwin, Richard. 2016. *The Great Convergence*. Cambridge, MA: Harvard University Press.

Bales, K. 1999. *Disposable People: New Slaves in the Global Economy*. Berkeley, CA: University of California Press.

Banday, M. U. L., S. Chakraborty, P. D'Cruz and E. Noronha. 2018. 'Abuse Faced by Child Labourers: Novel Territory in Workplace Bullying'. In *Indian Perspectives on Workplace Bullying—A Decade of Insights*, edited by P. D'Cruz, E. Noronha, A. Mendonca and N. Mishra, 173–204. Singapore: Springer Nature.

Barbier, Edward. 2016. 'The Protective Service of Mangrove Ecosystems: A Review of Valuation Methods'. *Marine Pollution Review* 109 (2): 676–681.

Barge, Sandha, M. E. Khan, Richard Anker, Martha Anker, Banwari Periwal and Mital Petiwale. 2018. *Living Wage Report: Tirupur City, India*. Global Living Wage Coalition. https://www.globallivingwage.org/wp-content/uploads/2018/05/urban-india-living-wage-benchmark-report.pdf, accessed 16 October 2018.

Barrientos, Stephanie. 2014. 'Gendered Production Networks: Analysis of Cocoa-Chocolate Sourcing'. *Regional Studies* 48 (5): 791–903.

———. 2019. *Gender and Work in Global Value Chains: Capturing the Gains?* Cambridge: Cambridge University Press.

Barrientos, S., and S. Smith. 2007. 'Do Workers Benefit from Ethical Trade? Assessing Codes of Labour Practice in Global Production Systems'. *Third World Quarterly* 28 (4): 713–729.

Barrientos, S., G. Gereffi, and A. Rossi. 2011. 'Economic and Social Upgrading in Global Production Networks: A New Paradigm for a Changing World'. *International Labour Review* 150 (3–4): 319–340.

Baruah, A., and I. Singh. 2020. 'Employment of Women in Rural Punjab: Deconstructing Agricultural Growth Policy'. *Economic and Political Weekly* 55 (26 and 27): 29–35.

Basu, Kaushik, and Pham Hoang Van. 1998. 'The Economics of Child Labor'. *The American Economic Review* 88 (3): 412–427.

Becattini, G. 1990. 'The Marshallian Industrial District as a Socio-Economic Notion'. In *Industrial Districts and Inter-Firm Cooperation in Italy*, edited by F. Pyke, G. Becattlni and W.Sengenberger, 37–51. Geneva: International Institute for Labour Studies.

Beck, Ulrich. 1992. *Risk Society: Towards a New Modernity*. London and New York: Sage.

———. 2005. *Power in the Global Age*. Cambridge: Polity Press.

Bedi, J. S., and C. B. Cororaton. 2008. 'Cotton-Textile-Apparel Sectors in India: Situations and Challenges Faced'. IFPRI DP No. 801, IFPRI, New Delhi.

Bedi, J. S., and R. Verma. 2011. 'State of Fabric Production Units in India'. *Economic and Political Weekly* 46 (4): 62–68.

Beitz, Charles. 2001. 'Does Global Inequality Matter?' In *Global Justice*, edited by Thomas Pogge, 106–122. Oxford: Blackwell Publishers.

Better Work. 2019. *Sexual Harassment at Work: Insights from the Global Garment Industry*. Geneva: ILO and IFC. https://betterwork.org/wp-content/uploads/2020/01/SHP-Thematic-Brief.pdf, accessed 5 March 2021.

Bhaskaran, Resmi, C. Upendranadh, Dev Nathan, and Nicola Phillips. 2010. 'Home-Based Child Labour in Delhi's Garment Production: Contemporary Forms of Unfree Labour in Global Production'. *Indian Journal of Labour Economics* 53 (4): 607–624..

Bhattacharjee, Anannya, and Ashim Roy. 2016. 'Bargaining in Garment GVCs: The Asia Floor Wage'. In *Labour in Global Value Chains in Asia*, edited by Dev Nathan, Meenu Tewari and Sandip Sarkar, 78–93. Cambridge: Cambridge University Press.

Bhattacharya, Tithi, ed. 2017. *Social Reproduction: Remapping Class, Centering Oppression*. London: Pluto Press.

BHRRC. 2019. 'El Salvador: Garment Workers Owed $2.3 Million Severance Pay after Sudden Closure of Global Brands Group Major Supplier; Global Brands Group Did Not Respond'. https://www.business-humanrights.org/en/el-salvador-garment-workers-owed-23-million-severance-pay-after-sudden-closure-of-global-brands-group-major-supplier-global-brands-group-did-not-respond, accessed 28 September 2021.

Bick, R., Erika Halsey, and Christine C. Ekenga. 2018. 'The Global Environmental Injustice of Fast Fashion'. *Environmental Health* 17: 92. DOI: https://doi.org/10.1186/s12940-018-0433-7.

Bitzer, V. 2012. 'Partnering for Change in Chains: The Capacity of Partnerships to Promote Sustainable Change in Global Agrifood Chains'. *International Food and Agribusiness Management Review* 15 (Special Issue B): 13–38.

Bloom, Nicholas, Benn Eifert, David McKenzie, Aparajit Mahajan, and John Roberts. 2013. 'Does Management Matter? Evidence from India'. *Quarterly Journal of Economics* 128 (1): 1–51.

Boehlje M., J. Akridge, and D. Downey. 1995. 'Restructuring Agribusiness for the 21st Century'. *Agribusiness* 11 (6): 493–500.

Bonds, Eric. 2007. 'Environmental Review as Battleground: Corporate Power, Government Collusion, and Citizen Opposition to a Tire-Burning Power Plant in Rural Minnesota, USA'. *Organization and Environment* 20 (2): 157–176.

Bourgois, Philippe. 1988. 'Conjugated Oppression: Class and Ethnicity among Guyami and Kuna Banana Workers'. *American Ethnologist* 15 (2): 328–348.

Boyed, D. E., R. E. Spekman, W. Kamauff, and P. Werhane. 2007. 'Corporate Social Responsibility in Global Supply Chains: A Procedural Justice Perspective'. *Long Range Planning* 40: 341–356.

Brake, Deborah L. 2005. 'Retaliation'. *Minnessota Law Review* 90 (18): 18–105.

Breman, Jan. 2013. *At Work in the Informal Economy of India: A Persepctive from the Bottom Up*. New Delhi: Oxford University Press.

———. 2020. 'The Pandemic in India and Its Impact on Footloose Labour'. *Indian Journal of Labour Economics* 63 Special Issue (October–December): 901–919.

Brock, G. 2015. 'Global Justice'. In *Stanford Encyclopedia of Philosophy*. https://plato.stanford.edu/entries/justice-global/, accessed 5 October 2021.

Brown, Drusilla, Rajeev Dehejia, and Raymond Roberrson. 2018. 'The Impact of Better Work: Firm Performance in Vietnam, Indonesia and Jordan'. Better Work Discussion Paper No. 27, August 2018. https://betterwork.org/portfolio/discussion-paper-27-the-impact-of-better-work-firm-performance-in-vietnam-indonesia-and-jordan/, accessed 6 January 2021.

Buccholz, Wolfgang, and Dirk Rubbelke. 2019. *Foundations of Environmental Economics*. Cham: Springer.

Burawoy, Michael. 2010. 'From Polanyi to Pollyana: The False Optimism of Global Labor Studies'. *Global Labor Journal* 1 (2): 301–313.

Butler, Sarah. 2012. 'Cambodian Workers Hold "People's Tribunal" to Look at Factory Conditions'. *The Guardian*, 2 February. https://www.theguardian.com/world/2012/feb/02/cambodian-workers-peoples-tribunal-factory, accessed 28 September 2021.

Campling, Liam, and Elizabeth Havice. 2019. 'Bringing the Environment into GVC Analysis: Antecedents and Advances'. In *Handbook of Global Value Chains*, edited by S. Ponte, G. Gereffi, and G. Raj-Reichert, 214–227. Cheltenham, UK: Edward Elgar. DOI: https://doi.org/10.4337/9781788113779.00019.

Carson, Rachel. 1962. *Silent Spring*. New York: Houghton Mifflin.

Carswell, Grace, and Geert de Neve. 2012. 'Labouring for Global Markets: Conceptualizing Labour Agency in GPNs'. *Geoforum* 44: 62–70.

———. 2014. 'T-Shirts and Tumblers: Caste, Dependency and Work under Neoliberalization in South India'. *Contributions to Indian Sociology* 48 (1): 103–131.

CCC. 2014. 'Stitched Up: Poverty Wages for Garment Workers in Eastern Europe and Turkey'. Clean Clothes Campaign. https://cleanclothes.org/livingwage/europe/europes-sweatshops, accessed 5 October 2021.

———. 2018. 'Indonesian Garment Workers Appeal to Uniqlo CEO in Letters to Take Action on Severance Debt'. Clean Clothes Campaign, 20 April. https://cleanclothes.org/news/2018/04/19/indonesian-garment-workers-appeal-ceo-uniqlo-in-letters-to-take-action-on-severance-debt, accessed 5 October 2021.

CCHR. 2014. 'Workers Rights Are Human Rights; Policy Brief: The Garment Industry in Cambodia'. Cambodian Center for Human Rights. http://cchrcambodia.org/admin/media/analysis/analysis/english/CCHR_Policy%20Brief%20on%20Garment%20Industry_ (January%202014)_eng.pdf, accessed 9 May 2016.

CENTRAL. 2018. *Rising Production Targets Undermining Minimum Wage Increases*. Center for Alliance of Labor and Human Rights. https://www.central-cambodia.org/wp-content/uploads/2018/12/Rising-Production-Targets-Undermining-Wage-Increases_CENTRAL_2018-1.pdf, accessed 28 September 2021.

Ceresna-Chaturvedi, L. 2015. 'A Study of Occupational Health and Safety in the Garment Industry in Bangalore, October 2015'. http://cividep.org/backdoor/wpcontent/uploads/2016/02/25-2-Occupationalhealth-safety.pdf, accessed 9 May 2016.

CETA. 2014. *Labour and Trade*, Chapter 24. Comprehensive Economic and Trade Agreement. https://ec.europa.eu/trade/policy/in-focus/ceta/ceta-chapter-by-chapter/, accessed 26 November 2015.

Chan, Anita. 2003. 'Racing to the Bottom: International Trade without a Social Clause'. *Third World Quarterly* 24 (6): 1011–1028.

Chan, Aris. 2009. 'Paying the Price for Economic Development: The Children of Migrant Workers in China'. Special report, *China Labour Bulletin*. https://clb.org.hk/sites/default/files/archive/en/share/File/research_reports/Children_of_Migrant_Workers.pdf, accessed 20 January 2021.

Chan, Jenny, Ngai Pun, and Mark Selden. 2016. 'The Politics of Global Production: Apple, Foxconn and China's New Working Class'. In *Labour in Global Value Chains in Asia*, edited by Dev Nathan, Meenu Tewari, and Sandip Sarkar, 353–376. Cambridge: Cambridge University Press.

Chancel, Lucas. 2020. *Unsustainable Inequalities: Social Justice and the Environment*. Cambridge, MA: Harvard University Press.

Chappell, Duncan, and Vittorio Di Martino. 2006. *Violence at Work*, 3rd ed. Geneva: ILO.

Chatterji, A. 2015. *Conflicted Democracies and Gendered Violence: The Right to Heal*. Delhi: Zubaan.

COAPCL. 2012. 'Cotton Value Chains and Traceability: Securing Supply Chains—Brands Investment in Organic Cotton'. Presentation at the Biofach, Nuremberg, Germany, 17 February 2012. Chetna Organic Agriculture Producer Company Limited, Hyderabad.

Coen Kompier, Archana Prasad, Sajjad Hassan, et.al. 2014. 'Labour Markets: Exclusion from "Decent Work"'. In *India Exclusion Report 2013–2014*, ch. 4. Delhi: Books for Change.

Costa, M., and C. B. Klein. 2006. 'Toxicity and Carcinogenicity of Chromium Compounds in Humans'. *Critical Reviews in Toxicology* 36 (2): 155–163.

Costanza, Robert, O. Perez-Maquero, M. L. Martinez, P. Sutton, S. J. Anderson, and K. Mulder. 2008. 'The Value of Coastal Wetlands for Hurricane Protection'. *Journal of Human Environment* 37 (4): 241–248.

Costanza, Robert, Ralph d'Arge, Rudolf de Groot, Stephen Farber, Monica Gasso, Bruce Hammont, Karin Limburg, Shahid Naeem, Robert V. O'Neill, Jose Paruelo, Robert G. Raskin, Paul Sutton, and Marjan van ben Belt. 1997.

'The Value of the World's Ecosystem Services and Natural Capital'. *Nature* 387: 253–260.

Costanza, Robert, Rudolg de Groot, Paul Sutton, Sander van der Ploeg, Sharolyn J. Anderson, Ida Kubiszeweski, Stephen Farber and R. Kerry Turner. 2014. 'Changes in the Global Value of Ecosystem Services'. *Global Environmental Change* 26: 152–158.

Crenshaw, Kimberle. 1989. 'Demarginalizing the Intersection of Race and Sex: A Black Feminist Critique of Antidiscrimination Doctrine, Feminist Theory and Antiracist Politics.' *University of Chicago Legal Forum* 1989 (8). https://chicagounbound.uchicago.edu/uclf/vol1989/iss1/8, accessed 5 October 2021.

Cruz, Adrienne, and Sabine Klinger. 2011. 'Gender-based Violence in the World of Work: Overview and Selected Annotated Bibliography'. ILO Working Paper No. 3.

csimarket.com. 2019. 'Levi Strauss & Co.'s Gross Profit Margin (Quarterly)'. https://csimarket.com/stocks/singleProfitabilityRatios.php?code=LEVI&net, accessed 15 January 2019.

CSO. 2015. *Main Characteristics of Industries, 2014–15*. Annual Survey of Industries, Central Statistical Office. https://www.ap.gov.in/wp-content/uploads/2018/05/ASI-2014-15-Publication.pdf, accessed 29 November 2021.

Curran, D. 2017. 'The Treadmill of Production and the Positional Economy of Consumption'. *Canadian Review of Sociology* 54 (1): 28–47.

Custers, Peter. 1997. *Capital Accumulation and Women's Labour in Asian Economies*. New Delhi: Vistaar Publications.

D'Cruz, Premilla, and Charlotte Rayner. 2012. 'Bullying in the Indian Workplace: A study of the ITES-BPO Sector'. *Economic and Industrial Democracy* 34 (4): 597–619.

D'Cruz, Premilla, Ernesto Noronha, A. Mendonca, and N. Mishra, eds. 2018. *Workplace Bullying: An Indian Perspective*. Singapore: Springer.

Davidson, D. J., and S. Frickel. 2004. 'Understanding Environmental Governance: A Critical Review'. *Organization and Environment* 17 (4): 471–492

Daystar, J. S., E. Barnes, K. Hake, and R. Kurtz. 2017. 'Sustainability Trends and Natural Resource Sue in U.S. Cotton Production'. *Bio Resources* 12 (1): 2362–2392.

De Hoop T., J. Mcpike, S. Vasudeven, C. U. Holla, and M. Taleja. 2018. *Social and Economic Impact Assessment of Cotton Farming in Madhya Pradesh*. Washington: American Institute for Research.

de Janvry, Alain. 1986. 'Peasants, Capitalism, and the State in Latin American Agriculture'. Working Paper No. 396, Department of Agricultural and Resource Economics, Berkeley, Working Paper Series.

de Marchi, Valentina, Eleonora Di Marchi, and Gary Gereffi, eds. 2018. *Local Clusters in Global Value Chains*. London: Routledge.

de Neve, Greet. 2009. 'Power, Inequality and Corporate Social Responsibility: The Politics of Ethical Compliance in the South Indian Garment Industry'. *Economic and Political Weekly* 44 (22): 63–71.

de Vivo, G. 1987. 'David Ricardo'. In *The New Palgrave: A Dictionary of Economics*, vol. 4, edited by John Eatwell, Murray Milgate, and Peter Newman, 183–198. London: Macmillan Press.

Degain, Christophe, Bo Meng, and Zhi Wang. 2017. 'Recent Trends in Global Trade and Global Value Chains.' In *Global Value Chain Development Report 2017: Measuring and Analyzing the Impact of GVCs on Economic Development*, 37–68. Washington, DC: The World Bank.

Delgado, N. A., and L. B. Cruz. 2013. 'When the Social Movement and Global Value Chain Literatures Meet: The Case of Fair Trade'. In *Sustainable Value Chain Management: A Research Anthology*, edited by A. Lindgreen, F. Maon, J. Vanhamme and S. Sen, 397–414. London: Routledge.

Deshingkar, P., and Farrington, J. 2009. *Circular Migration and Multilocational Livelihood Strategies in Rural India*. New Delhi: Oxford University Press.

Dev, Mahendra S. 2011. 'NREGA and Child Well-being'. IHD-UNICEF Working Paper Series, No. 10, IHD, New Delhi.

Devi, Indira, Lalit Kumar, Manjula M., Pranab Mukhopadhyay, P. Raghu, Devinder Sharma, R. Sridhar, and L. Venkatachalam. 2017. 'Payment for Ecosystem Services: Guaranteed Farm Income and Sustainable Agriculture'. *Economic and Political Weekly* 52 (17): 12–14.

Dhingra, J. 2014. *From Field to Fashion—Mainstreaming the Midstream: Better Cotton Fast Track Program End Year Report 2013*. New Delhi: Down to Earth.

Dick, Eva, and Einhardt Schmidt-Kallert. 2011. 'Understanding the (Mega-) Urban from the Rural: Non-Permanent Migration and Multi-Locational Households'. *disP—The Planning Review* 47 (187): 24–34.

Distelhorst, G., and D. Fu. 2018. *Wages and Working Conditions in and out of Global Supply Chains: A Comparative Empirical Review*. Geneva: International Labour Organization.

Dobbelaere, S. 2005. 'Joint Estimation for Price Cost Margins and Union Bargaining Power for Belgian Manufacturing'. IZA Discussion Paper 1466.

DtE (*Down to Earth*). 2013. 'Organic Thread: Cover Story'. 16–28 February 2013.

Dubash, N. 2000. 'Ecologically and Socially Embedded Exchange: "Gujarat Model" of Water Markets'. *Economic and Political Weekly* 35 (16): 1376–1385.

Durand, Cedric, and William Milberg. 2019. 'Intellectual Monopoly in Global Value Chains'. *Review of International Political Economy* 27 (2): 404–429. DOI:https://doi.org/10.1080/096922.

Ebert, Franz, and Anne Posthuma. 2011. 'Labour Provisions in Trade Agreements: Current Trends and Future Prospects'. IILS, Geneva. http://www.ilo.org/wcmsp5/groups/public/---dgreports/---inst/documents/publication/wcms_192807.pdf, accessed 1 December 2015.

ECCJ. 2019. *French Corporate Duty of Vigilance Law*. European Coalition for Corporate Justice. https://corporatejustice.org/news/405-french-corporate-duty-of-vigilance-law-frequently-asked-questions, accessed 20 January 2021.

Edwards, Remi, Tom Hunt, and Genevieve LeBaron. 2019. *Corporate Commitments to Living Wages in the Garment Industry*. Sheffield: Sheffield Political Economy Research Institute (SPERI).

Egels-Zander, Niklas. 2015. 'The Role of SMEs in Global Production Networks: A Swedish SME's Payment of Living Wages at Its Indian Supplier'. *Business and Society* 56 (1): 92–129.

Emmanuel, Arghiri. 1972. *Unequal Trade: The Imperialism of Trade*. New York: Monthly Review Press.

Ernst, Dieter. 2012. 'Production and Innovation Networks, Global'. In *Encyclopedia of Global Studies*, 1392–1396. Sage Publications.

Economic Times. 2020. 'India's Cotton Cultivation Consumes Too Much, Produces Too Little. That's Changing'. 5 August.

Evers, Barbara, Flavia Amoding and Aarti Krishnan. 2014. 'Social and Economic Upgrading in Floriculture Global Value Chains: Flowers and Cuttings GVCs in Uganda'. Capturing the Gains, Working Paper 2014/42. http://www.capturingthegains.org/publications/workingpapers/wp_201442.htm, accessed 16 December 2020.

FairWear Foundation. 2016. *Living Wages: An Explorer's Notebook*. Amsterdam: FairWear Foundation.

Fang, Cai, and M. Wang. 2010. 'Growth and Structural Changes in Employment in Transition China'. *Journal of Comparative Economics* 38: 71–81.

FAO and ICAC. 2015. *Measuring Sustainability in Cotton Farming Systems: Towards a Guidance Framework*. Rome: FAO.

Farmer, P. 2003. *Pathologies of Power: Health, Human Rights, and the New War on the Poor*. Berkeley, CA: University of California.

Fayet, L., and W. J. V. Vermeulen. 2014. 'Supporting Smallholders to Access Sustainable Supply Chains: Lessons from the India Cotton Supply Chain'. *Sustainable Development* 22 (5): 289–310.

Feldblum, Chai R., and Victoria A. Lipnic. 2016. *Report of the Co-Chairs of the Select Task Force on the Study of Harassment in the Workplace*. U.S. Equal Employment Opportunity Commission.

Flynn, G., and Robert O'Brien. 2010. 'An Internationalist Labour Response to the Globalisation of India and China'. *Global Labour Journal* 1 (1): 178–202.

Folbre, Nancy. 2020. *The Rise and Decline of Patriarchal Systems: An Intersectional Political Economy*. London: Verso.

Fox, Suzy, and Lamont E. Stallworth. 2006. 'How Effective Is an Apology in Resolving Workplace Bullying Disputes'. *Dispute Resolution Journal* 61 (2): 54–63.

Fraser, Nancy. 2009. *Scales of Justice: Reimagining Political Space in a Globalizing World*. New York: Columbia University Press.

Frassesn, L. 2015. 'The Effect of Global Value Chains on Relative Wages'. *European Trade Study Group*. Paris: ETSG.

Freedman, Josh, and Michael Lind. 2013. 'The Past and Future of America's Social Contract'. *The Atlantic*, 19 December. https://www.theatlantic.com/business/archive/2013/12/the-past-and-future-of-americas-social-contract/282511/, accessed 5 October 2021.

Freeman, Dena. 2003. 'Homeworkers in Global Supply Chains'. *Greener Management International* 43: 107–119.

Frey, R. Scott. 2015. 'Breaking Ships in the World-System: An Analysis of Two Shipbreaking Capitals, Alang in India and Chittagong in Bangladesh'. CSSJ Study Papers. University of Tennessee. https://trace.tennessee.edu/cgi/viewcontent.cgi?article=1001&context=utk_cssjpapers, accessed 18 December 2019.

FTF (Fairtrade Foundation). 2012. *Impact of Fair Trade Cotton, Summary and Management Response to an Independent Impact Study*. London: Fairtrade Foundation.

———. 2015. *Fairtrade and Cotton*. London: Fairtrade Foundation, March.

FTI. 2016. *Scope and Benefits of Fairtrade*, 7th edition. Bonn: Fair Trade International.

———. 2017a. *Creating Innovation, Scaling up Impact, Annual Report 2016–17*. Bonn: Fair Trade International.

———. 2017b. *Monitoring the Scope and Benefits of Fairtrade*, 8th edition. Bonn: Fair Trade International.

Fuquan, Yang, Yu Xiaogang, Yu Yin, Dev Nathan, and Govind Kelkar. 2016. 'Restricting Competition to Reduce Poverty: Impact of the Tourism Value Chain in the Upland Economy of China'. In *Labour in Global Value Chains in Asia*, edited by Dev Nathan, Meenu Tewari and Sandip Sarkar, 139–153. Cambridge: Cambridge University Press.

Gangwar, Santosh. 2020. 'Coronavirus I EPFO Settles 52 Lakh COVID-19 Claims, Disburses INR 13,300 Crore'. *The Hindu*, 16 December. https://www.thehindu.com/business/epfo-settles-52-lakh-covid-19-claims-disburses-13300-crore-santosh-gangwar/article33346095.ece, accessed 28 September 2021.

Gates, Hill. 1979. 'Dependency and the Part-Time Proletariat in Taiwan'. *Modern China* 5 (3): 381–408.

Gereffi, Gary. 1999. 'International Trade and Industrial Upgrading in the Apparel Commodity Chain'. *Journal of International Economics* 48 (1): 37–70.

———. 2019. *Global Value Chains and Development: Redefining the Contours of 21st Century Capitalism*. Cambridge: Cambridge University Press.

Gereffi, Gary, and Fritz Mayer. 2006. 'Globalization and the Demand for Governance'. In *The New Offshoring of Jobs and Global Development, Social Policy Lectures*. Geneva: ILO.

Gereffi, Gary, John Humphrey, and Timothy Sturgeon. 2005. 'The Governance of Global Value Chains'. *Review of International Political Economy* 12 (1): 78–104.

Gill, S., S. Singh, and J. S. Brar. 2010. 'Cotton Economy, Cotton Producers and Bt Cotton Cultivation in Indian Punjab: An Assessment of Economic Impact and Sustainability Issues'. In *Economic and Environmental Sustainability of the Asian Region*, edited by S. S. Gill, L. Singh and R. Marwah, 419–442. New Delhi: Routledge.

Gillson, I. 2004. *Developed Country Cotton Subsidies and Developing Countries: Unravelling the Impacts on Africa*. ODI Briefing Paper, July, ODI, London.

Gillson, I., C. Poulton, K. Balcombe, and S. Page. 2004. *Understanding the Impact of Cotton Subsidies on Developing Countries*. London: ODI WP, ODI.

Glover, David, and Ken Kustrer. 1990. *Small Farmers, Big Business: Contract Farming and Rural Development*. Hampshire: Macmillan.

Goger, Anneliese. 2014. 'Ethical Branding in Sri Lanka: A Case Study of "Garments Without Guilt"'. In *Workers' Rights and Global Supply Chains: Is Social Branding the Answer?*, edited by Jennifer Bair, Marsha Dickinson and Doug Miller, 47–68. New York: Routledge.

———. 2016. From Disposable to Empowered: Rearticulating Labour in Sri Lankan Apparel Factories. In *Labour in Global Value Chains in Asia*, edited by Dev Nathan, Meenu Tewari and Sandip Sarkar, 239–264. Cambridge: Cambridge University Press.

GoI. 2017. 'Status Paper of Indian Cotton'. DCD (Directorate of Cotton Development), January. Nagpur: MoAFW, Government of India.

Gould, K. A., D. N. Pellow, and A. Schnaiberg. 2003. 'Interrogating the Treadmill of Production: Everything You Wanted to Know about the Treadmill, but Were Afraid to Ask'. Paper prepared for the symposium on Environment and the Treadmill of Production, 31 October to 1 November 2003. University of Wisconsin, Madison.

Graham, D., and N. Woods. 2006. 'Making Corporate Self-Regulation Effective in Developing Countries'. *World Development* 34 (5): 868–883.

Greenhouse, Steven. 2010. 'Pressured, Nike to Help Workers in Honduras'. *New York Times*, 29 July. http://www.nytimes.com/2010/07/27/business/global/27nike.html?_r=0, accessed 17 December 2020.

Grosscurt, C., A de Groot Ruiz, and V. Fobelets. 2016. *The True Price of Cotton from India: Joint Report by IDH and True Price*. Amsterdam: True Price.

Hall, Stuart. 1985. 'Signification, Representation, Ideology: Althusser and the Post-Structuralist Debate'. *Critical Studies in Mass Communication* 2 (2): 91–114.

Handmer, J. W., and R. S. Dovers. 1996. 'A Typology of Resilience: Rethinking Institutions for Sustainable Development'. *Organization and Environment* 9 (4): 482–511.

Harding, Sandra. 2013. 'The Less False Accounts of Feminist Standpoint Epistemology'. In *Philosophical Profiles in the Theory of Communication*, edited by Jason Hanan. New York: Peter Lang.

Harvey, David. 2017. *Marx, Capital and the Madness of Economic Reason*. New York: Oxford University Press.

Harvey, Jenna. 2019. 'Homeworkers in Global Supply Chains: A Review of Literature'. WIEGO Resource Document No. 11.

Hearson, M. 2008. 'Cashing In: Giant Retailers, Purchasing Practices, and Working Conditions in the Garment Industry'. Amsterdam. https://archive.cleanclothes.org/resources/ccc/working-conditions/cashing-in.html, accessed January 2019.

Helper, Susan. 1991. 'Strategy and Irreversibility in the US Auto Industry'. *Business History Review* 65 (Winter): 781–824.

Hilmi, M. 2016. 'Developing Greener Food Value Chains: Environmentally Friendly Tomato Post-Harvest Operations in Four Cities'. *Food Chain* 6 (1): 2234.

Hirway, Indira. 2002. 'Employment and Unemployment Situation in 1990s: How Good Are NSS Data?' *Economic and Political Weekly* 37 (21): 2027–2036.

HNSA. 2020. *Working in Garment Supply Chains: A Homeworkers' Toolkit South Asia*. Bengaluru: HNSA/WIEGO.

Hobsbawm, Eric. 1968. *Labouring Men: Studies in the History of Labour*. London: Weidenfeld and Nicolson.

Hodson, Randy, V. J. Roscigno, and Steven H. Lopez. 2006. 'Chaos and the Abuse of Power: Workplace Bullying in Organizational and Interactional Context'. *Work and Occupations* 33 (4): 382–416.

Holdcroft, Jenny. 2015. 'Transforming Supply Chain Industrial Relations'. *International Journal of Labour Relations* 7 (1–2): 1–11.

———. 2019. 'Feature: Supply Chain Justice through Binding Global Agreements'. IndustriALL Global Union website. www.industriall-union.org/feature-supply-chain-justice-through=binding-global-agreements, accessed 19 September 2019.

Holmes, Seth. 2013. *Fresh Fruit, Broken Bodies: Migrant Farmworkers in the United States*. Berkeley, CA: University of California Press.

HRW. 2013. '"Work Faster or Get Out": Labor Rights Abuses in Cambodia's Garment Industry'. Human Rights Watch. https://www.hrw.org/report/2015/03/11/work-faster-or-get-out/labor-rights-abuses-cambodias-garment-industry, accessed 17 December 2020.

Humphrey, J., and H. Schmitz. 2002. 'How Does Insertion in Global Value Chains Affect Upgrading in Industrial Clusters?' *Regional Studies* 36 (9): 1017–1027.

ICAC. 2018. *Production and Trade Subsidies Affecting Cotton Industry*. Washington, DC: ICAC. https://icac.org/Content/PublicationsPdf%20Files/0a348d9d_7eb4_44ff_b237_f767b4c84c4e/Cotton_subsidies2019.pdf.pdf, accessed 5 October 2021.

Ichniowski, C., and K. Shaw. 2003. 'Beyond Incentive Pay: Insiders' Estimates of the Value of Contemporary Resource Management Practices'. *Journal of Economic Perspectives* 17 (1): 155–180.

IFAD. 2005. *Organic Agriculture and Poverty Reduction in Asia: China and India Focus, Thematic Evaluation*. International Fund for Agricultural Development Report No. 1664, July. Rome.

IHD. 2019. *Poverty, Development and Migration in Rural Bihar*. Delhi: Institute for Human Development (mimeo).

———. 2020. *Mapping Cotton Supply Chain in Telangana*. Draft report, IHD and ILO. New Delhi.

Illien, Noele. 2020. 'Plan to Hold Corporations Liable for Violations Abroad Fails'. *New York Times*, 29 November. https://nyti.ms/39kJITc, accessed 30 November 2020.

ILO. n.d. *Mininum Wage Setting*. International Labour Organization. https://www.ilo.org/global/topics/wages/minimum-wages/setting-adjusting/lang--en/index.htm, accessed 30 September 2018.

———. 1998. *Declaration on Fundamental Principles and Rights at Work*. Geneva: ILO.

———. 1999. *Report of the Director-General: Decent Work*. 87th Session, Geneva, June. https://www.ilo.org/public/english/standards/relm/ilc/ilc87/rep-i.htm, accessed 5 October 2021.

———. 2000. *Convention No. 177: Homeworkers*. Geneva: ILO.

———. 2012. *Indicators on Forced Labour*. Geneva: ILO.

———. 2016. *Child Labour in Cotton: A Briefing, Fundamentals*. Geneva: ILO.

———. 2018. *Global Wage Report*. Geneva: ILO.

———. 2019. *Convention C190: Violence and Harassment*. Geneva: ILO.

IndustriAll. 2017. 'MOU on Action, Collaboration, Transformation'. https://actonlivingwages.com/memorandum-of-understanding, accessed 1 September 2018.

ITC. 2011. 'Women in Cotton: Results of A Global Survey'. Technical paper, Doc. No. SC-11-208.E, International Trade Centre, Geneva.

Janvry, Alain de. 1971 *Peasant and Peasant Societies*. Edited by Teodor Shanin. Harmondsworth: Penguin.

Joshi Rai, K. 2011. *The Ikea Experience of Moving towards a Better Cotton Supply Chain-Making Sustainability Work*. IDH Case Study, Amsterdam. https://www.idhsustainabletrade.com/uploaded/2016/08/Ikea-booklet-def.pdf, accessed 5 October 2021.

Kabeer, Naila. 2002. *The Power to Choose: Bangladeshi Women and Labour Market Decisions in London and Dhaka*. London: Verso.

———. 2015. 'Women Workers and the Politics of Claims-Making in a Globalizing World'. UNRISD Working Paper 2015-13.

Kalecki, Michal. 1971. 'Class Struggle and the Distribution of National Income'. In *Selected Essays in the Dynamics of the Capitalist Economy, 1933–1970*. Cambridge: Cambridge University Press.

Kaplinsky, Raphael. 2005. *Globalization, Inequality and Poverty*. Cambridge: Polity Press.

———. 2019. 'Rents and Inequality in Global Value Chains'. In *Handbook of Global Value Chains*, edited by Gary Gereffi, Stephano Ponte and Gale Raj-Reichert, 153–168. London: Edward Elgar.

Kaplinsky, Raphael, and Mike Morris. 2019. 'Trade and Industrialisation in Africa: SMEs, Manufacturing and Cluster Dynamics'. *Journal of African Trade* 6 (1–2): 47–59. DOI: https://doi.org/10.2991/jat.k.190812.001.

Kaplinsky, Raphael, Mike Morris, and Daniel Readmond. 2002. 'The Globalization of Product Markets and Immiserizing Growth: Lessons from the South African Furniture Industry'. *World Development* 30 (7): 1177–1196.

Kara, Siddharth. 2019. *Tainted Garments: The Exploitation of Women and Girls in Indiaa's Home-Based Sector*. Berkeley, CA: Blum Center for Developing Economies, University of California.

Kaur, S. 2019. *An Economic Evaluation of Externalities of Pesticides Use in the Malwa Region of Punjab*. Report submitted to Inter-University Centre for Alternative Economics, a department of the University of Kerala.

Keashly, Loraleigh. 2001. 'Interpersonal and Systemic Aspects of Emotional Abuse at Work: The Target's Perspective'. *Violence and Victims* 16 (3): 233–268.

Kelkar, Govind, Girija Shrestha, and Veena N. 2002. 'Women's Agency and the IT Industry in India'. *Gender, Technology and Development* 6 (1): 63–84.

Kelly, Annie. 2021. 'Worker at H&M Supply Factory Was Killed after Months of Harassment Claims Family'. *The Guardian*. 1 February. https://www.theguardian.com/global-development/2021/feb/01/worker-at-hm-supply-factory-was-killed-after-months-of-harassment-claims-family, accessed on 29 September.

Kompier, Coen. 2014. 'Labour Markets: Exclusion from "Decent Work"'. In *India Exclusion Report 2013–2014*, edited by Centre for Equity Studies. Delhi: Books for Change.

Konduru, Srinivasa, Fumiko Yamazaki, and Mechel Paggi. 2013. 'A Study of Mechanisation of Cotton Harvesting in India and Its Implications'. *Journal of Agricultural Science and Technology* B 3: 789–797.

Kooistra, K., and A. Termorshuizen. 2006. 'The Sustainability of Cotton: Consequences for the Man and Environment'. Report 223, Science shop, April. Wageningen UR.

Kotiswaran, Prabha. 2019. 'Trafficking. A Development Approach'. UCL Working Paper Series. WP No 4/2019.

Kulkarni, H., and M. Shah. 2013. 'Punjab Water Syndrome: Diagnostics and Prescriptions'. *Economic and Political Weekly* 48 (52): 64–73.

Kumar, A., and A. Kumar. 2016. 'BLack Face of Green Revolution in Malwa Region of Punjab'. *Biological Insights* 1: 3–4.

Kumar, Ashok. 2020. *Monopsony Capitalism: Power and Production in the Twilight of the Sweatshop Age*. Cambridge: Cambridge University Press.

Lakhani, T., S. Kuruvilla and A. Avgar. 2013. 'From the Firm to the Network: Global Value Chains and Employment Relations'. *British Journal of Industrial Relations* 51 (3): 440–472.

Lan, Tu, and John Pickles. 2011. 'China's New Contract Labour Law: State Regulation and Worker Rights in Global Production Networks'. *Capturing the Gains.* Working Paper 2011/05. http://www.capturingthegains.org/publications/workingpapers/wp_201105.htm, accessed 5 October 2021.

LeBaron, Genevieve. 2017. 'Can the World End Forced Labour by 2030?' https://www.opendemocracy.net/en/beyond-trafficking-and-slavery/can-world-end-forced-labour-by-2030/, accessed 17 December 2020.

———. 2020. *Combating Modern Slavery: Why Labour Governance Is Failing and What We Can Do about It*. Cambridge: Polity Books.

Lei, Lei, and Sonalde Desai. 2021. 'Male Out-migration and the Health of Left-behind Wives in India: The Roles of Remittances, Household Responsibilities, and Autonomy'. *Social Science and Medicine* 280 (July) 113982: 1-11.

Lepawsky, J., and M. Billah. 2011. 'Making Chains That Unmake Things: Waste-Value Relations and the Bangladesh Rubbish Electronics Industry'. *Geografiska Annaler Series B, Human Geography* 93 (2): 121–139.

Lerche, Jens, and Alpa Shah. 2018. 'Conjugated Oppression within Contemporary Capitalism: Class, Caste, Tribe and Agrarian Change in India'. *Journal of Peasant Studies* 45 (5–6): 927–949. https://doi.org/10.1080/03066150.2018.1463217.

Levy, D. L. 1997. 'Environmental Management as Political Sustainability'. *Organization and Environment* 10 (2): 126–147.

Lewis, Arthur. 1954. 'Economic Development with Unlimited Supplies of Labour'. *The Manchester School* 22 (2): 139–191.

Lin, Xirong, Laura Babbitt, and Drusilla Brown. 2014. 'Sexual Harassment in the Workplace: How Does It Affect Firm Performance and Profits'. Better Work Discussion Paper No. 16.

Locke, Richard. 2013. *The Promise and Limits of Private Power: Promoting Labor Standards in a Global Economy*. New York: Cambridge University Press.

Lopez-Morales, Carlos A., and Maria Azahara Mesa-Jurado. 2017. 'Valuation of Hidden Water Ecosystem Services: The Replacement Cost of the Aquifer System in Central Mexico'. *Water* 9 (8): 571. https://www.mdpi.com/2073-4441/9/8/571, accessed 25 August 2020.

Lund-Thomsen, Peter. 2008. 'Global Sourcing and Codes of Conduct Debate: Five Myths and Five Recommendations'. *Development and Change* 39 (6): 1005–2028.

Lund-Thomsen, Peter, Khalid Nadvi, Anita Chan, Navjote Khara, and Hong Xue. 2012.

'Labour in Global Value Chains: Work Conditions in Football Manufacturing in China, India and Pakistan'. *Development and Change* 43 (6): 1–28.

Lutgen-Sandvik, Pamela. 2008. 'Intensive Remedial Identity Work: Responses to Workplace Bullying Trauma and Stigmatization'. *Organization* 15 (1): 97–119.

Makori, C. M. n. d. 'Reforming the Cotton Trade Order? An Analysis of Cotton Subsidies and Implications for Sustainable Development'. Unpublished.

Martinez-Alier, J., L. Temper, D. D. Bene, and A. Scheidel. 2016. 'Is There a Global Environmental Justice Movement?" *The Journal of Peasant Studies* 43 (3): 731–755.

Martin-Ortega, Olga, and Claire Methven O'Brien. 2017. 'Advancing Respect for Labour Rights Globally through Public Procurement'. *Politics and Governance* 5 (4): 69–79.

Marx, Karl. 1958. *Capital*, vol. 3. Moscow: Progress Publishers.

Maryudi, Ahmed, and Rodd Myers. 2018. 'Renting Legality: How FLEGT Is Reinforcing Power Relations in Indonesian Furniture Production Networks'. *Geoforum* 97 (December): 46–53.

McCormack, D., N. Djurkovic, A. Nsubuga-Kyobe, and G. Casimir. *2018*. 'Workplace Bullying: The Interactive Effects of the Perpetrator's Gender and the Target's Gender'. Employee Relations 40 (2): 264–280.

McKay, Ruth, and Jae Fratzl. 2011. 'A Cause of Failure in Addressing Workplace Bullying: Trauma and the Employee'. *International Journal of Business and Social Science* 2 (7): 13–27.

McMullen, A., and Sanjita Majumder. 2016. 'Do We Buy It? A Supply Chain Investigation into Living Wage Commitments from M&S and H&M'. Labour Behind the Label, Cividep, Stand up Movement, Center for Alliance of Labour and Human Rights (CENTRAL).

McPherson, P. 2011. 'Hundreds of Workers Collapse at Cambodian H&M Clothing Factory'. *Independent*. 29 August. http://www.independent.co.uk/news/world/asia/hundreds-of-workers-collapse-at-cambodian-hampm-clothing-factory-2345537.html, accessed 9 May 2016.

Mehrotra, Santosh, and Mario Biggeri. 2007. *Asian Informal Workers: Global Risks Local Protection*. London: Routledge.

Mei, Lixia, and Jici Wang. 2016. 'Dynamics of Labour-Intensive Clusters in China: Wage Costs and Moving Inland'. In *Labour in Global Value Chains in Asia*, edited by Dev Nathan, Meenu Tewari and Sandip Sarkar, 139–153. Cambridge: Cambridge University Press.

Meillasoux, Claude. 1981. *Maidens, Meals and Money*. Cambridge: Cambridge University Press.

Mendoza, A. 2018. 'Economic and Social Upgrading in Global Value Chains: Insights from Philippine Manufacturing Firms'. Munich Personal RePEc Archive. https://mpra.ub.uni-muenchen.de/94702/, accessed 5 October 2021.

Mertes, Tom. 2003. *A Movement of Movements: Is Another World Really Possible?* London: Verso.

Mezzadri, Alessandra. 2016. *The Sweatshop Regime: Labouring Bodies, Exploitation and Garments Made in India*. Cambridge: Cambridge University Press.

Mezzadri, Alessandra, and Sanjita Majumder. 2018. 'The "Afterlife" of Cheap Labour: Bangalore Garment Workers from Factories to the Informal Economy'. FEDI and Cividep Working Paper.

Mhaskar, Sumeet. 2019. 'The Roots of Maratha Unrest Lie in Mumbai's Changing Political Economy'. https://thewire.in/politics/maratha-unrest-linkages-mumbai-political-economy, accessed 3 November 2020.

Mies, Maria. 1982. *The Lace Makers of Narsapur: Indian Housewives Produce for the World Market*. London: Zed Press.

Milberg, W., and D. Winkler. 2011. 'Economic and Social Upgrading in Global Production Networks: Problems of Theory and Measurement'. *International Labour Review* 150 (3–4): 341–365.

———. 2013. *Outsourcing Economics: Global Value Chains in Economic Development*. Cambridge: Cambridge University Press.

Millenium Ecosystem Assessment. 2005. *Synthesis Report*. Washington, DC: Island Press.

Miller, Doug. 2013. 'Towards Sustainable Labour Costing in UK Fashion Retail'. Capturing the Gains, Working Paper WP14, http://www.capturingthegains.org/pdf/ctg-wp-2013-14.pdf, accessed 5 October 2021.

Miller, Doug, and G. Mooney. 2010. 'Introduction to the Themed Issue. Corporate Power: Agency, Communication, Influence and Social Policy'. *Critical Social Policy* 30 (4): 459–471.

Miller, Doug, and Klaus Hohenegger. 2018. 'Redistributing Value Added towards Labour in Apparel Supply Chains: Tackling Low Wages through Purchasing Practices'. ILO Conditions of Work and Employment Series No. 83. ILO, Geneva.

Miller, Doug, and Peter Williams. 2009. 'What Price a Living Wage? Implementation Issues in the Quest for Decent Wages in the Global Apparel Sector'. *Global Supply Policy* 9 (1): 99–125.

Mills, Mary Beth. 2003. 'Gender and Inequality in the Global Labor Force'. *Annual Reiew of Anthropology* 32: 41–62.

Minot, N., and L. Daniels. 2002. *Impact of Global Cotton Markets on Rural Poverty in Benin*. IFPRI MSSD Discussion Paper 48. Washington.

Mishel, L. 1986. 'The Structural Determinants of Union Bargaining Power'. *Industrial Labour Relations Review* 40 (1): 90–104.

Moore, Jason S. 2015. *Capitalism in the Web of Life: Ecology and the Accumulation of Capital*. London: Verso Books.

Morris, Jo, and Jane Pillinger. 2016. *Gender-based Violence in Global Supply Chains: Resource Kit*. Turin: ITCILO and Fair Wear Foundation.

Murphy, S., and K. Hansen-Kuhn. 2017. 'Counting the Cost of Agricultural Dumping'. Institute for Agriculture and Trade Policy, June. https://www.iatp.

org/sites/default/files/2017-06/2017_06_26_DumpingPaper.pdf, accessed 5 October 2021.

Murthy, Narayana. 2009. *A Better India, A Better World.* New Delhi: Penguin Books.

Namie, Gary, and Ruth Namie. 2009. 'U.S. Workplace Bullying: Some Basic Considerations and Consultation Interventions'. *Consulting Psychology Journal Practice and Research* 61 (3): 202–219.

Nanda, G. 2019. 'Is the Cotton Industry Fair and Sustainable?' https://www.iknockfashion.com/is-the-cotton-industry-fair-and-sustainable, accessed 20 October 2020.

Nathan, Dev. 2013. 'Industrial Relations in a GPN Perspective: From Tripartite to Quadripartite Machinery'. *Economic and Political Weekly* 48 (30): 29–33.

———. 2016. 'Governance Types and Employment Systems'. In *Labour in Global Value Chains in Asia*, edited by Dev Nathan, Meenu Tewari, and Sandip Sarkar, 471–502. Cambridge: Cambridge University Press.

———. 2018. 'Imperialism in the 21st Century: Global Value Chains and International Labour Arbitrage'. *Economic and Political Weekly* 53 (32): 33–39.

———. 2020. 'Knowledge, Oligopoly and Labour in GVCs'. *Global Labor Journal.* 11 (2): 134–151.

Nathan, Dev, and Abhishek Kumar. 2016. 'Knowledge, Education and Labour Practices in India'. *Economic and Political Weekly* 51 (36): 37–45.

Nathan, Dev, Anjum Shaheen, and Immanuel Dahaghani. 2018. 'Living Wages and Precarious Work in Garment Value Chains'. Society for Labour and Development Clean Clothes Campaign, New Delhi. Mimeo.

Nathan, Dev, and Govind Kelkar. 1999. 'Agrarian Involution, Domestic Economy and Women: Rural Dimensions of the Asian Crisis'. *Economic and Political Economy* 34 (19): 1135–1141.

———. 2012. 'A Political Economy Analysis of Crisis Response: Reflections on Thailand and India'. In *The Global Crisis and Transformative Social Change*, edited by Peter Utting, Shahra Razavi and Rebecca Varghese Buccholz, 218–236. London: Palgave Macmillan and UNRISD.

Nathan, Dev, and Harsh. 2018. 'Gaining Process Rents in Indian Garment Industry'. In *Development with Global Value Chains: Upgrading and Innovation in Asia*, edited by Dev Nathan, Meenu Tewari and Sandip Sarkar, 63–85. Cambridge: Cambridge University Press.

Nathan, Dev, Madhuri Saripalle, and L. Gurunathan. 2016. 'Labour Practices in India'. ILO Asia-Pacific Working Papers. https://www.ilo.org/wcmsp5/groups/public/—asia/—ro-bangkok/—sro-new_delhi/documents/publication/wcms_501117.pdf, accessed 5 October 2021.

Nathan, Dev, Meenu Tewari, and Sandip Sarkar, eds. 2016. *Labour in Global Value Chains in Asia.* Cambridge: Cambridge University Press.

Nathan, Dev, and N. S. Jodha. 2004. 'External Trade and Development of Upland Peoples'. In *Globalization and Indigenous Peoples in Asia: Changing the Global-*

Local Interface, edited by Dev Nathan, Govind Kelka, and Pierre Walter, 259–290. New Delhi: Sage Publications.

Nathan, Dev, and Sandip Sarkar. 2010. 'Blood on Your Mobile?' *Economic and Political Weekly* 45 (43): 22–24.

———. 2011. 'Profits, Rents and Wages in Global Production Networks'. *Economic and Political Weekly* 46 (36): 53–57.

Nathan, Dev, Sandip Sarkar, and Balwant Mehta. 2013. 'How Social Upgrading Drives Economic Upgrading by Indian IT Majors'. *Capturing the Gains*. Working Paper No. 27.http://www.capturingthegains.org/publications/workingpapers/wp_201327.htm, accessed 5 October 2021.

Nathan, Dev, and V. Kalpana. 2007. *Issues in the Analysis of Global Value Chains and Their Impact on Employment and Income in India*. Geneva: International Labour Organization.

Nathan, Dev, Varsha Joshi, Asha Wadhwani, Desh Raj Singh, Ramesh Sharma, Lakshmi Bhatia, and Govind Kelkar. 2018. *Business Strategies for Making Jaipur Child Labour Free*. London: Freedom Fund. https://freedomfund.org/wp-content/uploads/Business-Strategies-for-a-Child-Labour-Free-Jaipur.pdf, accessed 28 October 2021.

NCPCR. 2011. 'Gujarat Visit Report, Led by Dr. Yogesh Dube Member, National Commission for the Protection for Child Rights'. National Commission for Protection of Child Rights, Delhi.

Neilson, J., and B. Pritchard. 2009. *Value Chain Struggles: Institutions and Governance in the Plantation Districts of South India*. London: Wiley Blackwell.

Nelson, V., and S. Smith. 2011. 'Fairtrade Cotton: Assessing Impact in Mali, Senegal, Cameroon and India—Synthesis Report'. University of Greenwich and IDS Sussex, May.

Nuon, V., M. Serrano, and E. Xhafa. 2011. *Women and Gender Issues in Trade unions in the Cambodian Garment Industry*. Phnom Penh: ILO.

Ngai, Pun. 2005. *Made in China: Women Factory Workers in a Global Workplace*. Durham, NC: Duke University Press.

———. 2016. *Migrant Labour in China: Post-Socialist Transformation*. Cambridge: Polity Press.

Noronha, Ernesto, and Premilla D'Cruz. 2016. 'Still a Distance to Go: Social Upgrading in the Indian ITO-BPO-KPO Sector'. In *Labour in Global Value Chains in Asia*, edited by Dev Nathan, Meenu Tewari and Sandip Sarkar, 423–449. Cambridge: Cambridge University Press.

Nriagu, J. 2007. 'Zinc Toxicity in Humans'. School of Public Health, University of Michigan, Ann Arbor, MI.

NSSO. 2018. *Periodic Labour Force Survey*. New Delhi: NSSO, Ministry of Statistics and Programme Implementation, Government of India.

———. 2019. *Periodic Labour Force Survey*. New Delhi: NSO, Ministry of Statistics and Programme Implementation, Government of India.

Nussbaum, Martha. 2004. 'Beyond the Social Contract: Capabilities and Global Justice'. *Oxford Development Studies* 32 (1): 3–18.

O'Neill, Onora. 2001. 'Agents of Justice'. In *Global Justice*, edited by Thomas Pogge, 188–204. Oxford: Blackwell Publishers.

OECD. 2013. *Responsible Supply Chain Management*. Paris: Organisation for Economic Co-operation and Development.

———. 2018. 'Time Spent in Total, Paid and Unpaid Work by Sex'. http://www.oecd.org/gender/data/time-spent-in-unpaid-paid-and-total-work-by-sex.htm, accessed 1 September 2018.

Orden, D., A. Salam, R. Dewina, H. Nazli, and N. Mint. 2006. 'The Impact of Global Cotton Markets on Rural Poverty in Pakistan'. Paper presented at the AAEA annual meeting, 23–26 July. Long Beach, California.

Oxfam. 2002. *Cultivating Poverty—The Impact of US Cotton Subsidies on Africa*. Oxfam Briefing Paper No. 30, Oxfam International, September.

Oxfam Australia. 2017. 'A Sewing Kit for Living Wages'. Melbourne. https://www.oxfam.org.au/wp-content/uploads/2017/09/A-Sewing-Kit-for-Living-Wages, accessed 1 September 2018.

Pagano, Ugo. 2014. 'The Crisis of Intellectual Monopoly Capitalism'. *Cambridge Journal of Economics* 38 (6): 1409–1429.

Pal, Rupayan, and Udayan Rathore. 2014. 'Estimating Workers' Bargaining Power and Firms' Mark-up in India'. Paper presented at ISLE Conference, 18–20 December. Ranchi (mimeo).

Palanisami, K., K. Mohan, K. R. Kakumanu, and S. Raman. 2011. 'Spread and Economics of Micro-Irrigation in India: Evidence from Nine States'. *Economic and Political Weekly* 46 (26 and 27): 81–86.

Paludi, Michele A., and Richard B. Barickman. 1991. *Academic and Workplace Sexual Harassment: A Resource Manual*. Albany: SUNY Press.

PAN. 2017. *Is Cotton Concurring Its Chemical Addiction: A Review of Pesticides Use in Global Cotton Production*. Brighton, UK: Pesticides Action Network (PAN).

PAN, Solidaridad, and WWF. 2017. *Sustainable Cotton Ranking, 2017: Assessing Company Performance*. Brighton, UK: PAN UK, Solidaridad and WWF.

Pani, Narender, and Nikky Singh. 2012. *Women at the Threshold of Globalization: Garment Workers in Bangalore*. New Delhi: Routledge.

Parteka, A., and J. W. Derlacz. 2019. 'Global Value Chains and Wages: Multi-Country Evidence from Linked Worker-Industry Data'. *Open Economies Review* 30 (3): 505–539.

Pearce, David, and R. Kerry Turner. 1990. *Economics of Natural Resources and the Environment*. Baltimore: The Johns Hopkins University Press.

Phillips N. 2015. 'Private Governance and the Problem of Trafficking and Slavery in Global Supply Chains'. In *Vulnerability, Exploitation and Migrants. Migration, Diasporas and Citizenship*, edited by L. Waite, G. Craig, H. Lewis, and K. Skrivankova, 15–27. London: Palgrave Macmillan. https://doi.org/10.1057/9781137460417_2.

Phillips, Nicola, Resmi Bhaskaran, C. Upendranadh, and Dev Nathan. 2014. 'Social Foundations of Global Production: Unfree Labour'. *Third World Quarterly* 35 (3): 428–446.

Phongpaichit, Pasuk, and Chris Baker, eds. 2008. *Thai Capital after the 1997 Crisis*. Chiangmai: Silkworm Books.

Pickles, John, and Adrian Smith. 2016. *Articulations of Capital: Global Production Networks and Regional Transformation*. London: Wiley.

Pogge, Thomas. 2008. *World Poverty and Human Rights*. Cambridge: Polity Press.

Pollin, Robert, and Stephanie Luce. 2000. *The Living Wage: Building a Fair Economy*. New York: The New Press.

Pollin, Robert, Justine Burns, and James Heintz. 2004. 'Global Apparel Production and Sweatshop Labour: Can Raising Retail Prices Finance Living Wages?' *Cambridge Journal of Economics* 28 (2): 153–171.

Ponte, S., G. Gereffi, and G. Raj-Reichert, eds. 2019. *Handbook on Global Value Chains*. Cheltenham: Edward Elgar Publishing.

Porter, Michael. 1985. *Competitive Advantage*. New York: Simon and Schuster.

Prahalad, C. K., and G. Hamel. 1990. 'The Core Competence of the Corporation'. *Harvard Business Review* 68 (3): 79–91.

Preston, Joel, and Carin Leffler. 2014. *When 'Best' Is Far from Good Enough: Violations of Workers' Rights at Four of H&M 'Best-in-Class' Suppliers in Cambodia*. Oslo: Framtiden i våre hender.

Pun, N., A. Y. Liu, and H. L. Lu. 2015. 'Labour Conditions and the Working Poor in China and India: The China Team's Final Report'. Unpublished Final Report for the ESRC/DfID project 'Labour Conditions and the Working Poor in China and India'. Centre for Development Policy and Research, SOAS, London.

Purwanto, H. 2016. 'Twenty Five Million People Depend on Citarum River'. *Anatara News*, 28 July. https://en.antaranews.com/news/105951/twenty-five-million-people-depend-on-citarum-river, accessed 18 January 2020.

Quine, Lyn. 1999. 'Workplace Bullying in NHS Community Trust: Staff Questionnaire Survey'. *British Medical Journal* 318: 228–232.

Quirk, Joel, and Genevieve LeBaron. 2016. 'Introducing the Terms of the Debate: Regulation and Responsibility in Global Supply Chains'. *OpenDemocracy*. https://www.opendemocracy.net/en/beyond-trafficking-and-slavery/genevieve-lebaron-and-joel-quirk-intro/, accessed 5 October 2021.

Raj-Reichert, Gale. 2018. 'The Changing Landscape of Contract Manufacturers in the Electronics Industry Global Value Chain'. In *Development with Global Value Chains: Upgrading and Innovation in Asia*, edited by Dev Nathan, Meenu Tewari and Sandip Sarkar, 20–62. Cambridge: Cambridge University Press.

Ramaswami, B. 2019. 'Agriculture Subsidies–Study Prepared for XV Finance Commission'. Final Report. New Delhi: ISI. https://fincomindia.nic.in/

writereaddata/html_en_files/fincom15/StudyReports/Agricultural%20 subsidies.pdf, accessed 5 October 2021.

Randle, J., K. Stevenson, and I. Grayling. 2007. 'Reducing Workplace Bullying in Healthcare Organizations'. *Nursing Standard* 21 (2): 49–56.

Ranganathan, T., S. Gaurav, and I. Halder. 2018. 'Pesticide Usage by Cotton Farmers in India—Changes over a Decade'. *Economic and Political Weekly* 53 (19): 43–51.

Raveendran, G., R. M. Sudarshan, and J. Vanek. 2013. *Home-Based Workers in India: Statistics and Trends*. WIEGO Statistical Brief No. 10. Manchester, WIEGO.

Rawls, John. 1955. 'Two Concepts of Rules'. *The Philosophical Review* 64 (1): 3–32.

———. 1999. *The Law of Peoples*. Cambridge, MA: Harvard University Press.

Raworth, K. 2017. *Doughnut Economics: Seven Ways to Think Like a 21st-Century Economist*. White River Junction, VT: Chelsea Green Publishing.

Rayner, Charlotte, and Cary Cooper. 1997. 'Workplace Bullying: Myth Or Reality – Can We Afford to Ignore It? *Leadership and Organization Development Journal* 18 (4): 211–214.

Rice, James. 2007. 'Ecological Unequal Exchange: International Trade and Uneven Utilization of Environmental Space in the World System'. *Social Forces* 85 (3): 1369–1392.

Rodrik, D. 2016. 'What Do Trade Agreements Really Do?' NBER. https://www.nber.org/system/files/working_papers/w24344/w24344.pdf, accessed 5 October 2021.

Roemer, John. 1996. *Theories of Distributive Justice*. Cambridge, MA: Harvard University Press.

Rosenberg, Tina. 2007. 'Reverse Foreign Aid'. *New York Times Magazine*, 25 March. https://www.nytimes.com/2007/03/25/magazine/25wwlnidealab.t.html, accessed 29 October 2020.

Ross, R. B., V. Pandey, and K. L. Ross. 2015. 'Sustainability and Strategy in US Agri-Food Firms: An Assessment of Current Practices'. *International Food and Agribusiness Management Review* 18 (1): 17–47.

Rourke, Emily L. 2014. 'Is There a Business Case Against Verbal Abuse? Incentive Structure, Verbal Abuse, Productivity and Profits in Garment Factories'. Better Work Discussion Paper Series No. 15. https://betterwork.org/global/wp-content/uploads/2014/09/DP-15-web.pdf, accessed 5 October 2021.

Rowbotham, Sheila. 1999. 'Strategies against Sweated Work in Britain, 1850–1920'. In *Threads through Time: Writings on History and Autobiography*. London: Penguin Books.

Ryder, Guy. 2021. 'Foreword'. In *Maritime Labour Convention*. Geneva: ILO.

Sachitanand, Rahul. 2018. 'Why Indian IT Firms Are Hiring Teams Overseas'. *Economic Times*, 23 December.

Salaheldin, I., and Mohamed Zain. 2007. 'How Quality Circles Enhance Work Safety: A Case Study'. *TQM Journal* 19 (3): 229–244.

Samel, Hiram. 2012. 'Upgrading under Volatility in a Global Economy'. MIT Sloan School of Management. http://ssrn.com/abstract+2102643, accessed 9 December 2014.

Sarkar, Sandip, and Balwant Singh Mehta. 2016. 'What Do Workers Gain from Being in a GVC? ICT in India'. In *Labour in Global Value Chains in* Asia, edited by Dev Nathan, Meenu Tewari and Sandip Sarkar, 450–478. Cambridge: Cambridge University Press.

Sarkar, Sandip, Balwant Singh Mehta, and Dev Nathan. 2013. 'How Social Upgrading Drives Economic Upgrading by Indian IT Majors'. *Capturing the Gains*. Working Paper No. 2013/27. https://papers.ssrn.com/sol3/papers.cfm?abstract_id=2237520, accessed 25 July 2015.

Sassen, Saskia. 2014. *Expulsions: Brutality and Complexity in the Global Economy*. Cambridge: The Belknap Press of Harvard University Press.

Scanlon, Tom. 1998. *What We Owe to Each Other*. Cambridge, MA: Harvard University Press.

Schmidt-Kallert, Einhardt, and Peter Franke. 2010. 'Living in Two Worlds: Multi-Locational Household Arrangements among Migrant Workers in China'. *Die Erde; Zeitschrift der Gesellschaft für Erdkunde zu Berlin* 143 (3): 263–284.

Schrempf-Stirling, J., G. Palazzo, and R. A. Phillips. 2013. 'Ever Expanding Responsibilities: Upstream and Downstream Corporate Social Responsibility'. In *Sustainable Value Chain Management: A Research Anthology*, edited by A. Lindgreen, F. Maon, J. Vanhamme and S. Sen, 353–368. Surrey, UK: Gower.

Schwank, O., N. North, and M. Battig. 2001. *Freshwater and Cotton: Field Case Studies*. Zurich: WWF.

Scott, B. R. 2007. 'Health Risk Evaluations for Ingestion Exposure of Humans to Polonium-210'. *Dose-Response* 5 (2): 94–122.

Sen, Amartya. 2009. *The Idea of Justice*. London: Penguin Books.

SEWA Bharat. 2020. *Gendered Precarity in the Lockdown*. May. https://www.wiego.org/sites/default/files/publications/file/Gendered_Precarity_SB_Lockdown.pdf, accessed 5 October 2021, accessed 21 January 2021.

SF Gate. 2006. 'San Francisco-Garment Workers to Get Severance Pay'. 13 January. https://www.sfgate.com/bayarea/article/SAN-FRANCISCO-Garment-workers-to-get-severance-2543673.php, accessed 17 December 2020.

Sharma, S. K., and K. Bugaliya. 2014. 'Competitiveness of Indian Agriculture Sector: A Case Study of Cotton Crop'. *Procedia–Social and Behavioral Sciences* 133: 320–335.

Shih, Stan. 2010. 'Millennium Transformation: Change Management for New Acer'. Translated by Eugene Hwang. Aspire Academy Series. http://www.stanshares.com.tw/StanShares/upload/tbBook/1_20100817144639.pdf, accessed 4 July 2017.

Shiratani, Eisaku, Ikuo Yoshinaga, and Asa Miura. 2006. 'Economic Valuation of Cultivate Lands as Nitrogen Removal/Effusion Sites by Newly Proposed Replacement Cost Method'. *Paddy and Water Environment* 4 (4): 211–215.

Silliman Bhattacharjee, Shikha. 2020a. *Advancing Gender Justice on Asian Fast Fashion Supply Chains Post COVID-19*. Global Labor Justice–International Labor Rights Forum.

———. 2020b. 'Fast Fashion, Production Targets, and Gender-Based Violence in Asian Garment Supply Chains'. In *Labor, Global Supply Chains, and the Garment Industry in South Asia: Bangladesh after Rana Plaza*, edited by S. Sazena. New York: Routledge.

Silver, Beverley. 2003. *Forces of Labor: Workers' Movement and Globalization since 1870*. Cambridge: Cambridge University Press.

Silverstein, Ken. 2018. 'Indonesian Garment Workers Appeal to Uniqlo CEO in Letters to Take Action on Severance Debt'. 20 April. https://cleanclothes.org/news/2018/04/19/indonesian-garment-workers-appeal-ceo-uniqlo-in-letters-to-take-action-on-severance-debt, accessed 17 December 2020.

———. 2019. 'Blood Money: Indonesian Wage Theft and the Massacre Premium'. *New Republic*, 8 April. Clean Clothes Campaign, 2018. https://newrepublic.com/article/153248/blood-money-indonesian-wage-theft, accessed 17 December 2020.

Sindhi, S., and N. Kumar. 2012. 'Corporate Environmental Responsibility—Transitional and Evolving'. *Management of Environmental Quality* 23 (6): 640–657.

Singh, B. P. 2008. 'Cancer Deaths in Agricultural Heartland: A Study in Malwa Region of Punjab'. Master's thesis, IIGSEO Enschede. The Netherlands.

Singh, Gurpreet. 2020. 'India's Food Bowl Heads toward Desertification'. *Eos*, 30 July. https://eos.org/articles/indias-food-bowl-heads-toward-desertification, accessed 17 December 2020.

Singh, Sukhpal. 2009. *Organic Produce Supply Chains in India: Organisation and Governance*. New Delhi: Allied Publishers.

———. 2016. 'Sustainability Issues in Indian Agriculture: An Examination of Role of Corporate Social Responsibility v/s 3P Business Models'. In *Corporate Social Responsibility in India: Quest for Socio-Economic Transformation*, edited by R. S. Ghuman and R. Sharma, 31–56. Chandigarh: CRRID.

———. 2017. '"White Gold" for Whom? A Study of Institutional Aspects of Work and Wages in Cotton GPNs in India'. In *Critical Perspectives on Work and Employment in Globalizing India*, edited by Ernesto Noronha and Premila D'Çruz, 15–36. Singapore: Springer.

———. 2019. 'Competing for Space and Making a Difference? An Assessment of the Sustainability Standards in the Indian Cotton Sector'. In *Business Responsibility and Sustainability in India*, edited by Bimal Arora, Pawan Budhwar, and Divya Jyoti, 129–160. London: Palgrave Macmillan.

Sinha, Shalini, and Feroza Mehrotra. 2016. *Working in the Shadows: Women Homeworkers in Global Supply Chains*. Bangalore: HomeNet South Asia.

Sklair, L., and D. Miller. 2010. 'Capitalist Globalization, Corporate Social Responsibility and Social Policy'. *Critical Social Policy* 30 (4): 472–495.

Sneyd, A. 2014. 'When Governance Gets Going: Certifying "Better Cotton" and "Better Sugarcane"'. *Development and Change* 45 (2): 231–256.

SLD. 2018. *Migrant Workers at the Margins: Access to Rights and Entitlements for Internal Migrants in India.* New Delhi: Society for Labour and Development. http://www.sld-india.org/wp-content/uploads/2018/11/Migrant-Workers-at-the-Margin-1-SLD-1-Pages-format-For-Web.pdf, accesed 5 October 2021.

———. 2020. 'Garment Workers in India's Lockdown: Semi-starvation and Dehumanization lead to Exodus'. Society for Labour and Development. https://media.business-humanrights.org/media/documents/files/documents/Garment-Workers-in-Indias-Lockdown11.pdf, accessed 28 September 2021.

Smith, Adam. 2000 [1777]. *An Enquiry into the Causes of the Wealth of Nations.* https://scholarsbank.uoregon.edu/xmlui/bitstream/handle/1794/782/wealth.pdf, accessed 19 September 2021.

Smith, J. 2016. *Imperialism in the Twenty-First Century.* New York: Monthly Review Press.

Sood, A., and B. Arora. 2006. 'The Political Economy of Corporate Responsibility in India'. UNRISD Technology, Business and Society Program Paper No. 18, November. UNRISD, Geneva.

Srivastava, Ravi. 2011. 'Labour Migration, Inequality and Development Dynamics in India'. *Indian Journal of Labour Economics* 54 (3): 373–385.

———. 2020. 'Understanding Circular Migration in India: Its Nature and Dimensions, the Crisis under Lockdown and the Response of the State'. Working Paper 04/2020. Institute for Human Development. https://www.thehinducentre.com/publications/policy-watch/article33461900.ece/binary/IHD-CES_WP_04_2020.pdf, accessed 20 August 2020.

Stabile, Donald. 2008. *The Living Wage: Lessons from the History of Economic Thought.* Cheltenham: Edward Elgar.

Standing, Guy, ed. 1985. *Labour Circulation and Labour Process.* London: Croom Helm.

Statista. 2019. 'Market Share of Leading Chocolate Companies Worldwide in 2016'. http://www.statista.com/statistics//629534/market-share-leading-chocolate-companies-worldwide, accessed 4 March 2020.

———. 2020. 'Market Share of the Leading Coffee Chains in the United States as of October 2019, by Number of Outlets'. http//www/statista.com/statistics/250166/market-share-of-major-us-coffee-shops, accessed 4 March 2020.

Stohl, Cynthia, Michael Stohl and Lucy Popova. 2009. 'A New Generation of Corporate Codes of Ethics'. *Journal of Business Ethics* 90: 607–622.

Sturgeon, Tim, and Greg Linden. 2011. 'Learning and Earning in Global Value Chains: Lessons in Supplier Competence in East Asia'. In *The Dynamics of Local Learning in Global Value Chains*, edited by M. Kawakami and T. Sturgeon, 207–226. New York: Palgrave Macmillan.

Subrahmanyam, Sanjay. 1991. 'Connected Histories: Notes towards a Reconfiguration of Early Modern Eurasia'. *Modern Asia Studies* 31 (3): 735–762.

———. 1997. 'Connected Histories: Notes towards a Reconfiguration of Early Modern Eurasia'. *Modern Asian Studies* 31 (3): 735–762.

Swaminathan, Padmini. 2004. 'The Trauma of "Wage Employment" and the "Burden of Work" for Women in India: Evidences and Experiences'. Working Paper No. 186, Madras Institute for Development Studies.

———. 2014. 'Regulating Industrialization through Public Action and Legal Intervention: Interpreting an On-Going Experiment in Tamil Nadu'. In *Globalization and Standards*, edited by K. Das, 225–244. India Studies in Business and Economics. New Delhi: Springer.

Swaminathan, P., and J. Jeyaranjan. 1994. 'The Knitwear Cluster in Tiruppur'. Working paper No. 126, The Madras Institute of Development Stuies, Chennai, November.

———. 1999. 'The Knitwear Cluster in Tiruppur: An Indian Industrial District in the Making'. In *Economy and Organization: Indian Institutions under the Neoliberal Regime*, edited by A. K. Bagchi. New Delhi: Sage.

Swaminathan, Padmini, J. Jeyaranjan, R. Sreenivasan, and K. Jayashree. 2004. 'Tamil Nadu's Midday Meal Scheme: Where Assumed Benefits Score over Hard Data'. *Economic and Political Weekly* 39 (44): 4811–4821.

Tewari, Meenu. 2016. 'Diffusing Labour Standards Down and Beyond the Value Chain: Lessons from the Mewat Experience'. In *Labour in Global Value Chains in Asia*, edited by Dev Nathan, Meenu Tewari and Sandip Sarkar, 287–314. Cambridge: Cambridge University Press.

Tewari, M., and P. Pillai. 2005. 'Global Standards and the Dynamics of Environmental Compliance in India's Leather Industry'. *Oxford Development Studies* 33 (2): 245–267

Toye, Richard. 2003. 'The Origins and Interpretation of the Prebish-Singer Thesis'. *History of Political Economy* 35 (3): 437–467.

Truscott, L. Tan, E., Gosai, A., Emberson, L., Lambert, N., Worley, D., et al. 2016. *Organic Cotton Market Report, 2016*. O'Donnell, TX: Textile Exchange.

Turco, G. 2003. 'Dissecting the Cotton Value Chain, Part 1, The Farm Level'. *Australian Cottongrower* 24 (1).

UN. 1948. *Universal Declaration of Human Rights*. United Nations.

UNHRC. 2011. *Guiding Principles on Human Rights: Implementing the United Nations 'Protect, Respect and Remedy' Framework*. Geneva: UN Human Rights Council. https://www.ohchr.org/Documents/Publications/GuidingPrinciplesBusinessHR_EN.pdf, accessed 20 September 2018.

UN Women-ILO. 2019. *Handbook: Addressing Violence and Harassment against Women in the World of Work*. United Nations Entity for Gender Equality and the Empowerment of Women (UN Women) and International Labour Organization (ILO), UN Women Headquarters.

USEPA. 2021. 'Environmental Justice'. United States Environmental Protection Agency. https://www.epa.gov/environmentaljustice, accessed 28 September 2021.

Usher, A., K. Newitt, and L. Merouchi. 2013. *Better Cotton and Decent Work: Activities, Impacts and Lesson Learned* (executive summary). London: Ergon Associates.

Vaughan-Whitehead, Daniel. 2014. 'How Fair Are Wage Practices along the Supply Chain?' In *Towards Better Work: Understanding Labour in Apparel Global Value Chains*, edited by Arianna Rossi, Amy Luinstra and John Pickles, 58–102. London: Palgrave Macmillan.

Vaughan-Whitehead, Daniel, and Luis Pinero Caro. 2017. 'Purchasing Practices and Working Conditions in Global Supply Chains: Global Survey Results'. INWORK Issues Brief No. 19, ILO, Geneva.

Vega, G., D. R. Comer. 2005. 'Sticks and Stones May Break Your Bones, but Words Can Break Your Spirit: Bullying in the Workplace'. *Journal of Business Ethics* 58: 101–109.

Venkatachalam, L. 2015. 'Environmental Implications of the Manufacturing Sector: A Case Study of Textile Manufacturing in Tiruppur, Tamil Nadu, India'. *Review of Development and Change* 20 (2): 165–175.

Venkateswarlu, D. n. d. 'Child Labor in Carpet Industry in India: Recent Developments'. International Labor Rights Fund. https://laborrights.org/sites/default/files/publications-and-resources/child%20labor%20in%20carpet%20industry%20122706.pdf, accessed 20 January 2021.

Vijayabaskar, M. 2019. 'Constraints to Upgrading and Employment Expansion in the Tiruppur Knitwear Cluster'. Unpublished.

Viswanathan, P. K., and N. Lalitha. 2010. 'Does GM Technology Pay Rich Dividends? Reflections from Bt Cotton Farmers in Maharashtra'. In *Economic and Environmental Sustainability of the Asian Region*, edited by S. S. Gill, L. Singh and R. Marwah, 391–418. New Delhi: Routledge.

von Broembsen, Marlese. 2020. 'The World's Most Vulnerable Garment Workers Aren't in Factories—and Global Brands Need to Step Up to Protect Them'. WIEGO. https://www.wiego.org/blog/worlds-most-vulnerable-garment-workers-arent-factories-and-global-brands-need-step-protect, accessed 5 October 2021.

von Broembsen, Marlese, Jenna Harvey, and Marty Chen. 2019. 'Realizing Rights for Homeworkers: An Analysis of Governance Mechanisms'. CCDP 2019-04.

von Hippel, 2005. *Democratizing Innovation*. Cambridge, MA: MIT Press.

Wabi, Abdul Latif, and J. A. Usmani. 2015. 'Lead Toxicity: A Review'. *Interdisciplinary toxicology* 8 (2): 55–64.

Wagner, M. 2007. 'Integration of Environmental Management with Other Management Functions of the Firm'. *Long Range Planning* 40: 611–628.

Wang, W., S. Thangavelu, and C. Findlay. 2018. *Global Value Chains, Firms, and Wage Inequality: Evidence from China*. New York: Forum for Emprical Investigation in International Trade.

War on Want. 2011. *Stitched Up: Women Workers in the Bangladeshi Garment Sector*. London: War on Want.

———. 2012. Restricted Rights: Migrant Workers in Th ailand, Cambodia and Malaysia. Report. London: War on Want.

Ward, A., and A. Mishra. 2019. 'Addressing Sustainability Issues with Voluntary Standards and Codes: A Closer Look at Cotton Production in India'. In *Business Responsibility and Sustainability in India*, edited by B. Arora, P. Budhwar and D. Jyoti, 161–193. Geneva: Palgrave Macmillan (Springer Nature).

Watkins, K., and J. von Braun. 2003. 'Time to Stop Dumping on the World's Poor'. Annual Report 2002–03 IFPRI. http://ebrary.ifpri.org/utils/getfile/collection/p15738coll2/id/57353/filename/57354.pdf, accessed 30 November 2021.

Whittington, Dale, and Stefano Pagiola. 2012. 'Using Contingent Valuation in the Design of Payments for Environmental Services Mechanisms: A Review and Assessment'. *World Bank Research Observer* 27 (2): 261–287.

Willis, Jane. 2016. 'The Living Wage'. In *The International Encyclopedia of Geography*, 33–46. London: Wiley.

Wilson, Tamar Diana. 2012. 'Primitive Accumulation and the Labor Subsidies to Capitalism'. *Review of Radical Politics of Economics* 44 (2): 210–222.

Wolpe, Harold, ed. 1980. *The Articulation of Modes of Production*. London: Routledge and Kegan Paul.

WRC. 2013. 'Global Wage Trends for Apparel Workers, 2001–2011'. Worker Rights Consortium and Center for American Progress, Washington, DC.

———. 2020. 'Hunger in the Apparel Supply Chain: Survey Findings on Workers' Access to Nutrition during Covid-19'. Worker Rights Consortium, Washington, DC.

World Bank. 2020. *Trading for Development: In the Age of Global Value Chains*. Washington, DC: The World Bank.

WTO. 1998. 'Singapore Ministerial Declaration'. World Trade Organization. https://www.wto.org/english/thewto_e/minist_e/min96_e/wtodec_e.htm, accessed 5 October 2021.

WTO, ITE-JETRO, OECD, and the World Bank. 2019. *Global Value Chain Development Report*. Washington: World Trade Organization.

WWF and Yes Bank. 2012. *Cotton Market and Sustainability in India*. Delhi: WWF-India.

Young, Iris Marion. 2004. 'Responsibility and Global Labor Justice'. *The Journal of Political Philosophy* 12 (4): 365–388.

Yu, Zhu. 2003. 'The Floating Population's Household Strategies and the Role of Migration in China's Regional Development and Integration'. *International Journal of Population Geography* 9: 485–502.

Zhou, M. 2017. *Pakistan's Hidden Workers: Wages and Conditions of Home-Based Workers and the Informal Economy*. Geneva: International Labour Organization. https://www.ilo.org/islamabad/whatwedo/publications/WCMS_554877/lang--en/index.htm, accessed 5 October 2021.

Index